A History of East Central Europe

VOLUMES IN THE SERIES

VOLUME VIII

The Establishment of the Balkan National States, 1804–1920

A HISTORY OF EAST CENTRAL EUROPE

VOLUME VIII

EDITORS

Peter F. Sugar
University of Washington

Donald W. Treadgold
University of Washington

The Establishment

of the Balkan National

States, 1804–1920

CHARLES and BARBARA JELAVICH

UNIVERSITY OF WASHINGTON PRESS
Seattle and London

Library of Congress Cataloging in Publication Data

Jelavich, Charles.
  The establishment of the Balkan national states,
1804–1920.

  (A history of East Central Europe ; v. 8)
  Bibliography: p.
  Includes index.
  1. Balkan Peninsula—Politics and government.
2. Eastern question (Balkan) I. Jelavich, Barbara
Brightfield, joint author. II. Title. III. Series:
Sugar, Peter F. A history of East Central Europe ; v. 8.
DJK4. S93 vol. 8 [DR43] 949s [949.6] 76-49162
ISBN 0-295-95444-2

10-21-77

OCT 2 1 1977

Foreword

The systematic study of the history of East Central Europe outside the region itself began only in the last generation or two. For the most part historians in the region have preferred to write about the past of only their own countries. Hitherto no comprehensive history of the area as a whole has appeared in any language.

This series was conceived as a means of providing the scholar who does not specialize in East Central European history and the student who is considering such specialization with an introduction to the subject and a survey of knowledge deriving from previous publications. In some cases it has been necessary to carry out new research simply to be able to survey certain topics and periods. Common objectives and the procedures appropriate to attain them have been discussed by the authors of the individual volumes and by the coeditors. It is hoped that a certain commensurability will be the result, so that the eleven volumes will constitute a unit and not merely an assemblage of writings. However, matters of interpretation and point of view have remained entirely the responsibility of the individual authors.

No volume deals with a single country. The aim has been to identify geographical or political units that were significant during the period in question, rather than to interpret the past in accordance with latter-day sentiments or aspirations.

The limits of "East Central Europe," for the purposes of this series, are the eastern linguistic frontier of German- and Italian-speaking peoples on the west, and the political borders of Russia/the USSR on the east. Those limits are not precise, even within the period covered by any given volume of the series. The appropriateness of including the Finns, Estonians, Latvians, Lithuanians, Belorussians, and Ukrainians was considered, and it was decided not to attempt to cover them systematically, though they appear repeatedly in these books. Treated in depth are the Poles, Czecho-Slovaks, Hungarians, Romanians, Yugo-slav peoples, Albanians, Bulgarians, and Greeks.

There has been an effort to apportion attention equitably among regions and periods. Three volumes deal with the area north of the Danube-Sava line, three with the area south of it, and four with both areas. Four treat premodern history, six modern times. The eleventh consists of an historical atlas and a bibliography of the entire subject. Each volume is supplied with a bibliographical essay of its own, but we all have attempted to keep the scholarly apparatus at a minimum in order to make the text of the volumes more readable and accessible to the broader audience sought.

The coeditors wish to express their thanks to the Ford Foundation for the financial support it gave this venture, and to the Institute of Comparative and Foreign Area Studies (formerly Far Eastern and Russian Institute) and its three successive directors, George E. Taylor, George M. Beckmann, and Herbert J. Ellison, under whose encouragement the project has moved close to being realized.

The whole undertaking has been longer in the making than originally planned. Two of the original list of projected authors died before they could finish their volumes and have been replaced. Volumes of the series are being published as the manuscripts are received. We hope that the usefulness of the series justifies the long agony of its conception and birth, that it will increase knowledge of and interest in the rich past and the many-sided present of East Central Europe among those everywhere who read English, and that it will serve to stimulate further study and research on the numerous aspects of this area's history that still await scholarly investigators.

PETER F. SUGAR
DONALD W. TREADGOLD

Preface

THIS narrative deals primarily with the modern history of seven Balkan peoples—the Albanians, Bulgarians, Croatians, Greeks, Romanians, Serbians, and Slovenes—all of whom have a historical base of equal or greater antiquity than that of the western European states. The oldest are the Greeks, who claim an unbroken historical and cultural tradition of over four thousand years. Next come the Illyrians, the ancestors of the Albanians, who migrated into the peninsula at approximately the same time, the second millennium B. C. Third are the Romanians, described by their historians as the descendants of the Dacians and of Romans who controlled the province from A. D. 106 to 271. At the end of the sixteenth century a medieval Romanian kingdom under Michael the Brave embraced territories roughly equivalent to those of the modern state.

The other four peoples, the Slavic population, settled in the peninsula after the sixth century. The Bulgarians, whose name comes from a group of Finno-Tartar invaders who first conquered and then were absorbed by the Slavic inhabitants, experienced two periods of medieval grandeur. The First Bulgarian Empire reached its peak in the reign of Simeon from 893 to 927; the Second Empire, in that of John Asen II from 1218 to 1241. The Serbs can look back to a similar period of greatness and power, which reached its height during the reign of Stevan Dušan from 1331 to 1355. During the Middle Ages the Serbs, Greeks, Romanians, Bulgarians, and some Albanians also shared the experience of conversion to Christianity from the same Byzantine center. Thus, in modern times they all were, like Russia, members of the Orthodox church.

In contrast, the Croats and Slovenes became Catholic and henceforth were to remain culturally linked with the West. Like the other Balkan peoples described, Croatia too had an independent kingdom which

ix

came into existence in the tenth century. In 1102, however, after the dynasty had died out and the state was defeated by the Magyars, the Croatian nobility signed the Pacta Conventa with Hungary. In this document they recognized the king of Hungary as the ruler of the Triune Kingdom of Croatia, Slavonia, and Dalmatia, but they retained the right to administer their lands. For a brief period during the seventh century the Slovenes, too, had an independent state, but it soon fell under German rule. In the thirteenth and fourteenth centuries Albania enjoyed periods of independence or semi-independence as a principality.

Unlike the western European medieval states, the historical continuity of Balkan national development was interrupted by a long period of subjugation to outside rule. The Ottoman conquest was the great event that shaped the future life of all of the Balkan people. Two dates have particular symbolic significance in this regard. In 1389 at the Battle of Kosovo an army of Serbs, aided by Bosnians, Croatians, Bulgarians, and Albanians, was decisively defeated by the Ottoman forces. In 1453 Constantinople fell, thus bringing to an end the thousand-year Byzantine Empire. Thereafter, until the nineteenth century, the Balkan nationalities lived under a foreign rule. It should be emphasized that this period of almost five centuries marked the submergence but never the complete annihilation of national awareness. The Ottoman government did not attempt to assimilate or destroy the Christian people. Although the Balkan kingdoms disappeared, national identity was preserved through the church, the languages, and popular culture. The memory of the past was never completely erased. As shall be seen, the first step in the national revival of each nationality was the resurrection of the glories of the ancient or medieval history of their people by writers and historians.

In the following pages, therefore, we will be dealing with the national development of peoples with a long historical heritage, whose political evolution was halted by a foreign conquest. In addition, the Ottoman domination removed the region and its inhabitants from Western European influence, except in an indirect manner, as, for example, through Venice, for over four centuries. The great strides made in the West were consequently not reflected in the peninsula. The nineteenth century was thus to witness not only the revival of national feeling among the Balkan peoples, but also the growth of awareness of their economic, social, and political backwardness and the first attempts to remedy this situation.

In this book the authors have attempted to adhere to the statement in the editors' foreword and to present an introduction to the subject to the "scholar who does not specialize in East Central European history and the student who is considering such a specialization." The footnotes, in keeping with the policy of the series, have been held to a minimum. In addition, the books discussed in the bibliographical essay are almost exclusively in English, although the text itself is based primarily on works in other languages. The final volume in the series will contain a historical atlas and complete bibliography.

The spelling of names and geographic points in this study has presented certain problems because of the multiplicity of languages and the variety of forms used both in the nineteenth century and at present. Complete consistency has not been possible, but usually modern spelling has been adopted unless a person or place is better known under another form. *Constantinople,* not *Istanbul,* has been employed as the name of the Ottoman capital because it was the word regularly used throughout the nineteenth century. In general, the Library of Congress system of transliteration, with modifications, has been used for Bulgarian, Greek, and Serbian. Albanian, Romanian, and Turkish names follow their national forms unless they are better known in English in another spelling. At times, alternative versions are given, e.g., Bitola (Monastir), Durrës (Durazzo). Thus, for example, whereas the city is called Bitola, it is the vilayet of Monastir. First names are usually, but not always, anglicized. The authors recognize that some may disagree with their individual decisions in this matter, but they have tried to use the forms most readily understandable to English-speaking readers and ones which are most commonly used.

The authors are greatly indebted to their friends and colleagues who have kindly consented to read this manuscript. They are most grateful for the comments and criticisms which they have received on what are often controversial and complicated matters. All or a major part of the manuscript was read by Professors Keith Hitchins, University of Illinois; John R. Lampe, University of Maryland; John A. Petropulos, Amherst College; Marin V. Pundeff, California State University, Northridge; Traian Stoianovich, Rutgers University; and Wayne S. Vucinich, Stanford University. Professor Roderic H. Davison, George Washington University, and Professor Stanford J. Shaw, University of California, Los Angeles, read specific parts dealing with the Ottoman Empire. Professor Stavro Skendi, Columbia University, commented on the chapter on Albania. Professors Willis R. Barnstone and Ante Kadić, Indiana University, assisted with the chapter on culture.

The authors would also like to express their gratitude to Professor Michael B. Petrovich, University of Wisconsin, for having allowed them to read the manuscript of his excellent study, which is now published in two volumes entitled *A History of Modern Serbia, 1804–1918* (New York: Harcourt Brace Jovanovich, 1976). In addition, we appreciate the valuable suggestions of Professors Peter F. Sugar and Donald W. Treadgold, the editors of this series. We also wish to thank our two colleagues Professor Norman J. G. Pounds, who drafted the maps, and Mr. John M. Hollingsworth, who prepared them. Nancy Weil compiled the index.

Finally, Mark and Peter Jelavich have both read the entire manuscript and have offered important contributions.

CHARLES AND BARBARA JELAVICH

Contents

Maps

VOLUME VIII

The Establishment of the Balkan National States, 1804–1920

CHAPTER 1

The Ottoman Background

GENERAL CONDITIONS OF LIFE

AT the beginning of the nineteenth century the greater proportion of the Balkan territories formed part of the Ottoman Empire. Stretching over a wide expanse that embraced Asian, African, and European lands, this state occupied a strategic position which made its fate a matter of vital concern to all of the great powers. Within its European territories, comprising about 238,000 square miles and containing approximately 9 million people, the Ottoman government controlled a predominantly Christian population. Although these people were governed under a system, unique in Europe, which divided them according to their religious affiliation, an Ottoman administrative network nevertheless covered the peninsula.

The area was divided into five provinces: Rumelia, Bosnia, Silistria, Djezair (including the Peloponnesus and the Greek islands), and Crete. These were in turn organized into nine subdivisions: Rumelia, Bosnia, Belgrade, Shkodër (Scutari), Janina, Negropont, the Morea (Peloponnesus), Candia (Crete), and the Archipelago. Certain areas with wide rights of self-government were also attached to the empire: for instance, the two Romanian provinces of Wallachia and Moldavia and some Greek islands. This pattern underwent many changes in the nineteenth century. Each of these divisions was staffed by Ottoman officials appointed from Constantinople. The administrative head of each was usually supported by a council (*divan*) of assistants and by a hierarchy of state officials, including judges, tax collectors, police, and military officers. The primary concern of these men was the defense of the empire, the collection of taxes, the maintenance of public order, and the affairs of the Muslim inhabitants. Cities, towns, and villages also had similar officials.

Although this Ottoman administration exerted a great deal of direct influence on all of the Balkan people, the Christian communities in fact

3

enjoyed a large measure of autonomy through the system of church and local government adopted by the Ottoman conquerors. Considering themselves primarily as Muslims, they preferred to organize their empire according to the religious affiliation of their subjects. They thus established four major administrative divisions, called "millets," for their Orthodox, Gregorian Armenian, Roman Catholic, and Jewish population. There was also a Muslim millet, and a Protestant organization was recognized in the middle of the nineteenth century. Although other religions were accepted or tolerated, particularly Christianity and Judaism, they were in no sense regarded as equal. An individual in the empire could not join the ruling strata or hold a high position in the political or military hierarchy unless he were Muslim. Although no really determined efforts were made to convert the Balkan peoples, certain areas, in particular Bosnia, Hercegovina, Crete, Albania, and sections in the Rhodope Mountains, did become predominantly Muslim. Their inhabitants then enjoyed the privileges reserved for their faith.

The majority of the population of the Balkan Peninsula, however, remained with their church and therefore belonged to the Orthodox millet. As such they fell under the jurisdiction of the patriarch of Constantinople, who was regarded as an agent of the Ottoman government. He and his administration represented and spoke for the Orthodox population in its dealings with the Muslim authorities. On the local level they had jurisdiction over all legal and moral matters affecting their people. The main general effect of this system was the preservation both of national divisions that had existed before the Ottoman conquest and of local particularism. Through much of the Ottoman period the higher church administration was divided along national lines. The Greeks became predominant at Constantinople, where the patriarch was the highest ecclesiastical official of the Orthodox world, but the Serbs could look to their patriarchate at Peć and the Bulgars to an archbishopric at Ohrid. Despite this separation the Orthodox church as a whole did preserve a spirit of Christian unity against Islam. The faithful were taught that they had lost their freedom because of their sins, but that the day would come when their church would emerge triumphant.

In addition to the millet the Balkan Christians had much control over their own affairs on the local level. Although conditions varied widely throughout the peninsula, usually the peasant communities enjoyed a degree of autonomy under their own notables, who were called, among other titles, *kodza-bashi* in Greece, *starešina* in Serbia, and *chorbadzhiia* in Bulgaria. These men were either elected or appointed from among the leading and generally more prosperous members of the community. Their relative wealth rested on agriculture, trade, or tax farming. In general they represented their villages to the provincial Muslim administration and were responsible to that authority for tax collection and the maintenance of law and order. Like the church officials, the notables were part of Ottoman political life. Some areas, such as the Peloponnesus, enjoyed virtual autonomy; others, such as the Bulgarian lands, felt Ottoman control more strongly.

Along with these separate political authorities the Christian was also subject to three legal systems. At the top Muslim law applied to all members of that faith and any matters involving Christians and Muslims. The ecclesiastical law of the millet regulated, in particular, questions dealing with the family, such as marriage and morals. In time customary local law came to hold precedence in some communities. Here, as in other facets of Balkan life, secular interests tended to gain strength at the expense of the church.

In the local communities conditions were also favorable for the preservation, at least in a dormant form, of national divisions. The Ottoman destruction of the former Balkan states and their ruling classes produced a situation in which the Christian thereafter tended to identify himself with and give his first allegiance to his own family, his village and his church. After the establishment of Ottoman rule no effort was made either to destroy or to unify the divergent elements of the peninsula. Before the nineteenth century no attempts were made to provide a legal, political, or cultural basis for a common Ottoman citizenship embracing all of the diverse elements of the state. National and local particularism was enforced and increased. In some localities Muslim, Serbian, Bulgarian, and Greek villages existed side by side for centuries with little or no cultural or personal intermixing. In the towns the different peoples lived in their own quarters. When in the nineteenth century the Ottoman government tried to introduce the principles of the modern European state system, the attempt foundered because the empire had been organized on quite a different basis during the previous four centuries.

Although the Balkan nationalities themselves tended to remain apart, certainly the greatest division in the population was that between a privileged minority, the Muslims, and the majority, the Orthodox Christians. In the decaying Ottoman Empire individual Muslims often suffered as much as their Christian counterparts did from bad government, but they still enjoyed important basic privileges, such as a far better chance in court, fewer taxes, and a recognized superior status. The Christian population was fully aware of the difference of its position. Generalizations are difficult to make since conditions differed widely throughout the peninsula and changed with time. Christians, however, usually were supposed to observe certain prohibitions that were as galling to their personal pride as to their material interests. For instance, in theory they could not bear firearms, wear conspicuous or rich clothes, or don the color green, sacred to the Muslims. They were supposed to dismount when passing a Muslim on horseback; their houses could not be richer than or overlook those of their Muslim neighbors. Christian churches could not have bells or belltowers; new churches were not to be built, but old ones could be repaired. Despite the fact that by the nineteenth century many of these measures were no longer enforced, the Christian remained in a distinct and recognized inferior position. It was perhaps this aspect of Ottoman rule that was most resented by the subject population.

Next to the question of status, the tax burden that he was forced to shoulder made the Balkan peasant most discontented with his lot. The fact that by the nineteenth century the empire was not economically prosperous and had few of the basic prerequisites for healthy development made this condition more difficult to bear. Although the Christian was not required, indeed not usually allowed, to join the military forces, he was expected to provide the tax support for them and the other functions of the state. The Christian peasant thus paid taxes on the produce of his land and home industry and on his personal possessions, as well as a special head tax levied on all male Christians in place of the military service required of the Muslim. It should be noted that this payment was the chief tax that was also not required of the Muslim population. Together with the other inhabitants of the empire the Christian was subject to additional services and contributions. He was particularly unhappy about the obligation to work on roads and public works and to provide horses, oxen, and carts when called upon. In time of war these burdens were, of course, increased. When it is considered that other taxes in kind and in labor dues had to be paid for the use of the land he tilled, the gravity of the tax problem for the peasant can be understood.

The methods used for collecting taxes were as bad as the heavy burden of payments. The Muslim peasant, of course, also faced this problem. Government taxes were usually taken by tax farmers who won the right by competitive yearly bidding. This official, who could be Christian or Muslim, was concerned neither with the welfare of the peasant nor with the government; he was primarily interested in gaining a high profit. Great wealth could be acquired through this system, but the results for the individual peasant could be disastrous. One of the principal causes for peasant revolt in the empire was the almost impossible burden of state taxes coupled with the payments required for land usage. Although both Muslim and Christian suffered from the corruption and injustice of the empire's fiscal system, the basic payments were higher for the Christian, who also had much less chance of defending his rights against the police and in the courts.

It is interesting to note that despite the personal and financial disadvantages under which they labored, the Christian communities in the Balkans were on the whole healthier than the Muslim. By the end of the eighteenth century the Muslim population had entered a period of comparative economic and moral decline. Several explanations have been offered for this development. Certainly the fact that the Muslim population provided the soldiers contributed to its ultimate weakening. Their concentration in towns also made them more susceptible to the ravages of plague and other diseases. Turkish customs, particularly the practice of polygamy, played a part. This process of decay was clearly illustrated in the eighteenth century in the changing demography of the Balkan towns where Christian and national elements formed an increasingly larger proportion of the population.

With regard to the life of the average Balkan Christian under Ottoman rule, it is difficult to generalize because of the variety of conditions to be found in the peninsula. Nevertheless, it can be said that the mass of the Christian population were peasants who produced the food and provided the greater part of the tax base for the empire. Any individual's actual conditions of existence depended greatly on where he lived and how closely he was subject to direct Ottoman control. In remote sections, particularly in the less attractive mountain areas, he might occupy a relatively independent position, either as a herdsman or as a peasant farmer cultivating land that was in practice his private property. In contrast, where the land was better, as in the Maritsa valley, Thessaly, or Bosnia, he probably was a sharecropper on the estate of a landowner who was usually Muslim, but who could also be Christian. In Moldavia and Wallachia the land was held exclusively by Orthodox Christians. On the estates, again depending on local conditions, the peasant might have effective possession of his house and a garden area, but he was required to surrender from 10 to perhaps over 50 percent of the produce of the lands that he worked. He was also subject to numerous other dues in kind or to labor obligations to his landlord. These were, of course, in addition to the taxes owed to the Ottoman government.

Methods of cultivation were extremely primitive. While Western Europe had long outgrown medieval conditions, the Balkan peasant usually still relied on the three-field system and on the wooden plow drawn by oxen or buffalo. His lands might consist of small plots scattered over a wide area and far from his village. Traditionally, he raised wheat, maize, barley, millet, and rye, but during the eighteenth century he began to pay more attention to corn and cotton as market crops. He also raised horses, cattle, sheep, and pigs.

The peasant produced what was necessary for his own subsistence and for payments to those who controlled his land and to the political authorities. He paid in kind; money played little part in his life. He made his clothing and his household and farm equipment at home and conserved some food. The average peasant throughout the Balkans lived in an extremely simple mud, stone, wood, or brick house consisting usually of one or two rooms. His chief furniture was a small table and low stools; he and his family slept on blankets or on a raised platform. He cooked over a fireplace in his main room in clay pots using wooden utensils. In a rich village or house the furniture might be more complete and the floors covered with furs or richly decorated rugs. Here gaily embroidered pillows, towels, and curtains might brighten the home. The clothing of the peasant family again depended on the prosperity of the region and the family's circumstances. It could range from the most simple and basic covering to elaborate and beautiful folk costumes.

Most peasant homes were clustered together to form small villages and hamlets lying in the middle of the fields cultivated by their inhabitants. Within this fold the individual was subject to a highly conservative and traditional pattern of life, with the local church serving as the center of the community. Quite naturally definite social differences existed within this overwhelmingly agricultural society. Some peasants controlled good lands and were extremely prosperous; others were sharecroppers or agricultural laborers. Priests, merchants, craftsmen, teachers, and those connected with the local administration all had their established place. Within this scheme the community leaders, both the clergy and the notables, usually accepted the existing conditions; both groups showed themselves resistant to revolutionary change. Over the centuries they had learned to live within the Ottoman system; they had a privileged position within their own section. The church, in particular, was not likely to favor new movements that promised the westernization and secularization of Balkan society.

Despite the extreme poverty and backwardness of the peninsula under Ottoman rule, life was not necessarily drab or dull. The church gave a basic view of life, thoroughly intermixed with superstition and folk tradition, which explained each man's place in the wider scheme of life. This institution also offered a long series of religious holidays and festivals that broke the monotony of rural life. Each locality had its own songs, dances, and stories. The tight structure of the peasant family gave the individual security in precarious times and a definite position in his own society.

In contrast to the villages, which are here defined as primarily rural and peasant communities, the cities of the Balkans served as military and administrative headquarters and as commercial and handicraft centers. As could be expected, the larger cities lay on the principal routes to Europe where they served the needs of war or commerce. Particularly significant was the line Constantinople-Adrianople-Plovdiv-Sofia-Niš-Belgrade. The seaports Varna and Thessaloniki and the river ports of Vidin and Ruse were similarly important. Some cities, such as Sarajevo and Samokov, were major administrative centers.

In the period of Ottoman rule the silhouette and general appearance of the cities was formed by Ottoman public buildings, usually of stone construction. Typical of Ottoman architecture were mosques with minarets, caravanseries (inns), fountains, baths, covered markets, and distinctive bridges, tombs, and fortresses. In contrast, Christian building was of necessity modest. There were Ottoman restrictions on both ecclesiastical and private Christian architecture. In some cities, such as Plovdiv and Thessaloniki, wealthy merchants were able, in the course of the nineteenth century, to construct impressive private homes, but these are remarkable by their rarity.

Since the major cities were Ottoman administrative and military centers, they contained large Muslim, Turkish populations. Like the countryside, the cities were divided on a religious and national basis into quarters (*mahalle*). The handicraft industry was organized on the guild system. These organizations, which played a leading role in urban life, were formed by both artisans and merchants. They could be Muslim, Christian, or mixed in composition. They controlled the quality, quantity, and price of the items produced. Traditionally, certain crafts belonged to particular national or religious groups. For instance, metalworking and skillful leatherwork were usually the province of Muslim craftsmen.

In addition to the split between the Muslim and Christian population in town and country, basic divisions also developed among the Christian nationalities. Within the Ottoman scheme certain groups came to enjoy a privileged position and in fact to share in the benefits enjoyed by the ruling strata. By the end of the eighteenth century it was clear that among the Balkan people the Greeks occupied the most favorable place. In Greece proper the local communities, despite the wars and disorders of the time, ran their own affairs. More important, however, was the power and wealth that the Greek merchant and administrator had acquired. As has been mentioned, under Ottoman rule the church was the main governmental authority for the Christian people. Through the office of the patriarch of Constantinople, which was consistently in Greek hands, the Greek hierarchy was able to win and hold a position of preeminence in the cultural and religious life of the peninsula. Especially important was the collaboration of the patriarchate and the Porte [1] in securing the abolition of the Serbian patriarchate at Peć in 1766 and the Bulgarian archbishopric at Ohrid in the following year. Thereafter, the Serbian and Bulgarian ecclesiastical organizations were under the direct control and supervision of the patriarch at Constantinople and Greek officials. By the end of the eighteenth century the patriarch ruled about eight million Christians, a quarter of the population of the empire.

The Slavic and Romanian people naturally resented the Greek domi-

1. The term "Porte" or "Sublime Porte" was used to designate the Ottoman government. It refers to the building that housed the principal government offices.

nation of the Orthodox church. They saw Greek control as a sign of oppression and of the stifling of their own national rights. For many of them the attainment of national liberation was to mean the overthrow just as much of Greek ecclesiastic control as of Ottoman imperial domination. Moreover, the patriarchate and the church hierarchy under its control were exceedingly corrupt. Like the Ottoman government, its high offices were for sale and it held great wealth. Although in theory the representative of the oppressed Christians, it had a vested interest in the maintenance of the *status quo*.

Greeks not only dominated the Orthodox church, but by the eighteenth century they also participated actively in the Ottoman administrative system. The Greeks were certainly the best educated of the Christian people; their facility for languages, a talent particularly appreciated by the Ottoman rulers, gave them definite advantages. Because of their abilities and their ambition they were able to win important posts throughout the empire. By the beginning of the nineteenth century they had come to hold traditionally three high offices: grand dragoman, a quasi-minister of foreign affairs; the governorships (*hospodar*ships) of the Danubian Principalities; and dragoman of the fleet. These posts were administered with extreme corruption and some, like the *hospodar*ships, were used as vehicles of Greek political and cultural domination. The Greeks who participated in the Ottoman administration were generally known as "Phanariotes" after the district in Constantinople where many of the families lived.

In addition to these positions the Greeks, together with the Jews and the Armenians, held the principal commercial positions in the empire. The merchant group, with its opportunities to travel and its superior education, was to take a leading role in the Greek national movement. It should also be mentioned that the Greeks developed close ties with Russia, thanks to their religious, political, and economic activities. Many Greeks entered Russian state service, and in the Treaty of Kuchuk Kainardji of 1774 Greek merchants gained the right to sail under the Russian flag.

Second to the Greeks, the Romanians living in the principalities of Wallachia and Moldavia enjoyed a special position in the state. Situated relatively far from Constantinople, the provinces never came under direct Ottoman rule; they were not Turkish pashaliks (provinces). In theory Ottoman rights in the area were limited to the occupation of certain strong points, the exaction of a tribute, and the right to name the *hospodars* (princes or governors). After Peter the Great invaded Romanian lands in 1709 with the help of certain Romanian boyars, the Romanian political position deteriorated. Thereafter, the Ottoman government appointed not native Romanians, but Phanariote Greeks to the posts of *hospodar*. During the eighteenth century these offices became a source of power and wealth for Greek officials. The Romanian national movement was thus to commence with action against Greek cultural and political predominance.

In comparison with the Greeks and Romanians the Serbs and Bulgarians occupied a much less advantageous position. Primarily a peasant people living in impoverished circumstances, the Serbs suffered severely from the warfare and turbulence of the late eighteenth century. Even more difficult was the fate of the Bulgars. With their lands situated close to Constantinople and lying on the route of the Ottoman armies, they bore a higher burden of taxation and were more directly affected by the hazards of war than were their neighbors. Like the Serbs, their church fell under the control of the Greeks in the eighteenth century.

BACKGROUND OF REVOLT

Most of the conditions to which the Christian population objected had existed since the establishment of Ottoman control and particularly after the state started to decline gradually. Although there had been sporadic rebellions in the past, the nineteenth century was to usher in a period of concentrated national revolution. Between 1804 and 1878 the major national movements attained a large degree of success. Four independent states, Serbia, Greece, Montenegro, and Romania, were established, and an autonomous Bulgaria came into being. The Albanians were forced to organize when their territories were threatened by other national groups. The question thus arises of why, after enduring Ottoman rule for so long, the Balkan people were able, in a relatively short time, to regain control of their political destinies. Although this entire narrative will deal with this question, particular attention must be paid to the historical circumstances in existence at the end of the eighteenth and beginning of the nineteenth century. These conditions can best be discussed under the headings of, first, the changing economic and social conditions and, second, the growth of internal and external opposition to the authority of the sultan and the central Ottoman government.

SOCIAL AND ECONOMIC CHANGE: THE POLITICAL AND CULTURAL EFFECTS

By the end of the eighteenth century the Balkans had been strongly affected by European events. The previous century had marked a period of economic upsurge in Western and Central Europe, a development occasioned by technological advances and the beginnings of the industrial revolution. There was an increasing demand for Balkan raw materials, in particular for the new colonial crops of cotton and corn, and also for meats, hides, wax, silk, wool, tobacco, lumber, and other products. This rise in European demand was both preceded and paralleled by a change in the landholding system in the Balkans which allowed that area to produce the surplus necessary to supply the European market.

After the Ottoman armies conquered a territory, they regarded it as belonging to God; the sultan, as God's representative, had the right to redistribute it. This land became the economic base of the cavalry, the *spahis* (*sipahis*) who won the first great Ottoman military victories. In return for service in the military forces, or in the administration of the state, an individual, almost always a Muslim, received a grant of land, a *timar*, which he held on a nonhereditary basis. The peasant worked the land for a fixed set of dues, usually a tenth of the crop and a few additional labor and tax obligations. Except in rare cases he could not be removed from his land, so long as he performed his prescribed duties. Moreover, he was not legally bound to the soil.

The *timar* system remained effective as both an economic and a military support for Ottoman power until gunpowder was introduced and the infantry soldier with a musket became a more efficient instrument of war than the horseman. Thereafter, the janissary corps became the chief arm of the state. Recruited originally from the Christian population under the *devshirme* [2] system, this body of dedicated, converted Muslim soldiers ranked with the best troops in Europe. Despite the fact that the infantry now became militarily more important, the state still needed the estates as a source of food, military supplies, and taxes to support warfare. Although the *timar* officially remained in existence until its abolition in 1831, another type of estate, the *chiftlik*, (*çiftlik*) came to predominate.

With the *timar*, it will be remembered, the uses that could be made of the land and the dues and services that could be required of the peasant were limited. In time, however, certain individuals were able to gain control of large blocks of land on an extralegal basis and on terms which were, in operation, close to those of owners of private property in other societies, including hereditary possession. *Timar* lands were changed to *chiftlik* estates through different processes. A *chiftlik* owner might assemble his lands by acquiring leases from various peasants; he might also be a tax farmer and exploit this position to gain property. Pure force and armed mercenaries could also be used to gain peasant holdings. This land system had the great advantage that it could be adapted to capitalist farming methods and thus supply the increasing European demands for food and raw materials.

This development brought with it fundamental social and political

2. Approximately every five years the Ottoman authorities in the Balkans as a special tax levy could take about one out of every four boys between the ages of ten and twenty from the Christian population. This levy was called the *devshirme*. The boys were then converted to Islam. The most gifted received the best education possible at the time and were eventually assigned to the highest offices in the empire. The others often ended in the janissary corps. The system ended in the seventeenth century.

changes and a shift in the power balance between the central Ottoman government and the provinces. Most significant at this time was the rise to political prominence of local Muslim leaders known as *ayans* (*âyan*). The exact equivalent of the Christian notable, the *ayan*'s power was based on his economic prosperity as a landholder or trader and his relationship to the central government. Like the Christian notable, he was often the agent of the central administration in the local communities and was responsible for duties such as tax collecting, the supervision of the land system, and the maintenance of order. As the Ottoman central authority weakened during the disastrous wars of the eighteenth century, the *ayan* was able to increase his own independence in the countryside. The power of this group was considerably enhanced by the fact that these notables assembled their own private armies numbering sometimes thousands of retainers. These bands were used against rival leaders and the government, and to keep the peasants under control on the *chiftlik* estates.

The changing economic conditions benefited not only the *ayan*, but also the Christian merchant. In the eighteenth century the carrying trade of the empire was largely in the hands of Orthodox Christians. The sea trade was dominated by the Greeks, but the land routes to Europe were also important. Here Serbs, Bulgars, and Vlachs [3] shared with the Greeks and Jews the profits which could be made. Because of the conditions in the empire this wealth was generally put back into commercial ventures or into banking and moneylending. Trade with Europe provided equal rewards for the Christian merchant and for the Muslim *ayan*. The latter supplied the agricultural products and protected the trader. Both groups wanted a free and open trade system within the empire and opposed government regulation or control.

In contrast to the merchant and estate owner, the peasant found his condition steadily declining. On the *chiftlik* he was reduced to the position of a sharecropper. His obligations both in labor and in dues in kind were sharply increased. Instead of being subject to fixed obligations, he was now at the mercy of the *chiftlik* holder, who usually dominated the political authority of the area and used armed guards to control those who worked the land. *Chiftlik* villages predominated in some of the best agricultural areas, such as the Maritsa valley and parts of Bosnia. In the mountainous and remote areas individual peasant families had more control over the land and herds, but taxes were high and tenure sometimes uncertain. They were also at the mercy of those who held the political and police power in their region.

The dissatisfaction of the peasants inevitably had political repercus-

3. The Vlachs (Kutzovlachs, Arumanians, Tsintsars) were a nomadic or seminomadic people of Romanian ancestry who lived throughout the Balkans as shepherds, cattlemen, and traders.

sions as the power of the central government was eroded. The land problem and peasant unrest will form a constant theme in this narrative. The situation was bound to inflame religious hatred because the *chiftlik* owners were usually, but not always, Muslim and the peasants Christian. Poor conditions often forced the peasants to flee from the land or to join behind a strong military leader. Like the *ayan's* retainers, Christian armed bands became more numerous. Already certain groups known as *haiduks* or *klephts*, outlaws with a romantic reputation, were in existence. The turbulence of the period thus led to an increase in the number of men, either Muslim or Christian, who had the will and weapons to fight.

Not only the peasant, but also the city artisan was injured by the economic developments. Handworkers of all faiths and nationalities were harmed by the increasing importation of cheaper European finished goods of higher quality and by the failure of the Ottoman government to adopt protective measures. In the eighteenth century a process was thus begun which culminated a century later when the Ottoman Empire became primarily a source of raw materials and a market of the industrial products of the West. This development was accompanied by the virtual destruction of the empire's own internal industrial capacity.

Although the Christian Orthodox merchant benefited from these conditions, his increasing contacts with Western and Central Europe were to have a revolutionary effect on the Balkan world. Because of their maritime interests and their geographical position, some elements of the Greek population had always been in close touch with European intellectual developments. In the eighteenth century other Christian nationalities had similar opportunities. The principles of the Enlightenment and then of the French Revolution were to affect the attitude of some of the population not only toward the Ottoman government, but also toward their own church organization. In spite of the fact that the Orthodox church had been a major element in the preservation of Christian self-awareness, it was also part of the Ottoman system. In the past it had stood strongly against western influences and it had seen Catholicism as its main enemy. The new doctrines were to strengthen the national convictions of the Balkan leaders and give them a predominantly secular outlook. The Orthodox church, particularly the lower clergy, was to play an important role in the revolutionary movement, but the leadership lay in other hands.

In the intellectual revival that now occurred the Greeks were again to occupy a leading position. Greek merchants had previously been willing to invest their profits in schools, and they saw the value of sending their sons to Europe for an education. Among the Balkan peoples they were the first to establish a system of secular education based on western models. Although they were often attacked by other nationalities for their early monopoly of education, both secular and ecclesiastical, their schools did offer all Christians the opportunity to expand their knowledge of the world even though instruction was in Greek. At the end of the eighteenth century and the beginning of the nineteenth, the other nationalities also shared in a period of national cultural awakening, which was to be of great significance for future revolutionary movements. Even though their numbers were extremely limited and their direct influence on the affairs of the day circumscribed, scholars, writers, and national propagandists appeared to represent the interests of their nation. They shared a deep interest in their national language and history, and they generally had a close acquaintance with the Enlightenment. A brief description of the principal men in this group will be given because of their importance both in the national movements and in later national ideology.

Among the Greeks two names, Adamantios Koraes and Rhigas Pheraios, stand out. Born in 1748, Koraes did most of his work in Paris, but his books were imported into the Ottoman lands. Sympathetic with the rational and anticlerical aspects of the Enlightenment, he sought to revive in Greek minds the heritage of classical Greece and to establish that civilization as the direct ancestor of the modern Greeks. He was extremely critical of the Orthodox church. Especially significant for the future were his prefaces to editions of the Greek classics which he published. Since he did not approve of the vernacular Greek of the time, he tried to create a literary language closer to ancient forms. He thus began the unfortunate split in the Greek language between the written *katharevousa* and the spoken *demotiki*. In contrast to the scholar Koraes, Rhigas was a revolutionary agitator and a publicist. Born in 1757, he traveled extensively and also translated French works into vernacular Greek. Constantly involved in conspiracies, he was finally arrested by the Austrian government and turned over to the Ottoman authorities. Executed for his activities in 1798, he subsequently became a Greek hero and martyr. His revolutionary writings were widely circulated.

Activities similar to those of Koraes were undertaken by the Serbian scholars Dositej Obradović and Vuk Karadžić. Obradović was born in 1743 in the Banat. At first a monk, he later traveled widely and became acquainted with European thought. He was deeply interested in the language question, and he wished the Serbs, too, to have a literature in the vernacular. This interest was carried forward by Karadžić, the 'father' of the modern Serbian language. Like Obradović, he was concerned with the Serbian cultural heritage, and he collected popular Serbian poetry and stories. Most important, he compiled a grammar and a dictionary using the dialect of Hercegovina as his standard. This then became the literary language of the Serbs and Croats. Unlike Greek, written Serbo-Croatian was to remain close to the spoken language.

Similar developments in the Romanian principalities and in Bulgaria were delayed because of Greek dominance in the cultural life there. Because of the control of the Phanariote princes in Wallachia and Moldavia in the eighteenth century, Greek was the main language of culture and education. Later, French replaced it to an extent. Although the development of the national language was thus postponed, western ideas and literature did enter the country through the French ties. The Bulgarian cultural revival was to occur even later, but Bulgarian historians today emphasize the works of two early writers, Father Paisii and Bishop Sofronii of Vratsa. In 1762 Paisii, a monk at Mt. Athos, wrote a highly nationalistic history of Bulgaria which circulated thereafter in handwritten copies. Sofronii first taught school in Kotel, but in 1802 he moved to the freer atmosphere of Bucharest. While in Kotel, in 1765, he had copied Paisii's manuscript. Now he wrote his own works in the vernacular, including a memoir *The Life and Sufferings of Sinful Sofronii* and *Sunday Book* (Kiriakodromion), a collection of homilies.

Thus, by the end of the eighteenth century changes favorable to at least some sections of the Christian population had occurred in the social, economic, and intellectual atmosphere of the Balkans. Parallel with these developments and intimately connected with them were a series of events that threatened to bring about the disintegration of the Ottoman government at the center. The Porte was now under attack from two sides—on the one hand from the *ayan*s with their strong hold in the countryside and their private armies, and, on the other, from the great powers, who continued their pressure on the Ottoman possessions.

INTERNAL AND EXTERNAL THREATS: THE AYANS AND THE GREAT POWERS

The Ayans

Perhaps the most dangerous challenge to the Ottoman state came at this time not from the European powers or discontented Christians, but from the Muslim *ayan*s. With the disruption caused by war and civil turmoil the Balkan people needed some group to whom they could turn for protection. Moreover, in some places local notables were popular because they appeared to stand between the population and a rapacious and unreliable central authority. Since the government could not suppress these local leaders, it was usually forced to recognize them and appoint them to official posts. Civil and military crises also compelled the Porte to utilize these irregular armies and even bandit forces when the regular army was insufficient. Local notables were thus given major military positions. Unable to control the *ayan*s directly, the Ottoman government found its best weapon in playing them off against each other and establishing a balance of power; this was at best a dangerous game. In their turn the *ayan*s could support antigovernment forces such as the rebellious janissaries.

The problem of military weakness was recognized by the Ottoman leaders who were well aware of the declining power of their state before internal and external foes. The issue was not the necessity of reform, which was clear, but the direction in which these efforts should be turned. Some argued that the empire's basic weakness lay in its deviation from traditional practices and that former conditions should be restored. In opposition, a stronger current sought the abandonment of old ways and traditions in favor of what appeared to be superior western institutions.

The initial attempts at reform failed because of the opposition of local notables and their ability to exploit the catastrophes of the time. The first reforming sultan was Selim III, who came to power in 1789. In 1792 an interlude of peace allowed him to turn to the question of military reorganization. Previously, French military instructors had been used and the French government still wished to offer this assistance. The obvious weakness in the Ottoman forces was the janissary corps. This body had become more influential in Ottoman life as an organized political faction of a potentially dangerous character for internal policy than as an effective fighting force against foreign threats. Selim's major accomplishment toward reform was the formation of a parallel and rival infantry, the Nizam-i Cedid, or New Order, which received western style training and uniforms. Selim also attempted to carry through changes in tax policy and administration, but the military emphasis was stronger.

Unfortunately for the Ottoman state Selim proved too weak to carry through his ideas. He failed, in particular, to make adequate preparation for his reforms or to build a strong enough group of supporters to carry through the changes against those who had a vested interest in maintaining the old order. The janissaries remained a major political danger. They could not defeat foreign foes, but they could still threaten the government in Constantinople.

In 1807 a crucial struggle commenced between those who favored Selim and the opposition, which included conservatives, janissaries, and *ayan*s. The state was at war with Russia and, as will be shown, a rebellion had broken out in Serbia. In May a military revolt resulted in the overthrow of Selim and his replacement in July by Mustafa IV. Although Selim was allowed to live, a new regime dominated by Muslim conservatives and the janissaries was set up. Meanwhile, Selim's supporters and those who favored reform gathered in Ruse under the leadership of Mustafa Pasha, called Bayrakdar (the standard bearer), who was himself an *ayan*. In 1808 these forces moved on Constantinople. Faced with this danger, Mustafa IV had Selim assassinated. The new insurgents were nevertheless successful. Selim's cousin, Mahmud II, now came to the throne. Mustafa Pasha Bayrakdar died that same year, but Mahmud II was to remain in power until 1838 and to become the first successful reforming sultan.

The revolt of 1807 had involved the capture of the central government. Other actions by *ayan*s, janissaries, and discontented elements of the Muslim population threatened to dismember the state. Although this book is devoted primarily to the formation of the Balkan Christian nations, an account of the activities of the three most important rebels, Pasvanoglu Osman Pasha, Ali Pasha of Janina, and Mohammed Ali is necessary because their actions are intertwined with the first Balkan Christian revolutionary movements. Their careers are also important in that they illustrate the atmosphere of Balkan life at the end of the eighteenth and the beginning of the nineteenth century, which produced Muslim as well as Christian revolt. Like the national leaders, these three men sought to establish independent or autonomous principalities and to separate from direct Ottoman rule.

The career of Pasvanoglu Osman Pasha had a major effect on the beginnings of the Serbian revolution and on Bulgarian and Romanian national history. When Pasvanoglu's father was executed by the Ottoman government, the son fled to join outlaw groups. Later he fought with the Ottoman army in the war of 1787–92. Establishing a center at the city of Vidin on the Danube, he collected a large force of bandits and renegades. In 1795 he declared himself independent and thereafter remained in almost constant revolt against Constantinople. The efforts of the Ottoman government to control his activities will be discussed in connection with the Serbian revolution.

The activities of Ali Pasha of Janina, although similar in many respects, were even more spectacular. Born in 1750 in Tepelenë in Epirus, Ali was forced into a life of banditry when his father died. After an adventurous youth he succeeded in establishing a base at Janina. Through intrigue and violence he was subsequently able to increase his power and the number of his followers. At first he entered the service of the Porte and used his official positions to add to his personal strength. In 1788 he was appointed governor of the Janina district, whence he extended his rule over surrounding territory in Thessaly, Epirus, and Albania. The area under his control fluctuated in the following years, but it was always sufficiently extensive to serve as a power base for semi-independent rule. In 1799 the Porte, in dire need of his assistance, appointed him governor of Rumelia, a position which he held and lost several times. The Ottoman government particularly required his aid against Pasvanoglu and other bandit and *ayan* leaders. Continually alert to his own interests, Ali maintained close contacts with France. In 1809 he sent assistance to the Porte in the war against Russia.

Although Ali ruled from Epirus in the manner of an independent sovereign, the Porte did not attempt to destroy his power until 1820. At that time it prepared to move against him with naval and ground forces. In retaliation Ali concluded agreements with local Greek notables and encouraged other Balkan people to revolt. Unable to defeat the Ottoman troops, Ali was finally forced back into Janina, which was then surrounded. During the seige he died, in January, 1822.

Mohammed Ali was the most successful of the leaders. He failed to achieve his more ambitious goals, but his descendents ruled Egypt until 1952. Born in Macedonia in 1769 of a Turkish-Albanian family, he went to Egypt in 1798 at the head of an Albanian force to fight Napoleon. Although his troops were defeated, Ali remained in Egypt and subsequently rose in the military and administrative service. A master of the intrigue that plagued the empire, he was able to eliminate his rivals for power and in 1806 was named governor of Egypt. During the first part of his career he, like Ali Pasha, remained in the service of the Porte. At the same time he used his official rank to secure and strengthen his personal position. Active in the Sudan and in the suppression of local rebellions in Asia Minor, he was assisted by his extremely able son, Ibrahim Pasha.

In 1825 the Porte, unable to suppress the rebellion that had broken out in Greece, promised Mohammed Ali the island of Crete for himself and the governorship of the Peloponnesus for his son Ibrahim in return for military assistance. Although his forces were successful against the Greek rebels, the Ottoman defeat in the Russo-Turkish War of 1828–29 deprived Mohammed Ali of his expected reward. Because of this setback and his desire to gain more territory, he launched an attack on Syria in 1832 and caused a major European crisis. His intention at this time appears to have been to create a great Arabian kingdom centered on the Red Sea and embracing Egypt, the Sudan, and Arabian lands in Asia Minor. With the exception of Crete and the Peloponnesus he did not directly threaten lands inhabited by Balkan Christians. Like Pasvanoglu and Ali Pasha, Mohammed Ali represented the attempt to break up the empire by the formation of separate states under Muslim military leaders. Both his formidable armies and the character of his rule made his movement far more of a threat to the existence of the Ottoman state than the Serbian or Greek revolts.

The Challenge of the Great Powers

At the same time that the Porte was facing internal disintegration, it had to meet renewed attacks from outside powers. When Selim III ascended the throne in 1789, his government was still at war with both Austria and Russia. The Habsburg forces had occupied Belgrade, and Russian armies were operating along the Danube. In 1791 the Habsburg

Empire signed the Treaty of Sistova, returning Belgrade in exchange for gains of Bosnian territory. Peace was made with Russia the following year. In the Treaty of Jassy Russia extended her lands to the Dniester River, but surrendered Moldavia and Wallachia, which her troops had occupied. These two treaties marked the conclusion of what had been almost a century of intermittent cooperation between the Habsburg Empire and Russia against the Ottoman Empire. Over eighty years were to elapse before the two states were again to make a serious partition arrangement at the expense of the Porte. Both powers continued to show interest in Ottoman territory, but the partnership that had prevailed during the eighteenth century was interrupted.

The attention of all of the great powers was now drawn away from the Near East and concentrated first on Poland and then on revolutionary France. Poland was partitioned in three stages in 1772, 1793, and 1795. In 1792 war broke out in Europe. Thereafter the main emphasis in European international relations remained on continental affairs, but these events had wide ramifications in the Balkans and the eastern Mediterranean. In 1797, in the Treaty of Campo Formio, France annexed the Ionian Islands, an event that was to influence the Greek revolt. In the same agreement Austria took the remaining Venetian territories, thus bringing to an end the independent existence of the seapower that had formerly been a major Ottoman adversary.

In July, 1798, a period of direct French intervention in Ottoman lands commenced when Napoleon launched an invasion of Egypt. The French army quickly defeated the Mamluk soldiers. The Porte now entered into the conflict against France in alliance with Britain. Russia also took the Ionian Islands from France. In 1802 the Porte concluded a peace that lasted until 1806. In the intervening period French influence so increased in Constantinople that the Ottoman government shifted its allegiance and joined France against Russia and Britain. Although the period of warfare from 1806 to 1812 was not marked by continual hostilities, the Russian government attempted to use the opportunity to increase its influence in Serbia and the Danubian Principalities. In 1812 this conflict was concluded by the Treaty of Bucharest. Despite the fact that the Ottoman Empire was in a weak position, Russia asked only for the surrender of Bessarabia and withdrew from the Principalities. The Russian government was principally concerned with the impending French invasion. This change in boundaries was the single territorial loss suffered by the Porte after the Napoleonic Wars. In the Vienna settlement, in which the Ottoman Empire did not participate, the Ionian Islands were given to Britain and Dalmatia to Austria. These lands, however, had been part of the Venetian, not the Ottoman, Empire.

The Congress of Vienna was to mark the beginning of almost a century of relative peace for the great powers, but during that time the Ot-

Map 1. The Ottoman Empire, 1815

toman Empire was to lose most of its European possessions. In this period it was repeatedly demonstrated that the Porte was not capable of defending its territorial integrity or even of maintaining its political independence without outside aid. The empire continued to endure chiefly because of the strategic position of the Ottoman lands and their vital significance for the expanding European imperial states. Particularly important was the attitude of Russia and Britain. Their conflict over Constantinople and the Balkans became part of the great imperial contest waged between these two nations and extending from the eastern Mediterranean through Central Asia to China.

With the completion of the conquest of India in the eighteenth century, Britain regarded this land henceforth as the prime acquisition of her great empire. Her position as the first commercial and industrial nation of the world and as mistress of the seas, which was maintained throughout the nineteenth century, made her apprehensive and fearful of any power who threatened to rob her of supremacy in these fields. At the end of the eighteenth century and during the Napoleonic period she saw France as her chief competitor throughout the world, including the Near East. Thereafter, until the rise of a united Germany, Russia occupied this role. From a world standpoint, based on British commercial and naval preoccupations and the defense of India, the territories of the Ottoman Empire were the key to the imperial system. Britain feared constantly a Russian takeover of the Ottoman lands, either through a direct conquest of territory, domination of the government in Constantinople, or the establishment of satellite Balkan states. Because of this concern, Britain in the nineteenth century usually preferred to keep the Ottoman Empire intact. Her representatives in Constantinople did, however, consistently press the Ottoman government to reform its administrative system and to conciliate the Balkan nationalities.

The Russian position in regard to the Ottoman Empire was more complex. After Bessarabia was absorbed in 1812 the Russian government contemplated no more direct annexations. Nevertheless, the opportunities that subsequently arose for the extention of Russian influence were most inviting. Unlike the other great powers, Russia could expect to benefit from a triumph of the Balkan national movements. The peoples looked to her as the greatest Orthodox power; this feeling had been encouraged. In the Treaty of Kuchuk Kainardji of 1774 the base was laid for some sort of a claim to a religious protectorate, although in a very ambiguous form. Not only did the Balkan Christians expect aid from Russia, but important elements in Russian society were strongly attracted along both Orthodox and Slavic lines to the idea of giving assistance to the national movements. The Russian government was thus under pressure both from the appeals from the Balkans and from the reaction at home to do something for apparently oppressed Christians and Slavs.

In addition the Russian government was continually tempted to intervene in Ottoman affairs for prestige and an extension of her own power. Russia, like Britain, could not afford to see another power dominate the territory. In its dealings with the Porte the Russian government had several strong weapons, including its influence with the national movements, its large army, and regular opportunities to dominate the Ottoman government itself. In general the Russian leaders preferred to follow the policy adopted in the Treaty of Unkiar Iskelesi of 1833, namely, that of control from within.

Of the great powers directly concerned with Balkan events, the Habsburg Empire was perhaps in the weakest position. A multinational empire in an age of national revolution, she could win little by a change of conditions in the Ottoman lands. The acquisition of more territory in the area would only increase her minority problems; the establishment of independent states would give encouragement to her own national groups to follow a similar path. Although the monarchy usually cooperated with Russia, the dangers of such a course of action were clearly recognized. Habsburg policy was also limited by the fact that the military leaders never believed that they alone could defeat the Russian armies should a real crisis arise leading to a war in the Balkans. With her preference for the maintenance of the *status quo,* the Habsburg Empire should logically have cooperated with Britain since both countries feared Russian expansion. In such an alliance, however, the military burden and real risks would have fallen on the monarchy; the British navy would have been of little use in a land war against Russia.

Despite her enormous prestige in the previous centuries, France after the Napoleonic Wars wielded less influence in the empire than did the other three powers. Although French revolutionary ideology played a great role in the Balkan national movements, France herself from 1815 to 1848 was not a center of agitation. Thereafter, particularly during the reign of Napoleon III, French governments usually supported Balkan national movements. Without an army on the scene and with a navy second to that of her rival, Britain, France hesitated to intervene in the Near Eastern conflicts. This nation did, however, have designs on parts of Ottoman territory. In 1830 she established herself in Algeria; her influence at that time was paramount in Egypt. Later, in the 1840s and 1860s, she intervened in Syria and Lebanon. Because of her desire to expand her empire into Africa and Asia, France usually supported the formation of the national states and the weakening of the central government. She opposed any situation that would allow the entire area to fall under Russian or British control.

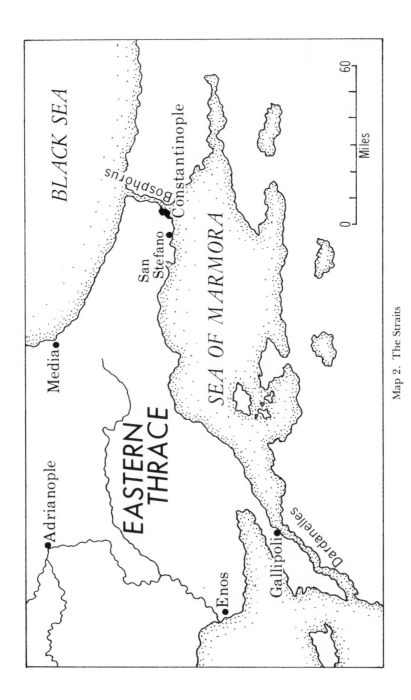

Map 2. The Straits

Unable to defend herself alone against the European states, the Ottoman Empire was forced to adopt a policy of balancing the influence of the great powers and playing one against another. In the nineteenth century this was to prove a losing struggle. The empire was compelled to grant concession after concession, both commercial and political, to Europe. The national movements made steady progress, usually with the support of one or of all of the European governments. It will be noted that although the Balkan revolts were commenced by the Christian people, the great powers made the final decisions over the establishment of the new states, their boundaries, and their forms of government. The European leaders were far from altruistic in their actions. Their own interests and the maintenance of the balance of power came first. Both the Ottoman Empire and the new Balkan states were to be subjected to the same policies and treatment that the powers employed in their other imperial adventures.

By the beginning of the nineteenth century it can thus be seen that conditions prevailed in the Balkan Peninsula that would be favorable to Christian rebellion. The weak Ottoman government could neither control rebellious Muslim notables nor defeat foreign armies. During this time of turmoil local centers of authority had appeared under strong military leaders. A tradition and habit of rebellion had thus been established. The Balkan Christian rebellions stemmed from this atmosphere and these conditions. The first, the Serbian revolution, was directly connected with the failure of the Ottoman government to maintain control over its local officials and its weakness before its Muslim opponents.

CHAPTER 2

The Serbian Revolution

THE center of the first successful revolt of a Balkan people against Ottoman authority was the pashalik of Belgrade whose administrative problems at the end of the eighteenth century in many ways reflected those of the entire empire under Selim III. Throughout the century this area had been the scene of repeated battles between Austria and the Ottoman Empire. Fighting occurred in 1716–18, 1737–39, and 1788–91. In these years the fate of the Serbian inhabitants had been deeply involved with that of the Habsburg monarchy. The wars and the extreme chaos associated with them had resulted in the emigration of large groups of Serbs into Austrian territory, primarily into southern Hungary. Particularly significant had been the mass migration of about seventy thousand Serbs under Patriarch Arsenije III in 1690. This group made Sremski Karlovci a religious and cultural center for the Serbian people. Thereafter, the Serbs in the monarchy, where conditions were much more favorable, remained in close touch with the events in Serbia proper. They were to have an important influence on the national movement, on cultural development, and on the administration of the Serbian national state in the nineteenth century.

During the wars the Habsburg government was often in administrative control of Serbian lands. Despite the opposition of the population to Ottoman rule, Austrian dominance was not popular, largely because of the activities of the Catholic church. Unlike the Ottoman Empire, which did not actively attempt to gain converts for its faith, the Catholic church, with Habsburg approval, did. Like the Greek experience with Venetian rule, the substitution of a Christian for a Muslim overlord was not attractive nor was it an aim that the Serbian population subsequently sought as a political alternative.

The chief result of these years of frontier warfare for the Serbian population was that it gave them experience in fighting. Serbs served as regular soldiers in the Habsburg army or as irregular guerrillas. They usually went into combat in their own units under their own officers. During the Austrian occupations Serbs also were given higher offices in the administration of the region than they held under the Ottoman. The experience gained in the war of 1788–91 proved particularly valuable. At this time many Serbs joined the Habsburg Free Corps, and they in fact carried the main burden of the battles. Simultaneously, Koča Andjelković organized an unsuccessful revolt, known as Koča's rebellion. Although no immediate benefits were gained from these actions the Serbian leaders obtained training in military organization and confidence in their own abilities.

The years of cooperation with Austria proved a great disappointment. The Serbs felt that the monarchy had failed to deliver promised supplies, and certainly the peace terms brought Serbia no advantages. Nevertheless, despite the fact that in the future the Serbian leaders were to turn more to Russia for aid, the Austrian frontier remained important because of its proximity. Even when the Habsburg government did not support Serbian actions, supplies and war material constantly crossed the Danube; at the same time refugees from Ottoman persecution continued to move freely into Habsburg territory.

As noted previously, the Peace of Sistova in 1791 and that of Jassy in 1792 gave Selim III a period in which to consider the reform of the empire. His desire for the establishment of peaceful and orderly conditions corresponded exactly with that of his Serbian subjects. After the devastating period of war the Serbs would have continued to accept Ottoman rule in return for the assurance of rights of local self-government and a guarantee of tranquility in the countryside. These conditions, however, could not be controlled by the central Ottoman administration. With the cessation of the fighting the janissaries and the irregular military units found themselves unemployed. They thus turned and preyed on the population. Bands of these men seized villages and their lands and converted the property into their own estates. Others joined rebel *ayan*s or bandit organizations and plundered peaceful Muslims and Christians alike. Under these circumstances the interests of the central government and the Christian population coincided; neither could tolerate a continuation of this situation.

Selim III, well aware of these problems, tried to conciliate the Serbs and alleviate the bad conditions. First, he appointed as local Ottoman administrators men who were directed to work with the people and to suppress the unlawful elements. Second, he issued three firmans (decrees), in 1793, 1794, and 1796, giving the Serbs essentially what they sought. Together these documents defined the relations of the Serbs to the Ottoman government. The Serbs now received much broader rights of local autonomy. They could collect their own taxes, bear arms, and form a militia. The abuses of the *chiftlik* system were to be corrected. These firmans became the political program of the Serbian leaders in the next years. Had these stipulations been carried out, the Serbian national revolt could probably have been postponed.

Unfortunately, Selim III and his supporters could not execute their own decisions. The problems of the empire in the following years proved too great. Moreover, Constantinople remained a center of traditional intrigue. Repeatedly, able and conciliatory commanders and administrators were removed from their positions by those whose basic interests were threatened by reform and, most important, by those whose religious sensibilities were hurt by concessions to Christians.

The chief problem in the pashalik of Belgrade remained the janissaries. One of Selim's orders in 1791 had been to forbid their return to Belgrade, a measure that these soldiers chose to resist. Their defiance of the central government was made easier by the parallel action of other, similar rebellious groups and of Pasvanoglu. The janissaries now made common cause with those who would not accept the authority of the Porte. To balance the military strength of this opposition, the Ottoman authorities were forced to call for Serbian assistance. The policy of relying on the Serbs and of granting them concessions was associated in particular with the governor of Belgrade, Hadji Mustafa Pasha, known as the "mother of the Serbs."

Within the Balkans at this time the major problem was that of controlling Pasvanoglu. Not content with the rule of extensive Bulgarian territories, he also wished to establish his friends the janissaries in Belgrade. Selim was now determined to act decisively. The Serbs were given new privileges and allowed to raise their own army under their own leaders. The population was thus fully armed. The alliance of official Ottoman forces with the Christians was successful. Pasvanoglu suffered repeated defeats until finally he retreated to his fortress at Vidin, which was placed under siege. Once again, however, general world conditions hindered Ottoman efforts. In 1798 Napoleon entered Egypt. The Porte was compelled to strip the Balkans of regular troops to meet the foreign invasion. Simultaneously pressures mounted in Constantinople. The policy of arming Christians against Muslims continued to offend deeply conservative opinion.

The new combination of circumstances proved disastrous for Serbian interests. Unable to press his military action, Selim was forced to pardon the janissaries and allow them to return to Belgrade on the condition that they promised to obey Hadji Mustafa Pasha. At the same time the sultan was also compelled to compromise with Pasvanoglu. Once back in a strong position, the janissaries returned to their old ways. They revolted against Hadji Mustafa and killed him. The balance of power thus shifted to the janissaries and Pasvanoglu at the expense of the central authority and the Serbs.

After a period of conflict and instability, during which the janissaries fought among themselves, four janissary officers, called *dahi* from their rank in the corps, emerged on top in 1802. The result of this seizure of power for the Serbs was immediately apparent; their autonomous rights were ended. The janissaries again terrorized the countryside. The events of the past repeated themselves. Large numbers of Serbs fled into the hills where they joined existing irregular bands or formed new ones. Throughout Serbia military units once more appeared. The most important area for the resistance was to be the hilly forest region of the Šumadija. Here a local notable, Karadjordje Petrović, was able to assemble by the spring of 1804 as many as thirty thousand armed men. Other centers under other local leaders were similarly organized throughout the pashalik.

These military bands were soon to be needed. At the beginning of 1804 the Serbs were faced with the fact that they would have to defend themselves or see their leadership literally destroyed. In January and February the janissaries began what was planned to be a massacre of the Serbian notables. In two months between 70 and 150 were killed. The entire province reacted. Aware of the obvious need for coordinated action and direction, about three hundred Serbian notables met at Orašac in the Šumadija in February and named Karadjordje as their commander. The Serbian revolution had begun. It now had a leader and a cause for which to fight.

The role of Karadjordje is so important in the revolution and in the first political organization of the Serbian state that a short summary of his career is in order. We know little about his early life. In fact, even the date of his birth is uncertain although it was probably 1768. His parents were poor, and the family was forced to move often in search of a livelihood. Karadjordje worked for a number of landlords before 1787 when his family left the Šumadija, perhaps because of his activities against the janissaries, and moved to the Vojvodina. There they became attached to the monastery at Krušedol. When the Austro-Turkish war broke out, Karadjordje joined the Free Corps and took part in the campaigns in western Serbia, where he gained invaluable military experience and learned Austrian military methods. After the Peace of Sistova he settled in Topola in the Šumadija where he became a livestock merchant trading with Austria. This business brought him in touch with many of his compatriots; these connections were later to prove invaluable. In addition he became a *buljukbaša* (the head of a military unit of about one hundred men) in the Serbian national militia which had been authorized by Selim III. In this capacity he cooperated with Hadji Mustafa against the janissaries and thus gained experience in Ottoman military organization. When the janissaries returned in 1801, Karadjordje, like many Serbs, foresaw that some measures of defense would have to be taken against these violent and undisciplined forces. With his military experience, Karadjordje's background was typical of many of his countrymen.

Karadjordje now became and remained the leader of the first Serbian insurrection, largely because of his personal abilities. As an outstanding military leader, he was attractive to the Serbs; he was brave, firm, and resolute. He was to show considerable good sense and judgment in handling the complex international situation during the Napoleonic period. Under his guidance the Serbian question was raised from an internal Ottoman problem to a matter of international concern. In domestic politics he was a skillful enough politician to judge accurately the mood of most of his countrymen and to hold the revolutionary movement together in face of innumerable conflicting forces and interests.

In fact, his abilities in domestic affairs were probably decisive in maintaining his leadership. Almost from the beginning of the revolution Karadjordje's authority was challenged by others. As was typical in the Ottoman system, political power lay in the individual villages and districts; there was no *Serbian* central authority for the pashalik. Even the reforms of the 1790s had not altered this situation. Consequently, each area had its own leaders and spokemen. In 1804 Karadjordje was well known and respected only in his district in the Šumadija. In the western part of the country Jakov Nenadović was the principal figure; in the eastern section Milenko Stojković and Peter Dobrnjac held a similar position. Soon sharp conflict broke out between these men with their followers and Karadjordje supported by his friends. Jealous of their position and anxious to profit from the situation, the opposition leaders fought all attempts to create a strong centralized national government for the Serbs. They did not wish to see their power in their individual localities weakened. They would agree to cooperate with a central authority only to the end of defeating the Turkish forces. As will be shown, they also attempted to enlist the support of the Russian government against Karadjordje.

In fighting his domestic opponents Karadjordje had to consider not only his personal interests, but also the obvious fact that a centralized regime with real power was necessary in a revolutionary period. Moreover, certain internal problems, such as the distribution of former Ottoman lands, taxation, and justice, had to be settled for the entire pashalik. Despite the undoubted need for a united leadership Karadjordje's rivals throughout the revolution kept up a constant pressure of criticism. They asserted that no Russian aid would be forthcoming unless he were replaced; they attacked his personal life and morals; they claimed he used excessive brutality, that he enriched himself from Turkish property, and that he was involved in various intrigues and acts of violence against other Serbs. Despite these unrelenting attacks Karadjordje, until his final military defeat, was able to maintain his personal position at the head of the first revolution. The centralization of leadership was an advantage enjoyed by the Serbian revolutionaries which was not to be shared by the Greeks later.

The divisive aspects of the Serbian internal scene were not apparent during the first days of the revolt. The sudden action of the janissaries in January of 1804 had produced a spontaneous national reaction for survival. At the meeting at Orašac in February, Karadjordje was chosen the supreme leader without opposition. At this time all of the Serbs recognized that a single strong executive authority was necessary. After May, 1804, Karadjordje was able to sign his orders and proclamations under such titles as "Supreme Vojvoda" (duke), "Commander of Serbia," and "Leader."

At first there was a unity not only in the leadership, but also in the goal to be achieved. It is most important to note that at this stage the aim of the revolt was not independence; rather it was directed against the janissary rule and toward the restoration of the autonomous rights already agreed upon by the Ottoman government. At this time representatives of the revolutionaries and the Porte were in regular communication on what the Serbs wished. Throughout the negotiations the Serbian purpose was to secure terms that would give them a position of autonomy within the Ottoman Empire. The immediate demand was the removal of the *dahis* and a full pardon for the Serbian rebels. The Serbs further wished the Porte to recognize their own head of state, a supreme *knez* (elder or chieftain), who would have authority over the Serbian population of the pashalik and who would be responsible for tax payments. He would also represent his people before the Ottoman government. The desire was also expressed that the tribute and taxes be set and that no arbitrary increases be made. In addition janissaries were to be forbidden to hold rural property, and the right of Muslims to reside in Serbian towns was to be controlled. Freedom of religion, trade, and communication were also to be guaranteed. While negotiating these points, the Serbian leaders turned to both the Habsburg and Russian governments for support.

The new situation found the Ottoman government faced with the now familiar problem. The janissaries were again technically in rebellion, but the forces against a reliance on the Christians were still strong. At first Selim III had no desire to take a stand against the Serbs. He therefore sent the popular vezir of Bosnia, Abu Bekir Pasha, who had previously negotiated successfully with the Serbian leaders, to Belgrade to put down the janissaries. By August, 1804, the *dahis* had been defeated;

again it appeared as though the janissary forces had been subdued. The situation, however, was not stable. Rebellious Muslim factions were still strong. Moreover, the Serbs now insisted upon some sort of foreign guarantee for the terms of their autonomy, a concession that the Ottoman government was loath to grant. In order to obtain outside support the Serbian government despatched a delegation, which included the prominent religious leader Matija Nenadović, to Russia. The group was received by the foreign minister Adam Czartoryski in November, 1804. Since Russia was now cooperating in foreign affairs with the Ottoman Empire against Napoleon, the Russian minister advised the Serbs to deal directly with the Porte.

The conditions in Serbia thus remained fluid. In preparation for possible future action the Serbian leaders now sought links with Christian groups in Bosnia and Hercegovina, with Greek *klepht* bands, and with the governors of Moldavia and Wallachia. On the opposing side the janissary and outlaw bands similarly organized to regain their position. In the winter and spring of 1805 they again moved into the countryside; once more chaos, terror, and anarchy prevailed. The Ottoman officials were too weak to control their own lawless elements. Under considerable pressure, Selim shifted his position. By the spring of 1805 he had come to regard the Serbs as rebels. Abandoning a policy of conciliation, he appointed the Pasha of Niš, Hafiz Pasha, as the new governor of Belgrade and sent him with an army to deal with the Serbs. Hafiz's forces were defeated in the first major clash between Serbian and Ottoman troops at Ivankovo in August, 1805. With this victory the Serbian forces proceeded to take full military control of the pashalik. Smederovo was captured in November and became the first capital of the new government. Belgrade fell at the end of the following year.

Meanwhile an important change had occurred on the international scene. Although the Ottoman Empire had at first been allied with Britain and Russia against France, French prestige in Constantinople rose sharply after the victories of Austerlitz and Jena in 1805 and 1806. Napoleon also sent an astute diplomat, General François H. B. Sebastiani, to gain an agreement with the Porte. As a result the Ottoman Empire now shifted its alliances and joined France. In the summer of 1806 fighting broke out between Russia and the Porte. This conflict was to have a decisive effect on the fate of the first Serbian revolution.

The Ottoman government, faced with Serbian forces in control of the pashalik and with renewed warfare, naturally wished to settle the Serbian question by negotiation and was willing to grant wide concessions. The new situation, however, changed both the Serbian and the Russian attitude. At war with the Ottoman Empire, the Russian government, of course, had an interest in the continuation of the revolt. For its part the

Serbian regime, having achieved success on the battlefield, was attracted to the idea that it could gain independence. The Porte had appeared prepared to give the Serbs a large measure of autonomy. The question was now whether more could be obtained and whether the Porte could be trusted to abide by its agreements and to enforce them. Under the circumstances the temptation to continue the rebellion with the objective of real independence was strong. The final decision was certainly influenced by Russian actions. Henceforth the attitude taken by the Russian government or its agents was to have a determining effect on the future of the Serbian national state.

In the summer of 1807 Colonel F. O. Paulucci arrived in Serbia to assess the political and military situation. He was to determine what assistance Serbia needed and what aid she could give Russia in the common war against the Ottoman Empire, but he was not authorized to make a binding agreement. From the evidence now available it appears that the Serbian authorities were not aware of the limited extent of this emissary's powers. On July 10 an understanding, commonly known as the Paulucci-Karadjordje Convention, was concluded. This agreement called for, among other stipulations, the appointment of Russian administrators in the Serbian lands, the establishment of Russian military garrisons in the towns, and the sending of Russian military and economic aid. Believing that he had firm assurances of effective Russian backing, Kardjordje now adopted a policy aimed at Serbian independence rather than autonomy under the Ottoman Empire. This decision was a grievous error. Between July 7 and 9 Alexander I and Napoleon met and signed the Treaty of Tilsit. One of the provisions of this pact was that France would attempt to negotiate a peace between the Russian and Ottoman empires.

The shift of the Russian attitude toward Napoleon was to have immediate disastrous consequences for Serbia. In line with the new Russian policies, the government concluded the armistice of Slobozia with the Porte in August. Although the Russian representatives to the negotiations had been instructed not to abandon the Serbs, the signature of the agreement and the end of the hostilities left the Serbian forces in an exposed military position. Meanwhile the hostility of the Ottoman government toward the Serbian rebels, of course, increased.

Despite the extreme difficulty of the situation the Serbian forces were nevertheless able to maintain control of the Serbian countryside. Their final fate would obviously depend on the evolution of world affairs. Meantime in Constantinople the crisis that resulted in the overthrow of Selim III and the eventual succession of Mahmud II was taking place. With the center of the Ottoman government paralyzed, the Serbian government was in a better position. Not only was the Porte unable to launch a major military campaign against the rebels, but it was more favorable to a negotiated settlement. Although discussions were held, it was still difficult to determine boundaries for the Serbian state.

Throughout this crucial period Karadjordje continued to face domestic opposition to his rule. In 1805 a council was established; in theory it was to be a check on his power. In 1808, however, he declared himself the hereditary supreme leader of the country, although he agreed to act in cooperation with a governing council, which was also to be the supreme court of the country. When the opposition intrigued with the Russian representative, Constantine Rodofinikin, who had arrived in August, 1807, Karadjordje sought assistance in France and Austria. The struggle over the authority to be allowed the council was not settled satisfactorily during this revolutionary period. Karadjordje, in general, was highly successful in maintaining his supreme control.

Despite his difficulties with the Russian representative Karadjordje recognized the unity of interest that bound Serbia to Russia. When fighting broke out again in 1809 between Russia and the Ottoman Empire, he was prepared to support the tsarist armies. Cooperation between and coordination of the two forces was not, however, effective. Although Karadjordje launched a successful offensive in Novi Pazar, he was subsequently severely defeated at Niš. The Ottoman troops then marched on Belgrade. In August, 1809, there occurred another mass flight of Serbs across the Danube, which included Rodofinikin. Although Serbia had not been completely reconquered, a turning point had been reached in the rebellion. Henceforth the Serbian forces were to remain on the defensive; the goal was simply to hold on to the territories that they still controlled.

In June, 1810, Russian troops arrived in Serbia for a second time. Some military cooperation followed; weapons, ammunition, and medical supplies were sent. Marshal M. I. Kutuzov, the great Russian military commander, participated in some of the planning for the joint actions. An air of optimism prevailed in the Serbian camp. With Russian assistance victory seemed at hand. But once again events in Europe intervened to destroy Serbian hopes.

Faced with the imminence of a French invasion, Alexander I now wished to sign a definitive peace treaty with the Porte in order to free his troops to meet the new attack. Again, as at the armistice of Slobozia, the Russian government acted against the interest of its ally. The Serbs were not even informed of the negotiations; they learned the final terms from the Ottoman government. The second Russian withdrawal came at a time when Serbian expectations were rising and Karadjordje had reached the height of his personal power.

In the negotiations that led to the Treaty of Bucharest of May, 1812, the Russian representatives once more attempted to do something for their former allies. Article 8 dealt with Serbia. Here it was agreed that the fortifications built by the Serbs during the revolt were to be destroyed unless they were of value to the Ottoman government. Ottoman installations that had existed before 1804 were to be reoccupied and garrisoned by Ottoman forces. In return the Porte promised a general amnesty in Serbia and certain autonomous rights. The Serbs were to control "the administration of their own affairs" and the collection and delivery of the tribute, which was to be fixed.

The reaction in Serbia was strong. Ottoman reoccupation of fortresses and cities caused particular concern. Fearful reprisals were expected. Moreover, the Serbian government had no guarantee that the Porte would implement Article 8. The Russian government instructed the Serbs to negotiate directly with Constantinople concerning the arrangements to be made, stating that Russian diplomatic support would be given. This assurance gave small comfort, particularly when it became apparent that Russian troops would not only be withdrawn from Serbia, but also from Moldavia and Wallachia. Once these armies returned to their own country, the Serbian apprehensions were fully confirmed. The Ottoman Empire was now at peace so its forces could concentrate on Serbia. The previous nine years of warfare had drained Serbian resources and manpower. Three Ottoman armies combined in the attack. In July, 1813, Karadjordje and many of the Serbian leaders crossed the Danube into Austrian territory. Ottoman armies re-entered Belgrade, a city that they had been forced to abandon in 1806. Severe reprisals were inflicted on the population. With these actions the first Serbian revolution ended.

Despite the final failure Serbia had achieved a great deal under the leadership of Karadjordje. A rebellion had been organized and the first separate national government established. International attention, particularly Russian, had been drawn to the Serbian question. Some attempt had been made to answer what was to become the great political question: whether a centralized regime or a government where the real power lay with the local communities was more advantageous. Great internal changes had been accomplished. Much Ottoman property—including land, houses, stores, and warehouses—fell into Serbian hands. It had, however, been made abundantly clear that the future of the country depended on the attitude of Russia and on the willingness of that power to back Serbian autonomy.

After the French invasion of Russia in June, 1812, the eyes of the Porte and of all of Europe remained focused on that area, next on the battles in Central Europe, and finally on the defeat of Napoleon and the occupation of France. During this period the Ottoman authorities wanted peace in their own lands and so again adopted a policy of conciliation. At the end of October, 1813, they declared a general amnesty.

Many Serbian leaders, including the head of the next phase of the Serbian national movement, Miloš Obrenović, took advantage of the offer and in return were confirmed in local positions of authority. As the Serbs returned to their homes, the Ottoman soldiers and many Muslims left the countryside. The Serbs were still armed, and the number of their potential opponents had decreased.

Despite the conciliatory actions of the Ottoman administration bad feeling continued to exist between the Christians and Muslims. As in previous situations nothing had been really decided. In 1814 a local revolt broke out. Miloš Obrenović, now the *oborknez* of Rudnik, offered to put it down on the condition that the rebels received amnesty. Although the governor of Belgrade, Suleiman Pasha, had given this assurance, many of the participants were massacred following the suppression of the rebellion. Again Serbian fears were aroused; some Serbs fled; others prepared for revolt. In April, 1815, Miloš abandoned his policy of cooperation with the Porte and this time headed the rebellion. Both domestic and world conditions now turned in favor of the Serbs. First, the Serbs had a decisive advantage numerically in comparison with the Ottoman forces. Second, the great period of warfare was ending in Europe; the Battle of Waterloo in June marked the final defeat of Napoleon. The Porte did not want a major uprising.

With the Porte in a passive mood and with Miloš also desiring negotiations, both sides could come to an agreement. Serbian delegates now went to Constantinople where they declared that their rebellion had been against Suleiman's misrule and not against the Porte itself. The Serbs were strengthened by Russian representations in their favor. The Russian government in fact warned the Porte that it should come to an agreement or Russia would bring up the question of the enforcement of Article 8 of the Treaty of Bucharest. Suleiman was removed and replaced by Maraşli Ali Pasha.

A final oral understanding was reached between Miloš and Maraşli Ali Pasha in November, 1815. Miloš now asked for the terms that the Ottoman government had accepted in 1807, but that Karadjordje had subsequently rejected when he decided to fight for independence. It was agreed that Miloš would be recognized as "supreme *knez* of Serbia," that in each province both Serbian and Ottoman officials would serve as judges in cases involving Serbs, and that a national chancery would be set up in Belgrade to act as the highest court in the land. Serbian officials were to collect the taxes, and land payments were to be settled by an official firman. Three months later Mahmud II issued a firman confirming the spirit of this arrangement. The Serbs were also given favorable tariff and trading privileges, and janissary families were excluded from owning land. A Serbian and an Ottoman official were to serve together in charge of towns and military installations. A full amnesty was also granted.

These terms did not make Serbia a truly autonomous state within the empire. Full autonomy was not achieved until 1830, but the period of active revolt and military conflict had been brought to a close. The next steps were to be achieved by diplomatic negotiations and by Russian pressure on the Porte. A Serbian administration, however, ran the country and there was a recognized national leader. A strong basis had been set for future national development.

The head of the new government was not, of course, the revolutionary hero Karadjordje, but Miloš who had excelled in negotiation rather than in fighting. Like his predecessor, Miloš soon faced opposition within the state, much of it coming from supporters of Karadjordje. In 1817 Karadjordje returned to Serbia to seek support for a planned Greek insurrection. Fearing his political strength, Miloš had him murdered and sent his head to Maraşli, who had it stuffed and presented to the sultan. The subsequent feud between the Obrenović and Karadjordjević dynasties, which colored so much of later Serbian history, arose from this event.

CHAPTER 3

The Greek Revolution

IN contrast to the Serbian revolution, which made little impression on general European diplomacy, the Greek revolt became the main international problem of the 1820s. In fact, outside intervention was to be more influential in determining the final outcome than were the actions of the Greek leaders themselves. In the same manner the subsequent evolution of Greek political life was to remain heavily dependent on the attitude of the great powers.

In addition the extreme social complexity of Greek conditions influenced the course of the revolution there. As we have seen, the Serbian revolt was carried on by a peasant people, fighting what was essentially a guerrilla war under local military leaders. Serbian society was not sophisticated or highly differentiated. Although there was a merchant class and large landowners, they were closely associated with the land and the village. The Greek world, as previously described, introduced other elements into the situation. The first direct steps toward revolution were taken by Greeks living outside of Greece proper—merchants in the cities and trading communities of the Black Sea and the Mediterranean, the Phanariotes of Constantinople, and Greeks living in the Principalities. These groups were joined by some of the notables and upper clergy of Greece proper. Once the revolution was underway in the Peloponnesus and Rumeli (mainland Greece) it involved military men and peasant followers. The essential split between the social and economic groups was reflected in a civil war that was waged parallel with the fight against Ottoman rule. In general, in the land held by the revolutionary forces, the notables of the mainland, the Phanariotes, and the wealthy shipowners found common cause against the military elements with their peasant followers. The situation, however, was never clearcut. Competition between individual military leaders and among the upper group for predominant power in the movement cut across social lines.

38

Regional differences were also significant. Men from Rumeli, the Peloponnesus, and the islands could compete with each other or form alliances.

Constantly shifting allegiances and the struggle between individuals prevented the rise of a strong leader. In contrast to the Serbian revolt there is no one man who stands out in the Greek revolution. Similarly, the Greeks were unable to form a single stable government to carry through the revolution. Repeated outbreaks of civil war prevented the formation of a united national government until 1827. The regime established at that time fell apart four years later when its president was assassinated. The final victory of the revolutionary movement found the land in a condition of political chaos.

As there was to be no permanent governmental authority, there was also no lasting military command. Individual military leaders, such as Theodore Kolokotrones in the Peloponnesus and George Karaiskakes in Rumeli, directed the operations of their own men. The Greeks fought not as a national army but in guerrilla bands. The geography of the land made this a practical and recommended method of warfare. The negative feature was the damage that these troops often did to their own countryside and their own people. The military commanders also used their troops against each other or against the civilian government. The same problems were to be found in the organization of the navy, which, although it became very effective against Ottoman shipping, was also plagued with problems of insubordination and revolt.

Reflecting well the divisions in the Greek world, the revolution had its origins in two separate spheres: the outer world of the merchant, the Phanariote, and the diaspora, and the inner world of the mainland of Greece with its military elements and its peasant people. The first revolt centered in the Danubian Principalities; the second arose from the conditions in Greece proper and from the attempt of Mahmud II to put down the revolt of Ali Pasha. The first was highly organized with an ideology greatly influenced by western thought; the second, similar to the Serbian revolt, arose on the old basis of the reaction of a Christian Orthodox peasantry against Ottoman misgovernment and general conditions of chaos and lawlessness.

The activities of the Greeks overseas centered in what was perhaps the most remarkable and successful of Balkan revolutionary organizations, the Philike Hetairia, or Society of Friends. Founded by three impoverished Greek merchants in Odessa in 1814, this group enlisted widespread support, particularly among merchant and professional groups on the lower level. Wealthy established merchants and peasants were seldom found among its members. Organized on the model of the Masons and other revolutionary bodies, it had an elaborate ritual and different grades and placed a great emphasis on secrecy and conspiracy.

In 1818 the Hetairia moved its headquarters to Constantinople, which, although it was the Ottoman capital, contained a large Greek population. Serious preparations were then made for revolt. The aim was to be a general Balkan uprising supported by the Russian government.

Russian assistance was central in the plans of the society. In fact, its leaders in arguing for their program gave every hint that Russian backing was assured. They spoke of a mysterious *arche* at the head of the society who might be Tsar Alexander I himself. In the past the Russian government had indeed shown an interest in Balkan resistance to the Ottoman Empire. In 1770 the Russian government had given encouragement to the ill-fated revolt in the Peloponnesus. In subsequent treaties Russia had extended at least a claim to be the protector of Balkan Orthodoxy and to have special rights to speak for the Serbs and Romanians. Moreover, many of the Russian consuls in the Balkans, who were mostly Greek, were members of the Hetairia; other Russian officials also knew of the society and its goals.

In preparation for the revolution the society needed a leader with prestige. The obvious first choice was John Capodistrias, a Greek from the Ionian Islands who was then Russian foreign minister. Although he declined, another Greek in Russian service accepted. Alexander Ypsilantes, the son of a former *hospodar* of Wallachia, and at the time an aide-de-camp of the tsar, now took charge of the organization of the revolt. Other influential Greeks in Greece proper were also recruited. Particularly important were Theodore Kolokotrones, Petrobey Mavromichales, an important notable in Mani in the Peloponnesus, and Germanos, the Bishop of Patras. Agents of the society combed Greece to gain converts and establish cells. Since the ideal of the society initially was a general Balkan uprising, attempts were made to enlist other nationalities. Here, too, much success was achieved; Bulgars, Romanians, and Serbs joined as well as Greeks. In time the society had hundreds of branches and a large membership.

Initially, the society planned that the first actions should be undertaken simultaneously in Serbia and in the Peloponnesus. Unfortunately, conditions in Serbia were not favorable for such an event. The Hetairia was successful in recruiting Karadjordje, who had been living in exile but who in 1817 returned to Serbia to present the Greek plans. The whole idea of an uprising, however, was in contradiction to the basic ideas of Miloš on how Serbia should act. Whereas Karadjordje favored revolutionary tactics, Miloš believed that Serbia could best gain her goals through evolutionary means and by cooperating with the sultan. Moreover, Miloš was at this time engaged in negotiations with the Porte on gaining the title of hereditary prince. He did not want these discussions interrupted, and he did not think that his country was prepared for another conflict. The entire issue also became involved in Serbian internal politics. Karadjordje had become a political rival; some of Miloš's other opponents, such as Stojković, had joined the society. The execution of Karadjordje in 1817 ended any possibility that Serbia might join in the plans for a general revolution.

The Danubian Principalities were finally chosen as an alternative. Although these lands were predominantly Romanian, there was a great deal of logic in this decision. First, it must be remembered that the Hetairia saw itself as leading a general Balkan uprising. The Principalities had become a center for Serbian and Bulgarian refugees. In addition, within Moldavia and Wallachia the chief political influence was Greek; the Phanariote regimes controlled the administration of both provinces. Michael Suţu (Soutsos), the *hospodar* of Moldavia, was a member of the Hetairia. Support was also to be expected from the Romanian upper clergy, which was Greek-dominated, and the large landowners, many of whom were Greek or had close ties with the Phanariote regime. Most important was to be the initial cooperation of Tudor Vladimirescu, who now emerged as the leader of a Romanian national movement based on the peasants and the small landowners. A member of the Hetairia, Vladimirescu at first joined in the Greek plans.

The choice of the Principalities was also determined by the weakness of the Ottoman forces stationed there. The few Ottoman soldiers in the land were concentrated in the Danubian forts. There were no Ottoman officials in the countryside where the local militia was in the hands of men whom the Hetairia considered dependable supporters.

Despite the favorable situation in the Romanian provinces Russian support was recognized as essential for success. The Hetairia expected that Russia would be forced to intervene should the revolt break out in the Romanian lands because she had exerted such great political influence there in the past. According to an agreement reached between Russia and the Porte in 1802, Ottoman troops could not be sent into the Principalities without Russian consent. The revolutionary leaders could well expect that the tsarist government would either send in troops itself or that it would prevent the entrance of Ottoman forces.

In the spring of 1821 the Hetairia commenced the revolt under the direction of Ypsilantes. The assured support of Vladimirescu and the fact that Ottoman forces were tied up with the suppression of Ali Pasha in Greece were factors in the determination of the time for action. The Hetairia kept in close touch with events in Greece proper, where it was expected that a similar revolt would soon break out.

From the beginning the revolution in the Principalities was a disaster. No general Balkan uprising followed; during the entire period Serbia did not move to hinder or embarrass the Porte. More important, not only did Russia not give assistance, but the tsar denounced the entire action. Alexander I was at the Congress of Laibach, which had been called to discuss the revolutionary movements in Italy and Spain, when he received word of the revolt. Under the influence of the Austrian minister Prince Metternich and the spirit of the Holy Alliance, the tsar saw this uprising as another instance of a general European conspiracy. He disavowed the revolt and did not move to prevent the entrance of Ottoman troops into the provinces.

The revolutionary movement also met severe reversals within the Principalities. When Russian intervention did not occur, the relations between the Greeks and Romanians began to deteriorate. The majority of Romanians, regardless of social strata, disliked the rule of the Phanariotes. The Hetairia was essentially a Greek nationalistic organization; there was no basic Romanian interest in a great Greek victory. Even more serious, under Tudor Vladimirescu the movement soon acquired a strong social character. Peasants throughout the country used the opportunity to rise against their landowners. Vladimirescu himself was in a very difficult position. Finally, realizing that the revolt would not succeed, he tried to save himself by initiating negotiations with the Ottoman authorities. The Hetairia, aware of this, kidnapped him. Ypsilantes then had him executed on May 27. With his death any hope of a united Romanian support behind the Hetairia died.

Meanwhile the Ottoman troops had entered the Principalities. At the beginning of the movement Greek forces had massacred the Ottoman populations of Jassy and Galați. Reprisals were to be expected. Ypsilantes and the "Sacred Battalion," as the strongest Greek unit was called, were decisively defeated at the Battle of Dragașani. In June Ypsilantes fled to Austria where he was imprisoned for the next nine years. The revolution in the Principalities was at an end.

Although the Hetairia had failed in the Romanian lands, by the summer of 1821 a similar revolt was well underway in Greece proper. Here the entire situation was to prove much more favorable, and conditions more closely resembled those in Serbia with the armed peasant population and the experienced military men. The Hetairia had, of course, been extremely active here, and preparations for revolution had been discussed. The involvement of Greek bands against Ottoman troops first occurred when Mahmud II decided to settle the problem of Ali Pasha. A situation soon arose that resembled Selim III's attempt to suppress the janissaries in Serbia.

Faced with a determined Ottoman army in 1819 and 1820, Ali Pasha found himself in a dangerous position. Although he relied on Muslim support and despite the fact that he had previously denounced the Hetairia to the Porte, Ali was forced to seek Greek and Albanian aid. He tried to make himself popular in the Christian villages through the reduction of taxes and labor dues. He appealed in particular to the *Kape-*

tanioi (captains, military men) of Rumeli to join him against the Ottoman forces.

At first Ali failed to gain Greek support. In August, 1820, Mahmud's troops began to move rapidly forward. Ali was finally forced to withdraw into the fortress of Janina with about two thousand supporters. Although the Ottoman army held the surrounding land, Ali was able to defend himself in the city. During these operations Greek military men had first fought with the Ottoman soldiers. When these forces began to ravage the land, however, the Greeks changed sides. By early 1821 some five to seven thousand Greek mountain fighters had joined Ali. The Ottoman army now found itself in the weaker position.

While Greeks were fighting Ottoman soldiers in northern Greece, the Peloponnesus became the center of what was to be the main Greek revolt. Although the Hetairia had a network in Greece, the movement here was not coordinated closely with that in the Principalities. By the time the news of Ypsilantes' crossing of the Pruth reached Greece, the events leading to the revolution were well underway.

Like the Danubian Principalities, the Peloponnesus was a logical place for the organization of Greek resistance. The area enjoyed at this time a type of political autonomy that was very similar to what the Serbs had sought and finally won only after years of fighting and negotiations. In each local community Greek officials were in control. Moreover, there were executive and legislative organs for the entire region. Each community elected representatives to a provincial body, which in turn chose members for the Peloponnesian Senate. This chamber had virtual control over administration and taxation of the area. In addition, the Greeks chose two representatives to sit with two Muslims to form the permanent council of the vezir of the Peloponnesus. The territory also had the right to send representatives directly to the Porte to discuss demands and grievances.

Although Greek nationals thus controlled the local government, the assemblies were in practice dominated by the large landowners. These notables, together with the higher clergy, were not under all circumstances interested in revolt against Ottoman authority. They were a part of the existing order, and they had vested interests in protecting the Ottoman regime. The clergy were also divided in their attitude. The revolutionary doctrines of groups like the Philike Hetairia could be in direct opposition to the tenets of Orthodox Christianity. In the past the church had not only cooperated in the Ottoman political system, but it had firmly resisted influences from the West. The secular and rational leanings of the revolutionary ideology were more of a threat to the power of the church than was the increasingly feeble Ottoman rule.

The hand of these groups was, however, forced by events. Because of rumors of impending revolt, as a test of loyalty the Ottoman authorities in March summoned the notables of the Peloponnesus to a meeting at Tripolitsa. A large number complied and were held hostage once the revolt broke out. Others, particularly those from the northern part of the peninsula, resisted. The revolution was officially proclaimed almost concurrently, around April 6, by Bishop Germanos in Patras and by Petrobey of Mani in Kalamata. It will be noticed that the movement in Greece proper thus contrasts with that in the Principalities. There was not a centrally organized and planned rising in the Peloponnesus. Agents of the Philike Hetairia had pressed circumstances to the point that some notables were so compromised that they had to proclaim the revolt. Others joined because of Ottoman measures. As in Serbia, the Greeks reacted to events; the first fighting was done by military groups and by peasant bands under local leaders. This pattern was to be maintained throughout the revolt.

The Ottoman reaction to the Greek defiance was at first weak. The authorities had already more than they could handle with the uprising in the Principalities, the problem of Ali Pasha, and a war with Persia which was also in progress. They were, however, forced to take some action. As in the Principalities, wholesale massacres of Muslim civilians had been among the initial acts of the Greek rebels. The destruction of the Muslim population of Tripolitsa in October, 1821, was particularly bloody. Ottoman reprisals followed a similar line. On Easter eve, before the first sizeable Greek massacres of Muslims in insurgent Greece, a group of janissaries hanged the patriarch of Constantinople and some of his bishops in front of their church. Greeks in the Ottoman capital and elsewhere were attacked and killed. Throughout the revolution both sides repeatedly committed atrocities; mutual reprisal and massacres were weapons in the type of guerrilla war waged. It was the Ottoman acts, however, and not the Greek, that received publicity and attention in Europe, including Russia. This fact was to influence strongly European public opinion and to be a cause of European intervention. The Ottoman massacre of an estimated three thousand inhabitants of the island of Chios in April, 1822, was to make a particularly strong impression.

Although the Ottoman forces did suppress the revolt in the Principalities, they were at first able to make little headway against the movement in Greece. Until Ali Pasha was finally defeated and died in February, 1822, the Porte did not have an army available. The war in the Greek lands was also very difficult to conduct; the Greeks were fighting on their own territory, and the terrain was ideal for guerrilla tactics. The Ottoman troops simply could not stamp out bands operating in inaccessible mountains. Moreover, the rebels early established a firm base of operations. By the summer of 1822 they held the Peloponnesus and many islands. The most important of these, Hydra, Spetsai, and Psara, became vital for the revolution as centers for the organization of a naval force and for supplies. North of the Isthmus of Corinth the Greeks were also able to hold Misolonghi, Athens, and Thebes with the surrounding area. Misolonghi became particularly significant. The revolt remained concentrated in this restricted area. Outbreaks in other parts of the Greek-inhabited lands were suppressed. The problem for the Ottoman government was to subdue this section. Its armies, setting out from Thessaly and Epirus, normally operated from Rumeli and from there organized campaigns into the Peloponnesus.

In the first period of the revolt, from 1821 to 1825, the rebels were able to hold their main positions. Aided by their close knowledge of the sea, they managed to organize very effective naval forces against Ottoman sea transport. These fleets operated more as pirates than as a formal fighting unit, but they did maintain contact with the outside world. Although the Greeks were thus able to meet the external threat of the Ottoman troops, they were to prove less successful in dealing with their internal problems. In fact, whenever pressure from the Ottoman military lessened, the revolutionary leaders turned against each other. Parallel with the struggle against the Ottoman Empire, we find in the Peloponnesus the outbreak of a civil war between the forces who had previously joined to support the uprising.

After the outbreak of the fighting the need to provide some sort of central authority was recognized. Also at this time, chiefly because of the reprisals taken against Greeks by the Ottoman authorities, prominent Greeks from the outer Greek world began to arrive in the country. They brought with them their more sophisticated political experiences, their better formal education, and often a belief in many of the political principles of the French Revolution. In June, 1821, Demetrios Ypsilantes, the brother of Alexander, arrived. The appearance of the Phanariote Alexander Mavrokordatos was also to prove politically significant. Ypsilantes now favored the convening of an assembly and the formation of a unitary state with a centralized leadership. Supported by the military leaders, in particular by Theodore Kolokotrones, he sought to place himself at the head of this government. In December, 1821, an assembly meeting at Epidaurus established a government and in January, 1822, issued a constitution. Here the civilian elements, the islanders and the Peloponnesian notables, with Mavrokordatos particularly prominent, were able to gain the regime that they wished. The model for the constitution of Epidaurus was the French Directory; the aim was specifically to prevent the concentration of authority in the hands of one man. The executive power was invested in a five-man committee headed by Mavrokordatos. Realizing that the real strength of the state remained in the regions of Greece, Mavrokordatos soon withdrew to Misolonghi to create a firm local base for himself. This government, dominated by notables and islanders, was not respected by Kolokotrones and his military and peasant followers.

In December, 1822, a second national assembly was held at Astros. Here some attempts were made to centralize the government, but the chief concern of the members was Kolokotrones. In an attempt to assure civilian control of the military actions, Kolokotrones was deprived of his military command. He reacted by kidnapping some members of the government and forcing others to flee. Two centers of authority now appeared. Kolokotrones held the important city of Nauplion; the civilian representatives settled at Kranidi where they were in close touch with Hydra and Spetsai. Here a government was formed under George Kountouriotes, who represented the islands and was the wealthiest man in Greece. He was joined by Andrew Zaimes, a Peloponnesian notable, and John Kolettes, who was to be important in future Greek politics. A Vlach from Epirus, Kolettes had come to the Peloponnesus in 1821. He had previously been connected with the court of Ali Pasha, and he had great influence among the military men of Rumeli. In the future he was to stand for the interests of that area.

In the struggle between the two centers the advantages lay with the civilian group at Kranidi, which was closer to a legitimate political authority. Its victory was assured when it received a British loan in 1824. Kolokotrones himself surrendered Nauplion in return for a sum of money. Despite this settlement the Greek political scene did not stabilize. At the end of 1824 civil war broke out again. The islands and Rumeli now fought against the Peloponnesus; soldiers from Rumeli made devastating raids into the Peloponnesus.

By 1825 the Greek and Ottoman forces faced a stalemate. The Porte could not crush the revolutionaries in the Peloponnesus and Rumeli; the rebels had not enlarged their area of control and they had squandered their resources in internal fighting. This balance was broken when Mahmud II decided to call in his vassal Mohammed Ali, the pasha of Egypt. This action was to change the entire situation in the eastern Mediterranean and to lead to foreign intervention.

Mohammed Ali placed a high price on his services. He was promised the island of Crete, and his son Ibrahim Pasha was to become the governor of the Peloponnesus. Crete was taken with little difficulty. In February, 1825, an Egyptian army landed in the Peloponnesus. The undisciplined Greek soldiers could not match the trained and modern Egyptian troops. The Greeks now paid the price for the years they had wasted in internal strife; they were not prepared to meet a major assault. Parallel with the Egyptian operations in the south, the Ottoman army pressed the attack in the north. In April, 1826, the major stronghold of Misolonghi fell; in June the Acropolis in Athens was in Ottoman hands.

The revolution appeared lost. Only a major foreign intervention could save the Greek cause.

The decisive importance of foreign, that is Russian, intervention in Serbian affairs and the disastrous effect of Alexander's denunciation of the revolt in the Principalities has already been shown. The Russian attitude toward the Greek national movement, however, was extremely complex. Alexander I was indeed at this time strongly conservative, and in Europe he joined with Metternich in demanding the repression of revolutionary activity. He was nevertheless the tsar of a country that had obligations toward Orthodox Christians and had already made claims to be the protector of the Orthodox population of the empire. The hanging of the patriarch and the massacre of Greek populations were not actions that could be so easily tolerated. The suppression of a political rebellion could be allowed; a Holy War was another matter. Russian economic interests were also involved with the fate of Greek shipping in the Black Sea and the Mediterranean. The civil war had disrupted commerce and made the seas unsafe. In the summer of 1821 the worsening of diplomatic relations between Russia and the Porte led first to an ultimatum and then to the severing of relations. In these negotiations the Russian government showed itself primarily interested in the protection of Orthodoxy and in conditions in the Principalities rather than in a movement for Greek liberation. This emphasis in the Russian attitude was to continue. In the first years after the Greek revolt began neither Russia nor the other European powers wanted a war in the Balkans over the issue.

Although Russian attention lessened after 1821, interest in Greek affairs in the West began to rise. In August, 1822, George Canning followed Robert Castlereagh as prime minister in Britain. British policy still called for the maintenance of the power and prestige of the Ottoman Empire as a check against Russia, but Canning was more flexible in his attitude. The revolt was also upsetting British commerce in the area and having an unsettling effect on the Ionian Islands, which were under British protection. When the Porte was unable to stamp out the rebellion, the British government felt itself drawn into the affair. What it wished to avoid at all costs was the establishment of an autonomous or independent Greece under Russian control. Canning now came to adopt a policy that called for cooperation with Russia and then with France on Greek problems. The aim was to bind the two powers in order to prevent them from acting in a manner damaging to British interests.

The British as well as other governments also had to face a strong wave of public opinion. The Greek cause was immensely aided by the great movement of romantic Philhellenism. All of the leading statesmen of Europe from London to St. Petersburg had received a classical education. They, like the other educated members of their society, tended to see in the modern Greeks the direct descendants of their schoolbook heroes. They imagined a noble, brave, and beautiful people, closely resembling classical sculptures, battling frightful Muslim hordes. Moreover, the first Greek constitutions were liberal in form and adopted from western models. European liberals thus saw in the revolt a social and political struggle sympathetic to their persuasions. Philhellenes came from all segments of society. Many, particularly from the German states, came to fight in Greece. Most influential for the Greek cause was to be the support of the Bavarian king Ludwig I and the poets Byron and Shelley. In Russia the religious note of embattled Orthodoxy was added.

On the basis of British self-interest and popular support Canning began to take a series of measures. In 1823 the Greeks were recognized as belligerents; this gave them certain advantages in naval warfare. In 1824 the City of London granted the Greek government a loan with a face value of three million pounds. This transaction was characterized by fraudulence and maladministration; nevertheless, it gave some British financiers a stake in Greece's future. Other loans were to follow. Even more significant was Canning's move toward cooperation with Russia. Certainly, both London and St. Petersburg had many interests in common in the Greek question despite their antagonism in other areas. Neither liked the involvement of Mohammed Ali; both had been harmed by the commercial interruptions and wanted peaceful conditions restored.

In 1825 Alexander I died and was succeeded by the more conservative Nicholas I. Nicholas proved to be an even greater opponent of revolutionary movements than his brother had been; he was also more decisive in his actions. Canning used the occasion of the coronation to send the Duke of Wellington to Russia. There, in April, 1826, the Protocol of St. Petersburg was signed. The two powers agreed to mediate between the Greek rebels and the Ottoman government with the aim of establishing an autonomous Greek state.

The signing of the agreement signified that Russia would cooperate with Britain on the matter of Greece. This question was not, however, of prime concern to the Russian government; the affairs of Serbia and the Principalities always took precedence. Russia now turned to settle the issues that had arisen in connection with these regions. In March, 1826, the Russian government sent an ultimatum claiming that conditions in Serbia and the Principalities were in violation of the treaties. The Porte was directed to remove its troops from the Principalities and to restore the situation that had existed prior to the Greek revolt. The stipulations of Article 8 of the Treaty of Bucharest were to be carried out in Serbia.

Once again the Ottoman Empire was in a period of severe internal crisis. In June Mahmud II, after careful internal preparation, finally took the great step of abolishing the janissaries. Although this measure was essential for the safety of the state, the Ottoman military forces were temporarily in disarray. The Porte could thus not easily resist the new demands that Russia now pressed. Therefore, in October, in the Convention of Akkerman, the Russian government received the terms that it had demanded. This agreement was of profound significance for future Serbian and Romanian affairs. Russia's position as the protector of these areas was acknowledged, and thus her right to interfere in their domestic affairs.

Meanwhile France had joined Britain and Russia in a common diplomatic front. The French government could not stand aside and allow a major Mediterranean crisis to be mediated without its participation. The French king, Charles X, was also a Philhellene. In the Treaty of London of July, 1827, the three signatory powers agreed to try to secure an autonomous Greece through mediation between the Porte and the rebels. The allies, however, did more than sign documents. They now cooperated in establishing a naval blockade of Greece designed to prevent communication between Egypt and its troops in the Peloponnesus. In October, 1827, the combined allied squadron entered the Bay of Navarino where a Turco-Egyptian fleet lay anchored. Shots were exchanged and general fighting broke out. As a result the entire Ottoman fleet was sunk. This action, planned by neither participant, inaugurated a chain of events that led to direct Russian military intervention in the Balkans.

The Navarino engagement occurred at a low point in Greek fortunes. Athens had fallen and the Egyptian troops were victorious. Moreover, the official British reaction to Navarino was not heartening. Canning had died two months before, and his successor, Wellington, condemned the allied action and in effect reversed Canning's policy. Wellington now allowed Russia and the Ottoman Empire to go to war. Angered by the Navarino episode and by other events the Porte denounced the Akkerman convention. War broke out between Russia and the Ottoman Empire in April, 1828. Although the Greek question was not really at issue between the two powers, the war did decide the question of the Greek national state.

After a difficult campaign in the Balkans, the Russian army finally reached Adrianople. There in September, 1829, the belligerents signed the Treaty of Adrianople. At this time the Russian government faced the question of whether it should seek the partition of the empire and its destruction as a truly independent power. It was decided that the state should be maintained, but that Russia should attempt to dominate it. The terms of the peace were thus not hard. Russia took her reward for victory in territory in the Caucasus and a confirmation of her protectorate over Serbia and the Danubian Principalities. The treaty also provided for the settlement of the Greek question by international mediation.

Meanwhile, political conditions had improved temporarily in Greece. The Kountouriotes government had been replaced by one under Zaimes after the fall of Misolonghi. Kolokotrones remained a problem. A third national assembly was held in 1827 and drew up the Constitution of Troezene. It also took the important step of inviting Capodistrias to come to Greece as president. Two British Philhellenes, Sir Richard Church and Alexander Cochrane, were chosen to head the Greek military and naval forces.

Capodistrias arrived in Greece in February, 1828. He had been dismissed from Russian service in 1822 and had been living thereafter in Switzerland. In Greek politics he had the support of Kolokotrones and his followers and of the Peloponnesian notables. An experienced administrator, he recognized that the country needed a strong, stable government and the support of the great powers. As a result of his past career and his acquaintance with European liberal political thought, he attempted to organize Greece according to the theories of the time. He wished to establish a centralized, bureaucratic administration which would govern the land justly with due regard for the interests of all of the social groups.

Immediately Capodistrias encountered a great deal of opposition; he was never popular with the peasants. He was also unable to control the distribution of the land. During the revolution Ottoman property that passed into the hands of the rebels, including the estates, was divided among those who held the political and military power: the notables and the military leaders. It was not shared among the peasants. In foreign relations Capodistria's position was weakened by the fact that both Britain and France unjustly considered him a Russian partisan.

Despite his difficulties Capodistrias did provide the necessary strong direction in Greek affairs. Unfortunately, he was assassinated in October, 1831. The next administration was headed by three men: Agostino Capodistrias, the brother of the president, Kolokotrones, and Kolettes. These divergent leaders soon quarreled, and the country was again plunged into a state of political anarchy. The failure of the Greeks to form a stable, lasting administration accounts for the form of government finally given the country by the great powers. It also helps explain why Greeks were allowed so small a political role in the first administrations established in independent Greece.

As political conditions degenerated in the country, the diplomats conferred on the future of Greece. It will be noted that the fundamental decisions, that is, those concerning the form of government and the person of the first ruler, were made by France, Britain, and Russia and not by representatives of the Greeks. The great powers now determined that Greece should be independent, not autonomous, but that the state should receive very reduced boundaries. It was also to have a monarchical form of government. The question of a constitution was left undecided. The important agreement for Greece was signed in London in February, 1830. The independent kingdom established in this treaty was expressly placed under the guarantee of the three powers.

The next task was the selection of a ruler. The crown was first offered to Leopold of Saxe-Coburg. Though he initially accepted, he later refused because he was not satisfied with the boundaries of the state or with the financial arrangements. He was also not encouraged by Capodistrias. The choice of a ruler was to prove difficult since the powers had agreed that no member of one of their ruling dynasties could hold this office. Finally, in 1832 the governments agreed on the selection of Otto, the seventeen-year-old son of King Ludwig of Bavaria. Otto arrived in Greece in 1833 with a new European loan and with the boundaries of the state finally set at the Arta-Volos line. He adopted the Greek form of his name, Othon.

By 1833 a Greek state with a foreign prince had thus been established. Despite the fact that the territories allotted included most of those held by the insurgents during the revolution, only about 800,000 Greeks inhabited the area. Three-quarters of the Greek people remained under Ottoman rule. Moreover, notwithstanding the apparent success of the revolutionary movement, it can be argued the Greek nation as a whole lost more than it gained. The privileged position previously enjoyed by the Greeks in the empire has already been emphasized. This situation changed after the revolt in 1821. Greeks continued to serve in high posts in the Ottoman service, but the prize offices were lost, in particular the *hospodar*ships of Moldavia and Wallachia, and with them the preeminent Greek position in the Principalities. In general, Greeks were now looked upon with suspicion and hostility by the Ottoman authorities. The effect was also felt in commercial and financial circles. In Constantinople Armenians replaced Greeks as the predominant element in banking. In the supplying of state and military needs Bulgarian merchants gained a stronger role. The Greek merchant communities remained, but their special position was lost. In addition, Greek shipping, on which so many fortunes had been based, had been severely damaged and had to be rebuilt. Equally tragic for the countryside was the legacy of ten years of civil war and revolt. Large areas, particularly in the Peloponnesus, were completely devastated and their population decimated.

A final negative aspect was the role that the three protecting powers were henceforth to play in Greek internal and foreign affairs. Although Greece, unlike Serbia, was now an independent state, she was to be subject to a degree of foreign interference almost as vexatious as Ottoman control had been. As already seen, Russia had by this time established herself as the recognized protecting power in Serbia and the Principalities, but these states had the advantage that they were dealing with one government. Greece, in contrast, had to deal with three powers who usually carried on radically opposing policies in their relations with Athens. Of the three Britain, with her paramount seapower in the Mediterranean, was in the strongest position. As will be shown, however, both France and Russia also exercised great influence on the future of the country.

CHAPTER 4

The Autonomous Serbian State

WITH the completion of the agreements of 1815 and 1816, which gave Serbia a condition of semiautonomy, the Serbian leaders next faced the task of setting up a national government and organizing the administration of the country. In the next years they confronted the same great problems that were to beset the statesmen of all of the successor states of the Ottoman Empire. First, they had to establish the basic framework of government and decide on the relationship between the central and local authorities; second, they had to determine the course of the foreign policy of their country; third, they had to concern themselves with their internal social and economic conditions.

The main internal political problems remained the same as those that had existed during the revolutionary period of both Serbia and Greece. The relationship between Miloš and opposition notables had yet to be settled. The question of the establishment of a council or an assembly to check the executive remained in dispute. In addition, the place of the Orthodox church in the secular state had to be defined.

In the question of foreign relations two problems were most obvious. Despite the agreements that had been made the exact status of Serbia within the empire was not clear. The goal remained the securing of full autonomy based on a treaty. In addition, the new state contained only a minority of the Serbian people. A decision had to be made concerning future expansion and the regions on which attention was to be concentrated. In foreign affairs relations with the great powers as well as with the suzerain Porte had to be regulated. Although Russia was by treaty the protector power, Austria, France, and Britain were to play a role in Serbian affairs. Russian influence, though strong, was limited by the fact that the two lands were not contiguous. Adjacent Austria was in a more advantageous position.

Finally, the Serbian leaders had to meet the enormous problem of

53

bringing their extremely backward country into the modern world. Since the overwhelming majority of the people were peasants, the land question was of first importance. The government was also faced with the necessity of establishing a network of communications, of creating favorable conditions for trade and commerce, and of setting up a national educational system. As will be shown, in the nineteenth century these aspects of national life were relatively neglected. As in the other Balkan states, Serbian attention remained fixed primarily on internal political controversies and on issues related to foreign expansion.

The first political form of the Serbian government was the creation of Miloš Obrenović and is unique among the Balkan nations. Unlike the situation in Greece, where foreign influence was predominant, Miloš was in control in Belgrade. Like Karadjordje, his position rested on his role in the revolution. He had been twenty-three when the revolt broke out. His brother Milan had played a major part in the anti-Karadjordje groups. When Milan was poisoned, his followers blamed Karadjordje, whose responsibility was never proved. Miloš continued to associate with his brother's friends. When Karadjordje fled in 1813 the fact that Miloš remained contributed to his prestige among his compatriots.

As has been seen, Miloš preferred to win advantages for his country by negotiation with the Porte rather than by insurrection. Although his methods, combined with a favorable international situation, did win gains for Serbia, the prince remained a controversial figure. He came to power in difficult times. In 1816 Serbia had neither an established central government and administrative system nor written laws. Miloš was thus faced with the necessity of setting up a state structure and at the same time dealing with the Ottoman government with the goal of gaining more rights and of preventing encroachment on those already attained. Miloš met the major political problem by simply taking the control of the state into his hands. It has been said that he ran the country like a Turkish pasha. Opposition came chiefly from those of relatively equal rank, namely, the notables prominent in the revolutionary period. By and large he remained popular with the great majority of the peasantry who had for centuries lived in a patriarchal society under an absolute authority. His methods of rule were not in contradiction to their understanding of political power.

Nor did Miloš hesitate to use his privileged position to make enormous profits. Of course, other leaders of revolutionary movements had and were to act similarly. What was unusual here was the degree of the prince's success. Miloš came from a poor family, but in 1837, two years before his abdication, his personal gross income was 1,600,000 groschen or 17 percent of the nation's gross income of 9,500,000 groschen. In order to acquire this wealth he had used many methods, such as seizing the choice lands of former Turkish owners, establishing a monopoly on livestock exports and the sale of salt, and maintaining the peasant labor dues on the land he acquired. He even came to own estates and twelve villages in neighboring Wallachia. In the 1840s, when he was in exile, he was regarded as one of the richest men in Europe.

Despite his evident corruption, at least by western standards, Miloš did establish a national regime and he did gain the recognition of Serbian autonomy. This second achievement was perhaps the most noteworthy of his career. Obviously, the conditions granted in 1815 were not satisfactory. Miloš had been recognized as supreme *knez* but not as a hereditary ruler. The boundaries of the state had not been set, and Ottoman officials still held some positions. The prince's first goals thus became the acquisition of the right of hereditary succession, the settling of the frontiers at their maximum possible extention, and the removal of all Ottoman officials and soldiers from Serbian territory.

In his relations with the Porte the prince continued to follow his former methods of negotiation, including the distribution of bribes. The delivery of the head of Karadjordje to the sultan and the refusal to aid in the Greek rebellion were part of his program of collaboration. For Miloš personally, of course, the recognition of his position as hereditary ruler was of first importance. In 1817 he had a hand-picked assembly proclaim him hereditary prince, but he needed the assent of the Porte to make this effective.

Miloš's first successes came not so much because of his own cleverness, but because he had Russian support. The Convention of Akkerman of 1826, as has been shown, called for the implementation of Article 8 of the Treaty of Bucharest and placed Serbia under Russian protection. This clause meant that the prince could expect Russian aid in international relations. The Treaty of Adrianople of 1829 confirmed these stipulations. In 1830 the sultan issued a *hatti-sherif* (imperial rescript) which established Serbia as a truly autonomous state. Miloš was now recognized as prince of Serbia with the right of succession in his family. By 1830 the Serbian leaders had thus gained control over their internal affairs. Serbian officials administered the country, collected the taxes, and regulated church affairs and other major aspects of national life. Ottoman nationals were forbidden to live in the countryside. The Muslim population was concentrated in the major fortress cities. Ottoman landed property was confiscated with the agreement made that the Porte would compensate the owners from the Serbian tribute.

The problem of the delineation of the Serbian boundaries remained. Both the treaties of Akkerman and Adrianople called for the inclusion in Serbia of the six *nahije* (districts) that Karadjordje had taken but Miloš had never ruled. Because of his preoccupation with the revolt of Mohammed Ali of Egypt, the sultan could not resist these demands. In November, 1833, he yielded the lands in dispute. Miloš's domain thus extended to the Timok River in the east and the Danube in the north; in the south the boundary ran east-west roughly north of the important city of Niš and then from Raška in a northwesterly direction to the Drina River, which formed the western frontier. Serbia developed within these borders until 1878.

With the settling of the crucial issues of autonomy and national boundaries, more attention could now be paid to the question of who would control the political power in the state. As has already been shown, this subject had caused constant difficulties for Karadjordje even in times of national danger. Two practical choices existed: either the government would be dominated by a strong leader and his followers, or it would be controlled by a group of notables. The establishment of centralized control in a sense contradicted Serbian traditions under Ottoman rule. On the eve of the revolution Serbian authority was patriarchal in nature and was based on the village and the *nahija* with the *knez* and the notables as the titular leaders. Karadjordje wished to replace this decentralized system with a strong personal rule. His opponents, basing their claims on the old system, wished to create a kind of union of local districts with a collective republican government. They tended to use western European terminology, talking of constitutions, but they wished in fact a return to the former order of rule. We have seen how they attempted to gain Russian support.

This pattern of political conflict continued throughout Miloš's reign. It will be noticed that relatively few individuals were involved actively in the political life of the country. Traditionally, there existed in Serbia the democratic institution of the skupština, which was an assembly of armed males who met outdoors to decide questions of general importance. During this period national assemblies of this type were indeed called, but they were not responsible deliberative bodies. They were generally summoned to ratify decisions or programs drawn up by the prince or the notables.

Throughout his reign Miloš, like Karadjordje, faced repeated challenges from the notables, who now stood for the introduction of a constitution or charter which would establish a council or chamber with the power to check the prince. They were joined in their stand by merchants, government officials, and others who did not like the prince's arbitrary methods. The agreement of 1815 between Miloš and Maraşli Ali Pasha had provided for the establishment of a Serbian National Chancery. Miloš appointed twelve of his supporters among the notables to the body and then proceeded to ignore it. In the 1820s several rebellions took place which Miloš was able to suppress. The *hatti-sherif* of 1830 called for an assembly and a council, but the prince refused to put this stipulation into effect. In 1835 the opposition was able to assemble about four thousand supporters at a meeting which drew up the so-called

Map. 3. The Expansion of Serbia, 1804–1913

Presentation Constitution. The provisions called for the establishment of an assembly and a council. Miloš appointed a council and again allowed it no power. The prince had the advantage in that at this time the Porte, Russia, and the Habsburg Empire were all against the introduction of constitutions providing for truly representative institutions.

Although Serbia had been hitherto fortunate in that it had been spared the type of incessant foreign interference suffered by Greece and the Danubian Principalities, intervention by the powers now determined internal political events. Both the prince and the opposition sought support in the foreign consulates which were established in the 1830s. An Austrian mission opened in 1835, a British in 1837, and a French in 1838. Since Serbia was not an independent state, any changes in her political structure were subject to the approval of the Porte, who was in turn open to outside influence. At this time the French and British governments came to stand behind the prince and absolutism while Russia supported the creation of a council of notables as called for in the 1830 *hatti-sherif*.

Negotiations on the subject were held in Constantinople. Here in 1838 the sultan issued the so-called Turkish Constitution, which was to be the basis of Serbian government until 1869. This document, which resembled the Organic Statutes at that time in force in the Principalities, was more an administrative statute than a constitution. It contained no general declarations of the rights and duties of citizens. The real power in the government was placed in the hands of a council of seventeen members who were appointed by the prince, but who held their offices for life unless they were dismissed for crimes. The ruler and the council shared the legislative functions. All laws and taxes had to be approved by the council, but the prince had the right of absolute veto. The ministers were made responsible to the council. In 1839 an amendment was introduced which provided that the ministers would have to be appointed from the members of the council. The constitution also regulated the civil service, the judicial system, and other aspects of state administration.

Despite its obvious deficiencies this constitution did end the period of absolute rule in Serbia. The prince was no longer supreme executive, legislator, and judge. The government of the country now rested on a written charter. For the next two decades, basing its control on this statute, the council held the real power in Serbian political life.

In addition to the establishment of the central government on a firm legal foundation, the reign of Miloš also witnessed the imposition of a centralized bureaucratic system on the local government of the country. At the beginning of his reign it was in the prince's interest to centralize the administration of the country; the communities were the focus of the opposition to his rule. It was thus important to the maintenance of his position that the local officials should represent the central government and not the areas to which they were assigned. He first assured this condition by seeing that the *oborknez* in the *nahija* was his appointee and paid by him. He also rendered the local assemblies powerless. His measures did effectively break the traditional system of local authority. From this time on in the communities the most important offices, including the police, were under the control of the central government.

To establish an effective national administrative system Miloš needed literate officials, a requirement that presented a problem in the Serbia of that day. He and his successors were forced to employ Serbs from the Habsburg Empire, where a better education was available. Miloš had a feeling of contempt for those who worked under him. He kept a firm hold on them and he tended to treat government officials as personal servants. Their numbers rose quickly. By the end of Miloš's reign they numbered 672 of which 201 were police. Naturally, these officials formed an interest group in the state. Their prime political objective came to be the protection of their own position and tenure in office.

Miloš also had to deal with the problem of the church and its relation to the state. Obviously, the church of the autonomous principality could not remain under the jurisdiction of the patriarch of Constantinople and of an institution that was largely Greek in national composition. In the *hatti-sherif* of 1830 the sultan agreed to restore the autonomy of the Serbian church which had been abolished in 1766. This settlement was confirmed by the patriarch in 1832. Serbian Orthodoxy was thus freed of Greek Phanariote control. Miloš was now able to regulate ecclesiastical matters as he wished. Like other Orthodox princes, he regarded the church as a state institution. The Metropolitan of Serbia was given the title of Metropolitan of Belgrade and of all Serbia. The most influential man to hold this post was Peter Jovanović, who held office from 1833 to 1859. Educated in the Habsburg Empire, he introduced reforms modeled on the Serbian church in the Austrian lands, an action which Miloš approved.

In foreign policy, as we have seen, the prince's efforts were directed primarily toward widening Serbian autonomy. Throughout his reign he consistently avoided foreign adventures and he refused to participate in national uprisings. His goal remained the attainment of further advantages from the Porte through negotiation.

For Serbia the question of economic and social development involved primarily the condition of the peasantry, who comprised 95 percent of the population. Their great aim was the full control of the land they tilled. The revolution did result in the end of Ottoman ownership of property in the countryside; for the mass of the people this was the major achievement of the revolt. Once the uprising had commenced life was made impossible for Turkish landowners in the villages. In 1815 the *chiftliks* were abolished; in 1830 the *spahis* lost the right to collect dues. The removal of the Ottoman system did not, however, bring any financial benefits to the peasant who now paid a 10 percent tax to the state, and his labor dues went to public works such as roads and bridges. Miloš, as we have seen, used the *corvée* to cultivate his private lands. In fact, autonomy brought the peasant higher psyments than he had carried previously.

The increase in the tax burden was due not only to the higher costs of the government, but to the changing economic conditions as well. Under Turkish rule the peasant had lived under a natural and not a money economy. He produced almost all that he needed; his taxes were in kind. With the foundation of the new state, which was endeavoring to set up a modern political structure, taxes had to be paid in cash. Moreover, desirable manufactured goods and luxuries were now available in the market. The peasant needed items like salt, but he had a strong desire to buy products such as coffee, sugar, tobacco, and candles. Imported or domestic machine-manufactured metal products such as nails, needles, and plows were obviously more efficient than crude handmade items. The necessity of earning a cash income led the peasant to become more interested in raising a crop that could be marketed than in providing for all of the needs of his family. This development also paved the way for the dissolution of inefficient rural collective agricultural units, such as the *zadruga*.

Miloš was personally concerned about the welfare of the peasants, who supported his position against the notables. Although the peasant had gained control of his land, it was soon apparent that he might lose it through unwise borrowing. The Homestead Act of 1836 was designed to prevent the peasant families from having all of their possessions confiscated by their creditors. The law set up a minimum—a house, a small plot of land, and some livestock—that was believed necessary to support a peasant household and that could not be taken away. In practice the enforcement of this measure was lax. In 1860–61 and 1873 further legislation was necessary.

Among the most impressive of the changes during Miloš's reign was the gradual alteration of the character of the cities. Previously, these had been market and administrative centers with a predominant Ottoman, Greek, and Jewish population. With autonomy the Ottoman officials and artisans began to leave. Serbian merchants slowly replaced their Greek and Jewish counterparts in the import trade, and they rapidly gained control of the export trade, mainly in livestock.

The question of the establishment of a national educational system also arose at this time. At first little was done. Moreover, the situation was difficult. Serbia had few schools and inadequate supplies of books and paper. There was a dearth of capable teachers. More attention was paid to the question after 1830. In 1833 the first law on elementary schools was passed. Although the state needed educated civil servants, a secondary school system was not established. In 1831 the first printing press was set up in Belgrade, but the problem of paper remained. Under these conditions the center of Serbian cultural life remained in the Habsburg Empire.

In 1839, almost immediately after the promulgation of the constitution, Miloš left the country, preferring not to rule under the restrictive conditions. His son and successor, Milan, died within a month. Michael, the second son, was only seventeen and thus governed through a regency. After three years, this regime was overthrown; Michael fled the country. An assembly, dominated by the opposition to the Obrenović family, then chose as the new prince Alexander Karadjordjević, the son of the revolutionary hero.

This radical change of leadership marked the complete victory of the backers of the Constitution of 1838 and what was now known as the Constitutionalist Party. That party was composed of notables, bureaucrats, merchants, and others who stood against absolute government such as that of Miloš. The group wanted to establish the rule of law and an orderly administrative system that would in fact benefit their own interests and which they could control. They stressed legality, greater economic freedom, and the advance of education. In theory they wanted written uniform laws which would be administered fairly by tribunals free from the control of the prince. They were not democratic or equalitarian, and they were not for the regulation of national life by the state. The leaders were Toma Vučić-Perišić, Avram Petronijević and, most important, Ilija Garašanin.

Despite the council's apparent strength with this group in control, the constitutionalist period was marked by a continual struggle of this body with the prince. In this contest Alexander was in a weak position; he did not have a strong character and he was not a hereditary prince. The right of automatic succession had been granted only to the Obrenović dynasty. Moreover, Alexander did not have a powerful following in the country. At issue, in particular, was the status of the cabinet of ministers, whose members were appointed solely from the council. Clashes between the supporters of the prince and those of the council became stronger after 1855. At that time Alexander's closest advisers, who resented the fact that they were powerless before the council and the Constitutionalists, urged the prince to dismiss the council members and other officials without seeking the concurrence of the Porte, as was required by the constitution. This recommendation, together with the discovery of a plot on his life, impelled Alexander to attempt to rid himself illegally of his opponents. When he did this, the Ottoman government forced him to return some of the officials to their posts.

Those in opposition to the prince wished to resolve this crisis by summoning an assembly, which would decide the limits of the prince's authority. The Constitutionalists thought they could use this means to get rid of Alexander. The proposal was also backed by those who desired to bring back the Obrenović dynasty and by the men who were to constitute the future Liberal Party. Composed primarily of young intellectuals who had been educated abroad, this group sought to go beyond the establishment of the rule of law and introduce guarantees of civil rights and democratic reform. Romantics at heart, they liked the idea of an assembly which they saw as the embodiment of the will of the Serbian people. They did not approve of the Constitutionalist's bureaucratic regime.

With Alexander's consent an assembly was summoned which met in December, 1858, at Kragujevac. The St. Andrew Assembly, as it was known, was out of the control of the Constitutionalists. It deposed Alexander, but it acclaimed the old Prince Miloš prince. The constitutionalist period thus came to an end; the former absolute ruler was returned by popular choice.

Despite their defeat at this time the Constitutionalists had achieved their aim of organizing a centralized, bureaucratic state system and of introducing a civil code which included criminal and administrative law as well as regulations concerning crafts, government officials, local government, and education. The great achievement of the party, the civil code of 1844, was taken over almost intact from Austrian prototypes. The system introduced protected the interests of the Constitutionalists in their position as state officials. Almost all government posts were held by men appointed by the government. The laws now assured that they would hold their positions for life. These provisions created a separate class of bureaucrats who felt apart from the peasant majority and superior to others in the state. The division was intensified by the fact that of necessity so many offices at first had to be filled by those born and educated outside of the former pashalik of Belgrade.

As previously explained, because of the lack of literate and educated men in Serbia, the practice of employing Serbs from the Habsburg Empire in the administration had been inaugurated during the reign of Miloš. They were known as *prečani* (men from across the river). Many of them were able, gifted, and patriotic, but others came because they could not gain a comparable position in Austria and they wished a comfortable life. Their great disadvantage was their division in manners and attitude from the peasant population they were to administer. A fine description of these officials and the reaction to them in the country has been given by one authority.

The transriparian Serbs regarded themselves as distinguished bearers of Western culture, destined to administer the illiterate and "half-savage barbarians" of the Principality. Dress, language and outlook divided them from the native Serbs. The new "men of the pen" looked down upon agricultural or manual labor, demurred against teaching their sons a craft or marrying their daughters to a craftsman, and for several years wore "German" clothing instead of the Serbian national dress. Instead of saying "thee" and "thou" in the homespun manner of the Principality, they employed the German habit— ridiculous sounding to Serbian ears—of addressing each other in the third person. Finally they refused to call other Serbians "Brother" in the customary fashion of the patriarchal society of Serbia.[1]

Their domination was not, however, to last. Although higher education was not soon available within Serbia, native-born Serbs were increasingly sent abroad at state expense for their education. Between 1839 and 1855 about fifty students went to institutions outside of the country. Although the substitution of natives did nothing to bridge the gap between the bureaucrat and the peasant, the issue of the *prečani* died down. Since the new group was more impressed by French civilization and manners, Paris, not Vienna, became the central point from which henceforth political and literary inspiration was to be drawn.

The Constitutionalist period, while witnessing a strengthening of the state structure, brought no advances in foreign policy. Nevertheless, the government was continually interested in the question of national expansion. The best statement of the Serbian views at this time is to be found in a plan, the Načertanije, drawn up by Garašanin in 1844 for the guidance of Prince Alexander. What the author wished was in fact the revival of the medieval empire of Tsar Dušan around the nucleus of autonomous Serbia. The lands that he wanted joined to Serbia were Bosnia, Hercegovina, Montenegro, Srem, Banat, Bačka, and northern Albania with an outlet on the Adriatic, territories that he regarded as basically Serbian in nationality. He planned first to inaugurate an elaborate educational and propaganda campaign among these people and the Serbs of Hungary. He recognized that the Habsburg Empire would be a permanent, unalterable foe of this program, and that Russia would also not give support. He proposed, therefore, that Serbia seek assistance in Paris and London. This program, as the subsequent plans of the Serbian government, laid emphasis on the acquisition of lands that were Serbian and Orthodox in population.

The fall of the constitutionalist regime and the return of Miloš did not solve the Serbian political problems. Three centers of power now existed: the prince, the council, and the assembly. The last-named body was not regularly organized, but it had just been the instrument for the change of rulers. Two political parties now began to emerge from this struggle for power within the state institutions. The Liberals remained

1. Traian Stoianovich, "The Pattern of Serbian Intellectual Evolution, 1830–1880," *Comparative Studies in Society and History*, 1 (March, 1959) 3:243.

the advocates of the supremacy of the assembly; the Conservatives favored the ruler and the council. In January, 1859, a law was passed calling for an assembly every three years, but one with only advisory powers. As before, Miloš wanted to rule as an absolute prince. After his death in 1860 he was succeeded by his son Michael who also became prince for the second time.

The first reign of Michael Obrenović, 1839–42, had been difficult because of his youth. He now returned at the age of thirty-seven, a mature and astute politician. Many regard him as the most effective ruler of modern Serbia. In exile he had traveled widely. He was well educated, experienced, and he had gained a realistic view of the international situation. His reign coincided with the great age of the national revolutions in Central Europe. In 1859 Wallachia and Moldavia united to form the basis for the modern Romanian state. In the 1860s both Italy and Germany became unified nations. With these events dominating the European scene it was natural that the prince should turn his greatest attention to territorial expansion.

The obvious next step for the Serbian state in international relations was to secure the complete removal of the Ottoman presence in the country, that is, the Turkish occupation of several fortresses. Preparation for the acquisition of neighboring Serbian lands could then be planned. To prepare for these moves Michael first wished to concentrate state power in his own hands so that he could act more effectively, and he wanted to strengthen the Serbian army. He also desired to contract alliances with the other Balkan Christian people in order to form a front against the Ottoman Empire.

During the reign of Miloš, as we have seen, the Serbian government was an absolute monarchy and under the Constitutionalist's regime the country was controlled by an oligarchy. Michael was now to give the government the form, if not the content, of a constitutional monarchy. Although he wished to hold supreme power, he was too wise to attempt to abolish the laws passed previously. He therefore moved to change matters legally. He was able to secure his position through assemblies which were held, as required, in 1861, 1864, and 1867, but which were in fact tools in his hands. He did not hesitate to use the police to gain governmental majorities, and thus the assembly could be induced to curb its own powers.

Michael also moved against the bureaucrats by introducing new measures that made them subject to dismissal under certain conditions. These measures were very popular since these officials had not endeared themselves to the population. For most of his reign the prince worked with the Conservative Party. His most prominent minister was Ilija Garašanin, who had also been important in the constitutionalist government. The Liberal Party, the opposition, was deprived of influence through the free use of repressive police measures. Its members were forced to go abroad to publish their attacks on Michael and to organize their resistance.

Since Michael's main interest was foreign policy, he was greatly concerned with the organization of an effective army. He increased the number of the militia and reintroduced the revolutionary concept of a nation in arms. By a law of August, 1861, all males from twenty to fifty years of age were made subject to military service. Thanks to these measures Serbia, with a population of 1,138,000 in 1863, was able to put 90,000 soldiers in the field. Although it was badly equipped and inadequately trained, the Serbian army was the most impressive in the Balkans. Michael also created a War Ministry and facilities for the training of officers.

The last signs of Ottoman rule were the garrisons of six fortress cities, especially Belgrade, which were the scene of constant incidents between Ottoman and Serbian nationals. In 1862 one such clash resulted in the shelling of Belgrade by Turkish soldiers. The Serbian government at once turned to the guarantor powers and demanded the evacuation of all Ottoman troops. Foreign pressure resulted in the withdrawal of two garrisons at this time and the rest in 1867. By that date only the flag over the Belgrade fortress and the annual tribute remained as signs of Ottoman suzerainty.

Michael's reign is best known for the system of alliances that he arranged with the neighboring Balkan states. All were, of course, directed against the Ottoman Empire. An agreement was signed with Montenegro in 1866, with Greece in 1867, and with Romania in 1868. He also had close relations with Bulgarian revolutionary groups. Enlarging on Garašanin's original concept, the prince considered the inclusion of Catholic Croatian lands in the nation that he wished to build around the Serbian nucleus. The negotiations that led to the conclusion of the pacts demonstrated the incompatability of the basic national ideas of the Balkan people.

Michael did not live to see the achievement of any of his major foreign policy objectives. As his reign progressed, the opposition to his autocratic measures increased. In June, 1868, he was assassinated. Since he had no children, he was succeeded by a cousin, Milan Obrenović, the son of a brother of Miloš. In no way was Milan prepared for the position. His childhood had been troubled and difficult. His mother had been the mistress of Alexander Cuza, the ruler of Romania. Since he was only fourteen at the time of his accession, he ruled first under a regency.

The principal achievement of the first part of Prince Milan's relatively long reign was the issuance of a new constitution in 1869. This document was prepared by a constituent assembly of five hundred delegates. It is significant that, unlike its predecessor of 1838, this constitution was formulated without outside interference even though Serbia was still a part of the Ottoman Empire. In the discussions the regents succeeded in gaining their desire for a strong executive, but many of the ideas of the Liberal Party were included. The assembly was now given a stronger role. In contrast, the council was reduced to the position of an administrative committee. In the assembly three-quarters of the delegates were to be elected and one-quarter appointed by the prince. The body was to meet yearly. It had the right to initiate legislation, but only indirectly. In theory no law could be issued, annulled, amended, or interpreted without the assembly's consent, but these rights were limited in other provisions.

The prince retained a strong, if not predominant, position in the state. The office was declared hereditary in the Obrenović family. As has been shown, the ruler appointed a quarter of the members of the assembly. Moreover, if this body refused to pass the budget, the prince could dismiss it and operate on the basis of the previous year.

The 1869 constitution, in contrast to that of 1838, contained general declarations on civil rights—including statements on the equality of all citizens, property rights, freedom of speech, religion, and the press, and the right to petition. No mention was made of freedom of assembly or association. Moreover, the civil rights granted were made subject to the law of land.

In the years preceding the accession of Milan the country witnessed some social and economic advances, despite the fact that the attention of the government was usually focused on political and foreign problems and not on questions of internal development. Beginning with the reign of Michael military expenses absorbed an increasing percentage of the national income. The growth of cities, mentioned before, continued. The country, however, remained without industrial development. The one heavy industry was an ironworks, which supplied the army. Handicrafts still dominated the scene. There were some improvements in internal communications. The number of roads and bridges increased under Michael. In 1855 the telegraph was introduced, and in 1868 Belgrade was connected with Vienna and Constantinople. Trade followed the former pattern with the principal partner still being the Habsburg Empire, followed by Romania and the Ottoman Empire. The chief exports were livestock and animal products, while the main imports were manufactured goods and luxury items.

In the countryside the main economic shift was the trend toward the production of more grain, chiefly corn and wheat, and the decline of animal husbandry, although the latter remained important for foreign trade. The great oak forests which had covered the Serbian landscape were fast disappearing. The peasant no longer had an ample supply of acorns to feed his livestock, and so he raised fewer pigs. He continued to face the problem of foreclosure. In 1873 a new homestead law set the amount of land that the peasant could not be deprived of because of debt at about eight and a half acres.

During this period further efforts were made to improve education. The supply of teachers increased, but in 1866 still only 4.2 percent of the population was literate. Michael, in particular, was interested in making his country, not Austria, the center of Serbian culture. In the 1850s the National Library and a museum were set up. A Serbian Royal Academy of Sciences was founded in the next decade. Interest was also shown in western European drama and music.

As has been shown above, the entire period of autonomous government from 1830 to the early 1870s was dominated by political concerns. The chief issue was the question of who would control the state—the prince, an oligarchy, or a democratically based assembly. Usually, the prince was able to maintain the strongest position. When he was not able to do so, an oligarchy ran the nation. During this period Serbia gained some additional territory and her rights of self-government were widened. By the 1870s, in fact, the Porte had lost all influence in determining the pattern of Serbian domestic life. At that time also a radical shift occurred in the main issues facing the Serbian leaders. Henceforth, questions of foreign policy and national expansion were the predominant Serbian interest.

CHAPTER 5

The Greek Kingdom

In 1830, as we have seen, three powers, France, Britain, and Russia, established Greece as an independent kingdom by international treaty. Thus, this state started on its political development, at least on paper, a step ahead of Serbia whose autonomy was only defined in that year. Greek reality, however, lagged far behind Greek appearances. Unlike Serbia, Greece was not a geographically isolated state of peripheral European concern. The Greek revolution had been a matter of major international interest. The country's position in the eastern Mediterranean made the political allegiance of its government of prime importance to the other European states. In addition, Greece was given not one, but three protecting powers with opposing interests in the Balkan and Mediterranean area. Contemporary international politics made it almost inevitable than Athens would be a point of conflict in their foreign policies, and that they would be drawn into internal Greek controversies. From the beginning it was clear that of the three protectors Britain would predominate, all other matters being equal. Her naval supremacy in the Mediterranean and the vulnerability of the Greek state from the sea assured that in a time of crisis Greek policy would be dominated by the strongest naval power in the region.

King Othon arrived in Greece in February, 1833. His first capital was Nauplion; not until 1835 was Athens in any condition to house the government. Since the new ruler was only eighteen, he was accompanied by a regency chosen by King Ludwig of Bavaria. Vitally concerned with the success of his son's reign, the king chose able and proven administrators. As president of the regency he appointed Count Joseph von Armansperg, who was known to be of liberal tendencies and who had gained much experience in Bavarian service. The other members were George Ludwig von Maurer, a well-known jurist and professor of law, and Major General Karl von Heideck, who had been in Greece during the revolution and was thus acquainted with the country. Karl von Abel was the secretary; Johann Greiner also came as an adviser. These men, with Greek assistants, immediately embarked on the task of giving the state an administration. They divided the work among themselves. Heideck concerned himself with military and naval affairs; Maurer, with law, the church, and education; Abel, with internal administration and foreign affairs; and Greiner, with economic problems. Each took examples for Greece from what was regarded as the most progressive and enlightened forms from western European experience. As in other states the Napoleonic internal order was of the greatest importance.

Unfortunately for Greek domestic harmony, the members of the regency soon came into sharp conflict. As a result of the struggle Armansperg secured the recall of Maurer in 1834 and reduced the influence of Heideck. In 1835 Othon came of age, but Armansperg retained his primary influence until 1837, when he was replaced by another Bavarian, Ignaz von Rudhardt. In the same year Greece received its first native prime minister: Constantine Zographos.

Greece, as we have seen, was established by the powers as an absolute monarchy despite the preference shown during the revolutionary period for constitutional governments with a limited executive. The protector states were primarily interested in securing order and peace in Greece and in ending the anarchy of the revolutionary period. Some sort of assurance appears to have been given by the Bavarian government that a constitution might be considered in the future, but certainly neither the powers nor the Bavarian king were initially enthusiastic about the idea. Ludwig I, who always wielded great influence over his son and thus over Greek affairs, was opposed to the concept. At the most he would allow that the ruler could concede a charter with limited rights. Until 1835 the absolute power of the monarch was exercised by the regency. Ultimate control lay, of course, in the hands of Ludwig, who could and did appoint and recall regents at will. The top administration of the first government of independent Greece was thus entirely Bavarian. There was a ministerial council of the heads of ministries, who were Greeks, but this body had no real power.

It must be emphasized that this nonnational government did attempt to establish what its members considered the best possible government in Greece. It may have made mistakes, particularly in financial matters, and it may have wasted large sums in trying to graft on to a backward Balkan state the framework proper for wealthier and more advanced states, but its members, with the possible exception of Armansperg, were not corrupt and they did put a great deal of effort into their task. From the Greek point of view they also had an advantage in that they were citizens of a weak state, Bavaria, and not of one of the protecting powers. They could thus not exert real pressure inside Greece except when they gained the backing of one of the protectors.

In the first years of the new state the regents proceeded to set up a system of local administration, organize a national church, regulate military and naval affairs, and establish educational, financial, and other institutions of a modern state. In the formation of a national administrative system the regents were faced with many of the same problems as those met by Miloš. Like the Serbian prince, Othon and his Bavarian advisers had every interest in curbing institutions that might become a source of opposition to the central power. On both practical and theoretical grounds they also favored a centralized system which, as in Serbia, would result in the destruction of the local self-government in effect in the Ottoman period.

A start in this direction had been made during the Greek revolution when the Greek leaders attempted to set up a government that would be strong enough to carry through a successful struggle. At that time the part of Greece under rebel control was divided into provinces, then into cities and communes (villages). A prefect (*eparch*), a secretary-general, and a chief of police were appointed for each province. The communes in this system were able to maintain much control over their own affairs. This administrative plan was never really put into effect because of the disturbed conditions of the revolutionary period.

The first steps toward the organization of a national administration were taken under Capodistrias. His desire to form a strong central government has already been discussed. An experienced administrator, he too wished to apply in Greece the widely accepted standards of government of an efficient centralized state with uniform laws and regulations. In April, 1828, a decree dividing the Peloponnesus into seven departments and the islands into six was issued. Each of these was subdivided into provinces, which were in turn divided into towns and villages. A uniform system of municipal government was then introduced. Since Capodistrias needed experienced, educated officials, and since he wished to assure their loyalty, he appointed to local positions men from outside of mainland Greece, for example, from Constantinople and the Ionian Islands. These men, like the *prečani* in Serbia, were separated from the local populations by their manners and by their own personal interests.

These tendencies continued during the reign of Othon. Like Capodistrias, the regents wished to centralize the government and apply uniform laws and standards. In 1833 Greece was divided into ten provinces (*nomarch*ies); these were then split into counties (*eparch*ies) and further into municipalities (*deme*s). The chief official of the first two levels was appointed by the central government. The municipalities were also so organized that the real power lay in the hands of the central government. After the kingdom was established, the same separation between governors and governed that had occurred in the revolutionary period continued. The leadership of the Greek state in the first decade was usually Bavarian or composed of Greeks from outside of Greece proper. Later the local officials appointed by the central government to the rural areas came from the ranks of the educated youth, who, as in Serbia, often had interests quite different from those of the natives of their region.

The status of the Greek Orthodox church was also regulated by the regency. As in Serbia the establishment of a national state led immediately to the desire for ecclesiastical institutions independent of the patriarch in Constantinople who was under the direct control of the Porte. A move toward separation had already taken place during the revolution. Under Ottoman pressure the patriarch had excommunicated the Greek church. During the revolt ecclesiastical affairs, like other matters, degenerated into chaos. With the return of peace a regulation of the church was obviously needed. The settlement reached at this time was largely the work of George Ludwig von Maurer and a synod of bishops. A liberal Protestant, Maurer used the examples of the Orthodox church in Russia and the Catholic church in Bavaria. In both places the church was a department of the state.

In 1833, when the new regulations were issued, the Greek church was declared independent of the patriarchate. It was to be administered by a synod whose members would be appointed by the crown. The head of the Greek church became now in fact the Catholic king. A wholesale reform of the monasteries, whose affairs were in a deplorable condition after the events of the revolution, was also undertaken. Monasteries with less than six members were closed. Their properties reverted to the government and in theory were to be used for ecclesiastical and educational expenses in the future.

This entire settlement was controversial. It was carried through by Greek leaders who were in favor of secularizing and westernizing influences. It was naturally not popular with the conservative elements of the Greek church. The regulation, in particular the position of the Catholic king in the hierarchy, became henceforth a major issue in Greek internal and foreign affairs. Moreover, a serious split occurred with the patriarch who, despite the fact that he had recognized a Serbian separation, refused to accept a similar arrangement in Greece. The change had been made without negotiation with Constantinople, and it marked a break with an organization that was also largely Greek in nationality. Russia, deeply involved in religious affairs and intensely interested in preserving Orthodox unity, also became concerned in this matter.

The breach was not healed, and a final settlement was not reached until 1850. With Russian mediation the patriarch finally agreed to recognize the separate organization in return for some relatively minor concessions. A new law was passed in 1852. The church remained under a synod whose president was the Archbishop of Athens. No decision was valid, however, until it was signed by the government representative, the procurator. The church thus remained dependent on the authority of the civil government.

Unlike Serbia where the irregular contingents that fought in the revolution were reabsorbed into their villages, the status of the military and particularly of the veterans became a major problem in the first years of Greek independence and one that did not find a satisfactory solution. Othon came to Greece with a force of thirty-five hundred soldiers, the majority of whom were German or Swiss. The great powers wished to make sure that the new monarch had troops on whom he could depend. As far as Greek soldiers were concerned, at the end of the revolution there were approximately five thousand irregulars and seven hundred regulars. It was to the interest of both the great powers and the Greek government that this force be disbanded because of its contribution to the anarchy of the period. This was not, however, so easily done. These soldiers received no regular payments; they lived off the localities where they resided. Many could not return home because their lands were still under Ottoman control. Plans were made to add Greeks to the regular army, but this process was difficult. Othon needed a reliable army, which would back his authority and which would maintain order in the state. He also required soldiers who were amenable to European military discipline and dress. The Greek military men did not like western uniforms or drill. Some were indeed brought into the regular army or the gendarmerie. Many simply returned to their villages, but others became bandits either within Greece or on the other side of the Ottoman border. Bands of robbers continued to pose a problem throughout Othon's reign.

Whether foreign or native in personnel, the military forces were an enormous expense for the new state. Here, as in Serbia, they took far too great a share of the very limited financial resources of the kingdom. Not only were the foreign troops expensive, but the army was simply too large. In 1835 the army, including the gendarmerie, had about seven thousand men; that meant that for about every hundred Greeks there was one soldier. Of these about half were Greek; the rest were foreign mercenaries. This force absorbed more than half of the state budget. Although foreign influences were strong in the army, the navy established at this time was dominated by Greeks.

The regency also organized other aspects of national life. A system of primary and secondary schools was set up. In 1837 the University of Athens was founded. This institution was to train the future administrators of the state and to wield great political influence. Later in Othon's reign the very controversial language question was regulated. In 1849 *katharevousa*, the artificial literary language, replaced the spoken *demotiki* as the official language for government, education, and the newspapers.

This change has been bitterly debated ever since. The existence of two languages, one of which was not used by the majority of the people, seriously complicated the political life and education in the kingdom.

At this time Maurer organized the legal system of Greece and directed the codification of the civil laws. The regency and King Othon also devoted a great deal of attention and expense to the city of Athens. At the end of the revolutionary period Athens was little more than another provincial Ottoman town graced by the Parthenon and other impressive ruins. The Philhellene Bavarians and the Greeks themselves were passionately interested in making their capital the worthy successor of the ancient city. The modern city of Athens dates from this period.

In the first years of Othon's reign much had thus been accomplished toward the organization of the state. Great problems, however, remained to be settled. Although an absolute ruler, Othon was not a Miloš or a Karadjordje, nor was he an intriguer. A weak and well-meaning monarch, he did not have the strength of character to control firmly the complicated political situation in Athens. In November, 1836, he married a Protestant, Duchess Amalia of Oldenburg. The queen and the alliance were popular, but the marriage remained childless. This was a political disaster for Othon. Basically, the king faced truly difficult problems. Of greatest significance were the economic weakness of the state and the existence of treaties that allowed the protecting powers to interfere continually in Greek internal affairs.

After the revolution the territory of independent Greece was in ruins. Vineyards, olive groves, and orchards had been destroyed. The entire tax-collecting system had been disrupted. Moreover, the land itself was naturally poor; only 25 percent was arable, yet the peasantry constituted about 75 percent of the population. The first government was faced with the problem of setting up a modern administrative system with an empty treasury and few resources. What remained of the Greek wealth in commerce and shipping was largely out of the control of the government in Athens. Moreover, the debts incurred during the revolution had to be paid. Financial problems were to plague the nation until the end of the century when bankruptcy was finally declared.

The economic situation was made worse by the bad system of revenue collection which had changed little since the Ottoman times. The Greek like the Serbian peasant was soon to discover that independence was more costly than Turkish rule and that the avoidance of payments was more difficult. He continued to pay his tithe, but the methods of collection often meant that he was forced to surrender far more. In fact, the extortionate means used quite equaled the Ottoman period. Under Othon taxes usually continued to be farmed. The right of collection was auctioned. Unlike the case in Serbia, payment was usually in kind. The tax farmer and his agent had to assess the crop in the field. The peasant could not harvest his grain until he had permission from the tax farmer. He also had to collect it under conditions controlled by the collector. Since crops are perishable, he often had to bribe the official to get his taxes assessed. Not only was the entire system a disaster for the peasant, but the prevalence of corruption meant that the central government received only a proportion of the amount paid. The regency and the later ministries all recognized the problem. Efforts were made to make the collection more efficient and to make certain that the tax farmers paid the sums they owed.

In addition to the financial considerations, the Greek government had to deal with a difficult internal situation, which allowed much outside interference. Greece was in theory an absolute monarchy, but it had in no sense a repressive or absolutist regime. Throughout Othon's reign vocal opposition parties always existed. In the first two decades the political scene was dominated by three parties who had their origins in the revolutionary period. Unlike Serbia, where the first political groups were the Constitutionalists, the Liberals, and the Conservatives, that is, parties formed primarily on the issue of the conflict between the ruler and the notables, Greece developed a system based on the three protecting powers.

The French, British, and Russian parties, as they were known, had their centers in the individual legations on which they leaned for support. Each represented a definite stand in Greek politics; each also reflected the policy of the patron power. Of the three the French party was probably the most popular in the years before the Crimean War, chiefly because it could champion a program of national expansion. Its leader was the extremely able politician, John Kolettes, who had close ties with the July Monarchy in France and who represented his country for eight years in Paris. The Russian, or Napist, party was probably next in influence. Conservative and Orthodox in direction, it was first led by Kolokotrones and Capodistrias during the revolutionary period and, after the death of these two, by Andrew Metaxas. The British party was probably the least influential, although it was able to exert great pressure at times on the Greek government because of British naval strength in the area. Hampered by the fact that the British government was usually a strong upholder of Ottoman integrity, this party could not champion a great national policy. During the first part of Othon's reign it supported Armansperg. Mavrokordatos remained at its head throughout the period. Its programs in general favored internal reform and constitutional government. All three parties were primarily interested in political power. When any individual party enjoyed a privileged position in the government, it supported the king. When it was out of power, it intrigued against the central authority and whatever party was predominant.

The main problems of the first five years of Othon's reign have already been indicated. Othon had, as it can be seen, no organized faction to support him; there was no Bavarian party. He also had to carry the burden of the resentment of Bavarian rule, the 'xenocracy' as it was called, even though Greeks gradually took over almost all the administrative posts. By the end of the 1830s Greek soldiers were slowly replacing foreign troops; they were not enthusiastic royal partisans and were not reliable. Moreover, throughout his entire reign the king suffered in popularity from the fact that he was a devout Catholic. His failure to have a son who could be raised in the Orthodox faith added to this problem. His greatest fault in the eyes of his people, however, was his failure to make any progress in the one field that engaged ardent Greek sympathies, the question of joining other Greek lands to the independent state. In 1841, when the island of Crete rose against the Ottoman government, Othon was unable to act.

By the 1840s Othon was faced with a condition of real internal crisis. Discontent with his rule and with his internal and foreign policies was at a height. The entire situation was made worse by the pressure now exerted by the powers on Greece in connection with the debt. In 1838 Greek finances had been put under a French supervisor, Artemonis de Regny. By 1843 the entire financial situation of the country was disastrous. With the exception of a single year the state had been run on deficit spending. Payments on the loan had been suspended for four years. Interested primarily in protecting their investment, the powers now pressed the Greek government to reduce sharply its internal expenditures. One of the obvious items that could be cut was the large military budget. This action directly affected the interests of the army. The military disatisfaction with the situation was shared by other groups. At this time the French party, in close cooperation with Othon, was in power; the Russian and British were out. In 1842 Alexander Karadjordjević had become the Serbian prince through a military coup. The issue in this revolt had been the question of the power of the executive. The idea of controlling the monarch through a constitution was part of the British party's policy. The question of the personal power of Othon and its possible limitation now became of immediate Greek political concern.

The combination of these issues resulted in the revolution of 1843. In September of that year an army corps stationed in Athens marched on the palace and seized the king and his government. The leaders of the revolt demanded that Othon form a new government and summon a constitutional assembly. The movement was a military *coup d'état,* supported by the British, Russian, and a part of the French parties. It was not a great popular uprising. The aim was to limit the power of the king through a constitution. It will be noted that this was also the beginning of the Constitutionalist period in Serbia.

Faced with the alternatives of accepting a constitution or abdicating,

Othon agreed to the demands of the revolutionaries. A constitutional assembly met from September, 1843, to March, 1844. It included representatives from Macedonia, Epirus, and Thessaly, lands that were, of course, part of the Ottoman Empire. The leading roles in the deliberations were taken by Mavrokordatos, who returned from Constantinople where he had represented Greece, and Kolettes, who came back from Paris. The two western protecting powers, France and Britain, gave constant advice on the making of the constitution. The Russian government stood aside, because of the convictions of Nicholas I on revolutionary activity.

The chief issue in drawing up the constitution became the question of defining the relationship between the king and the projected representative assemblies. Although both the British and French supported the idea of constitutional government, neither wished too much power given to the legislative bodies. After all, neither France of the July Monarchy nor Britain, even after the Reform Bill of 1832, had regimes based on real popular control. Both states were primarily concerned with assuring a stable government in Athens. For that reason the constitution adopted in 1844 was conservative and resembled the July Monarchy, which Kolettes knew so well. It established a two-house legislature. The chamber, or vouli, was elected on the basis of universal manhood suffrage; a senate, the gerousia, had members appointed for life from among distinguished Greek citizens by the king with the approval of the prime minister. The king had an absolute veto over legislation. He could appoint and dismiss the ministers, who were responsible to him. The constitution had a bill of rights containing the usual declarations on the equality of citizens, freedom of the press, assembly, etc.

Thus in 1844 Greece became a constitutional monarchy. In actual practice, however, the constitution had little direct effect on the actual governing of the country. As in Serbia, the Greek leaders adopted western political principles and constitutional forms, but modified them according to their own customs and traditions. The three parties returned to their former practices and continued the struggle for political control. During the year in which the constitution was debated the parties had cooperated. The revolt resulted in the formation of a government headed by Metaxas; it was replaced by a Mavrokordatos-Spyridon Trikoupes ministry, which was considered pro-British. It held power during the elections for the constituent assembly and during the assembly's meetings. The constitution itself was primarily the work of a committee of twenty-one, of whom Mavrokordatos, Trikoupes, and Kolettes were the most prominent members. The Russian party remained apart, it will be remembered, because of the tsar's attitude.

Once the constitution was accepted politics returned to normal. The first election gave the victory to Kolettes. A Kolettes-Metaxas coalition was then formed to the exclusion of the British party. In 1845 Kolettes assumed full control and remained in power until his death in 1847. During this period he established the system of government that was to prevail until Othon's expulsion in 1862. Although the country remained under a constitutional framework, Kolettes used the centralized system of administration to assure that government candidates won the elections. He put, of course, his partisans in all of the appointive positions. Using force and patronage to assure victory, he and his successors were not above recruiting bandits and organizing street riots to intimidate the opposition. With government candidates regularly elected, the chamber could not become an effective center of opposition to the regime in office.

Despite its methods the government of Othon and Kolettes did enjoy wide support. Kolettes was able to use the national program to gain popular approval, and he became the spokesman for the plan of expansion known as the Megale Idea, or Great Idea. The Greek state established in 1830 fell heir to a double tradition: that of ancient Greece and that of Byzantium. Although in many ways the two legacies were in principle in conflict, this great heritage played an active role in Greek politics. We have already seen the importance of the classical Greek legacy in the language question and in the Philhellene movement, which so aided the Greek revolution. In foreign policy and in national expansion, however, it was to be the Byzantine past that was to predominate. The national program, the Great Idea, was directed essentially to securing a revival of the Byzantine Empire. The capital of the future state was to be Constantinople, not Athens. Although the lands to be joined in this empire were not closely defined, they usually included Epirus, Thessaly, Macedonia, Thrace, the Aegean Islands, Crete, Cyprus, the west coast of Asia Minor, and the territory between the Balkan and Rhodope Mountains, later known as Eastern Rumelia. The emphasis was not on territory that was ethnically strictly Greek, but on the lands in which Hellenic civilization was believed predominant. The control of the Greek hierarchy over ecclesiastical affairs and education in areas inhabited by Slavic peoples was thus exploited to lay the foundations for political control.

The intensity of the conviction of Greek intellectuals in the justice of their claims was to be shown throughout the next years until the entire Great Idea went down in defeat in 1922. It was particularly apparent in the violent negative reaction of these circles to the writings of Jacob P. Fallmerayer, who, in a book published in 1836, claimed that Slavic migrations in the seventh and eighth centuries had decimated the Greek population. Thus, modern Greeks were Hellenized Slavs. The Greek national viewpoint was also expressed in the work of Constantine Paparregopoulos, whose *History of the Greek Nation* was published between 1860 and 1872.

The classic statement on the Great Idea was delivered by Kolettes before the constitutional assembly. Here on January 15, 1844, he declared:

> The kingdom of Greece is not Greece; it is only the smallest and poorest part of Greece. Greece includes not only the kingdom, but also Janina and Thessaloniki, and Serres, and Adrianople, and Constantinople, and Trebizonde, and Crete, and Samos, and any other country where Greek history or the Greek race was present. . . . There are two great centers of Hellenism, Athens and Constantinople. Athens is only the capital of the kingdom. Constantinople is the great capital, the City, *i Polis*, the attraction and the hope of all the Hellenes.[1]

These national goals brought Greece into direct conflict with Britain. Throughout Othon's reign repeated episodes or European diplomatic crises occurred which appeared to offer an opportunity for national gains; in each the determination of Britain to maintain the *status quo* blocked action. The uprising in Crete in 1841 has already been mentioned. In 1848–49 there were minor revolts in the Ionian Islands. In 1850 the Greek government became engaged in a major quarrel with Britain, now under the Liberal cabinet of Lord Palmerston. The British prime minister at this time backed the claims of Don Pacifico, a Portugese Jew of British citizenship, whose house had been plundered by a mob, and of the historian George Finlay some of whose property had been confiscated by the Greek government. The ownership of two small islands was also in dispute. In order to enforce its claims the British government sent a fleet to Piraeus. Although the financial settlement was finally arbitrated, the episode had the advantage of making Othon more popular for his stand against the great power. British opposition to Greek actions also brought about an improvement of relations with Russia, as the settlement of the church question by agreement with the patriarch indicated.

Should Greece expand, the natural next step would be the annexation of adjacent Ottoman territory in Thessaly and Macedonia. Three times during Othon's reign the Porte was involved in crises that might have created conditions that would allow the Greek government to move. In 1831–33 and 1839–40 Egypt challenged her suzerain; in 1853 the Crimean War commenced, bringing two of Greece's protectors, Britain and France, into war with the third, Russia. Although the Egyptian crises could not be exploited, the Crimean War seemed to offer real opportunities. Greek sympathies were with Orthodox Russia, who was also at war with the Porte. At the beginning of the conflict, which commenced with the outbreak of hostilities between Russia and the Ottoman Empire in 1853, irregular bands supported by Greece began to act in Ottoman ter-

---

1. Edouard Driault and Michel Lhéritier, *Histoire diplomatique de la Grèce de 1821 à nos jours,* (Paris: Presses universitaires de France, 1925), vol. 2, pp. 252–53.

SERBIA

BULGARIA

Bitola

Western Thrace

1919

Constantinople
(Istanbul)

ALBANIA

Macedonia

Kavalla

1913

Thessaloniki

IMBROS

Epirus

Janina

Thessaly

1881

CORFU

TURKEY

Misolonghi

Izmir
(Smyrna)

1832

Athens

Peloponnesus

Nauplion

IONIAN ISLANDS
(Acquired 1863)

HYDRA

DODECANESE
(Italian)

0   100
Miles

CRETE

1913

Map 4. The Expansion of Greece, 1821–1919

ritory. Although the Ottoman forces were capable of subduing these movements, the hostile Greek attitude brought a strong reaction from the western powers. From 1854 to 1857 a British-French fleet was anchored in Piraeus. Under its pressure Othon was forced to appoint a government headed by Mavrokordatos and the British party. The defeat of Russia in 1856 dampened any Greek hopes that the *status quo* would be changed. Until the end of Othon's reign international conditions were to preclude any Greek territorial gains.

Despite the disappointments in foreign policy this period did witness limited progress within the country. The nation, it must be remembered, started with the liabilities of few resources and a large foreign debt, which had been badly if not corruptly administered. In addition, the country suffered from the fact that the revolutionary land settlement had primarily benefited the notables. The majority of the peasant population either lived on extremely small plots or worked the lands of others. The peasant was further hampered by the ruinous methods of tax collection and by the same problem of accumulating debts that we have seen in Serbia.

Moreover, Greece had to contend with basic difficulties not shared by the other neighboring Balkan nations. After her revolution Serbia enjoyed the benefit of sufficient agricultural land and large, unexploited forests. In contrast, Greece could not produce the cereal crops needed to feed her own population. The country was forced to concentrate on growing export corps, particularly grapes, currants, olives, citrus fruits, and tobacco, to pay for cereals and also for manufactured goods. In this early period there was virtually no industrial development. The handicraft industry in fact suffered from competition with imported machine-made products. In contrast with this bleak picture, Greek shipping based in free Greece did revive.

Although economic conditions in the independent kingdom remained bad, the position of Greek nationals abroad improved. Despite the fact that Greek preeminence was lost, Greeks remained in Ottoman service and regained their importance in the economic life of the empire. Greek merchants still prospered in the Balkan cities, in Egypt, and in the Danubian and Black Sea trade. The real center of Greek economic power remained in the Ottoman Empire—in Constantinople, Thessaloniki, and Smyrna (Izmir). None of these financial resources, of course, were of service to the Greek state. Greeks from outside the kingdom did invest in the state, but the government could not control or tax the wealth of these people. It must be strongly emphasized that the major problem of independent Greece was financial. With a basically poor country and with such a large proportion of the state's income devoted to the army and the debt, there was not an adequate surplus for internal improvements even if the leaders of the state had wished to embark on such policies.

Under these circumstances it was inevitable that discontent with the rule of Othon should rise. After the death of Kolettes the system of royal ministries was continued. In 1862 Admiral Constantine Kanares, then prime minister, tried to influence Othon to reform the government and to limit royal interference, but with no success.

Meanwhile, in Greece, as in Serbia, a new generation had arisen which had different ideas and wanted positions of power. The former dominant class of notables and rich merchants was now challenged by a politically conscious commercial middle class and by those in government service. Apparent also was the rising influence of the young men who had been educated either at the University of Athens or abroad and who were impatient with the regime in power. They were joined and supported by a group of reform-minded politicians, best exemplified by Epaminondas Delegeorges, who attacked the institutions established by the constitution of 1843. They wished the establishment of true parliamentary democracy, a curbing of royal authority, and an improvement of the administration of the country. They were influenced by events in France where in 1848 the July Monarchy had been overthrown. The new concepts were reflected in a basic change in the political field in Athens. After the Crimean War the parties based on foreign consulates were replaced by loose factions headed by prominent political figures, such as Delegeorges, Dimitrios Voulgares, and Thrasyvoulos Zaimes.

In addition to his other problems, Othon's failure to produce an heir continued to be a major impediment to his popularity. The constitution of 1843 stipulated that the next king would have to be of Orthodox faith, but there was no obvious successor who could fulfill this condition. Othon's brothers, also Catholics, showed no inclination to change their religion for the Greek throne. The king's personal position was further weakened by European events. In 1859 war broke out between Austria and France on the question of Italian unification. Greek sympathies were with the Italian national cause; Othon, born a German prince, supported Austria. These problems, together with the failure to achieve further national goals, gradually eroded the king's political position.

The revolt in 1862, which led to Othon's abdication, was, like its predecessor of 1843, primarily a military *coup d'etat* and not a national rising. Led by junior and noncommissioned officers, it was backed by opposition politicians. In February, 1862, a revolt broke out in the garrison at Nauplion. Although it failed, the conspiracy spread and in October the Athens garrison rebelled. Othon and Amalia were at the time touring the provinces. They were advised by the foreign consuls not to come back to Athens. Othon took the opportunity to return quietly to Bavaria. A new government was set up with a regency composed of Voulgares, Kanares, and Venizelos Roufos and with a cabinet whose most prominent members were Delegeorges, Zaimes, and Alexander Koumoundouros. A second constituent assembly was then summoned. All three of the protecting powers had approved the departure of Othon. Thereafter, they concerned themselves deeply in the choice of a new monarch and the formulation of a new constitution. Again these states named the king. The Greeks themselves would have preferred Prince Albert of Britain, a son of Queen Victoria, under the mistaken assumption that with this prince as ruler they would receive not only the Ionian Islands, but also British backing for further expansion. The British government refused to consider this nomination; all three powers were still in agreement that no member of one of their ruling dynasties should be king of Greece. The final choice was in fact the British candidate, Prince Christian William Ferdinand Adolphus George of Denmark, who now became George I of Greece. The second son of the heir to the Danish throne, he was eighteen years old at the time of his selection. Reigning until 1913, he was to be an extremely successful and popular ruler, largely because he tended to stand aside in Greek politics. His nomination was accepted by a constitutional assembly in March, 1863. His title was "king of the Hellenes"; in other words his subjects in theory also numbered Greeks outside of the kingdom. On his acceptance Britain surrendered possession of the Ionian Islands. In 1866 George married the Russian Grand Duchess Olga.

Although the assembly accepted the prince designated by the powers, it did frame a constitution after its own desires. This time the liberal Belgian constitution of 1831 became the model. With the aim of limiting royal power Article 21 declared that: "All powers are derived from the nation and are exercised in the manner prescribed by the constitution." The senate, which had been a mainstay of the king's authority, was now abolished. The legislature was to consist of one chamber elected by direct secret manhood suffrage. It was to number not less than 150 members who were to be chosen for four years. The ministry was responsible to this body. Nevertheless, the king did retain important prerogatives, which could be used by a strong ruler. He appointed and dismissed ministers, he could dissolve the chamber, and he could declare war and make treaties.

The constitution was ratified in October, 1864. Kanares headed the first government, to be replaced in 1865 by Koumoundouros. Thereafter a period of rapid change followed. From 1864 to 1881 there were nine elections and thirty-one governments. Despite the liberal framework, politics thus returned to their former state with the exception that the monarch no longer controlled the process. The multiparty system, where the parties were in fact factions clustered around a leader, added to the instability of the situation. The membership in the parties and the alliances between them shifted constantly. Electoral questions were now predominantly those of personality and not of issues or ideology. Moreover, the centralized administrative system, with the gift of appointment to office in the hands of whoever won the elections, made the temptation to cheat irresistible. Unlike Serbia, where tenure in office was at least at times assured, a change in Greek government could mean a complete shift of the personnel of all offices from top to bottom. Under these circumstances fraud and violence were bound to continue to accompany the electoral process. Former reformers like Voulgares and Delegeorges showed themselves willing to adopt methods similar to those they had previously attacked to maintain their own political power.

Although internal politics remained much the same, the reign of George was to mark an active period in foreign policy and to witness the achievement of some of the Greek objectives. By this time the Greek government in foreign affairs not only had to consider the policies of the great powers and the Porte, but also those of its Balkan neighbors. Autonomous Serbia was joined in the 1860s by a unified Romania, but most important for Greece was to be the rising and in many respects competitive Bulgarian national movement.

CHAPTER 6

Wallachia and Moldavia before 1853

In the preceding chapters we have seen two national liberation movements, the Serbian and the Greek, attain partial success with the establishment of autonomous or independent states. In both countries the fighting in the revolution was carried on by peasant troops under local military leaders. With the conclusion of the conflict with the Ottoman Empire, the network of Ottoman administration was removed and separate governments were set up. Although certain similarities to Serbia and Greece can be found, the national developments in the Danubian Principalities differ, chiefly because these provinces at the end of the eighteenth century had evolved along a divergent political and economic path.

First, as described earlier, in the eighteenth century the Principalities were under a Christian, although Phanariote Greek, regime. The Ottoman government did not administer the area directly. The first step in the national movement thus involved as much the removal of the alien Greek control as a struggle against Ottoman suzerainty. Second, unlike the other Balkan countries, the Principalities had a native aristocracy of large landowners, the boyars; this group had survived the Ottoman conquest. Large *timar* or *chiftlik* estates under Muslim control were not to be found in the land. The boyars in the nineteenth century were to be in a strong political position not only because they were the natural leaders of the country, but also because they could profit so greatly from concurrent European economic developments.

Like Polish, Hungarian, Prussian, and Russian lands, the Romanian estates were to be a source of food supplies for the expanding western industrial states. In contrast to other Balkan areas, the rich soil of the Principalities was suited to grain cultivation for export on a large scale. Under these circumstances it was in the boyar's best interest to gain direct control of as much land as possible and to assure himself of an ad-

84

equate labor supply. Since the peasant's aims were to secure absolute control over a single plot and to free himself from feudal obligations, there was a natural antagonism between the two classes. Thus, we seldom find here the combination of local notable and fighting peasantry so evident in Greece and Serbia. The main stages in the achievement of Romanian independence were the result of diplomatic negotiation. Not only were the two periods of revolution, that of Tudor Vladimirescu in 1821 and the uprising in 1848 in Wallachia, unsuccessful, but they also demonstrated the political consequences of this division between the peasantry and the boyars.

A third contrast between the Romanian events and those previously discussed arose because of the geographic position of the provinces. Situated on Russia's land route to Constantinople, the region was the scene of repeated Russian occupation: in 1711, 1736–39, 1769–74, 1787–92, 1806–12, 1828–34, 1849–51, and 1853–54. The presence of a foreign army and one with definite political objectives was bound to be of vital importance in national development. Although usually the Russian actions were beneficial to the national movement, they did represent foreign interference. To a lesser extent the Habsburg Empire exerted a similar pressure. Her army was in occupation during the Crimean War, 1854–57. The presence of these two great and often conflicting powers on their borders forced the Romanian leaders to put more emphasis on diplomacy than on armed action to gain their aims. They could not hope to withstand their more powerful neighbors, and they did not want to turn their lands into a battlefield.

Because of the unique aspects of the Romanian conditions, the national movement can best be divided into two periods. The first, discussed in this chapter, extends to the outbreak of the Crimean War in 1853. In these years Phanariote Greek control was overthrown only to be replaced by a Russian protectorate that involved interference in all aspects of national life. The second, extending from 1853 to 1878, saw the attainment of independence and with it the creation of a situation in the Balkans that allowed the Romanian government to balance between the great powers.

The process that finally resulted in the substitution of primary Russian influence for Greek and Ottoman in the provinces commenced in the eighteenth century with the Treaty of Kuchuk Kainardji. This agreement, which did limit the abuses of Ottoman rule, marks the first step in the Russian acquisition of treaty rights in the Principalities. In Article 16 the Porte gave the assurance that amnesty would be granted to those who had fought with Russia, a free exercise of the Christian religion was promised, and it was agreed that the tribute would be fixed. In addition, the *hospodar*s of the Principalities were to have an agent in Constantinople. Most important, Russia could now speak in behalf of the provinces, and the Ottoman government promised "to listen with the consideration shown to friendly and respected powers." In 1779 in the Convention of Aynali Kavak, which dealt primarily with the Crimea, it was stipulated that the tribute would be paid every two years, and Russian rights of intervention were defined. In 1780 the first Russian representative was appointed in Bucharest.

The privileges of the Principalities were further delineated in other ordinances issued by the Ottoman government. In 1783 and 1792 the Porte agreed that Russia could make representations on financial charges imposed on the Principalities. A *hatti-sherif* of 1784 recognized the disastrous effect of the frequent changes of princes and directed that they were only to be deposed for crimes. No extraordinary contributions were to be levied in the future; only the tribute was to be paid. Supplies needed by the Porte were to be purchased at market prices.

These stipulations, however, were never carried out. The internal administrations of the Principalities continued in the old pattern of repeated changes of rulers; between 1792 and 1802 there were six such actions in Wallachia and five in Moldavia. In addition, like Serbia and the Bulgarian lands, Wallachia suffered from the attacks of Pasvanoglu and from expeditions of pillage launched from the Ottoman Danubian fortresses.

In 1802 the deprivations caused by Pasvanoglu brought another crisis in the relations of the Porte and the Principalities. At this time the boyars, backed by Russia, gained from the sultan a *hatti-sherif* that confirmed their former privileges and significantly extended these rights. *Hospodars* were now to be chosen for seven years. They were not to be deposed except for crimes and with the consent of Russia. All taxes and requisitions imposed after the decree of 1783 were to be abolished. The amount of foodstuffs and other provisions to be sent to the Porte was to be regulated by firmans and not determined arbitrarily; current prices were to be paid. With the exception of certain merchants carrying firmans, Muslims were forbidden to enter or to live in the Principalities. In addition, the *hospodars* were ordered to take into consideration the advice of the Russian representatives. This act thus limited Ottoman interference in the provinces and at the same time opened the door to increased Russian influence.

After 1802 the *hospodars* were the Phanariote Greeks, Constantine Ypsilantes and Alexander Moruzi. In 1806, when war again broke out between the Porte and Russia, the area once more became a battlefield. The Principalities were also an object of barter between Napoleon and Alexander I at their meetings at Tilsit in 1807 and at Erfurt in 1808. At this second conference Russia was given definite control of the provinces. A consolidation of the Russian hold was, however, prevented by the subsequent rupture in relations between Russia and France. In 1812, in preparation for an expected French invasion, the Russian government was forced to make peace. Despite the fact that her armies were occupying the Principalities, Russia, in the Treaty of Bucharest of 1812, returned these territories with the exception of the land between the Dniester and the Pruth, known as Bessarabia. This area, which belonged to Moldavia and was inhabited primarily by Romanians, was then annexed to Russia. This action was to prove a major block to good Romanian-Russian relations in the future. Although Russia thus returned Moldavia and Wallachia to the Ottoman Empire, her influence remained paramount. The *hospodars* were now Ioan Caragea in Wallachia and Scarlat Callimachi in Moldavia.

Despite the destruction caused by the wars, this period opened wider possibilities for the sale of Romanian agricultural products. After the loss of the Crimea to Russia in 1783, the Porte depended increasingly on the Romanian provinces for supplies for Constantinople. With the assurance given that a market price would be paid by the Porte, Romanian landowners had the opportunity to make real profits. They also began to set up, on their own estates, small enterprises involving the processing of their agricultural products, such as tanneries, alcohol distilleries, and facilities for smoking of meats. With these possibilities for wealth the boyars naturally desired to enlarge their estates and assure the continued availability of peasant labor. They also wished to rid themselves of the limitations that Ottoman rule still imposed on their activities.

The position of the peasant had been regulated in the middle of the eighteenth century during the administrations of Constantine Mavrocordat in both Wallachia and Moldavia. The peasant was legally emancipated, but the questions about his rights to the land and about the payments that he should make for its use were not settled. In 1774 it was decided that the peasant communities in a locality would be guaranteed the use of two-thirds of the boyar's land in return for twelve days of labor (the *clacă*). These days, however, were defined in terms of tasks to be accomplished so that the time actually required amounted to from twenty-five to forty days. In practice it was difficult to enforce these rules on a still sparse and mobile peasant population which depended chiefly on animal husbandry for support. The labor obligations were often commuted to a money payment or simply refused. The tithe that the peasant paid was the chief source of revenue for the boyars until the middle of the nineteenth century. The peasantry was also subject to a great many other dues and taxes, from which the boyar was completely exempt. In the future it was to be to the interest of the landowner to extend the labor dues and to bring under his control land, such as forest and pastures, formerly under common use.

In addition to the estates of the boyars, large tracts of land belonged to the Orthodox church. About a fifth of the Romanian territory was controlled by the so-called Dedicated Monasteries. These institutions, which were under Greek direction, gained wealth and strength during the Phanariote period. They did not pay taxes, and they were not under the authority of the civil government. Their profits were in theory "dedicated" to the support of Holy Places such as Mt. Athos, Mt. Sinai, and the Holy Sepulchre. They usually enjoyed Russian favor since Russian armies used them during their frequent incursions into the Principalities. Conditions for the peasants were particularly harsh on those lands.

Although the interests of the peasant and boyar clashed, both opposed Ottoman suzerainty and the Phanariote regime. The boyar resented the controls that the Ottoman regime placed on his activities. He wanted a completely free market for his products. The peasant suffered from the fact that Ottoman rule had not guaranteed him conditions of law and order in the countryside. Like the Serbian peasant, he had been the victim not only of his own ruling class, but also of bandit groups and the exactions of occupying armies. In addition, the small native class of artisans and traders were dissatisfied in particular with the capitulatory [1] regime in effect in the empire. They saw foreigners occupying privileged positions in their own trading communities and enjoying exemptions from taxes and the controls that hampered the activities of the natives. All groups—boyars, peasants, and merchants—desired a change in the political life of the country.

These views made their influence felt during the insurrection of Alexander Ypsilantes and Tudor Vladimirescu. The reasons that the Principalities were selected for the opening of the Greek revolution have been explained; Vladimirescu's role is more complex. The son of a Wallachian family of the free peasantry, the Romanian leader at the time headed a movement that had strong social overtones and expressed the desire of the peasant to be rid of the *corvée* and other oppressive dues. In his speeches he attacked the privileged position of the boyar.

In March, 1821, as we have seen, Ypsilantes entered Moldavia with a band of Greeks. From the beginning of the revolt cooperation between Greeks and Romanians of any social class proved difficult. The Greeks first massacred Turkish merchants at Jassy and Galați, and in general they behaved in Moldavia in a manner to arouse anti-Phanariote feeling. The entire success of the Greek action hinged, of course, on Russian involvement. The Philike Hetairia had been quite free in its promises of Russian aid. According to the treaties Ottoman troops could not enter the Principalities without the consent of the protecting power. The revolutionaries hoped to create a situation in the provinces that the Porte

1. After the middle of the sixteenth century the Ottoman government concluded with the European powers treaties called capitulations, which granted special privileges, exemptions, and rights of extraterritoriality.

could not handle and that would force Russian intervention, much in the manner that Austria was acting at this time in Italy under the sanction of the Holy Alliance.

When the Russian government refused to move and, even more important, sanctioned the entrance of Ottoman troops into the land, not only was the revolt doomed but Greek-Romanian cooperation became even more strained. Although at first he cooperated with Ypsilantes, the impending defeat of the movement led Vladimirescu to get in touch with the Porte. At the same time the anti-Greek feeling of the Romanian boyars rose. In their negotiations with representatives of the Porte, Vladimirescu and the boyars emphasized that their chief grievance was not Ottoman suzerainty but the Phanariote regime. In other words, their arguments resembled those of the Serbian leaders from 1790 to 1805 when they had attacked janissary rule instead of the sultan. Informed of the Romanian actions, Ypsilantes had Vladimirescu kidnapped from among his own troops and subsequently executed for treason. Thereafter some of his troops joined Ypsilantes, others went home.

After the defeat of the Greek rebellion, the elimination of Vladimirescu, and the dissolution of his army, the Romanian boyars were able to negotiate, with Russian backing, more favorable political conditions for the Principalities. Although the uprising had caused serious economic losses in the country and was to lead to a sixteen-months Ottoman occupation, important political goals were achieved. Of obvious prime importance was the end of the long Phanariote rule. In 1822 two native rulers were appointed: Gregory Ghica in Wallachia and Ioniţa Sturdza in Moldavia. In the future the country was to be governed by Romanian boyars assisted by boyar councils (*divans*). Although families of Greek descent were still to be prominent in the affairs of the country, the Greek revolution here as elsewhere brought about the destruction of the paramount influence which had existed previously.

The continuation of the Greek crisis with the uprising in the Peloponnesus was to cause further decisive political changes in the Principalities. In the Convention of Akkerman of October, 1826, in addition to the sections concerning Serbia, Romanian rights against the Ottoman suzerain and Russian rights to intervene were both strengthened. The *hospodars* were now to be elected by the boyar *divans* for seven years. Both their appointment and their dismissal were subject to Russian and Ottoman approval. The convention also provided that the boyars in each province should draw up a new statute, or organic regulation, for the administration of the provinces.

The Treaty of Adrianople of 1829, which followed the Russo-Turkish War, confirmed and widened the Akkerman provisions. *Hospodars* were now to be elected for life. The Ottoman fortresses on the left bank of the

Danube were to be evacuated. Ottoman subjects were to leave the provinces and to sell any land that they had to natives within eighteen months. The question of the tribute was finally regulated. There were to be no more payments in kind, and in 1834 the amount was set at the nominal sum of three million piastres. The Ottoman right of preemption on the purchase of Romanian grain, cattle, and sheep was surrendered. A national militia was also to be organized. Finally, the stipulation of Akkerman regarding the drawing up of an administrative regulation was repeated.

The Treaty of Adrianople completed a process commenced with Kuchuk Kainardji. Ottoman control over the Principalities was now nominal. In contrast, the Russian position had become predominant. Moreover, in the peace Russia annexed the Danube delta, which gave her a controlling position on the river, and her armies of occupation were to remain in the provinces until the Ottoman war indemnity had been paid. Fully conscious of its position, the Russian government immediately proceeded with the reorganization of Romanian political life.

Fortunately for the Romanians, the Russian administrator, Count Paul Kiselev, was to prove a remarkable statesman. In charge of the area from 1829 to 1834, he was directly responsible for the changes that now took place. He first devoted his attention to the immediate crises arising from the wartime conditions and to medical problems including dealing with a cholera epidemic and re-establishing the Danube quarantine. His greatest achievement, however, was his supervision of the completion of the Organic Statutes. When he arrived, committees were at work in both provinces in accordance with the provisions of both Akkerman and Adrianople. In each Principality the committee consisted of four boyars, two of whom were appointed by the *divans* and two by the Russian government. Drafts of their proposals were sent to St. Petersburg where they were examined by another committee under the chairmanship of Prince I. A. Dashkov. The documents were then forwarded to the Porte and back to the *divans*. The final statute for Wallachia was promulgated in 1831, and that for Moldavia in 1832.

The Organic Statutes established similar and parallel regimes in both Principalities. As such they were a step forward toward a possible eventual unification. The documents resembled lengthy administrative statutes rather than political constitutions. They covered all phases of national life from the organization of the executive, legislative, and judicial branches of the government to small details concerning public health and local administration. In general they set up the type of government that would be of the greatest benefit to the boyar class. Like the Serbian constitution of 1838, the power in the state fell into the hands of a group of leading landowners at the expense of that of the executive. Again the peasantry was excluded from a direct share in the government. In accordance also with the direction in both Serbia and Greece the administrative system was highly centralized with the control of local affairs held by prefects appointed by the central government.

In theory at least the governmental structure provided for a division of power. The executive branch consisted of a *hospodar* assisted by a council. The *hospodar* was to be elected from among the high boyars for life by a special assembly of 150 members. Here the boyars were to hold the greater share of the representation although twenty-seven were to be chosen from the merchants and the middle class. There were no peasant representatives. The legislative branch was composed of an assembly of forty-nine boyars, again chosen on a franchise which gave this group control. The *hospodar* could veto the decisions of the assembly and could prorogue but not dissolve it, but only with the consent of Russia and the Porte. The assembly voted the budget; it could not dismiss the *hospodar*. Both the assembly and the prince could appeal to Russia and the Porte separately. This system, in which the executive and legislative branches could effectively thwart each other's actions, gave the Russian government unlimited opportunity for interference.

The boyars, having received a political system that accorded with their interests, were also intent upon gaining further advantages for their economic position. Not only did they remain exempt from taxation, but they also strengthened their control of the peasantry. For the first time, in the Organic Statutes, the boyar was designated as the owner of the land; the peasant's rights were limited to a share in two-thirds of the land of the estate. For this he continued to pay state taxes, and his labor dues were increased as well. The number of days remained at twelve, but the tasks he was required to complete meant that the time actually worked would be about thirty-six days in Wallachia and perhaps twice that number in Moldavia. These and other burdens signified that the peasant would in all owe approximately fifty-two days in Wallachia, where the obligation was largely paid in money rent, and eighty-four or the equivalent in Moldavia. Although in theory not attached to the soil, the peasant had to give six months notice before leaving his plot, and he had to pay his share of the taxes first. It should be emphasized, however, that in the first part of the century the peasant obligations, in particular the labor dues, remained difficult to enforce.

The Organic Statutes thus put the landowner in a position to benefit from the end of the Ottoman right of preemption and the rise in the demand for agricultural products in Europe. In the next years a great expansion of Romanian agriculture occurred, particularly after the Crimean War. More land was put into use and rents rose sharply. Attempts were made to improve methods and land use. As in Serbia, the increase in grain production was paralleled by a relative decline in livestock. This change was to the detriment of the peasant and his daily diet. In general, Moldavian estates were directly administered by the boyar. In Wallachia, in contrast, many landowners preferred to live in Bucharest and to contract out their estates or to work the land on a sharecrop basis.

The Organic Statutes, it will be noted, preceded both the Serbian Constitution of 1838 and the Greek constitutions of 1844 and 1864. Like these documents, they reflected much of the constitutional thought of Western Europe. Control of the government lay in the hands of the 'men of substance,' usually to the detriment of the power of the central executive and to the exclusion of the majority of the people. This condition was also to be seen in the British Reform Bill of 1832 and the system of the July Monarchy in France. The Balkan nations thus reflected in their institutions the political system of western Europe. Russia, the sponsoring power, remained an absolute monarchy.

The Organic Statutes with their provisions for the establishment of a regular national government in both Principalities should have represented an advance toward national independence. In fact, the adoption of these documents marked the beginning of a period of increasing Russian interference. In 1834, in the Convention of St. Petersburg, Russia and the Porte settled the questions of the Ottoman war indemnity and the evacuation of the Russian forces. The two powers then chose new *hospodars*. Although the Organic Statutes called for lifetime appointments, the powers agreed that the first princes should only hold office for seven years. Alexander Ghica now became *hospodar* of Wallachia and Michael Sturdza of Moldavia. In the next years it soon became apparent that three separate and conflicting centers of power had been established: the *hospodars*, the assemblies, and the Russian consulates. Both the Organic Statutes and the treaties between the Porte and Russia allowed for unlimited intrigue by both the suzerain and the protecting power and by the assemblies against the *hospodars*. In the period of the Russian protectorate to 1856, many of the bad aspects of the Phanariote period again came to the fore.

In general, the boyars were not basically discontented with the political situation. Some large boyars were to prove strong Russian partisans. The Russian protectorship guaranteed them a conservative government that would secure their economic and social advantages and their political privileges. It should also be remembered that at this time the governments of the Principalities had no alternative but to cooperate with St. Petersburg. In 1833 Russia and the Porte signed the Treaty of Unkiar Iskelesi, which put the Ottoman Empire in a position of virtual subservience. The subsequent signing of the Treaty of Münchengrätz in 1834 between the Habsburg Monarchy and Russia signified the renewed cooperation of the two great conservative states. The Principalities could thus not hope for outside assistance in resisting St. Petersburg. France and Britain, although willing to intrigue in Bucharest and Jassy against Russia, could offer no positive support.

During the period of the Russian protectorate affairs went relatively more smoothly in Moldavia than in Wallachia. There Michael Sturdza proved an enterprising and strong ruler, even though he was also corrupt and conniving. Although there was some friction, he was able to work with the Russian consuls, first Besak and then K. E. Kotsebu. The *hospodar* put his chief efforts into reforming the country along the lines of the Organic Statute. Considerable improvements were made in the roads, the postal system, and in particular in education. As could be expected, he faced much opposition from the Moldavian boyars, but he was able to control them through expert political maneuvering.

The situation in Wallachia was more difficult. Here Alexander Ghica, like Sturdza, faced personal opposition from among the boyars. Moreover, he soon clashed with the Russian representatives. In 1837 the Russian consul, P. I. Rikman (Rückmann), demanded that the Wallachian Assembly accept the so-called additional article for the Organic Statute which stated that no change could be made in the document without the consent of Russia and the Porte. The Russian consulate justified this action by claiming that the stipulation had inadvertently been "left out" of the original draft. Since this clause would deal a real blow to the autonomy of the country, the assembly refused to accept it. A second assembly, held after the first was prorogued, not only objected to the article, but was also strongly hostile to the *hospodar*. When its members appealed to the Porte and Russia, both powers sent commissioners to investigate. Ghica was deposed in 1842. In December of that year a special assembly, as directed by the Organic Statute, was held. George Bibescu received the majority of the votes and became the first *hospodar* elected in this manner.

The new prince faced the same problems as his predecessor: boyar intrigues and Russian pressure. When the first assembly held during his reign had a hostile majority, he prorogued it. When it met again, in 1844, another major crisis concerning Russia occurred. The incident involved the requests of a Russian engineer, Alexander Trandafilov. Representing a Russian mining company, he sought permission to survey the country and to exploit for twelve years those mineral rights that he discovered after compensation had been paid the state and the owners of the property. The prince and his council agreed to the terms, but the assembly would not. In 1844 it was prorogued. The grant was finally refused. In 1847 an assembly was elected in which a majority supported the prince, but intrigues against him continued, including constant charges that he was too pro-Russian. At this time in Bucharest, as in Belgrade and Athens, the Russian, French, and British consuls with their opposing stands made the life of the prince difficult.

Like Sturdza before him, Bibescu, despite a shortage of funds, did succeed in bettering the general condition of the province. Means of communication were further improved. More primary and secondary schools were organized. A theater was opened in Bucharest, and the great swampland in the center of the city was turned into a park. Of particular importance were two legislative measures. In 1847 a law on naturalization was passed, which made it a simple process for a Moldavian to gain Wallachian citizenship. In the same year a customs union was established between the two provinces. The economic union was the second major concrete step toward unification, the passing of the parallel sets of statutes having been the first.

The period of the Russian protectorate coincided with the years of the greatest rise in Romanian national feeling, particularly among the educated and the privileged sections of society. Patriotic societies were organized, and the educational system reflected the growing national self-awareness. Since at this time Russian interference in Romanian affairs was more obvious than any actions resulting from Ottoman suzerainty, the chief object of attack became the Russian protectorate. For the future, the most important group from whom the leaders of the movement would be drawn were the young men, sons of boyars, who were sent to Western Europe, particularly to Paris, to complete their education.

From the 1840s onward increasing numbers of young Romanians began to gather in Paris. They were greatly attracted by the lectures of such men as Alphonse de Lamartine, Jules Michelet, and Edgar Quinet, all partisans of romantic nationalism. The majority preferred to study at the Collège de France where there were no degrees and no examinations. They devoted most of their activities to national propaganda, to the formation of various societies, and to frequent meetings. Although they had no single political goal, they had certain ideas in common. Most important they all advocated the unification of Romanian lands in an independent state. They stood also for constitutional government and for a program of civil rights. Unfortunately, many sections of the standard liberal program, such as equality of taxation for all classes, equality before the law, and a truly representative government, would have undermined the political and economic foundations of the rule of their class in the Principalities. Moreover, from their French education and their family background these young men had never had the opportunity to gain knowledge or understanding of the peasant and his problems and outlook. The "people" remained for them an abstract concept gained from books. Nevertheless, it was from these students that the national leadership for most of the rest of the century was to come. In the future Alexander Cuza, Nicholas and Radu Golescu, C. A. Rosetti, Ion and Dumitru Brătianu, and Nicholas Bălcescu were to be particularly prominent. The historian Michael Kogălniceanu, a Moldavian educated in Berlin, was to have a similarly important political career.

In February, 1848, when the revolt against Louis Philippe broke out in Paris, most of the Romanians went home to take a leading role in the events that subsequently took place in the Principalities. Jassy was the center of the first actions. Here on April 8 about one thousand men gathered, the majority of whom were liberal landowners. Among them were Alexander Cuza and Emanoil Epureanu. A committee of sixteen was then chosen to draw up a petition, which called for moderate social and political reform such as the guarantee of personal liberty, ministerial responsibility, the establishment of a national bank, the organization of a national militia, the end of censorship, and the election of a new assembly. About eight thousand people signed this petition of thirty-three articles. Although this was no true revolution, Sturdza acted promptly to put the entire movement down by force. Some of the leaders were arrested; others went into exile.

In contrast, in Wallachia the situation became far more serious. A revolutionary government actually held control in Bucharest for three months. After their return from Paris the Brătianu brothers, Rosetti, Bălcescu, and others immediately prepared plans for an insurrection. They also got in touch with Romanian leaders in Transylvania. The main thrust of their movement was to be against the Russian protectorate, and they sought the cooperation of the *hospodar*, Bibescu. The first step in the revolt occurred on June 21 at Islaz, a city on the Danube. Here the revolutionaries issued a manifesto containing twenty-two basic demands. These included a call for equal taxation, the convocation of an assembly with representatives from all classes, and the election of a chief executive, who could be from any class, for a five-year term. Article 13 supported the emancipation of the peasants with indemnification for the landowners. From the beginning of the revolt the leaders emphasized that they were acting against the regime of the Organic Statutes and Russia, not against the Porte. They wished only a return of their former rights.

Having issued their manifesto, the revolutionaries next set up their first provisional government, which included Christian Tell, Ştefan Golescu, Radu Şapca, and Nicholas Pleşoianu. They then moved on to Craiova on June 25. Meanwhile, events in Bucharest had proceeded along the same road. Bibescu signed the Islaz proclamation and made no overt attempt to put down the rebellion. On June 26 another provisional government was formed, including some members of the Islaz group. Metropolitan Neofit was named president. On June 25-26 Bibescu abdicated and went to Braşov in Transylvania. In complete control this regime adopted a new flag, blue-yellow-red in color, with the words *Dreptate-Frătie* (Justice-Fraternity) on it. From the beginning the revolutionary government had the support of the city of Bucharest. A series of meetings held on the Field of Liberty and attended by thousands showed the degree of popular participation.

The provisional government was, nevertheless, in a most precarious position. It was in constant danger of a conservative counter-revolution; furthermore, its members were not in agreement on the social and political program they should introduce. On July 1 the government was seized in a conspiracy led by Colonel Ioan Odobescu and Ioan Solomon and only freed by the Bucharest crowd. Within the ranks of the leaders a split had now become obvious between those who wished only political changes and others, like Bălcescu, who wished thorough social and economic reform, in particular the execution of Article 13 of the Islaz proclamation concerning the status of the peasant. Meanwhile, however, the provisional government did attempt to put into practice some of the provisions of the manifesto, such as the abolition of corporal punishment, and the death penalty.

More serious, however, than the dangers from within were those from without. The great question was the Russian reaction. In July Russian armies occupied Jassy in preparation for an eventual march into Transylvania against the Hungarian revolution. Rumors immediately swept through Bucharest that Russia might also occupy Wallachia. The provisional government therefore left Bucharest, and Neofit set up a new administration based on the Organic Statute. A *caimacamie* (regency) composed of Theodore Văcărescu and E. Băleanu and supported by Odobescu and Solomon was set up, but it was soon overthrown.

Having returned to Bucharest, the provisional government next planned to call a national assembly to be elected on the basis of universal manhood suffrage. At the same time attempts were made to come to an arrangement with the Porte. On July 9 a message was sent to Constantinople emphasizing that the new regime did not wish to break away from the empire. Equally apprehensive of possible Russian moves, the Ottoman government now sent Suleiman Pasha and an army of twenty thousand men to Ruse. Suleiman then went alone to Bucharest where he was warmly received. Although he did not recognize the provisional government, he did accept the formation of a new *caimacamie* containing members of the revolutionary regime. This arrangement, however, was subsequently rejected by the Porte. Another commissioner, Fuad Efendi, accompanied by Ottoman troops, entered Bucharest on September 25. There they encountered some resistance, but the revolutionary forces were too weak to organize a real military opposition. On September 27 Russian troops also entered the Principality. The Ottoman representatives now chose as sole *caimacam* (regent) Constantine Cantacuzino, a conservative boyar. The revolutionary leaders went into exile.

With Russian troops in Moldavia and Russian and Ottoman forces in Wallachia, a new and more repressive political regime was instituted. In May, 1849, Russia and the Porte signed the Convention of Balta Liman, in which it was agreed that the *hospodars* would henceforth be named by Russia and the Ottoman Empire rather than be elected. They would serve for seven years. The assemblies were to be replaced by so-called *divans ad hoc*, whose members would be nominated by the *hospodar*. Russian troops remained in the Principalities until 1851.

The new *hospodar*s were Barbu Ştirbey, a brother of Bibescu, in Wallachia and Gregory Ghica in Moldavia. Despite the difficult situation, both princes tried to work for the improvement of the provinces. For the future the most significant legislation was the Land Law of 1851. Here the days of *corvée* owed by the peasant were increased, but limits were placed on what had to be done during the period. The law benefited the boyar, whose aim remained the attainment of full control over the land with the assurance of an adequate supply of peasant labor.

The major Romanian revolutionary movement in the nineteenth century thus ended in failure. The leadership was simply too weak to carry through a program against the combined opposition of Russia and the Ottoman Empire. Concurrent events in Transylvania had also not aided the rebellion in the Principalities. The Romanian population of the Habsburg Empire was primarily interested in winning an equal position with the Hungarians. They thus sided with the Russian intervention and the Habsburg dynasty against the Hungarian revolution. In addition the revolt in the Principalities had demonstrated the division within the revolutionary command. A real national program had to include peasant emancipation. However, only a few of the leaders, such as Bălcescu, were willing to embrace a genuine land-reform program, which would inevitably undermine their economic and social privileges.

Although the revolutionary leaders in exile adopted no uniform political proposals, most of them moved to the right. The men of the revolution of 1848, who were known subsequently as the 'forty-eighters,' in the future came to stand for what was a comparatively conservative and limited national program. Instead of a national state embracing all the Romanian lands and a real social program, they now confined their objectives to the unification of Wallachia and Moldavia and to the naming of a foreign prince. Moreover, many recognized the futility of armed revolt. So long as the three great empires stood opposed to Romanian national demands, there was little hope that they could gain their goals by force. Many, like Ion Ghika, now pressed for an emphasis on diplomatic means.

Despite the fact that the refugees formed no single organization abroad, they did all act along the same lines. In no way discouraged by their recent failure, they prepared for the future. A real propaganda offensive was launched; meetings were held and articles were written. Romanian leaders made a great effort to speak with and to influence prominent European statesmen. They achieved their greatest success when they won the sympathy and support of Napoleon III. In contrast, in Britain where the government continued to stand for the maintenance of the Ottoman Empire as a bulwark against Russian expansion, little progress could be made. Even with the assured support of influential westerners, however, it was clear that even the limited Romanian national program, that is, the unification of the provinces, could not be attained unless some event occurred that would remove the Russian protectorate. The Crimean War was to be exactly this welcome occurrence.

CHAPTER 7

The Ottoman Empire to 1876: the Reforms

IN THE preceding chapters the steps taken by three of the Balkan national groups to secede from the empire and establish their own autonomous or independent regimes have been discussed. The parallel establishment in these countries of constitutional forms of government along European lines has also been covered. It is interesting to note that during this same period the Ottoman government, whose authority still extended over all of the peninsula with the exception of the small Greek state, faced many of the same problems and adopted some of the same solutions as the Christian peoples.

Throughout the century in both internal and foreign policy the Ottoman Empire had to deal with one single, overriding problem: that of holding the empire together under highly adverse circumstances, many of which have already been described. The Porte had to face the challenge not only of the Christian nationalities and the Muslim *ayans*, but also of the great powers who pressed to control, directly or indirectly, the decisions of the Ottoman state. The same conditions that led to the establishment of a French-British-Russian protectorate in Greece and a Russian protectorate in Serbia and the Danubian Principalities resulted in similar measures of domination in Constantinople at various times by either Russia or Britain.

The leaders of the Ottoman state realized that unless their national life were reformed they would not be able to stand against either foreign pressure or internal subversion from both Christian and Muslim elements. The military in particular needed a thorough reorganization. Change was, however, quite difficult to accomplish. With relatively little difficulty the Christian people were able to establish governments in which the church became in effect a department of the state, and the ruler of the country its nominal head. Despite their anti-Muslim tone, the revolutions had not been predominantly religious struggles. Moreover, the Serbs, Romanians, and later the Bulgarians viewed the Greek-dominated heirarchy of the Orthodox church as a block to their own aspirations. The patriarchate was a part of the Ottoman political structure.

In contrast, the religious influence remained predominant in Constantinople. The state was still a Muslim, not a Turkish, entity. For five hundred years religion had provided the basis for a great and conquering empire. The successes of the past made it difficult to change radically ancient institutions and ideas. At the beginning reforms could only be carried out when they were justified as a return to old ways. Moreover, despite the often desperate position of the empire, too many of its citizens continued to have a vested interest in the maintenance of conditions as they were.

As has already been seen, Balkan revolt was not always a clear case of Christian against Muslim. It was also a class and social struggle between those who were benefited by the system and those who were harmed or felt stifled by it. Christian millet leaders often discouraged Ottoman reform because they saw it as damaging to their position and as leading to a further secularization of their society. Some Christian merchants and notables also profited greatly from cooperation with the empire and had no wish to change the political order. The situation was, of course, much more difficult within Ottoman society. The *ulema* (learned men of Islam), who controlled education and the law, saw no advantage in progressive reform measures which would lead to a system of public education on the European model or to the adoption of a legal system separate from Muslim law. Both Christian and Muslim conservative church leaders opposed western ideas because they saw that they would lead inevitably to a secular state in which religious institutions would be reduced to a clearly subordinate position.

The path to reform in the Ottoman Empire was to proceed in the direction already taken by the Balkan states. First, an attempt was made to establish a centralized, orderly administration whose members would be loyal to the government, and to draw up uniform laws and regulations applicable to the entire country. These initial reforms were determined by the sultan and a small group of administrators close to him. Second, the representative principle was introduced into some phases of the government, and, third, an attempt was made to transfer the real control of the government to a legislature chosen by a general election. The third stage was achieved by a revolutionary action.

In addition to the problems already mentioned, it must be emphasized that in the nineteenth century the Porte, unlike the Balkan states, was faced with almost continual warfare—either at home or abroad. Often reform had to be undertaken during severe crises and usually under strong pressure from outside powers. Moreover, whereas the Christian states could usually count on the friendship of one or more great powers in their national struggles, the Porte could never be sure of support. After the middle of the century it often felt more endangered by its supposed friends, particularly Britain, than by its usual enemy, Russia.

A real effort to reform the empire was begun, as we have seen, during the reign of Selim III. At a time when it appeared that the state would collapse from inner rebellion, from both Muslim *ayans* and Christian rebels, the sultan recognized the primary need of military reform. Some efforts along this line had commenced in earlier reigns. Since France was recognized as the great military state of the age, and since she was the oldest European ally of the empire, the Porte had naturally turned to her for assistance and had received French military advisers. Selim's attempt to establish a modern army organized on European lines failed disastrously. In 1807 his plans were abandoned, and in 1808 he was assassinated and replaced by Mahmud II.

Few rulers have faced the conditions that now confronted the new sultan. It was obvious that his empire could not long withstand the internal and external threats. With rebellious *ayans* still in control of strong centers, with the Serbs in revolt, and with a war with Russia on his hands, he could do little before 1812 when the Treaty of Bucharest was signed. Given the prospect of a period of freedom from foreign war, the sultan first turned to crushing the rebellious *ayans*. Although he was successful in subduing Ali Pasha of Janina and Pasvanoglu, he was unable to curb Mohammed Ali. Ali remained in Egypt and assumed the attitude of an independent ruler rather than a subject of the sultan. Moreover, the problem of Christian rebellion remained. After the settlement of Serbian affairs in 1815, the Greek and Romanian movements in the Principalities and the revolt in the Peloponnesus again placed the empire in grave danger. The great powers did not intervene until 1827, but the threat of Russian action was imminent after 1821.

Like Selim III, Mahmud recognized that his chief military problem was the weakness of the janissaries, which was again demonstrated during the Greek revolution. Unable to put down the rebellion with his army, the sultan was forced to appeal to Mohammed Ali in 1825. The Egyptians with their modern army performed well against the rebels. The Porte could not, of course, continue to rely on a vassal state led by a man of the caliber of Mohammed Ali. The sultan needed forces loyal to his person. Unlike Selim, Mahmud prepared his moves well in advance. Since the Muslim state was obviously threatened, he was able to win the support of the *mufti* (interpreters of the law) and the *ulema* for the establishment of what was in fact a form of the New Model Army of Selim. Once again, the janissaries refused to accept any diminution of their power and rebelled. This time the sultan was ready; in 1826 the revolt was crushed and the janissaries abolished. At the same time Mahmud dissolved the religious Bektaski Dervish order, which had been a main support of the janissaries. The conservative forces in the empire thus lost their one great source of military power.

The abolition of the janissaries, although a necessary move, left the Ottoman state in a weak and exposed position. In that same year, it will be remembered, Russia imposed the Convention of Akkerman on the Porte; in 1827 the French, British, and Russian governments cooperated in the joint blockade which ended in the disaster at Navarino and ultimately in the Russo-Turkish War. In 1829 in the Treaty of Adrianople the empire surrendered the Danube delta to Russia and was compelled to consent to the establishment of the Russian protectorship over Serbia and the Danubian Principalities. The year 1830 saw the formal establishment of independent Greece and the recognition of Serbian autonomy. At this same time France began its expansion in Algeria, a move that heralded a century of European encroachment on the North African lands associated with the Ottoman Empire. Unfortunate as these losses were, an even graver threat was presented by the actions of Mohammed Ali.

This clever, highly ambitious ruler with his reorganized state and his excellent army now prepared to move. Although he had received Crete as payment for his services in the Greek revolution, he naturally could not obtain the promised Peloponnesus. He therefore wished Syria as compensation. When Mahmud refused, the Egyptian forces attacked, and at the Battle of Konya in December, 1832, they inflicted a grave defeat on the Ottoman army. Once again the empire was in serious danger; Constantinople lay open to attack. In this hour of peril the sultan was forced to accept Russian assistance; Russian troops and ships arrived in the Straits. In July, 1833, the Ottoman Empire and Russia signed the Treaty of Unkiar Iskelesi. A treaty of alliance and mutual defense, this agreement was important because it appeared to assure Russian dominance in the affairs of the empire. The Porte was saved from the Egyptian danger, but in the peace treaty Mohammed Ali did receive terms which gave him the effective control of Syria. Conclusion of peace allowed the empire another brief respite from foreign wars.

Although, as we have seen, the sultan had already commenced his efforts to reform the empire, the major changes occurred after the Russo-Turkish War. Mahmud II has often been referred to as the Peter the Great of the Ottoman Empire because of the nature of the measures that he introduced during his reign. His efforts were directed to turning his state toward the West, and he was interested in altering the appearance as well as the content of state institutions. Like Selim, he continued to place emphasis on strengthening the army, which had not performed well against the Greeks or against the Egyptians. Again foreign instructors were sought. In 1835 Helmut von Moltke and a group of Prussian officers arrived to train the army; British advisers were secured for the navy. Turkish students were also sent abroad for military training.

Mahmud then turned to the pressing problem of political reorganization. By this time the sultan had absolute control in his own domains, with the exception, of course, of the regions under the Mohammed Ali's rule. No other local *ayan*s were able to challenge his authority. His chief concern henceforth was to strengthen the central authority and to create state institutions that would serve this purpose. He also wished to give his regime the outward appearance of the European governments. He thus changed the titles of officials so that he had, for instance, a minister of foreign affairs, of the interior, and of the treasury. The grand vezir, the chief Ottoman official under the sultan, now became the prime minister, although the original title was restored a few months later. A ministerial council headed by the prime minister was established; it resembled a European cabinet. In local government measures were taken to tighten the hold of the central government on the provinces. An Ottoman census and a survey were taken in 1831 for purposes of taxation and conscription.

Like the leaders of the new Balkan states, Mahmud was faced with the problem of finding officials who could fill the offices of state. The modern bureaucratic system demanded a supply of literate, trained officials. Some attention was therefore turned to the problem of secular education, but little progress was made. In 1827 a medical school was established, but no further great advances were made at this time. As in the Balkans teachers were simply not available.

With his reign dominated by problems of foreign affairs, Mahmud recognized the need to improve relations with the European courts. In 1834 permanent embassies in the major capitals were opened. These posts became exceedingly important for the future development of the country, because through them many of the chief reformers and statesmen, such as Ali Pasha and Fuad Pasha, received their basic training and their experience with life in Europe. As direct relations with European states increased the question of languages was posed. Very few Turks had customarily learned foreign languages. The Porte had in the past leaned heavily on Greek and Armenian interpreters. Since the Greeks could no longer be completely trusted after the revolt, other provisions had to be made. A Translation Bureau was established to handle the correspondence with other governments, which was in French. Here Turkish students could learn that language and also receive instruction in subjects such as history and arithmetic.

Other important developments during Mahmud's reign included the appearance of the first Turkish language newspaper in the 1830s and the establishment of a postal system in 1834. Like Peter the Great, Mahmud was concerned with the dress of his officials. He introduced new uniforms in the European style, and he replaced the traditional turban with the fez. With these changes in dress, education, and manners the process began that we have already seen in the Balkan countries. A bureaucratic elite began to emerge; it ran the government, but it became increasingly separated from the mass of the people.

Although Mahmud's reign ended in another foreign disaster, his accomplishments must be acknowledged. The first steps were taken to change the state organization so that it could better withstand assaults from foreign powers and from dissident groups within the country. The central power of the government was strengthened. Moreover, with the abolition of the janissaries a more efficient fighting force could be established and the conservative and reactionary elements were less able to topple the government. Mahmud's desire to establish an efficient administration and to end corruption in public office was not accomplished, but at least one of the major complaints of all of the Ottoman subjects had been recognized.

Throughout his reign Mahmud had been faced with the problem of Mohammed Ali and his obvious ambition to erect a great state for himself and his family. The sultan had also not forgotten the humiliation of 1832. By 1839 he decided that his reformed army was strong enough to challenge his vassal, and in that year he unwisely declared war. The results were tragic. Again Ibrahim Pasha, a truly great general, defeated the Ottoman army. In this crisis Mahmud died, to be succeeded by the sixteen-year-old Abdul Mejid. At this critical point most of the Turkish fleet switched sides and joined Mohammed Ali. All three of these events, the defeat of the army, the death of the sultan, and the loss of the navy, occurred within two weeks.

Again the Ottoman Empire appeared at the point of collapse. The issue now in European diplomacy was not a Russian threat, but rather the close association of France with victorious Egypt. Fearing an upset in the balance of power in the Mediterranean, Russia, Britain, Austria, and Prussia joined to re-establish the *status quo*. Faced with this combination, France dropped her support of Mohammed Ali. Despite his early successes, in the final settlement the pasha of Egypt received little more than the right of hereditary rule in Egypt and the Sudan. He could defeat the Ottoman army, but he could not withstand the combined pressure of the great powers. At this time Russia let the Treaty of Unkiar Iskelesi lapse and joined with the other powers in a new agreement. The Convention of the Straits of 1841 put the area under international control for the first time and in effect limited the authority of the sultan over his own territory. The treaty provided that in time of peace the Straits would be closed to foreign warships. These terms were a compromise between Russian and British interests. With the closure British ships could not menace the Russian shores of the Black Sea; in turn, Russian squadrons could not endanger British shipping in the Mediterranean.

The reign of Abdul Mejid inaugurated the great period of Ottoman reform known as the Tanzimat. The aim of the measures passed at this time was exactly the same as Mahmud's: to save the empire. For the Balkan peoples the significance of this endeavor lay in the question of whether the empire could so change its structure that it would either be more attractive to the non-Muslim inhabitant than the national alternative, or so strong that revolt would be impossible. From the beginning the task assumed by the reformers ranged on the impossible. The Christian Balkan leaders did not seek equality in an Ottoman state; they wanted a separate national existence. The concept of Ottoman citizenry brought forth at this time offered limited appeal. In the same manner no significant body of Muslims actively sought the reformation of the state on the lines of religious and national equality. If change were inevitable, the non-Turkish Muslims tended to prefer the Egyptian example and a similar separation.

Unlike Mahmud II, Abdul Mejid did not provide firm direction for change. The leadership lay more in the hands of active, energetic statesmen like Mustafa Reshid Pasha. An excellent example of the new Ottoman official, Reshid had been ambassador in France and Britain before becoming the grand vezir. The sultan himself was a mild but intelligent man who allowed his ministers much latitude. This period of bureaucratic supremacy corresponded with an unusually long era of tranquility in international affairs in the Near East. From the conclusion of the Egyptian crisis until the outbreak of the Crimean War, Russia and Britain were usually in agreement in their eastern policies. British influence was usually stronger in Constantinople, but the Russian government made no active effort to reverse the situation. The British government was particularly interested in the maintenance and reform of the empire after the signature of the very favorable commercial Treaty of Balta Liman in 1838. This agreement opened the empire to British imports on a virtually free-trade basis.

The two landmarks of the Tanzimat period are the Hatti-Sherif of Gülhane and the Hatti-Hümayun of 1856. The first was issued in the middle of the Egyptian crisis. Reshid wished to impress upon the powers that the empire could reform and maintain itself as a viable state. The document was a statement of the program that the government intended to introduce. Its goal was the further centralization and bureaucratization of the state and the winning of popular support by the sultan and his officials as against provincial loyalties and local notables. In this document assurances were given that measures would be passed ensuring the security of life, honor and property, equal taxation, an improved system of taxation, and a better system for recruiting soldiers. The guarantees were offered to all Ottoman citizens regardless of religion. It is interesting to note that these declarations had to be justified by stating that they were a return to the past basis of the empire:

> In the last one hundred and fifty years a succession of accidents and divers causes have arisen which have brought about a disregard for the sacred code of laws and the regulations flowing therefrom, and the former strength and prosperity have changed into weakness and poverty.[1]

Despite the strong British influence in Constantinople, the Ottoman reformers usually preferred to follow French examples in their administrative changes, in a manner similar to the Balkan states. In 1840 a new law code was issued based on the premise of the equality of all the citizens. Improvements were also made in the system of secular education. For the Balkans the most significant measure was probably the introduction of a new system of local government in 1840. The power of the provincial governor was now to be limited by the establishment of a council of notables on which non-Muslims would be represented. In practice these bodies, whose members were appointed by the governor, were not only dominated by Muslims, but they also came to represent those who had vested interests in the *status quo* and were not particularly interested in reform. In addition, in the field of local administration attempts were made to improve the quality of the officials sent to the provinces and to end graft. More of these men were made responsible directly to the central rather than to the local governments, and regular salaries were paid.

Unfortunately for the Porte, the process of change was again interrupted by a foreign crisis and a revival of the contest among the great powers for control of all or a part of the empire. Russian influence in Ottoman lands, the importance of which has been amply demonstrated in the preceding pages, was based on her military power, on her relations with the Balkan national groups, and on a series of treaties giving her a protectorate over Serbia and the Danubian Principalities and certain rights in regard to the Orthodox Christians in general. The question of exactly what the Russian position was in regard to the Orthodox church became a matter of international concern as a result of a quarrel between the Orthodox and Catholic churches over their respective rights in certain Holy Places in Jerusalem. In this conflict Russia backed the Orthodox position, France the Catholic. When in 1852 the Ottoman government made a judgment favoring the French, the Russian reaction was violent. Part of the army was mobilized and a special representative was sent to Constantinople.

The Russian delegate, Prince Alexander Menshikov, arrived in Febru-

---

1. J. C. Hurewitz, *Diplomacy in the Near and Middle East: A Documentary Record* (Princeton: D. Van Nostrand Co., 1956), vol. 1, p. 114.

ary, 1853, armed with considerable latitude to negotiate. Adopting a tough and arrogant manner, he presented to the Porte demands that included a clear Ottoman recognition of Russia's right to protect the Orthodox Christians, and a treaty similar to Unkiar Iskelesi. These conditions, which changed the issue from a quarrel over the Holy Places to one of the control of the Ottoman Empire, brought a strong British reaction. The energetic British ambassador, Stratford Canning, apparently counseled the Porte to resist. When the Russian terms, which were presented in the form of an ultimatum, were rejected, Menshikov left Constantinople and diplomatic relations were broken. Russian troops then entered the Principalities. This was, of course, an act of war since the provinces were under Ottoman suzerainty despite the Russian protectorate.

The Russian actions now engaged all of the great powers. Britain, France, and Austria could not allow the change in the balance of power that would occur should the Ottoman Empire accept the Russian conditions and thus become a satellite of the great Slavic nation. No state, including Russia, wished to go to war, but each government was drawn into the conflict. Feeling in a strong position because of the apparent support of the western powers, the Ottoman Empire declared war on Russia in October, 1853. At the same time the French and British fleets entered the Straits. In November the Ottoman navy suffered a disastrous defeat in an engagement with Russian ships at Sinope. The entire Ottoman fleet was sunk with the loss of four thousand men. After another four months of complicated negotiations Britain and France finally declared war on Russia in March, 1854. Then in August, 1854, Austria forced Russia to evacuate the Danubian Principalities, which were placed under a joint Austro-Turkish occupation.

The main event of the Crimean War was the British and French invasion of the Crimean Peninsula. For once an eastern war was not waged chiefly on Ottoman territory, although fierce fighting did take place near Kars. The ultimate defeat of Russia and the terms of the Treaty of Paris of 1856 created a favorable international situation for the Porte. Russia, as we have seen, had consistently been the chief foreign threat to the Ottoman Empire. She had endangered the state by her claims to Ottoman territory, by her attempts to control the government after the Treaty of Adrianople, and by her patronage at times of Christian revolt. The peace terms appeared to give the Ottoman government the assurance that Russian pressure would be at least temporarily contained. Of utmost importance was the stipulation that the Black Sea was to be neutralized and that no fortifications were to be built on its shores. This condition applied equally to the Ottoman Empire, but that state could maintain a fleet in the Straits. In contrast, southern Russia would be completely without maritime defenses. Other terms of the pact also favored the Ottomans. Russia was now pushed back from the Danube River. The delta was returned to the Ottoman Empire; Moldavia was given three districts of Bessarabia bordering the mouth of the river. The Danube was then internationalized. In addition, the Russian protectorship over Serbia and the Principalities was abolished, and the states were placed under the guarantee of the great powers. In the treaty the Ottoman Empire was expressly admitted to the "concert of Europe," or the European community of nations. The Porte promised to reform its internal administration, while the other powers agreed that they would not interfere in Ottoman internal affairs.

The Crimean War and the peace treaty led to another period of reform. The war itself had brought many Europeans to the Ottoman capital. These people associated with the Ottoman upper classes, and the latter's partial adoption of western clothes and habits aided the Tanzimat supporters. By this time Constantinople had also become the home of many political refugees, in particular Poles and Hungarians, many of whom entered into the service of the Ottoman state. They, too, provided a channel to acquaint Ottoman society with European developments. These years thus brought to the fore another generation of reformers. These men often had been educated in Europe, and they carried on the work of their predecessors in reforming the state along European lines. Of these men the most important were to be Ali Pasha and Fuad Pasha.

The new era of reform marked a continuation of the emphasis on the equality of all citizens regardless of religion. In 1855 the poll tax for non-Muslims was abolished, and they were allowed to bear arms. Together with rights came, of course, the obligation to serve in the military. These measures were greeted with little enthusiasm in the Balkans. There was certainly no eagerness to fight in the Ottoman armies. The Christians preferred to pay a tax exempting them from service. For their part, the Muslims were reluctant to serve with Christian soldiers or obey Christian officers.

The major document to appear now was the Hatti-Hümayun of 1856, issued in connection with the Treaty of Paris. It had been formulated under foreign pressure, and it was a declaration of intentions. Again the equality of all of the citizens in matters such as justice, education, religion, and tax payments was proclaimed. And again either these stipulations were to remain largely unfulfilled or their implementation failed to appease Christian dissatisfaction.

The 1850s and 1860s also saw continuing efforts to improve communications. In 1855 the telegraph reached Constantinople, placing that capital in close touch with Europe. The network was subsequently extended throughout the empire. In the 1860s the building of railroads commenced and hereafter their construction was to play a major role in the relations of the Porte and the Balkan governments with foreign powers. The railroads were to serve as yet another means of European political and economic penetration into the area.

Despite growing criticism the reforms were continued during the first part of the reign of the new sultan, Abdul Aziz, who came to the throne in 1861. Fuad and Ali continued to alternate in office as his chief ministers. Attention was turned to the problem of local government. In 1864 the Law of Vilayets (provinces) reorganized the empire; again French examples were followed. The governors of the provinces were still to be appointed by the central government, but administrative councils and provincial assemblies representing both Muslim and non-Muslim elements of the population were now associated with them. A standard body of regulations was issued for all of the divisions. The efforts to centralize and standardize local administration were thus continued.

Changes were also made in the central government. The ministerial council was enlarged and charged with the drawing up of new laws; a High Court of Justice was established. The continuation of legal reform resulted in the issuance of a new civil code, the *Mecelle,* between 1868 and 1876, which was based on traditional Muslim law. Education was further improved. In 1868 the Lycée of Galatasaray was opened with French as the language of instruction. Its goal was to provide a modern education on the secondary level.

Once these measures were passed the impetus toward reform began to die. Among the reasons for the waning enthusiasm were the defeat in 1870 of France, whose example had been so important for the reformers, and the deaths of both Fuad and Ali by 1871; no minister of equal ability replaced them. In the next years the sultan took more power into his own hands. His chief minister, Mahmud Nedim, relied more on Russia than on Britain. By this time criticism of the Tanzimat was strong. The aim of reform had been the preservation of the state, yet the process of dissolution was obviously continuing unchecked.

After the Crimean War repeated incidents occurred that resulted in a further weakening of the Ottoman position. Between 1859 and 1861 the Danubian Principalities, in violation of the treaties, united. In 1860–61 the great powers intervened in a revolt in Syria and Lebanon, compelling the Porte to grant autonomy to that area. In 1866–68 Crete again was the scene of a rebellion involving European interference. The efforts of Prince Michael of Serbia to stir up Christian resistance have already been discussed. Most significant, in October, 1870, the Russian government denounced those clauses of the Treaty of Paris that provided for the neutralization of the Black Sea. That state was now free to embark on an active eastern policy. In July, 1875, a massive insurrection broke out in Hercegovina and Bosnia. It was thus obvious that reform measures were not bringing Balkan peoples under Ottoman administration closer to their government. Throughout the area signs of resistance and extreme discontent were evident.

Not only was reform not producing the desired results among the Christian population, but the financial basis of the empire was fast weakening. Like the Balkan states, the Porte found that modern internal improvements were costly. Since the Ottoman government could not finance them from its own resources, it too resorted to foreign loans. Expensive foreign technicians were often employed since the Ottoman educational system did not provide men with the necessary skills. The officials themselves had scant experience with financial matters. At first little attempt was made to coordinate the expenditures of the various departments of state. The government resorted to indiscriminate printing of money at times and to borrowing on unwise terms. Although efforts were made to remedy the situation after Abdul Aziz came to the throne, the conditions continued to worsen. The first loan was taken out in 1854. By 1860 the government was paying 20 percent of its income on the service of the debt, and by 1875 it was paying 50 percent. In 1876 payments on the debt were suspended; the state was thus technically bankrupt.

The Tanzimat period witnessed an increase in the volume of Ottoman trade, but again the results were unfavorable for the state. The empire was not only hampered by the capitulations, but also by the terms of its commercial treaties, particularly with Britain. Operating under a free trade policy, which benefited mainly the industrial countries, the Porte found its markets filled with imported manufactured goods. The Ottoman craftsman and home industry, whether Muslim or Christian, were severely harmed. These economic difficulties caused much criticism of Tanzimat policy.

The measures discussed above were formulated to improve the administration of the state and to remove the obvious abuses. They were not designed to improve general social and economic conditions in the countryside. In the empire, as in the autonomous areas, the major social problem was the condition of the peasant and the question of the distribution of the land. No specific laws were enacted by the Porte regulating landholding, with the exception of the land law of 1858. This act placed the control of the state lands involved into the hands of leaseholders or tax farmers to the detriment of the peasant who actually worked the land and who now became a sharecropper or a tenant. Turkish agricultural policy thus continued to give the advantage to the holder of the large estate. It should be strongly emphasized in this connection that the position of the peasant throughout the empire was in general declining. He suffered from high taxes and extortionate methods of collection. In this regard the Muslim was no better off than his Christian counterpart. The Tanzimat reforms did not alter this situation, nor were they intended to do so.

Probably the greatest criticism that can be made of the reform period was that it did not accomplish its basic aims. It did not prevent the loss of further Ottoman territories, nor did it reconcile the Christian people to membership in the empire. It did not create a common citizenship. In addition, the reforms were imposed from the top by a small minority influenced by European thought, and they were simply grafted on to a civilization based on other principles. A major underlying difficulty also lay in the failure of the majority of both Christians and Muslims to accept the spirit and intentions of the reforms. Most Muslims were content with the conditions that existed, in particular with the maintenance of the secondary status of the Christians. These people in turn wanted national independence rather than a reformed empire.

Moreover, as in the Balkan nations, the creation of a bureaucratic state apparatus brought forth a class of officials quite divided in manner, sympathies, and education from those below them. The aim under the reforming sultans was to establish an efficient administration free of bribery and corruption. The goal was not accomplished. Commenting on this question, one authority has written concerning the reign of Mahmud:

> Some of the officials were competent and industrious, whatever their degree of westernization. But the majority were not, and many looked only for sinecures, of which there were never enough to go around. It was estimated that half the people of Istanbul lived off the state in some way. Many, both in Istanbul and in the provincial capitals, became unsalaried hangers-on of pashas, hoping that position or graft would come their way. The crowd of relatives and parasites in the anterooms of every high official was one of the great curses of Ottoman administration, leading to favoritism, inefficiency, and bribery.[2]

To this criticism should be added the fact that despite numerous declarations and decrees the Ottoman administration in the Balkans did continue to be dominated by Muslim officials who did not regard Christians as equals. The repeated complaints by the nationalities that the promises made in the reform edicts were not carried out were justified.

The attitude of the great powers was also harmful to reform efforts. Although all of the powers were critical of Ottoman rule, they did nothing to make the task of the Porte easier. They insisted on the maintenance of their capitulatory rights, and they pressed for special privileges for their client nationalities. In their mutual struggle for influence each

2. Roderic H. Davidson, *Reform in the Ottoman Empire, 1856–1876* (Princeton: Princeton University Press, 1963), p. 34.

was willing at different times to support strongly national programs for their own ends. Thus, France encouraged Greek plans and Russia at times backed resistance movements among the Slavic peoples. Given the possibility of foreign aid, the Balkan peoples saw less need to find a satisfactory political accommodation with the Porte.

By the 1860s the reform program was under attack not only by those who claimed that it failed to work because it violated Ottoman traditions, but also by those who believed that the chief problem was that it had not gone far enough. The latter group wished the reform to proceed from administrative reorganization to the establishment of organs of representative government. As in the Balkan states, the reforms and the educational improvements had produced an intellectual class composed of civil servants, army officers, writers, and some businessmen who were in touch with European developments and who were not satisfied with the rate of progress in the Ottoman Empire. In 1865 some of these joined together in the Young Ottoman Society. Among their numbers were many talented writers, the best known being Namik Kemal. Combining progressive ideas with an emphasis on Islamic traditions, they criticized the Tanzimat because they believed that it had given too much to the Christians at the expense of the Muslims. They disliked Ali Pasha personally and considered him too dictatorial in his methods. This group admired certain parts of European civilization. They wished to adopt what it had to offer in science, technology, education, and economic advances, but they emphasized their Muslim and Ottoman identity. Their slogan was Liberty (*hürriyet*) and Fatherland (*vatan*). They sought to join Christian and Muslim in a common Ottoman citizenship. Regarding specific changes in the government, they desired a limitation of the absolute power of the sultan and the introduction of representative institutions.

In 1876 the Young Ottomans had the opportunity for a brief time to put their program into practice. At that time, in another period of grave international crisis, Midhat Pasha led a coup which succeeded in dethroning first Abdul Aziz in May and then his mentally unstable successor Murad V in August. Abdul Hamid II came to the throne after having promised a constitution. This document was drawn up and subsequently issued in December, 1876. Essentially conservative in spirit, the constitution allowed the sultan broad powers. He appointed the ministers, approved legislative acts, and summoned and dissolved the legislature. He was also proclaimed caliph, and his person was sacred. The legislative branch consisted of a senate responsible to the ruler and a chamber elected indirectly. A bill of rights and provision for an independent judiciary were also included. All citizens were declared equal, but Islam remained the state religion. National unity was strongly emphasized.

The first chamber chosen under this constitution met in March, 1877. In April Russia declared war to open the fourth Russo-Turkish war of the century. The Tanzimat reforms were now to be put to a practical test. It remained to be seen whether the empire could resist alone the power that had been its main threat for over a century.

CHAPTER 8

The United Principalities to 1876

T HE early 1850s had been a difficult time for the Romanian nationalist. The failure of the revolutions of 1848 had resulted in renewed Russian and Ottoman intervention in the internal life of Wallachia and Moldavia. Unless some international event were to occur to deter these two powers, it seemed most unlikely that the program of the nationalists for the unity of the Principalities and a foreign prince could be achieved. The Crimean War provided such an opportunity. The terms of the Treaty of Paris guaranteed both that Russia alone would not be able to determine the affairs of the provinces and that Ottoman control would not be re-established. It will be remembered that the agreement replaced the Russian protectorate with a guarantee by the great powers. The mutual distrust and competition among these states assured that they were not likely to exert real influence over the Principalities. Similarly, the neutralization of the Black Sea and the Russian surrender of three districts of southern Bessarabia to Moldavia were favorable developments.

Most advantageous for the Romanians was the fact that the peace conference gave Napoleon III the opportunity to support the nationalist position. At the end of the war Austrian and Ottoman troops occupied the country. The powers were faced with the problem of what regime was to replace the Russian protectorate and the Organic Statutes. In their discussion on this question the powers naturally followed their traditional interests in the area. Napoleon III, who now emerged as the patron of European national movements, argued for the full unionist program of the joining of the Principalities under a foreign prince. His position was backed by Prussia and Piedmont, themselves in a period of national upsurge, and by Russia who had joined with France in what was to be the beginning of a brief period of cooperation in international affairs. Against them stood the Porte, who saw union as an infringement of its treaty rights and a step that would inevitably lead to independence.

Now and later the Habsburg government supported the Ottoman position, principally because of its fears over Transylvania, a territory claimed by the Romanian nationalists. At first Britain also disapproved of union because of her desire to maintain a strong Ottoman Empire.

Since the powers could not come to an understanding at the congress in Paris, it was agreed that an attempt would be made to consult the wishes of the Romanians. In order to do this the powers decided to hold elections for so-called *divans ad hoc* in each Principality, which in turn would express an opinion on the organization to be given the country. The first election, held in July, 1857, was clearly fraudulent. As a result of Ottoman and other pressures, conservatives who wished to maintain the separation of the provinces won a clear majority in Moldavia. This event caused a crisis between France, who wished the elections annulled, and Britain, who was still primarily interested in upholding Ottoman rights. In a compromise the French finally agreed not to press for unification and the British accepted new elections. These, held in September, 1857, resulted in the choice of unionist candidates, who in October voted for union and a foreign prince. Since the powers would not accept this solution, the Porte dissolved the two bodies and the matter again was referred to international consideration.

In May, 1858, the representatives of the great powers met in Paris to discuss the Romanian question. As before France stood for union; the Habsburg Empire and the Porte were the chief opponents. A compromise was again achieved and resulted in the conclusion of the convention of August 19, 1858. This document, which now replaced the Organic Statutes, provided a new political organization for the Principalities. The provinces were to be known as the United Principalities of Moldavia and Wallachia and were to remain under the suzerainty of the sultan and be guaranteed by the powers. Like the Organic Statutes, the convention provided that the provinces were to have parallel but separate institutions with two *hospodars,* two ministries, and two assemblies. As a sop, however, to nationalist feeling, a Central Commission at Focşani and a single court of appeals were to be established. The *hospodars* were still to be elected by special assemblies and approved by the sultan. The legislative power was divided between the assemblies and Central Commission. The assemblies were to be elected every seven years with the ministries responsible to them. They controlled the budget and taxation. Elected on a highly restrictive franchise, their membership guaranteed that the boyars would continue to control the state.

Like the Organic Statutes, the new convention introduced changes in the land system. Article 46 stated:

> All the privileges, exemptions or monopolies which certain classes still enjoy will be abolished, and the revision of the law which regulates the relations of

the landlords with the farmers will be undertaken without undue delay with a view to improving the conditions of the peasant.[1]

The same article provided that all citizens were to be "equally liable to taxation and equally admissible to public service in both Principalities. Their individual liberties will be guaranteed."

Although the Convention of August 19 did mark certain advances toward union, it obviously did not meet the desires of the nationalists, politically the most active group in the Principalities. To them the most favorable feature of the document was the introduction of a Central Commission to enact measures of interest to both Principalities. It could, however, act only with the approval of the two chambers and the *hospodars* under a complicated procedure. Given the division of the great powers on the question of Romanian unity, the terms of the convention were the best that could be expected.

With the signature of the agreement the two Principalities proceeded with preparations for the elections to choose the new *hospodars*. As in the preceding years, these took place amid confusion and recrimination. Each Principality was under the charge of a *caimacamie* of three. The functions of these bodies were not clear, and their membership was split between those who wished union and the conservatives who did not. The first elections were held in the last week of December in Moldavia. Although they did not dominate the assembly selected at that time, the unionists nevertheless succeeded in securing the election of Alexander Cuza on January 17, 1859. In Wallachia the voting took place at the beginning of February. Again the unionists did not win, but the conservatives were split between rival candidates. During the meetings of the assembly in Bucharest, there was considerable agitation in the streets in favor of the unionists. Divided among themselves, the members of the assembly finally also chose Cuza. The election was the victory of the liberal leaders and certainly a great step toward achieving the program of the forty-eighters. The two Principalities were now linked in a personal union.

Since this action broke the spirit if not the letter of the August convention, the powers again consulted on what should be done. As could be expected, France was the main supporter of the Romanian union and was again backed by Russia who wished to maintain the entente with Paris established after the Crimean War. The Ottoman Empire and Austria remained opposed; Britain wished a compromise. The chief problem for those who desired a strict observance of the convention was how

1. The text of the convention is given in D. A. Sturdza, *Acte şi documente relative la istoria renascerei României* (Acts and documents relating to the history of the Romanian renaissance) (Bucharest: Carol Göbl, 1900–1909), vol. 7, pp. 306–16.

the Principalities could be compelled to hold new elections. No power was willing to allow the Porte to send troops to enforce the decisions previously reached.

The Romanian cause was, however, to be strongly aided by the outbreak of war in Italy between France and Austria in April. The Italian crisis now effectively removed Austria from the diplomatic negotiations on the Principalities. Faced with military defeat in Italy, the monarchy was in no position to enforce her views on the Romanian question. In September, 1859, the powers finally agreed to recognize as an exception the double election of Alexander Cuza. The principle of the separation of the Principalities was reconfirmed; only the personal union for the lifetime of Cuza was accepted.

At first glance Alexander Cuza, a prince whose period of rule was to witness real reform in the Principalities, did not seem particularly well qualified for the role he was called on to play. His past associations had been with the Liberals, and he had joined in the revolutionary movement in Moldavia in 1848. After a short period in exile he had returned in 1849 and had served in the administration under Ghica and Nicholas Vogorides. His election in Jassy came as a complete surprise; he had not sought the office. He was not a personally impressive man, nor did he have a party or a clique behind him. He suffered from an additional disability in that he was obviously considered only a poor substitute for a foreign prince by his Liberal supporters. With these handicaps he had to deal with a difficult internal situation, the constant rivalry of ambitious politicians, and pressure from abroad.

The double election had done little to simplify the complicated political organization set up by the August convention. The provinces had one *hospodar,* but there were still two separate assemblies, two administrative systems, and the Central Commission. During his first period in office Cuza could not accomplish much. The two political parties, the Liberals and the Conservatives, dominated the political life of the country. Representing, for the most part, the great landowners, the Conservatives had no real program or competent organization. Because of the restrictive franchise they controlled the assemblies, but partisan politics within the party made the presentation of a united front difficult. In contrast, the Liberals were better politicians. Their numbers were made up of the smaller landowners, state officials, and some men from the professions and business. They had formed the leadership of the revolutionary movement in 1848, and they were to provide the Principalities' most effective statesmen in the years to come. In contrast to the Conservatives, who wished to preserve the political, social, and economic *status quo,* some Liberals were, at least in theory, for land reform. These parties, which represented but a small minority of the Romanian population, provided the same sort of opposition to Cuza as did similar groups to other Balkan princes.

The combination of the cumbersome state machinery and the political rivalries made the Principalities most difficult to govern. Moreover, like other Balkan leaders, Cuza was aware that a further move toward national unity was the one issue on which all competing factions would unite. Even the Conservatives, who were in opposition to Cuza, would in the majority approve the next step, that is, the administrative union of the two provinces. The prince wisely decided to work toward this goal, not through another *fait accompli*, but through negotiation with the suzerain power. In the spring of 1861 he was able to gain the consent of the Porte to the establishment of a single ministry and assembly and to the abolition of the Central Commission. Like his appointment, this union was to last only for Cuza's lifetime. Since these changes involved an alteration of the August convention, the consent of the powers was necessary. Here Russian opposition marked a change in the position of that power toward the Principalities. The Russian government now argued that this would be just another move toward the accession of a foreign prince and the further breaking of treaties. Since the Ottoman government did not oppose the move, however, in December, 1861, the powers accepted the full unification of the administration of the provinces, although only for the duration of Cuza's reign. This measure was a major accomplishment for the Romanian nationalists. For the first time in modern history a true Romanian state existed. In December Cuza could proclaim: "Romanians, union is accomplished. The Romanian nationality is founded! . . . *Long live Romania*." [2] On February 3, 1862, the first single government was formed under the Conservative Barbu Catargiu; on February 5 the united assembly convened. Bucharest now became the capital of the country.

The change did not diminish Cuza's problems. He still faced the necessity of dealing with domestic opposition and two great interrelated internal problems: agrarian reform and a widening of the franchise. As long as the electoral law was so restrictive, it was inevitable that the assemblies would be dominated by Conservatives who would try to maintain the *status quo*. At this time Catargiu led the Conservatives, and Ion Brătianu and Michael Kogălniceanu, the Liberals. In June, 1862, Catargiu was assassinated; in July Nicholas Crețulescu became premier. The pressing national question was land reform, but as long as the Conservatives dominated the assembly, nothing could be accomplished.

In October, 1863, Cuza finally took a decisive step and appointed the Moldavian Liberal Kogălniceanu as prime minister. Under his leadership the country embarked upon its greatest period of social and eco-

2. Quoted in T. W. Riker, *The Making of Roumania* (Oxford: Oxford University Press, 1931), p. 340.

nomic change. The two landmarks were the secularization of the lands of the Dedicated Monasteries, and the Agrarian Law. Kogălniceanu handled the first of these problems at once since this question caused little disagreement. With the end of the Phanariote rule of 1821, each succeeding government in both Principalities had attempted to deal with the matter and to free what was approximately a quarter of the Romanian acreage from foreign control. The provinces naturally wished to get hold of these rich lands and their revenues, but this action was not so easily taken. The heads of the monasteries argued that they were not subject to the jurisdiction of the state. Their stand was supported by Russia who wished to do nothing to weaken the ecumenical patriarchate at Constantinople. All classes in the Principalities opposed the special privileges of the monasteries and their holding of such vast territories. The Romanian clergy resented this remnant of Greek domination. The boyars hoped to secure the property for their own exploitation. The peasants knew that those who worked on the ecclesiastic lands were worse off than those on the private estates.

After 1821 real efforts were made to negotiate a satisfactory agreement. In 1843 the monasteries agreed to pay a fixed amount to the state, but the offer was not satisfactory from the Romanian viewpoint. The matter was still unsolved at the time of the union of the Principalities. In the subsequent discussions both sides adopted an unyielding attitude. The monasteries would not concede on any major point; the Romanian government wanted complete control over the lands. Russia, the logical mediator as the only Orthodox great power, remained biased on the side of the Patriarchate. As negotiations dragged on, Cuza decided to act, in December, 1863. He ended the negotiations and declared the lands secularized. When the Porte and the powers protested, he insisted that this was a purely Romanian internal affair. The assemblies approved the expropriations, but they also offered compensation. The Patriarchate remained adamant and in the end received nothing.

The sequestration of these lands was a very popular measure. In contrast, the next question, that of land reform, aroused much domestic opposition and led to a political crisis. In April, 1864, the Conservative assembly voted a motion of censure against Kogălniceanu. Cuza nevertheless refused to dismiss this ministry and instead dissolved the assembly on May 14. He then announced that he would hold a national plebiscite on a new statute, which would both increase his own powers and also widen the franchise. This action, a veritable *coup d'état,* was successful. Using the powers of the central government to influence the voting, Cuza won by 682,621 to 1,307; 70,220 abstained. Since stipulations of the August convention were involved, the powers had to approve these actions. Despite the protests of the Porte, not only were the changes accepted, but it was now agreed that the guarantor states would henceforth only intervene in questions relating to the vassal-suzerain relationship of Romania with the Ottoman Empire.

With the election of a compliant assembly assured, Cuza and Kogălniceanu could proceed with their greatest reform measure, the Agrarian Law. It will be remembered that Article 46 of the August Convention of 1858 called for legislation in this field. The Conservative boyars had already formulated their conception of land reform; they wished to enact measures that would leave the peasant without land. They would thus not only control all the land, but they would be assured of a more than adequate labor supply. The Agrarian Law introduced in July, 1863, avoided this extreme, but its provisions were not unfavorable to the boyar, who was required to surrender no more than two-thirds of his land. The peasant was to be the full owner of his share. Allotments, as was customary in Romania, were based on the number of cattle that a peasant family owned. If a landowner did not have sufficient property to fulfill the law, state lands were to be provided. All payments and services owed by the peasant to the landowner were abolished. The boyar, however, received compensation for these losses from the state. The peasant paid a fixed amount over a fifteen-year period. The intention of the law was to create a class of prosperous, free peasants. The newly acquired land was declared inalienable for thirty years to prevent the peasant from selling it back to the boyars. In addition to these peasants there were approximately 107,000 others who already controlled their own lands.

The law, which was hastily drawn up, was full of loopholes. The great difficulty was the lack of proper supervision to assure that the provisions would be fairly carried out. The boyar obviously was in a stronger position than the peasant, and he dominated his locality. There were no adequate surveys or statistics on which to base the division of the estates. The boyar thus was able to take the best sections and to control the ownership of the forests and pastures. Peasant holdings were not only often from the poorest soil, but the individual could receive scattered plots far from his home village. One of the greatest problems was, however, to come in the future. From 1859 to 1899 the Romanian population grew 54 percent. The grave social consequences of the repeated subdivision of plots thus soon arose here as elsewhere in the peninsula. The unfortunate position of peasant was shown in the continual unrest in the countryside culminating in the great uprising in 1907. Although grain exports increased sharply for the rest of the century, few of the benefits of this trade were passed on to the peasant. More and more peasants were forced to go into debt, rent land, or become agricultural laborers on a large estate. In 1866 and 1872 laws on agricultural contracts were passed that placed the peasantry almost in a position of bondage to the great landowner. The reform thus did not result in the formation of a class of stable and contented peasant proprietors. Romania remained a land of great estates where production was directed toward fulfilling the demands of a large grain export trade.

In addition to these measures, other reforms were passed under Kogălniceanu's ministry. A national system of education was established providing for primary and secondary schools throughout the country and for universities in Bucharest and Jassy. A civil code was issued based on the Code Napoleon. Local government was reorganized, again along French lines. In the future the strong centralization of the administration allowed the authorities in the capital to control the localities through the prefects and the police. As in Greece and Serbia, this system gave the ministry in power control over elections. The reign of Cuza also saw the inauguration of a period of foreign investment in Romania, which was to have important repercussions later.

Despite, and even because of, the magnitude of these reforms, Cuza faced increasing opposition. The Conservatives, who represented the great landowners, hated the prince because of the land and electoral laws. The Liberals, who had never wholeheartedly backed Cuza and who were also divided on the agrarian question, became increasingly discontented. Moreover, Cuza was anything but a model prince. He was not ambitious and he does not seem to have concerned himself with adopting regal ways. He also had a private life which, although not in outright contradiction to Romanian customs, was not well regarded in the head of a state. Living apart from his wife, he had as his mistress Marie Obrenović, whose son Milan was to become the first king of Serbia. The prince also had no legitimate heir so the problem of succession existed.

In February, 1865, Cuza finally broke with Kogălniceanu. Since he had now estranged both the Conservatives and Liberals, it was inevitable that members of both parties should conspire together to remove him. The leaders of this movement were Lascar Catargiu, Ion Ghica, Ion Brătianu, the Golescu brothers, and Rosetti. Once again the leaders of the Wallachian revolution of 1848 headed an insurrection. Rosetti took the principal role in Romania; Ion Brătianu went to Paris to try to assure French support for a change of rulers and, most important, to find another candidate for the throne.

One night in February, 1866, a group of army officers who had been won over to the conspiracy entered the prince's rooms and forced him to sign an abdication. He later left the country. A regency was immediately formed composed of General N. Golescu, Ion Ghica, and Colonel N. Haralambie. The revolutionary government now proclaimed as its goals a program calling for unity, autonomy, a foreign prince, and the establishment of constitutional government. The assembly then proceeded to chose Philip Count of Flanders, a brother of King Leopold II of Belgium, as prince. This candidate, who did not have French support, declined at once, but in the meantime Brătianu had found a suitable substitute.

Although the exact role taken by Napoleon III in the selection of the next ruler of Romania is not clear, he certainly approved the candidate now designated by Brătianu, Prince Charles of Hohenzollern-Sigmaringen. The second son of Prince Karl Anton, the head of the Catholic southern branch of the Prussian ruling dynasty, Charles was by birth as much French as German. On his mother's side he was related to Napoleon III; on his father's to the Prussian king. In March Brătianu met with the prince and his father. Shortly after this visit he was able to telegraph Bucharest that Charles would accept the position. In April, 1866, the provisional government held a plebiscite to confirm this choice. Given the political conditions in the country, it is not surprising that Charles was approved by 685,969 votes to 224. Once again the Romanian leaders were to be aided by the course of international events. The danger existed that a war might soon break out between Prussia and Austria. Charles, as a Prussian officer, was forced to slip through the Habsburg Empire in disguise. He arrived in Bucharest in May, 1866, where he was welcomed as the long-desired foreign prince. As the international situation worsened, the powers were thus forced to deal with another Romanian *fait accompli.*

According to the treaties, after the abdication of Cuza the Romanian provinces should have returned to the separate status that they had held in August, 1858. No power expected this to happen since all had recognized, even when limiting the unification to the lifetime of Cuza, that the union could not be undone. More serious was the question of the foreign prince. Luckily for Romania the powers were as divided in 1866 as they had been in 1859 and 1861. As usual, France remained the chief support of the national program; the Porte, Austria, and Russia were against it. As before, the prime question was how to force Charles off the throne and again enforce the treaties. No power would allow a Turkish intervention. Moreover, in June the Austro-Prussian War broke out. The impressive Prussian victories nullified Austrian opposition to the events in Bucharest. The acceptance by Charles of the Romanian throne had been approved by the Prussian king and by his chancellor, Otto von Bismarck.

Meanwhile, the provisional government proceeded in haste to prepare the constitution that it had promised. The resultant document was based on the Belgian constitution of 1831. As in similar documents discussed above, freedom of speech, press, assembly, and the equality of all citizens were guaranteed. The prince was given a relatively strong position in the state. He could name and dismiss ministers, and dissolve the assembly; most important, he had an absolute veto over legislation. The legislative branch of the government consisted of two houses: a senate and a chamber. Indirect elections assured that the landowners and those who held political power in 1866 would retain control of the government. The chamber was to be elected for four years and was to have regular annual sessions. It had control over the budget. In what was to become a controversial article in the future, the constitution stated that "only foreigners who are Christians can become citizens." Despite its liberal phraseology, the document, like those of Serbia and Greece, did not guarantee a truly representative government. The centralized administrative system still allowed a strong ministry or a determined prince to dominate the electoral procedure. Nevertheless, the year 1866 did mark the achievement of goals set by the Romanian national leaders in 1848. The country was united, and it was ruled by a foreign prince.

Despite the revolutionary basis of his authority, Charles was able to gain the recognition of the powers. In October, 1866, he was invested by the sultan. In addition, the Porte now conceded him the right to issue his own coinage and to have an armed force of thirty thousand men. The prince, a highly ambitious and able man, came to Romania with the expressed determination to establish orderly government and economic prosperity. Highly conscious of his personal position, he disliked the fact that a Hohenzollern prince should be the vassal of the sultan. Nevertheless, in foreign affairs he followed an extremely cautious policy until 1877, when events allowed him to act otherwise. As a Prussian officer he placed great emphasis on building up an efficient Romanian militia, which could be used if further gains in foreign policy were possible. In 1867 he joined, as we have seen, in a secret alliance with Prince Michael of Serbia, but it is safe to assume that he would only reluctantly have gone to war against the Porte. In 1869 he made a very popular marriage with Princess Elizabeth of Wied, a Lutheran. Since he was a Catholic, Charles, like Othon, had agreed to bring up his children in the Orthodox faith. Elizabeth, writing under the name of Carmen Sylva, did much to introduce Romania to Europe.

Although Charles was to become a strong and popular ruler, his first years found him involved in continual political controversies. During the period of national crisis that followed Cuza's fall, the Conservatives and the Liberals had joined hands to preserve the interests of their country. Once the external dangers were removed, the parties returned to their factional disputes. Charles was not an experienced political leader, nor had he come to his throne with an adequate knowledge of the country. He was soon quarreling with those very persons who had been chiefly responsible for his selection, Brătianu and the Liberals. The fall and winter of 1870–71 were to prove particularly difficult for the prince. In July, 1870, France declared war on Prussia; in the next months it was soon clear that the Romanian patron would be militarily crushed. Feeling ran high. As a Prussian officer and a patriotic German, the prince made no attempt to hide his sympathies or his opinion that Prussia would win. In August, 1870, an uprising backed by republican elements occurred in Ploeşti. Although it was repressed, the prince was most disturbed when a jury freed the participants. This action seemed a direct challenge to his authority.

To add to the political troubles, a scandal connected with the building of railroads also damaged the prince's position. At the beginning of his reign Charles, interested in the modernization of Romania, had favored the swift construction of railroads. As was to be the case in all of the Balkan countries, the Romanian lack of capital and skilled technicians meant that the lines had to be constructed by foreign firms and with loans. Although most of the companies involved in enterprises in the country fulfilled their tasks, one railroad contractor, a Prussian Jew by the name of Strousberg, fell into financial difficulty and could not pay dividends to his stockholders. He then attempted to compel the Romanian government to shoulder his financial liabilities. The affair also revealed the involvement of some Romanian politicians in fraudulent transactions. In addition, Bismarck strongly backed the stand of the Prussian citizen. The incident was used to damage the prince, and it coincided with a period of rapidly increasing anti-Semitism.

Charles was now becoming increasingly depressed. He was convinced that he could not continue to reign with a constitution that allowed the political parties, which, of course, represented only a fraction of the Romanian people, to thwart constantly his actions. The same struggle between the prince and the rival parties that we have seen in Greece and Serbia and during the time of Cuza was thus being repeated. Fully prepared to abdicate if necessary, the prince, in the fall of 1870, wrote a personal letter to the protecting powers concerning his difficulties in ruling, given the political situation in the country. Unfortunately for the prince, he chose the wrong moment to act. Not only were France and Prussia at war, but in October Russia had denounced the Black Sea clauses of the Treaty of Paris. No European power wanted another complication. Moreover, most of the governments misunderstood the aim of the letter. They thought that Charles was preparing the ground to declare Romanian independence.

Charles' personal position became even more precarious after an incident on the night of March 22–23, 1871. That evening the German colony of Bucharest was holding a dinner to celebrate the Prussian victory and the founding of the German empire. They were attacked by a mob while the police stood by. This event, together with the problems previously discussed, led Charles to inform Lascar Catargiu and Nicholas Golescu that he would resign. Faced with what would obviously be a dangerous situation, the two statesmen assured the prince of Conservative support. Lascar Catargiu then succeeded in forming a cabinet which lasted for five years. George Costaforu became foreign minister. Since the central government could control the elections, the assemblies in this period were dominated by the ministry.

The formation of the Catargiu government heralded a brief period of calm in Romanian internal affairs. The Conservative regime wished the country to be a Belgium at the mouth of the Danube and not to engage in foreign adventures. Conditions in Europe were also favorable for such a policy. After the Prussian victory and the unification of Germany, this power, Russia, and the Habsburg monarchy came together to form the informal coalition called the Three Emperors' Alliance. Romania's two neighbors were thus now allies. The Romanian link with the triumphant Hohenzollern dynasty gave additional prestige to the nation.

With the strengthening of his own position, Charles was free to concentrate more on forwarding the Romanian interests in international relations. Like previous Romanian statesmen, he preferred to rely on diplomacy to advance the national cause. His government thus proceeded to attempt to conclude various treaties and conventions with other powers to test how far the autonomous state could go in conducting an independent foreign policy. First, postal and telegraphic conventions were arranged. Then, diplomatic agencies were opened in the major capitals—Vienna, Berlin, Rome, and St. Petersburg—in the 1870s. From now on Romania's closest ties were to be with Germany and the Habsburg monarchy. Defeated France was not to play such a large role in the Romanian alliances until after the outbreak of the First World War.

In the diplomatic offensive the most important move was the Romanian attempt to conclude separate commercial conventions and to set its own customs rates. Both Britain and the Porte refused to recognize this right. They argued that Romania was legally bound by the commercial treaties concluded by the Ottoman Empire, which, incidentally, were usually favorable to British interests. For Romania the issue involved was political not economic. The successful negotiation of such an agreement would signify a further step toward independence.

The state that had the greatest interest in the question was the Habsburg Empire, with its primary economic interests in Romania and its leading position on the Danube. In order to put pressure on Vienna, in June, 1874, the Romanian government introduced a new set of customs dues, which would mean that nations not having agreements would pay higher rates. The Habsburg government agreed to start negotiations, which led to the conclusion of the first Romanian commercial convention in June, 1875. Although the economic terms were favorable to the monarchy, the Romanian government, concerned primarily with the political aspects, regarded the treaty as a victory. In March, 1876, a similar agreement was signed with Russia and later with the other powers.

As can be seen, great progress had thus been made in the years from

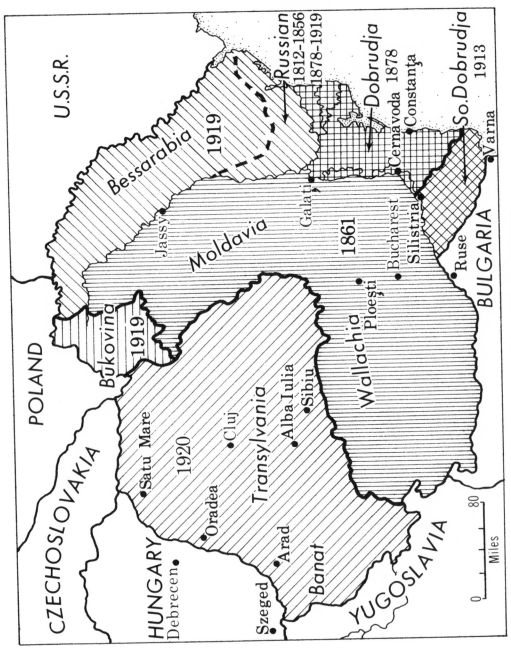

Map 5. The Expansion of Romania, 1861–1920

1856 to 1876. The program of the forty-eighters, the union of the Principalities and a foreign prince, had been accomplished. An agrarian reform act had been passed and a constitution adopted. A truly national government was in existence, although the country was still under the suzerainty of the Porte. The most important advances in the national program had been made by diplomacy and by presenting the powers with a *fait accompli*. Romania had taken advantage of other nation's wars; she had not fought herself. Each change had been in violation of international treaties, but the great powers, divided among themselves, were unable to agree on how the Romanian acts could be reversed.

Despite the great gains of these two decades, much was left to be accomplished. The final Romanian goal, like that of the Greeks and Serbs, was the acquisition of all the lands inhabited by their nationals. Transylvania, Bukovina, and most of Bessarabia lay outside the Romanian state. It was obvious at this time that it was impossible to annex these lands since they were held by Russia and the Habsburg Empire who were in alliance. The Romanian nationalist did, however, have one objective that did not seem so remote, the achievement of independence, an aim that was also particularly appealing to the prince. In the summer of 1875 the Ottoman provinces of Bosnia and Hercegovina were the scene of a peasant rebellion which could not be suppressed. In May, 1876, a Bulgarian uprising occurred; in the summer of that year Serbia and Montenegro went to war against the Porte. The entire eastern question was thus again reopened. The problem for the Romanian government was to determine where in an extremely complicated situation its best interests lay. It also had to deal with a new national movement arising in the neighboring Bulgarian lands.

CHAPTER 9

The Bulgarian National Movement
to 1876

The national development of Bulgaria, the last of the Balkan states to obtain an autonomous or independent regime in the nineteenth century, lagged considerably behind the areas already studied. Perhaps the best explanation of this condition lies in the simple geographic fact that the Bulgarian lands lay closer to Constantinople and were therefore more easily controlled. In addition, of the Balkan peoples the Bulgarians probably suffered the most from the lawless conditions of the late eighteenth and early nineteenth centuries. During this period bands of janissaries, demobilized soldiers, and bandit groups, called *kirdzhali*, whose activities resembled those of the *dahi* in Serbia, roamed the area between the Balkan Mountains and the Danube. Pasvanoglu, as we have seen, assembled many of these outlaws around himself in his center at Vidin. They reduced sections of northern Bulgaria to a wasteland and forced the population to flee into the foothills and mountains.

The Bulgarian lands, like the Danubian Principalities, were also the scene of constant warfare. In the nineteenth century Russian troops fought here during the war with the Ottoman Empire that lasted from 1806 to 1812 and again in 1828–29. In these conflicts some Bulgarians joined the Russian army and had hopes that the tsarist victories would bring them political gains. As mentioned previously, however, the Russian government was primarily interested in Serbia and the Danubian Principalities. The peace treaties contained no clauses concerning the Bulgarians. Nevertheless, throughout the century the Bulgarian national leaders did consistently look to Russia as their best hope among the foreign powers.

After the conclusion of the Napoleonic Wars and with the establishment of generally stable conditions in the empire, life in Bulgaria began to improve. Like the Greeks and the Serbs, the great majority of the population were peasants, and, like other Balkan peoples, they lived in villages under the direction of their notables, known here as *chorbadzhiis*. Like the Orthodox church hierarchy and the Phanariote Greek, these men were a part of the Ottoman state system and had a general interest in its maintenance. As their counterparts elsewhere on the peninsula, they often showed a great interest in national revival and national culture, but they were hesitant to adopt radical measures to attain political liberation. It should also be emphasized that early in the century the higher church offices and what education was available was exclusively Greek controlled. This influence had to be removed before any political moves could be undertaken.

The Bulgarian position was greatly improved by the Greek revolution and by the changes in the status of the Principalities. The first event removed the predominant Greek influence in Constantinople; in fact, Greeks generally became objects of suspicion. Like the Armenians, the Bulgarian merchants used the opportunity to strengthen their position in Constantinople. The end of preemption rights over the products of the Principalities in 1829 led the Porte to turn more toward the Bulgarian lands for supplies for both the army and Constantinople. It will be remembered that in 1826 Mahmud II began the formation of a modern regular Ottoman army. Thereafter, Bulgaria became the chief supplier of food and of textiles for uniforms, blankets, and other military needs. From 1830 until 1878 the country enjoyed the market of the entire empire. It traded its agricultural products, including grains, honey, wax, silk, cattle, wine, and also manufactured goods such as pig iron, leather items, iron and metal work, and shoes and clothing. An active cottage industry specializing in woolen cloth developed in the Balkan Mountains. Although after 1856 signs of decline were apparent because of the increasing penetration into the empire of foreign manufactured goods, this period of relative prosperity provided a material basis for the national movement.

Moreover, despite the continued complaints about the tax system and land payments, the Bulgarian peasant did enjoy improving conditions. As in other Balkan countries, the free peasants living generally in the hill and mountain regions had a better life than did those on the *chiftlik* estates situated on the more fertile lands. The *chiftlik* system itself, however, was in the process of change. Faced with rising competition from neighboring countries, the *chiftlik* holder was finding that the estates were no longer so profitable; he was willing to sell land to the peasant. Thus in Bulgaria, in strong contrast to Romania, more land was passing to the Bulgarian small holder. This period of economic upsurge coincided with the Tanzimat reforms. Although the decrees were not carried out satisfactorily, the general atmosphere did improve. In fact, as will be seen, there was some peasant participation in revolutionary activities, but never the mass involvement that has been shown in Greece and Serbia.

Rising prosperity and the parallel increase in political awareness created the same conflicts in interest and attitudes between social classes and national groups that we have seen elsewhere. The Bulgarians, like the Romanians, faced the necessity of freeing their national life from the double burden of Greek cultural and ecclesiastical control and Ottoman political domination. Within the country certain circles were particularly active in working for national goals. In the cities the commercial and artisan groups took the lead. Bulgarian merchants in competition with Greeks became more deeply aware of their separate identity. Of particular importance were the activities of the guilds. Organized in a manner similar to their western European counterparts in an earlier period, the guild members were willing to support educational and cultural projects.

The first major step in the Bulgarian national movement was the establishment of secular educational institutions free from Greek control. As elsewhere in the Balkans, education at the beginning of the century was closely connected with the church. Although higher education was exclusively Greek, Bulgarian cell schools existed in certain churches and monasteries. Here the pupils learned to read religious works in Church Slavonic and to write. These schools were obviously unsatisfactory for a population that was expanding its economic activities and becoming more conscious of a wider world. Of the Greek institutions the most important were the so-called Helleno-Bulgarian schools, which had been set up by Greek merchants in major trading centers. They specialized in the subjects necessary for commerce. Here students had access to courses in mathematics, history, French, and geography. Many Bulgarians were attracted to these institutions. Since Greek was the general language of commerce, they also had an interest in learning this tongue. Moreover, not only were these schools secular, but through them the Bulgarian student came into contact with European political thought, in particular with that associated with the French Revolution. Liberal and national convictions were thus acquired in these establishments.

The foundation of the first modern Bulgarian schools was the result of the activities of Vasil Aprilov. Orphaned, Aprilov was taken to Moscow by his brothers, who were merchants. There he was enrolled in a Greek school because of the importance of this language for trade. Although he appears to have been at first favorable to Greece, in 1831 he read a history book that was to play a significant role in the Bulgarian national movement, the *Ancient and Modern Bulgarians*, written by a Ukrainian, Iuri Venelin. Aprilov thereafter became intensely patriotic and turned his attention to the education of his countrymen. He saw the establishment of a system of national education as a sure step toward eventual political independence. As a result of his efforts the first modern school was established in Gabrovo in 1835. It became subsequently the model for similar institutions which were opened thereafter in Kazanlik, Kalofer, Triavna, Sofia, Panaguirishte, Koprivshtitsa, and elsewhere. These cities, it will be noted, were trade and craft centers.

As in Serbia and other Balkan countries, the Bulgarian schools lacked good teachers. Most schools at first adopted the Bell-Lancaster system, where the best pupils were used to teach the others. In addition, as in the other states, Bulgarian young men began to go abroad for their higher education. Some went to Central Europe or to France, but a significant group received Russian scholarships. It will be noted that the over-whelming number of the subsequent revolutionary leaders were trained either in Greek schools or in foreign institutions.

In addition to the problem of teachers, the Bulgarian students lacked books and materials in the national language. Because of combined Greek and Ottoman pressure, the first Bulgarian books were produced in Belgrade, Bucharest, Constantinople, and other cities rather than in the Bulgarian lands. Only after the Crimean War did a significant number of books appear that were printed in Bulgaria. As had been true elsewhere, a standard literary language had to be established. Wisely avoiding the Greek example, Bulgarian writers did not choose Church Slavonic despite its close association with the great period of their national history. Since a majority of the better authors came from eastern Bulgaria, this dialect subsequently became the literary language.

Significant as were these economic and cultural advancements, national life was still stifled by the control of the ecumenical patriarchate over the church. The establishment of a national church was a logical move. In Serbia, Greece, and the Principalities action had already been, or was to be, taken in the direction of freeing the national religious institutions from control from Constantinople. In these lands, however, the attempt to separate from the patriarchate was made after the achievement of an independent or autonomous government. By contrast, in Bulgaria it was to precede the acquisition of a better political position. In fact, from the second quarter of the nineteenth century initiatives were taken to try to re-establish the independent religious authority abolished in 1767 in Ohrid.

Most significant for the religious question was the issuance of the Hatti-Sherif of 1839. Although the intent of this declaration was to equate Muslims and Christians, the Bulgarians saw in it an assurance of the equality of Bulgarian and Greek Orthodoxy. The leadership in forming a separate church was now taken by Neofit Bozveli and Ilarion Makariopolski, first in Turnovo, and after 1845 in Constantinople. A thriving Bulgarian commercial community lived in that city. Many were wealthy and willing to contribute to the cause. The demand was first made that the Bulgarians should have bishops of their own nationality, chosen by them, and that they should have a representative at the Porte. In addition, they wished to build a church in Constantinople and to publish a newspaper.

Any conflict involving the authority of the ecumenical patriarchate was bound to involve Russia, the greatest Orthodox nation. At this time in regard to the Bulgarian desires, as previously in the question of the Dedicated Monasteries and the establishment of the autocephalous Greek church in 1833, the Russian government stood opposed to any move that would weaken the power of the patriarch. It therefore agreed that strong action should be taken against Neofit and Ilarion for their activities. Neofit subsequently died in jail; Ilarion was released only in 1850. Despite these setbacks and the Russian attitude, the Bulgarian leaders did make one gain. In 1849 the sultan issued a firman allowing the "Bulgarian millet" to open a church in Constantinople. This act recognized for the first time the existence of a separate Bulgarian nation.

The issuance of the Hatti-Hümayun of 1856 gave added impetus to the Bulgarian insistence on an equal position with the Greeks. Although opinion diverged concerning how far they should go, the Bulgarian leaders were in full agreement concerning the direction in which they should proceed. Faced with this continued challenge, the patriarch acted to preserve the unity of the institutions still under his control. In 1858 he called into session the first of seven church councils, to be held between 1858 and 1872. As a token gesture, three Bulgarians were included among the more than thirty members of the first council. The Bulgarian demand for their own bishops in Bulgarian dioceses was, however, rejected. Instead, the patriarch would only agree to confirm one Bulgarian, Ilarion Makariopolski, as a bishop. Not satisfied with this arrangement, Ilarion on Easter Sunday, 1860, took the dramatic step of conducting services without the patriarch's approval. Moreover, during the ceremony he deliberately substituted the name of the sultan for that of the patriarch, thus signifying the separation of his church from the jurisdiction of the patriarchate.

The patriarch answered by convening a second church council. Here the patriarchs of Jerusalem, Antioch, and Alexandria joined in the condemnation of Ilarion and the anathematizing of his supporters. The strength of the Bulgarian opposition, nevertheless, gained them further concessions. Bulgarian bishops were now to be allowed to write in their own language and to print religious material in Bulgarian on the condition that the contents were first approved by the patriarchate. Despite his condemnation Ilarion, supported by his congregation, continued to conduct services. Subsequently, he and two other church leaders were forced into exile.

At this point the Bulgarian cause was greatly aided by a change in the Russian attitude. The Uniate movement, which sought to have the Orthodox accept the primacy of the pope at Rome, was receiving considerable attention in Bulgaria. Neither the Uniates nor the American Protestant missionaries, who were also active there, were a real threat to Orthodoxy. Their activities, nevertheless, seriously upset the metropolitan of Moscow, Filaret. He now came to favor the establishment of a Bulgarian national church that would remain in union with the patriarchate.

In 1864 the Russian government appointed Count N. P. Ignatiev as ambassador to Constantinople. A Panslav, Ignatiev also sought to maintain the unity of the Orthodox people. He thus wished to find a compromise between the Greek and Bulgarian positions. He won Bulgarian favor by securing the return of Ilarion and his two supporters who had been in exile since 1861. The ambassador could not, however, obtain the real cooperation of the patriarch, who felt his interests threatened throughout the Balkans. In 1864, it will be remembered, the Romanian government had seized the lands of the Dedicated Monasteries. Three church councils were held concerning the Bulgarian problem, in 1863, 1864 and 1866, but little progress was made. In 1866, in exasperation, the Bulgarian church leaders themselves acted and expelled the Greek bishops from their lands. This act meant that patriarchal authority had *de facto* ceased to exist in Bulgaria. The problem was now to obtain legal recognition of this situation.

Meanwhile, the Ottoman government had become deeply concerned. Signs of Christian revolt were again apparent throughout the Balkans. As a result of the bombardment of Belgrade in 1862, Ottoman officials had been compelled to evacuate Serbia completely by 1867. In 1866 Crete was once more the scene of a major revolt. The Porte naturally wished to prevent Bulgaria from becoming an area of disorder and rebellion. The government therefore urged the contestants to mediate their differences and itself took definite action. The issue now shifted from the establishment of a Bulgarian church to the territories over which that organization would have jurisdiction. The entire problem was, of course, fraught with strong political implications. Correctly estimating that the extension of Bulgarian ecclesiastical authority would foreshadow eventual political domination, both the patriarchate and the Greek government, now involved in the dispute, sought to limit Bulgarian control as narrowly as possible.

With religious and political rivalry thus correlating, the two religious bodies could not settle their disputes alone. The Bulgarian lands were the last remaining major source of revenue for the patriarchate. In addition both the Greek government and the patriarchate were most reluctant to abandon the large Greek colonies in Bulgaria, particularly in

Plovdiv and Varna, despite the fact that the surrounding countryside was completely Bulgarian. Nor did the Greek church wish to yield the diocese of Veles in Macedonia. The situation was immensely complicated when the Serbian government entered the conflict with the claim to Peć, their former patriarchal seat, and also Ohrid, the historical Bulgarian ecclesiastical center. Given these bitter disagreements, it can be understood why the mixed Bulgarian-Greek commissions created by the Porte could not come to a settlement. Finally, arguing that the issue was no longer primarily religious but political, the Ottoman government, in 1870, issued a firman settling the main problems and establishing a Bulgarian exarchate. The territorial boundaries of its jurisdiction were also defined and encompassed Plovdiv and Varna. Moreover, Article 10 provided that if two-thirds of the inhabitants of a district desired to join the exarchate, their wishes would be fulfilled. This provision opened the door to the intense, bitter, and bloody conflict that was to break out in Macedonia between the Greeks, Serbs, and Bulgars.

The firman did not, of course, end the ecclesiastical conflict. Orthodox tradition required that the new church receive the endorsement of the patriarch. Although the matter was under discussion for two years, the participants remained unable to settle the religious or political issues involved in the drawing of the boundaries of their jurisdictions. When a settlement by negotiation failed, the Bulgarians again acted alone. On Epiphany, January 6, 1872, the sultan's firman was formally accepted. Both the patriarch and Ignatiev attempted unsuccessfully to block the action. A sixth patriarchal council was subsequently convened where the Bulgarian bishop Ilarion and several others were excommunicated. In March, 1872, Antim I was designated as exarch. His first official action was to read a proclamation declaring the independence of the Bulgarian church. This open defiance caused the patriarchate to declare the exarchate schismatic. It is interesting to note that neither the Russian, Romanian, or Serbian churches, nor the patriarch of Jerusalem, accepted this judgment. The other patriarchs, and of course the Greek church, endorsed the action of the patriarchate at Constantinople.

On the question of the establishment of an independent Bulgarian church with a wide jurisdiction, there had been little division among the Bulgarian leaders. They had won their objectives with assistance from the Ottoman government, which wished to retain the loyalty and gratitude of this important part of its domains, and with reluctant Russian support for the final creation of the exarchate. On the next question, that of achieving a separate political status, a comparable unity of opinion was not to be found. Parallel with the efforts to form the exarchate, other groups had worked to secure an autonomous relationship with the Porte or even independence. The majority of these came to favor revolutionary methods rather than the slow process of negotiation that had brought victory in the church question.

Although the major revolutionary activities occurred in the second half of the century, a few minor actions took place before that time. For the future the most significant event was the organization of a small armed detachment, a *cheta,* by Vasil Hadzivulkov and a Serbian, Captain Vladislav Tatić. In 1841 this band, organized in Braila in Wallachia, crossed the Danube and landed on Bulgarian soil, hoping to precipitate a general rebellion. Like its successors, this group failed, but *cheta* organizations remained characteristic of Bulgarian revolutionary activity until 1868 when the emphasis was placed on actions within Bulgaria rather than on the formation of bands on foreign soil.

During this period there were also signs of peasant unrest, and local disturbances took place. Their cause was, however, economic and not political, and they reflected peasant discontent with the tax system and the conditions of the *chiftliks.* Uprisings of this type occurred in 1835 in northwest Bulgaria; in 1841 especially in the Vidin region; in 1841 and 1842 in Braila; and in 1850 again in the Vidin area. These movements were poorly organized and easily crushed by the Ottoman authorities.

After the Crimean War signs of renewed revolutionary activity were soon apparent. The events of the war and in particular the Russian defeat indicated that the Bulgarian leaders would have to act on their own and not expect foreign assistance to gain political advances. Moreover, both Serbia and the Principalities now had autonomous regimes; the temptation to strive for a similar goal was attractive. The difficulty lay in obtaining agreement as to the path to be followed. The country was enjoying a period of relative economic prosperity. Those that benefited from this situation, the merchants, artisans, and *chorbadzhii*s, naturally did not want to endanger their own interests. They were nationally minded, but they preferred to seek political gains through diplomacy and negotiation within the framework of the empire. In other words, they wished to use the methods which were to be successful in the Principalities; they did not want a revolution on the Greek or Serbian model.

Others disagreed with this position. Like the forty-eighters in Moldavia and Wallachia, the core of this group was made up of young men, sons of well-to-do merchants or professional men, who had enjoyed the opportunity to travel and who had been educated in foreign schools. Like their Romanian counterparts, they were deeply affected by current European political ideology. They were not "men of the people" like Karadjordje, Vladimirescu, Kolokotrones, and similar peasant leaders; essentially they were intellectuals whose ideas were formed by their studies and not by experience.

Whereas the Romanian youth had their views shaped by their French education, the Bulgarians were influenced by their studies in Greek schools, in Russian institutions and to some extent in the colleges of the American Protestant missionaries in Bulgaria and Constantinople. In all of these places they were exposed to the liberal-national political ideology. Most interesting, however, was the effect on some of their Russian education. In 1858 the Moscow Benevolent Society was formed. A Panslav organization devoted to furthering the welfare of the Orthodox Slavic peoples, it provided scholarships for young Bulgarians to study in Russia. Once there, these students came into contact with the radical Russian youth of the sixties. The writings of Alexander Herzen, N. G. Chernyshevsky, N. A. Dobroliubov, and D. I. Pisarev appealed more to the Bulgarians than the example of autocratic tsarist Russia. The Bulgarian youth thus came home not with admiration for the tsarist empire, but with a firm belief in social revolutionary programs.

Because of the strong Ottoman surveillance and the opposition of many Bulgarians to revolutionary activity, the first plans for action were formulated in Serbia and the Danubian Principalities. The governments of these states either closed their eyes to the Bulgarian conspirators or actively aided them, hoping to obtain benefits for their own cause. The leaders of the Bulgarian movement were never united on their goals. Ideologically oriented, they devoted much energy to debating principles. The chief problems facing them were four: first, should they strive for autonomy within the Ottoman Empire or for total independence; second, should they join a Balkan federation and if so, what kind; third, should they rely on outside aid or only on their own efforts; and fourth, what kind of internal organization should the Bulgarian state have.

The most important revolutionary leaders were to be George Rakovski, Liuben Karavelov, Vasil Levski, and Khristo Botev. Each represented a stage in the development of the national movement; their ideas can thus best be understood against the background of the events. Since in the early sixties Serbia was the center of the Bulgarian activities, Rakovski had his headquarters in Belgrade and Novi Sad. The Serbian government aided him both in his organization of a Bulgarian Legion and in the printing of books and pamphlets. In 1861 he founded the journal *Dunavski Lebed* (Danube Swan). Like Vasil Levski later, he believed that *cheta* tactics were not enough, and that a revolt would have to be organized within the Bulgarian lands. As far as the future of the state was concerned, he was willing to enter into a federation with the Serbs and Romanians, but not the Greeks. Although he had been educated at Greek schools, Rakovski wished to exclude Greek influence. In his political philosophy he followed the standard program of Balkan liberalism.

The Bulgarian activities were not carried on without friction with Serbian nationalist groups. Very soon Rakovski and his followers clashed with their Serbian supporters over the entire question of Balkan Slavic unity. At this time Serbia too had adopted an expansionist program aimed at achieving predominance in South Slav areas also claimed by the Bulgarians. In 1862, after the conclusion of the crisis over the Ottoman shelling of Belgrade, the center for the Bulgarian movement shifted to Bucharest. Close cooperation was nevertheless maintained with Serbia, particularly during the reign of Michael. Despite disagreements among the participants underground preparations for a general Balkan revolt went forward parallel with Prince Michael's endeavors to unite the Balkan governments.

Romania offered even better opportunities for Bulgarian conspiracies. The Liberal Party in that state looked with sympathy on the movement. Bulgarian territorial objectives were not yet openly contradictory to those of Romania. A large colony of Bulgarian merchants lived in Bucharest and in the Danube port cities. In this favorable atmosphere Rakovski continued his activities. In April and May, 1866, two companies of Bulgars were sent across the Danube to continue the *cheta* tactics. When these bands failed, the Bulgarian merchants became opposed to such actions. A year later Rakovski died of tuberculosis.

Despite these unsuccessful actions the *cheta* continued to play a major role in revolutionary planning. A major attempt was made in 1868. At that time the Bulgarian revolutionary societies organized the Hadzhi Dimitur and Stefan Karadzha *cheta*. It was directed to cross the Danube and proceed to the Stara Planina where it was to establish a revolutionary government which would then direct a general Bulgarian uprising. In July, 1868, 120 men crossed the Danube. The group was discovered by a Turkish patrol, and within two weeks its members were wiped out.

After Rakovski's death Karavelov, Levski, and Botev dominated the revolutionary movement. Of these Karavelov was the most moderate. At one time he had considered a relationship with the Ottoman Empire similar to the Ausgleich (Compromise) which had just been arranged in the Habsburg monarchy. Under this system the sultan would be the king of Bulgaria. The advantage of a continued association with the Porte was that it might block Serbian and Greek acquisition of lands claimed by the Bulgars. Later Karavelov abandoned this plan and came to favor the establishment of a Balkan federation. So far as revolutionary tactics were concerned, he believed that a general Balkan uprising would be necessary to obtain Bulgarian freedom. Politically liberal, he was apprehensive about Russian domination in the future.

Of the three men Vasil Levski best fitted into the romantic revolutionary tradition. He wished to achieve Bulgarian separation from the Ottoman Empire through a mass peasant revolt. He did not want to rely on other states in the initiation of the action. Like Rakovski, he believed that it was essential that a revolutionary network be established throughout the Bulgarian lands. In 1869 he went to Bulgaria to set up committees to prepare for the future revolt.

The third figure, Hristo Botev, was Bulgaria's greatest modern poet. In contrast to the others he was a socialist and he hoped that a mass revolution would occur that would lead not only to political freedom, but also to social change. He saw the future Bulgaria as a republic joined in a Balkan confederation of states with similar governments. Although he had acquired his beliefs as a student in Russia, he felt little attachment to that country.

In 1870 the conflicting groups and leaders finally joined together in a new organization, the Bulgarian Revolutionary Central Committee. In 1872 a meeting was held which included representatives from Bulgaria as well as from other emigrant organizations. Here a compromise between the different programs was at least partially achieved. It was agreed that revolutionary means, not negotiation, should be used to gain the goal of liberation from Ottoman control. The chief objective was to be the formation of a federation, including Bulgaria, Romania, Serbia, Montenegro, and Greece, in which each nation would be autonomous. The extreme divergence of views prevented the group from agreeing on the internal organization of the future Bulgaria.

Although Karavelov was president of the Central Committee, Vasil Levski and his chief assistant, Dimitur Obshti, were given the task of returning to Bulgaria to organize the revolution. This endeavor soon resulted in disaster. In order to secure money Obshti, without the approval of the committee, robbed the Turkish mail and was apprehended. In order to demonstrate to his captors and to Europe that he was not a common criminal but a respectable political conspirator, he confessed the general plans for the insurrection to the Ottoman authorities. With this information they were able to capture Levski and others. Levski and Obshti were hanged. Deeply affected by this failure, Karavelov and others left the committee in 1874. They were now convinced that foreign assistance, particularly from Serbia and Montenegro, was absolutely necessary if they were to achieve their aims. They also realized that they had to work to indoctrinate their conationals in Bulgaria with a more militant spirit.

Despite these disappointments and defections plans for insurrections continued to be made. In 1875, when the revolt broke out in Bosnia-Hercegovina, which was to precipitate another great eastern crisis, the new leadership of the Bulgarian Revolutionary Central Committee, in particular Hristo Botev and Stefan Stambolov, went ahead with the preparations for an uprising to be centered in Lovech, Stara Zagora, Sliven, Shumen, Turnovo, and Ruse. Hastily conceived, poorly planned, and ill-timed, the so-called Stara Zagora revolt met the same fate as its predecessors had. Again, the lack of support within the country was clearly evident. For example, at Chirpan the committee had expected to find three hundred volunteers, but only twenty-four appeared; a mere twenty-five joined at Ruse and sixteen at Shumen. Needless to say, the Ottoman authorities had little difficulty dealing with this action.

These disasters still did not discourage the Bulgarian leadership abroad. With the continuation of the revolts in Bosnia-Hercegovina and the obvious preparations for war being made in Serbia, Montenegro, and Greece, the opportunity for a successful revolt seemed highly favorable. The Ottoman government now had its hands full in other regions of the Balkans; troops were no longer available for action in Bulgaria. Under these circumstances another great uprising was planned, this time under the direction of George Benkovski. Once again, arms and supplies were collected in Romania and plans were drawn up for a revolt to take place in May, 1876. For purposes of organization Bulgaria was divided into four sections with headquarters at Turnovo, Sliven, Vratsa, and Plovdiv. In January, 1876, the organizers of the revolt crossed into Bulgaria; Plovdiv was to be their center.

At the end of April representatives of the revolutionary groups held a meeting at which the date of May 13 was set for the uprising. The plans, however, were discovered by the Ottoman authorities. Because of this disclosure revolts broke out prematurely first on May 2 at Koprivshtitsa, then in Panagiurishte and Klisura. The fighting remained largely confined to this Balkan Mountain area, although there was some action also in the Rhodope Mountain region. Once again there was no mass Bulgarian uprising.

Occupied elsewhere, the Ottoman government had only a limited number of regular soldiers to send against the rebels. Consequently, it was compelled to use irregular detachments. Ottoman feeling was very strong since the Bulgarian insurgents, like other Balkan people in similar circumstances, had massacred resident Turkish civilians. Moreover, the revolt was put down only after heavy fighting and after atrocities had been committed on both sides. The Ottoman reprisals, the so-called Bulgarian horrors, received great publicity in Europe where only the Bulgarian side of the story was known. Estimates of the actual number of Bulgarians killed in the suppression of this revolt vary: the Ottoman figure is 3,100; [1] the British, 12,000; the American, 15,000; and the Bulgarian, from 30,000 to 100,000.

In that same month Botev led the last Bulgarian attempt to organize an insurrection. At the end of May he and about two hundred of his followers boarded the Austrian steamer Radetzky. Once on the river the

1. David Harris, *Britain and the Bulgarian Horrors of 1876* (Chicago: University of Chicago Press, 1939), p. 22.

conspirators seized control of the ship and forced it to land them on the Bulgarian shore. Again the Ottoman authorities learned of the action immediately. Botev was killed and his men dispersed.

The Bulgarian revolutionary movement thus ended in total failure. The tactics adopted could only have worked if indeed a mass peasant uprising had occurred when the small bands crossed the Danube or if the majority of Bulgarians had followed the directives of the revolutionary committees. Even then foreign intervention would probably have been necessary to achieve the desired political goals. Thus, in the end the Bulgarian nationalists too were forced to await the moment when general European events would be favorable to their cause.

Despite the failure to achieve any political objectives, by the summer of 1876 a separate ecclesiastical organization, the exarchate, had been set up. The victory in the religious field had been achieved through negotiation and with the eventual support of both Russia and the Ottoman Empire. In the negotiations with the patriarchate and in the organization of revolutionary societies on foreign soil, the dangers blocking the attainment of the Bulgarian national aims had become clearly apparent. Until this time, in the events leading to Greek independence and to Serbian and Romanian autonomy, there had been some significant mutual assistance between the Balkan peoples, and, equally important, little outright enmity. Territories with a varied ethnic composition had not been in question. The Bulgarian movement, as shown in the quarrels over the jurisdiction of the exarchate and in the question of the Serbian position in a South Slav organization, involved the political future of lands with a mixed population and a complicated history. The quarrels arising from this condition were to lead the peninsula into a different historical age.

CHAPTER 10

The Crisis of the Seventies

In the preceding chapters the internal development of the Ottoman Empire, Serbia, Greece, and Romania has been traced. During the nineteenth century these three Christian states were able to achieve varying degrees of freedom from the Porte and to establish national regimes. In each nation similar political organizations were adopted, in which the Christian groups who had been in power before the revolutions, or who had risen to power during the period of national revival and the establishment of the new state apparatus, maintained their superior positions. The national movements thus brought about political but not social change. Although all of the new states adopted more or less liberal constitutional systems, practical political control rested in the hands of a relatively small percentage of the population. Organized into competing factions and political parties, these men fought for control of the government and associated patronage. Against the combined power of this group, the prince in each state was usually at a disadvantage. Except for Miloš at the beginning of his reign, no Balkan prince exercised autocratic powers. The rulers of Greece and Romania after 1866 were foreigners with no party of their own in the country; the prince of Serbia was always threatened by a rival dynasty.

Faced with almost constant domestic opposition, the Balkan rulers usually found that the best way to protect their own authority and unify their countries was to adopt active national programs for either gaining more political rights from the Porte or for territorial expansion. By this time all of the nations had formulated national goals, which included not only the acquisition of regions in which they were clearly the predominant nationality, but also of ethnically mixed lands where they could put forward historical, cultural, geographic, or strategic claims. As we know, three programs typifying this trend were the Greek Megale Idea, the greater Serbian plans as expressed in the Načertanije, and the Roma-

141

nian desire for the union of Transylvania, Bukovina, Bessarabia, and later Dobrudja and the Banat with Wallachia and Moldavia. Prior to the 1870s the states had not come into outright conflict over the division of the Balkan territories since an Ottoman buffer zone covering the Bulgarian lands, Macedonia, Albania, Bosnia, and Hercegovina still existed. During this decade, however, the possibility arose that Ottoman rule would be removed from at least some of these regions, most of whom were difficult to divide on strictly national lines. The rival claims to these areas introduced a new element into Balkan relationships. Moreover, it must be remembered that in each state questions of foreign policy had become deeply embedded in the domestic political balance. Princes or parties who failed to advance national interests gravely endangered their own positions.

As the Ottoman rule in the peninsula weakened, the great powers gained more direct control over the governments. At the beginning of the century no European state had a predominant influence on the life of any one of the Christian peoples. By the time of the Crimean War three-power supervision had been established in Greece, and a Russian protectorate over Serbia and the Principalities had been set up. In the Treaty of Paris the signatories jointly assumed the duty of guardians. Intervention of the powers in quarrels between the Porte and its subjects eventually meant that all Balkan boundaries were determined by international treaties. They therefore could not be altered without the approval of the signatories. This situation meant that the Balkan peoples, even if they had been able to agree among themselves, could not have arranged their affairs alone. The great powers had to consent to all changes. Since in international affairs the principal nations concerned, Russia, Britain, and the Habsburg Empire, were intensely jealous of each other, most controversies were settled on the basis of the balance of power, that is, on the principle that no one of these states should acquire a predominant influence in the entire area. These solutions often did violence to the legitimate interests of the Balkan nations and added one more complicating factor to a difficult situation.

The crisis of the 1870s, which was to bring these problems into the open, was precipitated by a revolt of Christian peasants in Hercegovina and Bosnia and by the deep involvement in the event of neighboring Serbia and Montenegro. Before proceeding to this affair, however, brief mention should be made of the development in the nineteenth century of both Montenegro and Bosnia.

Intermittently, Montenegro, under the rule of a prince-bishop, played an important role in the Balkans despite its size and poverty. From 1781 to 1830 the ruler, Peter I Petrović, was able to strengthen the state internally and to double its territory. He fought against the Porte both at the time of the Ottoman campaign against Ali Pasha of Janina from 1819 to

1821 and again during the Russo-Turkish War of 1828–29. His successor, Peter II, better known as Njegoš, was a poet and the author of the *Mountain Wreath*, one of the chief South Slav literary accomplishments. He continued the task of attempting to extend the authority of the state over the rebellious and independent tribes of the area, and in 1832 he too fought the Ottoman troops. A major change took place when the next ruler, Danilo I (1852–60), wished to marry and thus secularize the state. The princely office was now made hereditary in the Petrović family. In 1852 and 1858 there was renewed fighting with the Porte. In 1860 Nicholas I, sometimes called Nikita, ascended the throne where he was to remain until 1918. During the first part of his reign the constant conflicts with the Ottoman Empire continued. The chief issues concerned the territories in dispute, involving usually Bosnian, Hercegovinian, or Albanian lands, and the exact status of the Montenegrin state, which the Porte claimed was a part of the empire. Because of their mutual interests, their common Serbian nationality, and their Orthodoxy, Serbian and Montenegrin relations were usually close. There was, nevertheless, always an undercurrent of rivalry between the rulers for leadership in Serbian and South Slav affairs. The Montenegrin princes were also tempted to use the dynastic disputes between the Karadjordjević and the Obrenović families for their own advantage. By the 1870s Montenegro was chiefly interested in securing a port on the Adriatic and the possession of Hercegovina.

Like Montenegro, Bosnia and Hercegovina remained a constant problem for the Porte, but for very different reasons. Montenegro was a continual center of Christian rebellion; Bosnia, at least during the first part of the century, stood stubbornly for maintaining old ways and against reform. During the reign of Selim III it was a stronghold of *ayan* power. It will be remembered that Bosnia was one of the few areas in which there were mass conversions to Islam after the Ottoman conquest. The notables of the area, known as *beg*s, were thus both Muslim and Slavic. They fought stubbornly at this time to maintain their authority both against Constantinople and over their Christian peasants who were, of course, of the same nationality and who spoke the same language. The *beg*s revolted against the Porte in 1821, 1828, 1831, and 1837. They were able to maintain a condition of almost complete local autonomy until 1850 when Ottoman troops under Omer Pasha managed to defeat them and to reassert the authority of the central government.

Despite the fact that both *beg* and peasant were of the same nationality, the condition of the peasant in Bosnia and Hercegovina was one of the worst in the Balkans. Both the tax levels and the *corvée* dues were exorbitant. It has been estimated that they absorbed over 40 percent of the peasant's income. Ottoman reforms were also not enforced here. Peasant revolts aimed at bettering economic conditions and not at political change occurred in 1857–58 and 1861–62. The worst crisis came in the mid-seventies. The bad harvest of 1874 caused much distress. In July, 1875, an insurrection broke out in Hercegovina and then in Bosnia which the Ottoman authorities could not suppress. Like the Greek and Serbian rebellions earlier in the century, Ottoman soldiers could not defeat determined peasants fighting under local leaders and using guerrilla tactics. The main grievances of the rebels remained the miserable agrarian conditions.

With Bosnia and Hercegovina in rebellion, it was inevitable that Serbia and Montenegro would be drawn in. The people of both states were, of course, sympathetic with the rebels, and some Serbs had been involved in the organization of the uprising. The most important question, however, was the reaction of the Serbian government. During most of the first part of the reign of Milan, Jovan Ristić was in charge of Serbian foreign policy. The diplomatic situation in the Balkans was now very different from what it had been during the reign of Michael. Belgrade was no longer the center for the organization of Balkan rebellion against the Porte. Although the government tolerated the presence of groups such as those of the Bulgarian revolutionaries, it did not actively encourage them.

In this period of relative calm the news of the Bosnian revolt jarred Serbian opinion. Again national and religious sympathies were deeply stirred. Elections held in August, 1875, returned an assembly in which the Liberals, who were in favor of action to aid the insurgents, had the majority. In August the former Conservative ministry gave way to a Liberal government under Stevča Mihajlović, with Ristić as foreign minister and Jevrem Grujić as minister of interior. Since these men openly favored intervention, Milan was in disagreement with the assembly and his own ministry. Pressure on the prince continued to increase. By August, 1875, Nicholas of Montenegro had shown himself willing to act, but Milan held firm. He realized that his country was not prepared, and he was receiving warnings from the great powers not to move. In October he set up a coalition government under Ljubomir Kaljević to replace that of Ristić and Grujić; it stayed in office seven months. Meanwhile, the Bosnian revolt had become an international crisis. As could be expected, the Serbian government looked to St. Petersburg for direction, but it was not clear what that country wished. Official Russia, along with the other powers, warned Serbia not to become involved in the rebellion, but at the same time unofficial Panslav circles made their great enthusiasm for the insurgents clearly apparent.

Although the Conservatives, who were in the minority, continued to stand for peace, Milan was soon forced to change his policy. International events also seemed to compel him to act. In May, 1876, the Bulgarian uprising occurred. It was followed by the great internal crisis in

Constantinople in May, which in turn resulted in the deposing of Abdul Aziz and the succession of Murad V. In the same month General M. G. Cherniaev, a hero of the Russian Central Asian campaigns, arrived in Belgrade and offered his services. A large number of Russian volunteers sent by the Panslav committees also streamed into the country. It seemed indeed as if Russian opinion, despite the official declarations, strongly supported Serbian intervention.

In May the coalition cabinet was replaced by a government again headed by Ristić and Grujić. This ministry and public opinion were strongly for war. At the end of June the decision to fight was finally made. The Serbian military plans called for campaigns in Bosnia, in the Sanjak of Novi Pazar, and in the Niš and Timok areas. It was hoped that another Bulgarian uprising would occur and, of course, Serbia had the assistance of the Bosnian revolt which was still in progress. In July, 1876, Serbian and Montenegrin forces invaded Ottoman territory. As their objectives, the governments hoped that the war would result in the annexation of Hercegovina by Montenegro and Bosnia by Serbia. Although the Montenegrin operations were to be successful, the Serbian action soon became a military disaster.

As Milan had feared, Serbia was not prepared to fight. Her peasant soldiers, under badly trained officers, could not defeat the well-equipped, well-led Ottoman forces. Cherniaev proved an inept commander, and the Russian volunteers were soon a national scandal. Great friction developed between the Serbian and Russian elements in this ill-coordinated campaign. Serbian efforts were also weakened by the fact that no great Balkan revolt took place. The Bulgarians did not rise again; the Romanian and Greek governments waited for indications of the possible outcome. Most disastrous, however, was the failure of the Russian government to offer any practical aid.

The powers attempted to stop the fighting as soon as possible; they had every interest in bringing the affair to a conclusion. Although an armistice was arranged in August, it was broken by the Serbs in the next month. In October the Serbian army suffered a devastating defeat, which opened the path into the Morava valley to Belgrade for the Ottoman forces. This time Russia did intervene. After receiving a Russian ultimatum the Ottoman government agreed to an armistice on November 3. Although peace was now re-established, the war had a disastrous effect on Serbia, both materially and morally. Her casualties amounted to fifteen thousand men, and it had been made clear that her armies were no match for the Ottoman opponent.

With the war now over, the problem of the Bosnian revolt remained. The great powers found themselves drawn again into the settlement of the questions that had caused the peasant rebellion. Certainly, none of these governments had welcomed a resurgence of the eastern question.

After the Crimean War the Balkan area had been relatively quiet. The great events had taken place in Central Europe and Italy, not in the Near East. For future Balkan affairs Prussia's defeat of the Habsburg monarchy in 1866 and the reorganization of the state in the Ausgleich of 1867 were particularly important. Thereafter the monarchy, now usually referred to as Austria-Hungary, was divided into two administrative sections united in the person of the emperor and with a common minister of war, foreign affairs and finance as it related to these two offices of government. The next event, the Franco-Prussian War and the unification of Germany under Prussian leadership, resulted in the formation of a powerful state whose policies were henceforth to have great influence on Balkan affairs. Prussia, as we have seen, had previously played only a minor role in the peninsula.

It should be noted that German unification was accomplished with the approval and assistance of Russia. That state used the opportunity to denounce the Black Sea clauses of the Treaty of Paris and to gain international approval of the act. Although the Russian government did not thereafter embark on a real program of naval construction, the path was now open for Russia again to pursue an active Balkan policy.

After these events the governments of Russia, Germany, and Austria-Hungary joined together in the early 1870s in the Three Emperors' Alliance. This informal association was based on the exchange of visits and communications between the heads of the three nations; it was not a formal alliance. It did, however, make it probable that the states would cooperate if another eastern crisis arose. In 1875 they did act together because none was prepared for a major upset in the area. They wished the Bosnian revolt to be settled peacefully, if necessary by outside mediation; they did not want it to lead to a great Christian rebellion in the Balkans.

Of the three courts the Russian government was under the greatest pressure. In the past it had often claimed a special relationship with the Balkan Christians. The feeling always existed that if Russia had the right to intervene in their behalf, she also had the duty to act if Christian rights were indeed endangered. Unfortunately, the Bosnian crisis also coincided with a period when great enthusiasm was felt in Russian society for things Slavic. The racial tie of Panslav feeling was thus added to the religious issue of Orthodoxy. Although Panslav programs differed, all looked to the freeing of Orthodox Slavic people from foreign control, either Ottoman or Habsburg, and their unification in some sort of a federation in which Russia would play the predominant role. Prominent Russians including the heir to the throne, the future Alexander III, N. P. Ignatiev, and many generals adhered to these ideas. The Panslavs naturally wished to aid the Balkan peoples against the Ottoman Empire.

It was their committees who had despatched volunteers and supplies to Serbia.

In contrast, most of the responsible members of the Russian government disliked the implications of the program for the current crisis in the Balkans. They feared that Russia would be drawn into a war with the Ottoman Empire which in turn would involve the other great powers. The events of the Crimean War could thus be repeated; Russia might face a coalition of European states who did not wish the balance of power overturned. The official Russian policy was thus that a solution should be reached through negotiation among the powers and in close association with Vienna and Berlin. The Panslavs continued to insist on Russian aid to the Balkan rebels and that the final settlement of the problem should be on a bilateral Russian-Ottoman basis.

Since the official Russian position coincided with the interests of Vienna and Berlin, these three governments did cooperate during this crisis. Among the powers the major disturbing element was Britain. This government under the leadership of Benjamin Disraeli, did not wish to see Ottoman interests threatened and disliked the close association of the three conservative courts, which gave these powers a predominant influence in European affairs. When it became obvious that the Porte would not be able to quell the disturbance in Bosnia and Hercegovina, the three powers cooperated to secure reform measures. In December, 1875, such a program was proposed by the Habsburg foreign minister, Julius Andrassy. It was accepted by the Porte, but not by the insurgents. In May, 1876, a second plan suggested by the three states was rejected by Britain and therefore by the Ottoman Empire. Meanwhile, the Bulgarian uprising had taken place and the Balkan states were preparing for war. Constantinople was in the midst of the crisis that brought Murad V to power in May and Abdul Hamid II in August.

The outbreak of the war between the Porte and her vassals, Serbia and Montenegro, did not disturb the Three Emperors' Alliance. In July, 1876, the Russian foreign minister, A. M. Gorchakov, and Andrassy agreed upon the Reichstadt Convention. Although there was later disagreement on exactly what had been decided, the pact did preserve the balance of great power interests. The statesmen decided that if the Balkan states were defeated in the war, Austria and Russia would cooperate to maintain the *status quo*. If, on the contrary, the Balkan armies should be victorious, the two great powers would proceed to partition the Ottoman Balkan territories, but with the provision that no great Balkan state should be established. Autonomous regimes were to be set up in Bulgaria and Rumelia; Constantinople was to be a free city; Greece would receive Thessaly and Crete. Russia, for her part, would take southern Bessarabia and territory in Asia Minor. Austria's share was to be Bosnia and Hercegovina. It will be noted that the chief Serbian territorial objective in the war was thus to go to the Habsburg Empire, an action that, incidentally, was also in complete contradiction to the Panslav idea.

After the conclusion of the war of the Balkan states against the Ottoman Empire in 1876, the powers continued to try to negotiate a settlement which would appease the Balkan people and satisfy great power interests. They made a final attempt to save the situation in December, 1876. At that time in the Constantinople Conference new reform proposals were formulated. On December 23, however, the Porte announced the introduction of the constitution for the empire and proclaimed the reforms unnecessary. A declaration of war by Russia became now almost inevitable. In January and March, 1877, two more arrangements were made by Russia with Austria-Hungary to assure the latter's neutrality. Bosnia-Hercegovina was still to go to Vienna, but the status of the Sanjak of Novi Pazar, a strip of territory separating Serbia and Montenegro, was to be decided later. Russia also agreed that her troops would not fight inside the territory of these two states.

After signing an agreement with Romania Russia declared war on April 24, 1877. The campaign was to prove surprisingly difficult. The chief Russian obstacle was the inability to capture the Ottoman stronghold of Pleven (Plevna). From July until December the Russian advance was stalled at this point. The delay placed the Balkan states in a terrible position. Expecting at first a short war, the Russian government had not wished their active cooperation. After the check at Pleven Romanian, Serbian, Montenegrin, and Greek assistance was desired. Except for Romania none of the other governments responded with eagerness. All sought money for military preparations and territorial guarantees for the future. Uncertain of the general situation, Serbia and Greece delayed their entrance into the war. The Romanian government, in contrast, believed that the time had come to achieve certain national goals.

The revolt in Bosnia-Hercegovina, like previous Balkan crises, presented the Romanian government with both opportunities for advancement and threats to its interests. The Romanians, like the Greeks, did not welcome the possibility of the creation of strong, independent Serbian or Bulgarian states linked with St. Petersburg. Nevertheless, it was seen that the situation did offer the chance to press for more privileges from the Ottoman government. During the next three years, keeping these conditions in mind, the Romanian leaders remained concerned primarily with three aspects of the international scene. First, as already mentioned, they wished to exploit the difficult position of the Ottoman government; second, they hoped, to make territorial gains and achieve full independence should a general war occur; and, third, they did not want Russia to acquire again a predominant position in their state. In the conduct of foreign policy Prince Charles played the leading role. Until April, 1876, the Conservative ministry of Lascar Catargiu remained in power. It was replaced in May by a Liberal government. After this time the two Liberal party leaders Ion Brătianu and Michael Kogălniceanu, cooperating closely with the prince, shared with him the chief responsibility for the decisions reached. The Liberal Party, in contrast to its previous stand, now stood strongly behind the throne.

During the first two years of the crisis, with the revolts in Bosnia-Hercegovina and Bulgaria and the war between the Ottoman Empire and Serbia joined by Montenegro, the Romanian government maintained an official policy of neutrality. At the same time it put pressure on the Ottoman government to obtain more rights and privileges within the empire, and gave limited assistance to the neighboring Christian belligerents. Some arms and volunteers passed through the country to Serbian battlefields; Bulgarian bands continued to organize on Romanian soil. During this period, however, the general situation did not evolve to the Romanian advantage. Victorious over the Balkan armies, the Ottoman government rejected the Romanian demands. The same conditions, the defeat of the Slavic Christian people and Ottoman intransigence, were also likely to bring Russian intervention, an action feared by the Romanian government. Obviously, should Russia go to war with the Ottoman Empire, Romania would either have to allow the Russian armies passage or risk the danger of becoming a major battlefield. In view of their country's past history Romanian statesmen of all political parties were most hesitant to accept the presence of a Russian army.

Russia's immediate intentions were made clear in October, 1876, when Brătianu and a delegation of Romanians visited Alexander II at Livadia. At this time and later the Russian government pressed for an agreement with Romania, but one which would only cover questions arising from the passage of the Russian army to the Danube. The Romanian leaders, in contrast, wished a full political understanding, and one that would expressly protect their territorial integrity. In particular they feared the loss of the three southern Bessarabian districts gained in 1856.

During the negotiations with Russia, which lasted until April, 1877, alternate paths of action were thoroughly explored. Discussions were continued with the Ottoman Empire. Representatives were also sent abroad to seek the support of the other guarantor powers should Romania decide to resist Russian pressure. The results of these moves were discouraging. In the Ottoman constitution of December, 1876, Romania was declared an "integral part" of the empire and numbered among the "privileged provinces." This was exactly the issue at stake between the two governments. Regarding the possibility of outside assistance against Russia, the picture was even bleaker. The Habsburg monarchy, bound by secret understandings with Russia, advised Romania not to sign an agreement, but simply to allow the Russian army to march through the country. The Romanian army should withdraw to western Wallachia. Germany, in contrast, favored full acquiescence to Russian wishes. France was, of course, of no assistance because of her military weakness at the time. The British government both could not and would not offer aid.

The agreement with Russia, signed finally on April 16, 1877, was thus almost forced upon Romania, particularly once the Russian government had agreed to a formal political treaty with a clause guaranteeing Romanian territorial integrity. It should be noted that there was little enthusiasm in Romania at this time for war against the Ottoman Empire in alliance with Russia. At a crown council held on April 13 and attended by the Romanian ministers and other prominent men, the majority favored maintaining neutrality and withdrawing the army to western Wallachia away from the Russian line of march to the Danube. The subsequent decisions, from cooperation with Russia to the eventual entrance into combat, were largely those of the prince supported by Brătianu and Kogălniceanu.

The question of active participation in the Russo-Turkish conflict did not, however, arise at once, largely because of Russian reluctance to accept Romanian military assistance. The Russo-Romanian pact provided for Russian passage only; technically Romania thus remained neutral after the war broke out on April 24. Prince Charles, with a well-trained army of thirty thousand, found this position most uncomfortable, particularly after Ottoman forces made attacks on Danubian ports. On May 21 the Romanian chambers voted a declaration of independence; a state of war with the Porte now existed. Nevertheless, the Russian government continued to show little interest in Romanian military support. It would accept Romanian troops only to guard prisoners or to garrison towns. Prince Charles sought a more glorious role; he wanted to conduct an independent action and to maintain the Romanian troops as a separate unit in battle.

The Russian attitude toward Romanian participation in the war changed abruptly in August, 1877, after the disaster at Pleven. In sore need of Romanian manpower the Russian leaders now offered the command of the entire operation to Charles. Intensely flattered, the prince abandoned his previous insistence that the Romanian forces should operate separately. He also neglected to use the opportunity to specify what Romania should receive in the future peace negotiations. During the assault on Pleven relations between Russian and Romanian leaders remained relatively good.

A sudden change in both the Romanian attitude toward the war and the Russian treatment of their ally came with the fall of the Ottoman stronghold in December, 1877. Throughout the war the Romanian government had considered as its goals recognition of independence, an indemnity, and the acquisition of the Danube delta and as much land as possible on the right bank of the river, including Dobrudja. The maintenance of Romanian territorial integrity, however, was soon to become more important than these issues. Although Russia did not openly and officially notify the Romanian government of its intention to retake southern Bessarabia until January, 1878, rumors reached Bucharest from many sources. It was this issue that was henceforth to form the central theme of Romanian diplomacy. The government was in fact divided on how to deal with the matter. Brătianu, whose policy triumphed, felt that public pressure would force the government to remain steadfast on the question. The prince and Kogălniceanu, believing the cause hopeless, preferred to use the question as a bargaining point, perhaps to gain the Ruse-Varna line for Dobrudja.

In contrast to the Romanian attitude, Serbia was not so eager to enter the war. The final peace treaty had only been signed with the Ottoman Empire in March, 1877; the Serbian forces were exhausted. Moreover, no assurances could be obtained concerning territorial gains. Serbia wanted lands primarily in Bosnia and Old Serbia, but Russia, bound by the secret agreements with the Habsburg Empire, could not give Belgrade any promises concerning future peace arrangements. Moreover, other dangers had arisen. It was quite clear to Serbia that Russia was now solidly behind the Bulgarian interests. At the Constantinople Conference Ignatiev had wanted to award Niš, Skopje, and Prizren to Bulgarian control despite the Serbian claims. Thus, when the Russian government pressed Serbia for assistance after the defeat at Pleven, the Serbs took a long time in replying. First, they wished financial assistance and a clear indication of the lands they would receive. Finally, three days after Pleven was finally captured, on December 10, Serbia entered the war. Russia provided some money, but she would still give no territorial promises.

Like Serbia, Greece too acted only at the last moment. During the Bosnian rebellion and the Serbo-Turkish War the Greek government, under strong pressure from Britain, had taken no action to aid her neighbors. This entire crisis, following as it did the exarchate dispute, had made clear what difficulties were to face Greece. It was not the Ottoman government, but the rival Slavic Balkan states who now threatened to block the accomplishment of Greek national aims. The Greek government wished in the future to incorporate Crete, Thessaly, Epirus, Thrace, and as much of Macedonia as possible. Although the Greek position in the first three areas was strong, Bulgarian claims now rivaled those of Athens in Thrace and Macedonia. A successful campaign of the Balkan peoples against the Ottoman Empire would thus not assure Greece advantages and might indeed create a worse situation. Despite these hard realities the same division of opinion existed in Greece as has been seen in Serbia and Romania. Many Greeks feared that if they did not fight they would be left out of any future peace arrangement. Moreover, as in Serbia a great fund of public enthusiasm existed for any action against the Porte even when conditions were not favorable. Great pressure was exerted by these circles on the king and the government.

In 1876 Alexander Koumoundouros headed a ministry that stood for the maintenance of peace and the achievement of territorial objectives through diplomacy. His regime was naturally under attack from those who wished to declare war on the Porte and to foment rebellion in Macedonia. The Greeks became even more apprehensive when at the Constantinople Conference, which they had not been invited to attend, plans were developed for a great Bulgarian state holding lands claimed by Athens. In June, 1877, at this time of national danger, a coalition cabinet under Admiral Kanares replaced that of Koumoundouros. It contained four former premiers; Charilaos Trikoupes was the foreign minister. Attempts were now made to strengthen the Greek military position, and troops were concentrated on the Ottoman frontier. When after the Pleven debacle the Russian government asked for the Greek participation, the government found itself in an impossible situation. On the one hand, the British put strong pressure on the country not only not to enter the war, but also to aid in holding down rebellions in Ottoman territory. Should Greece go to war, the danger existed that Britain might in fact aid the Porte. The Greek military forces were also not ready. On the other hand, should Greece not act, it was probable that the Slavic states would reap the full benefit of a Russian victory. Serbian as well as Bulgarian conflicting interests in Macedonia were feared.

In these negotiations neither Britain nor Russia would give the Greek government any definite assurances on the territorial question. During the Pleven crisis the Russian government did make some vague promises concerning Thessaly and Epirus, but it remained silent on the controversial Macedonia and Thrace. Despite the fact that its diplomatic efforts failed, the Greek government was faced with the reality that public opinion was becoming increasingly belligerent. The possibilities for action remained twofold: Greece could enter the war, or she could incite revolts in Greek-inhabited Ottoman territories.

The fall of Pleven in December jolted the Greek as well as the Serbian government. Fears were now strong that the war would come to an end and the Greek claims be forgotten. The fall of Adrianople on January 20, 1878, made this possibility all the more probable. By this time the expressions of dissatisfaction from the Greek public had become so strong that King George feared that he would lose his throne. He thus mobilized the army and sent it to the border. Since this act was unconstitutional, it caused an immediate internal crisis. A new government under Koumoundouros was formed with the belligerent statesman Theodore Deliyannes as foreign minister. Riots were now taking place in Athens. The government, clearly for war, gave directions for the commencement of rebellions in Thessaly, Epirus, and Macedonia. On February 2 it announced that Greek troops would enter Ottoman territory to "protect Christians" from the effects of these same revolts. Like Serbia, the Greek government acted too late. On February 3 it learned that on January 31 an armistice agreement had been signed between Russia and the Ottoman Empire. Its terms made no mention of Greece. The situation that Athens had feared had thus arisen. The Ottoman army could now concentrate against the Greeks. The Greek forces withdrew behind their own boundaries; the powers intervened to prevent further Ottoman actions. With the conclusion of the hostilities the Greek government found itself in a weak position with regard to the future peace terms. It could be expected that Russia would support the Slavic states; Britain had not wished Greece to go to war.

The end of the conflict and the Russian victory thus caused little joy and much apprehension in Romania, Serbia, and Greece. The terms of the armistice agreement of January foreshadowed Russian intentions in the Balkans and were a profound shock to these three states. Most important was the provision for the creation of a great Bulgarian state. The full Russian program was more precisely expressed in the Treaty of San Stefano of March 3, 1878. This agreement, negotiated bilaterally by Russia with the Porte broke a series of international treaties, including the pacts that had been made with Austria-Hungary prior to the war. The outstanding features of this treaty, like the armistice agreement, were the sections concerning the establishment of a Bulgaria embracing territory north and south of the Balkan Mountains, Thrace, and most of Macedonia. This state, potentially the strongest in the Balkans, was obviously designed to be under Russian control, with the Russian army in occupation for two years. In addition, Montenegro, who still enjoyed Russian favor, made huge gains and tripled in size.

The other Balkan states received comparatively little or, in the case of Greece, nothing at all. Serbia, who had wanted the pashaliks of Niš, Prizren, Skopje, and Novi Pazar in addition to Vidin and some surrounding territory, received only Niš and some other pieces of land, amounting in all to an increase of about 150 square miles. Russia's ally Romania received perhaps the worse treatment of all. Despite the fact that the Russian government had signed a pact with Romania guaranteeing her territorial integrity, it now reannexed the three districts of southern Bessarabia lost after the Crimean War. In return, the Porte was to cede the Danube delta and Dobrudja to Romania. As in the armistice agreement, Serbia, Romania, and Montenegro were declared to be independent states.

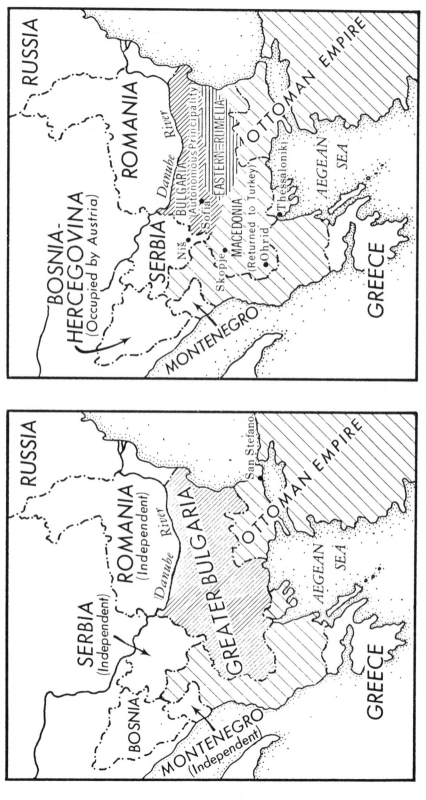

Map 6. The Treaty of San Stefano; The Congress of Berlin

Not only were the Balkan nations dismayed by this settlement, but Austria-Hungary and Britain found it impossible to accept the terms. Neither power could contemplate the establishment of a Bulgarian state that would command strategically the peninsula and put Russian armies within close marching distance of Constantinople. In addition, the agreements that gave Bosnia and Hercegovina to the Habsburg Empire had been ignored and in the treaty Russia had taken Asiatic territory of the Ottoman Empire to the detriment of Britain. An international crisis followed immediately. After a period of constant negotiation Russia agreed to submit the treaty to revision by the powers at a congress to be held in Berlin in June. Before this conference convened Russia and Britain came to terms over many of the basic changes to be made, the most significant of which was that the Russian government accepted the division of the large Bulgarian state.

Before the opening of the congress the Balkan states found themselves in a helpless position. The great decisions were being made in Berlin, London, Vienna, and St. Petersburg. The fate of the small nations would depend on the bargains made in their behalf by their patron great powers. Perhaps the strongest reaction to the terms of the peace came from Romania. The state had been deprived of national territory. Moreover, the Russian army was still in the country. A clause in the Treaty of San Stefano had provided for the passage of Russian troops through Romania during the proposed two-year occupation of Bulgaria. The Russian government now pressed Bucharest for a new convention to cover this question. Fearing that a prolongation of the presence of Russian troops would lead to the re-establishment of a Russian protectorate, the Romanian government resisted the action and appealed abroad for aid. Although Romania had no real friends or sponsors among the powers, the Habsburg government wished to keep Romanian friendship so long as the possibility existed that war might break out over the terms of the peace. Bucharest and Vienna thus remained in close touch.

Serbia was in a similarly unfortunate plight. The terms of San Stefano had clearly indicated the Russian abandonment of Belgrade. In fact, Serbian representatives were told plainly by Russian diplomats that they should seek assistance in Vienna. The Serbs were extremely bitter that San Stefano had created a Bulgarian state far more powerful than their own. With no other alternative available, the Serbian government thus turned to Vienna to obtain the backing of at least one great power. In return, the Habsburg government insisted on the immediate negotiation of a favorable economic agreement. On July 8, 1878, Ristić and Andrassy signed a pact which was indeed advantageous for the monarchy, but not really harmful to the economically backward Balkan land. The agreement covered commercial and railroad problems as well as the right of the Habsburg Empire to improve the navigation of the Danube at the Iron Gates. A provision was included for a future trade treaty or a customs union.

Although none of the Balkan states was allowed to participate fully in the congress, each was able to send representatives to state its views in the sessions devoted to questions directly related to its area. In no case were these arguments able to alter a major decision. Brătianu and Kogălniceanu both spoke at length protesting the loss of southern Bessarabia, but to no avail. The Greek government, with Deliyannes as the chief spokesman, made strong claims to Thrace, Thessaly, and Crete. Although for a time it appeared that Britain would sponsor Greek claims as a check to Slavic gains, France in fact was of chief assistance to Athens.

The final outcome of the congress, the Treaty of Berlin, was the single most important agreement for the Balkan nations during the nineteenth century. The main difference between its terms and those of San Stefano concerned the status of the Bulgarian lands. The great Bulgarian state was now divided into three parts. Bulgaria proper, an area north of the Balkan Mountains but including Sofia, was established as an autonomous, tributary principality. Eastern Rumelia, the territory south of the mountains, was to be a semiautonomous province with a Christian governor, who would be chosen by the Porte and approved by the powers. Macedonia and Thrace were returned to Ottoman control. Although clearly within the tsarist sphere of influence, Bulgaria was to be occupied by Russian troops only for nine months. The gains of Montenegro were also considerably reduced, but that state still received a respectable extension of territory. Serbia, with the acquisition of Niš, Pirot, and Vranje, obtained an addition of 200, not 150, square miles. The Romanian settlement remained much the same as provided for in the treaty of San Stefano. Montenegro, Serbia, and Romania were now all recognized as independent states. The recognition of Romanian independence, however, was tied to conditions regarding the Jewish question, which will be discussed subsequently.

Greece received no territory directly. The congress directed Greece and the Ottoman Empire to negotiate an adjustment of their frontiers in Thessaly and Epirus, and indicated in Article 24 of the treaty that should these efforts fail the great powers would mediate. As could be expected, the Greek government attempted immediately to implement this decision while the Porte delayed as long as possible. Finally, in February, 1879, delegations from the two powers met at Preveza. When they could not come to an agreement, the powers were forced to intervene. A conference was held at Constantinople from August to November, 1879, when it broke down. The Greek cause was aided immensely by the establishment of a Liberal ministry in Britain in 1880 under the Philhellene William Gladstone. At a conference held in Berlin in June of that same year, the powers awarded Greece a favorable frontier settlement. The problem of enforcement remained. Not only did the Ottoman government object, but here, as well as in the question of the Montenegrin frontier, the Albanian populations affected by the border decisions resisted any changes. The powers finally settled the question in July, 1881. The Greeks received less than they wished, but Thessaly and a part of Epirus joined the independent kingdom. The final boundaries were set in 1882.

Not only the small states, but also the great powers received extensions of territory. Russia took southern Bessarabia, while Austria-Hungary received the right to occupy and administer Bosnia and Hercegovina and to administer the Sanjak of Novi Pazar. Moreover, in addition to the losses in Europe the Porte was forced to yield Asiatic territory to the European states. Russia received Batum, Kars, and Ardahan. In the separate Cyprus Convention, Britain took that island. The chief victim of the treaty was, of course, the Ottoman Empire. Serbia, Montenegro, and Romania were now independent; Bulgaria was autonomous. The Porte, however, had been able to maintain control over Thrace, Macedonia, and the Albanian lands. The fate of these territories was not to be determined for another thirty-five years.

After the Congress of Berlin the major continental powers reformed their alliance groupings. Although France remained isolated until the 1890s, in 1879 Germany and Austria-Hungary concluded the strong Dual Alliance. In 1882 Italy joined the alignment, which was now referred to as the Triple Alliance, a combination that was to last until the First World War. Previously, in 1881, Russia and Austria-Hungary had at least temporarily healed their differences and together with Germany signed an agreement which revived the Three Emperors' Alliance. Article II of this pact concerned the Balkans. Here the signators agreed to act together should further changes occur in the area. As regards specific questions, Germany and Austria-Hungary were to support the Russian interpretation of the international agreements on the closure of the Turkish Straits; all three nations were ready to accept the Russian desire for a future union of Bulgaria and Eastern Rumelia and the annexation of Bosnia-Hercegovina by Austria-Hungary should an opportune moment for these actions arise. With this pattern of alliances in effect, a new equilibrium between the great powers had been established.

CHAPTER 11

Autonomous Bulgaria to 1896

DESPITE the establishment of a separate Bulgarian church and the creation of the autonomous state of 1878, the Bulgarian nationalist viewed the events of the 1870s with bitter disappointment. From this time on he regarded the boundaries of the Treaty of San Stefano as the true border of his state. Nevertheless, much had in fact been attained. Although still under Ottoman suzerainty, the autonomous state, with its capital at Sofia, was to have its own prince and a constitutional regime, which would be guaranteed by the powers. Even Eastern Rumelia was given a special organization. The territory was to have an organic statute and to be administered by a Christian governor-general appointed by the sultan with the approval of the great powers. Moreover, at Berlin the diplomats had realized that the separation of Bulgaria and Eastern Rumelia was of a temporary nature, and that the two provinces would eventually unite. Only the third part of the Greater Bulgaria of San Stefano, Macedonia, was returned outright to the Ottoman Empire.

These political advances, however, had their drawbacks. Like the Principalities after the Russo-Turkish War of 1828, Bulgaria was to find that the weakening of Ottoman control was to be accompanied by a sharp increase in Russian influence. The Bulgarian lands were of the utmost strategic importance to Russia because of their proximity to the Turkish Straits and Constantinople. The tsarist government was determined to make Sofia a reliable outpost of Russian interests. Since the great powers had in fact recognized Russia's predominant position in the new state, Russian officials were relatively free to act as they wished here. As previously in the Principalities during the administration of Kiselev, these men were sincerely interested in establishing as fine an administrative system as possible and in creating the basis for a real Russian-Bulgarian friendship in the future.

Two problems demanded immediate Russian attention: first, a constitution had to be drafted; second, a prince elected. The question of the constitution was of primary importance. At the Congress of Berlin, it will be remembered, it had been decided that the Russian army of occupation would leave Bulgaria nine months after the treaty was ratified. In order to prevent political and administrative chaos, which could serve as a pretext for the intervention of the Porte, Britain, or Austria-Hungary in Bulgaria's internal affairs, the Russian government was determined to secure the adoption of a constitution before its troops withdrew. Thus, in November, 1878, the imperial commissioner in Bulgaria, Prince A. M. Dondukov-Korsakov, and his aides drafted a constitution modeled on those of neighboring Serbia and Romania.

This document was then sent to St. Petersburg where it was examined by both the foreign and war ministries and by a special committee. In his comments the acting foreign minister, N. K. Giers, argued that the principal power in the state should be entrusted to the executive branch, that is, to the prince. His colleague, D. A. Miliutin, the minister of war, contended that Russia's influence in Bulgaria depended upon popular support and not upon that of a foreign prince, as yet not chosen. Therefore, the ultimate authority should rest in the legislature, not in the ruler. Miliutin also raised two other considerations. First, he believed that the Bulgarian constitution should not be more conservative than that of either Romania or Serbia; Bulgaria should be an example to them and not vice versa. Second, the document should be more progressive than the Organic Statute which was being drafted for Eastern Rumelia. If this were achieved, the people of that province would agitate for a prompt union with Bulgaria. In other words, he wished Bulgaria to become a model progressive state in the Balkans. Since his point of view prevailed, Giers instructed Dondukov-Korsakov to inform the Bulgarian constitutional assembly, which was in the process of being elected, that the constitution submitted by Russia was only a proposal, and that the delegates were to have "complete freedom" to express their own views and reach their own decisions. Consequently, during the debates the Russian government did not exercise any overt pressure on the members of the assembly.

In February, 1879, the constitutional assembly was convened in Turnovo. It was composed of 231 representatives, 89 of whom were elected on the basis of one delegate for every 10,000 males. The others were chosen from the church hierarchy and from city and town officials. It quickly became apparent that the assembly was divided into two opposing groups, which became the Conservative and Liberal parties. The Conservatives tended to be more prosperous and better educated. Among their members were Dimitur P. Grekov, Todor Ikonomov, Gregory D. Nachevich, and Constantine Stoilov. Prior to 1878 they had supported an evolutionary policy toward the Porte and had resisted revolutionary programs. So far as the constitution was concerned they believed that the executive branch should be dominant in the new state. Since they did not think that the electorate had sufficient political maturity, they wanted a strong, paternal ruler who would guide and educate his subjects. Further, they favored a bicameral legislature and they did not support a free press. In foreign policy they were pro-Russian. Their views generally coincided with those of the Russian foreign ministry.

The standpoint of the Liberals, in contrast, was nearer that of the Russian minister of war. Most of the members of this party, some of whom were Petko Karavelov, Petko R. Slaveikov, Stefan Stambolov, and Dragan Tsankov, came from the urban areas and had previously been more involved in revolutionary movements. Because many of them had been educated abroad or exposed to western ideas, they were more democratic and thus were uncompromising champions of a strong parliament and civil liberties. Among them were many eloquent orators. In the assembly their views finally prevailed. The Turnovo constitution of 1879 was thus an extremely liberal document. In it the principal power in the government lay in the legislative branch.

The constitution provided in fact for two assemblies—the National Assembly, the traditional legislative body, and the Grand National Assembly, whose purpose was to handle extraordinary matters such as the cession of territory, amendments to the constitution, and the election of a new ruler. The National Assembly had one representative for each ten thousand inhabitants based upon universal manhood suffrage. This body was given the right to introduce legislation and to control the budget. Although the prince was authorized to issue ordinances when the assembly was not meeting, he was obliged to submit them for ratification at the next session. He could not, in addition, impose new taxes; that task was the sole prerogative of the assembly. Its members could freely express their views in the sessions, and they were to be immune from prosecution. The assembly could not convene itself, but the prince was obliged to call it into session at least once every year for two months beginning on October 15.

Despite these strong legislative powers, the prince had much authority. He convened and closed the National Assembly, which he could also prorogue but only for two months. He appointed the cabinet ministers and all state officials. The ministers were responsible jointly to him and to the assembly, although the constitution was not precise on what would happen should a conflict arise on this question. All laws required the signature of the prince and the countersignature of the responsible minister. The prince also had, of course, the traditional authority of a head of state. He was commander-in-chief of the army, and he conducted the foreign relations of the country.

For administrative purposes the country was divided into departments (*okruzi*), districts (*okolii*), and communes (*obshtini*). The departments were directed by a prefect appointed by the prince. The prefect was assisted by a departmental council elected for three years by universal suffrage. Its duties were to assess taxes, prepare budgets, and administer departmental property. The districts were subdivisions of the departments and were administered by subprefects, who were in charge of the police and responsible for public order. The smallest administrative unit was the commune. Since this division had played such a significant role in Bulgarian life under Ottoman rule, its existence and functions were protected by the constitution. It had an elected council, from which the mayor and two assistants were chosen. The mayor administered the town or village and served as the link with the higher offices of government. In other words, in contrast to the neighboring states Bulgaria retained a large degree of local self-government.

The constitution also provided for a judicial system, and civil liberties were guaranteed. As in the other Balkan countries, freedom of speech, press, assembly, and association were assured. Private property was protected, unlawful search prohibited, mail and telegrams were regarded as secret and inviolable, and the right of petition was guaranteed to all. As elsewhere, the application of these assurances was to leave much to be desired.

Once a liberal constitution had been adopted, the next problem was the selection of a prince. Here, as previously in Greece, the great powers named the candidate. At Berlin they had agreed that the prince could not be a member of any of the major ruling dynasties. After much consideration they chose Alexander of Battenberg, a prince of Hesse, a twenty-two-year-old German army lieutenant. Thus Bulgaria, like Greece and Romania, received a German prince. Alexander seemed at first an excellent choice from an international viewpoint. His aunt was the empress of Russia; hence he was a nephew of the tsar. Since it was assumed that Russia would have predominant influence in the new state, this relationship was important. It is interesting to note that neither the tsar nor his wife envied the young man. When his name first came up for consideration, Alexander II said that he would "never" wish such a difficult position for his nephew. Although the tsar eventually changed his mind, the tsarina remained firmly opposed to exposing her relative to the problems that he would face in Bulgaria.

Alexander accepted the position as prince because he had no prospects within the German army. Despite his excellent dynastic connections his military training and his aristocratic background gave him little preparation to govern a peasant state with a highly liberal constitution. Like Prince Charles of Romania, Alexander intended to rule his country. He had little sympathy with constitutional restrictions or the ideas of the predominant Liberal Party. The inevitable clash came when the prince made his first major decision. Instead of selecting a member of the majority Liberal Party to form his first government, or of creating a coalition ministry as some had urged, Alexander entrusted this task to T. S. Burmov, a Conservative. The prince wished to establish the fact immediately that he intended to rule the nation notwithstanding the constitution and the Liberal strength.

In order to defend itself and to prepare for future unification with Eastern Rumelia, the principality needed a disciplined and well-equipped army. For this Russian support was indispensable. Although Alexander was at liberty to choose his own minister of war, it was understood by all that he would act in consultation with his uncle, the tsar. A Russian general, P. D. Parensov, was thus appointed to this office. It was his task to train the Bulgarian army. Reflecting the views of his superior, Miliutin, Parensov soon quarreled with the prince and came to support the Liberals. Despite the general's political activities he could not be removed since he was a Russian officer appointed by the tsar.

To complicate the problem further, the Russian consul general in Sofia, A. P. Davydov, who received his instructions from the foreign ministry, threw his support behind the prince and the Conservatives. In other words, the two responsible Russian officials in Bulgaria were pursuing diametrically opposed policies. Understandably, the prince, the two political parties, and the Bulgarian citizenry, who followed developments closely through the partisan press, were confused.

The conflict between the prince and the Conservatives, on the one side, and the Liberals, on the other, intensified over the next two years. The prince's opponents were suspicious of his German advisers, and they were particularly alarmed when he sought to introduce German officers into the army. It appeared as if Alexander were trying to gain control of the army to prepare for a *coup d'état*. For his part, the prince became increasingly convinced that he would have to suspend the constitution or find ways of circumventing it. In order to prepare for a possible change in the document, Alexander and members of his family appealed to the tsar, but to no avail. Then, unexpectedly, Alexander II was assassinated in 1881 and succeeded by his reactionary son, Alexander III. Because of his cousin's conservative attitude Prince Alexander was now able to suspend the constitution with official Russian sanction.

Although the prince believed that he could govern the country effectively, he was soon faced with a serious problem. Alexander III was an autocrat who demanded respect and deference from all, including Prince Alexander. Moreover, he considered Bulgaria as little more than a Russian satellite or as a province of his own empire. In contrast, Prince Alexander believed that he could treat the tsar as a relative and his equal. A conflict between these two strong-willed rulers was inevitable.

Moreover, paralleling this strain in personal relations at the top, it was increasingly apparent that Russians and Bulgarians were not cooperating smoothly on the lower levels. The most serious conflict developed in the army between the junior officers and noncommissioned personnel of Bulgarian origin and their Russian superiors. All of the ranks in the Bulgarian army from captain up were reserved for Russians, and so capable, proud, and ambitious young Bulgarians soon realized that their careers were restricted. Similar clashes also developed in the administration of the country because of the increasingly overbearing attitude of some Russian officials.

As a result of this situation Russian-Bulgarian relations declined precipitously. By 1883 even the Liberals, who had strenuously fought the prince, had become convinced that they had merely exchanged Ottoman for Russian domination. Eager to prove that they were capable of governing themselves, the rival political parties rallied behind the prince to present a united front before the Russian officials. For his part, Alexander agreed to restore the Turnovo constitution. He was now the true head of the Bulgarian state; for the first time since 1879 there was a semblance of unity in the country. This victory, however, permanently estranged the tsar, who was determined to oust the prince. Moreover, it was clear that so long as he remained the Bulgarian ruler, Russia would oppose the unification of Bulgaria and Eastern Rumelia. By this time events had evolved in that province in such a way that the question of union might soon arise.

Whereas Russia had been entrusted with the organization of Bulgaria in 1878, Eastern Rumelia had been placed in the hands of an international commission of the great powers. This body completed its work on the Rumelian Organic Statute in April, 1879, the same month that Bulgaria adopted the Turnovo constitution. In contrast to the Bulgarian document, which was carefully drawn, the Organic Statute with its 495 articles was completely unworkable. The commission entrusted with its formulation had not functioned as a unit. Instead, each of the powers was given the task of preparing a certain section. Thus, the British drew up the electoral laws; the Italians drafted the financial sections; the Austrians were responsible for the legal system; the French introduced their own administrative system; and the Russians and French collaborated on the organization of the militia. Local customs and needs were largely ignored. In order to administer this province the powers approved the sultan's appointment of Aleko Pasha, a Christian, as governor-general. Associated with him were a German as director of finance, a Britain as chief of the gendarmes, and a French citizen in charge of the militia, whose officers were Russians or Russian-trained Bulgarians. The province also was given an assembly of fifty-six members, twenty of whom were nominated and thirty-six elected. Eastern Rumelia was hardly a model state. Its citizens could easily be attracted to Bulgaria with her constitutional regime, as Miliutin had hoped.

The two principal problems that now confronted Aleko Pasha concerned the fate of the lands formerly owned by Muslims, but which had been abandoned and then appropriated by the local population, and the continual agitation for union with Bulgaria. The first question was resolved essentially by frightening the former owners with threats of reprisals for actions during the war, so that they would not return to claim their lands. Those who did come back found that a tax of 10 percent had been assessed upon the estimated value of their property. They usually had to sell their possessions to pay this. These former Ottoman homes, lands, and estates were purchased principally by Rumelian peasants. The former land tenure system thus ended, and this province, like Bulgaria to the north, became basically a land of small proprietors.

The issue of unification was much more dangerous. The population overwhelmingly favored the measure and was ready to take steps to realize it. Moreover, at first Russian representatives in the country showed the same enthusiasm and encouraged the citizenry to work for this goal. Russian officials, with or without the approval of their government, fostered intrigues and secretly armed the population. Although the Treaty of Berlin limited the size of the militia, they organized and trained so-called gymnastic societies, which could easily be transformed into military units if necessary.

This initial cooperation between the Russians and the Rumelian population on the question of union was brought to an end over many of the same basic issues that we have seen in Bulgaria proper. Some Russians in Rumelia sought special favors and economic concessions; the young native officers in the militia resented their Russian superiors. In addition, many of the members of the Bulgarian Liberal Party, who were forced to leave Sofia after Alexander set aside the constitution with the tsar's endorsement, fanned this anti-Russian sentiment. By 1884, when the prince and the tsar had become lasting antagonists, Aleko Pasha, too, found himself the object of Alexander III's dislike. Whereas the tsar could not easily force Prince Alexander's abdication, he could have the governor-general removed. Aleko Pasha's appointment had been for five years. In 1884 Russia refused to agree to a second term. The powers then chose Gavril Efendi Krustevich, who was acceptable to Russia largely because the man appeared weak and thus could be easily controlled. His ardent national sympathies were unknown at the time.

By 1885 the unionist movement in Rumelia was active and strong. Local committees existed throughout the province. Finally, on the night of September 17–18, 1885, the Rumelian leaders, supported by the militia, proclaimed the overthrow of their government and union with

Bulgaria. Krustevich made no effort to resist his removal from office. The Rumelian revolutionary regime now called on Prince Alexander to assume the leadership of a united nation.

This appeal presented the prince with a difficult decision. He knew that union was strongly desired by his subjects, and that if it were achieved under his leadership his personal position in the country would be virtually unassailable. If he chose not to assume command, he would have to prepare to abdicate. At the same time the risks were high if he did accept. First, he had assured the Russian government in August that he would not be a party to any unification movement. To reverse himself a month later would make his relations with St. Petersburg even worse. Second, the unification could reopen the entire eastern question without any guarantee that the ultimate outcome would be beneficial to Bulgaria. Nevertheless, when told bluntly by one of his advisers that his choice was either to lead the country or to leave it, he chose the former course.

Although the union was not completely unexpected, it caused a major diplomatic crisis, since it violated the Treaty of Berlin and thus involved the great powers. The question of territorial compensation for Greece and Serbia came up at once. The strongest reaction, as could be expected, came from Russia. To express his total disapproval, the tsar withdrew all of the Russian officers from Bulgaria. The purpose was to convince the Bulgarians that without Russian support the union would be in jeopardy and that they should take steps to overthrow the prince. Whereas the tsar acted from personal anger, the foreign ministry looked at the problem from the aspects of national interest. It was concerned about the strain that this event might put on the Three Emperors' League. The Russian government also feared that Austria-Hungary might seize the opportunity to annex Bosnia-Hercegovina, and that Greece and Serbia might move into Macedonia. In order to prevent a major Balkan upheaval, Russia called for an ambassadorial conference where she proposed the restoration of the *status quo ante.* In this she was supported by her allies, Austria-Hungary and Germany. In contrast, Britain changed her policy of 1878 and now supported the union. Since the united Bulgaria was anti-Russian, the state was a bulwark against and not an outpost for Russian influence in the Balkans. The major problem for the powers was precisely the one that had arisen during various stages of the Romanian national movement, namely how to reverse the action. Only the Ottoman government wished to use force to dissolve the union; not even Russia would endorse this step.

The Bulgarian position was considerably eased by an ill-considered action of King Milan of Serbia. This ruler recognized that the union would upset the political balance among the Balkan states and give Bulgaria a decided advantage in the ensuing struggle for Macedonia. In order to

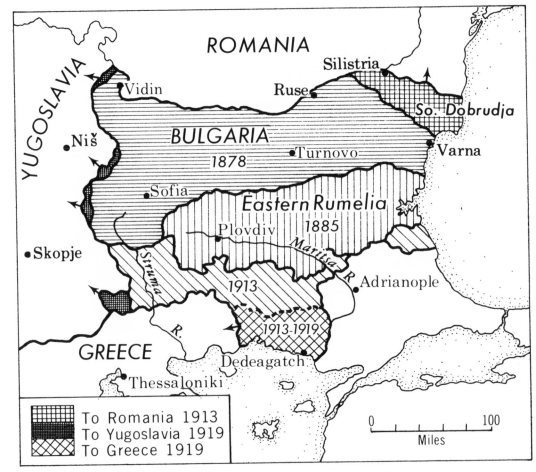

Map 7. The Expansion of Bulgaria, 1878–1919

protect the Serbian interests, he declared war on his neighbor. He did not, however, make his aims clear to his subjects, who showed little enthusiasm for the conflict. Although most observers expected Serbia to triumph, Prince Alexander and his army, led by young officers who admirably filled the posts vacated by the Russians, soundly defeated the Serbian forces. After this decisive victory, even the Russian government was forced to agree to the union. In 1886 the great powers accepted the prince of Bulgaria as governor-general of Eastern Rumelia for five years. Alexander was not named specifically. Despite this form, the powers understood that the union would be permanent.

Prince Alexander had thus emerged triumphant. Seven years after the Treaty of Berlin was signed, two of the three lands claimed by Bulgaria were united. The prince was praised for his skillful diplomacy and honored for his military victory over Serbia. This good fortune was not without its price. Alexander III had been deeply humiliated. Convinced that the prince was the sole obstacle to amicable Russo-Bulgarian relations, the tsar approved the overthrow of his rival. The Russian representatives in Sofia now actively plotted to oust the prince. These actions were done with the knowledge of the tsar, his foreign minister, and his minister of war. Support was found among some disgruntled army officers, who believed that they had not been properly rewarded for their role in the Serbo-Bulgarian War, and among some strongly pro-Russian politicians. These Russian partisans were also convinced that Macedonia could only be gained with Russian assistance. They were ready to sacrifice the prince for the achievement of the San Stefano Bulgaria. After careful planning the conspirators carried out a *coup d'état* in August, 1886. Prince Alexander was forced to abdicate and was escorted out of the country.

Metropolitan Kliment, a loyal supporter of Russia, then formed a new government, but the prince's popularity and political strength were soon proved. Led by Stefan Stambolov, a prominent participant in the uprising of 1876 and a former minister, a popularly supported counter-revolution forced the resignation of the Kliment government after a few days. Within ten days of the coup the prince was back on Bulgarian soil. In the crowd that came to greet him was a Russian vice-consul. Alexander took this as a sign that the tsar had forgiven him. Seeking the tsar's blessing, he sent a telegram to his cousin, without consulting Stambolov. In it he expressed his devotion and promised: "As Russia gave me my crown, I am prepared to give it back into the hands of its Sovereign." [1] The tsar's reply was brutal and frank. He did not approve the prince's

---

1. Egon Caesar Conte Corti, *Alexander von Battenberg,* tr. by E. M. Hodgson (London: Cassell, 1954), p. 239.

return and stated: "Your Highness will appreciate what you have to do."[2] With no choice left, Prince Alexander abdicated for the second time.

Although Bulgaria was now left without a prince, she did have a strong political leader in Stefan Stambolov. Two problems confronted the government: the intense pressure from St. Petersburg had to be resisted, and a new ruler had to be chosen. The Bulgarian constitution called for the election of a Grand National Assembly to approve the choice of a prince. Claiming that the country was in turmoil and that an orderly election was not possible, Russia insisted that the action be postponed. In order to secure his desires the tsar sent a special emissary, General N. V. Kaulbars, to argue the Russian case. When Stambolov, supported by the overwhelming majority of the leading Bulgarians, refused to heed his advice, Kaulbars toured the country, openly threatening, cajoling, and haranguing the Bulgars in a flagrant display of interference in Bulgarian affairs. Two Russian warships were also dispatched to the Black Sea port of Varna. Still Stambolov would not yield. The election was held, and the assembly prepared to decide on a new ruler. The Russian government seized upon an insignificant incident to sever diplomatic relations. Only eight years had passed since Russia had gone to war for the Balkan Slavs and had supported the formation of the Great Bulgaria of San Stefano.

The selection of a new prince was not easy because the great powers still had to approve the choice. The Russian government was determined to veto any nomination. Thus, the first candidates named by the assembly refused the position. However, in August, 1887, another German prince, Ferdinand of Coburg, accepted even though he did not have the approval of the powers. As a result, his first years as prince were precarious. In internal politics he was dependent on Stambolov who had backed his candidacy. Nevertheless, his government did have the support of the country. The Bulgarians resented plots and intrigues which the Russian partisans continued to organize. A climax was reached in 1891 when assassins killed the minister of finance; Stambolov had been their real target. In order to counter these acts and maintain his popularity with the electorate, Stambolov gained the Porte's approval for new Bulgarian bishoprics in Macedonia. In 1893 he also had the constitution amended to permit Ferdinand to marry a Catholic princess, whose children would not have to be christened in the Orthodox faith. This action was a direct challenge to the defender of Orthodoxy, Russia, and it marked the zenith of Stambolov's career. Only a year later, in 1894, he was to be dismissed from office.

Prince Ferdinand was a proud, ambitious, and shrewd ruler. He

2. *Ibid.,* p. 240.

dreamed of leading Bulgaria to the position of the predominant power in the Balkans. Because of his difficult situation in the first period of his rule, he let Stambolov carry the burden of responsibility for the actions of the government. In time, nevertheless, he came to realize the dangers of his own position and the necessity of a reconciliation with Russia. After seven years in Sofia he still had not been recognized officially by any great power as the legitimate prince of Bulgaria. Moreover, without Russian support expansion into Macedonia would be impossible. Stambolov now seemed the major obstruction to a reconciliation. Thus, in 1894, when Stambolov threatened to resign over a minor issue, a tactic he frequently used to intimidate the prince, Ferdinand accepted the resignation. In October, 1894, Alexander III died and was succeeded by Nicholas II. The path was now open for a renewal of Russo-Bulgarian relations.

First, however, Ferdinand had to lay the groundwork. Of primary importance was the conversion of Boris, the prince's infant son, from Catholicism to Orthodoxy. This action reversed one of Stambolov's greatest successes. In addition, a delegation led by the pro-Russian Metropolitan Kliment went to St. Petersburg where it placed a wreath on the grave of Alexander III. Nicholas II then received the group. Some pro-Russian politicians who had been imprisoned were also released. Finally, in 1896 relations were formally re-established. This action paved the way for the recognition of the prince by the other powers, who approved his nomination as ruler not only of Bulgaria, but also of Eastern Rumelia. The union of 1885 was thus formally accepted.

Once recognized by Russia and the powers, the prince was free to concentrate on the internal development of the state and, even more important, on the question of national expansion. After 1878 the overriding issue in Bulgarian political life was the fate of Macedonia. This was the one issue that could rally the nation and unite the political parties. The realization of the boundaries set at San Stefano had now become the national program of Bulgaria. The struggle to attain this goal was to shape much of the future history of the country.

CHAPTER 12

The Balkan States: Internal Political Developments to 1914

With the recognition of the independence of Serbia, Romania, and Montenegro and the establishment of an autonomous Bulgaria, the basis for the modern Balkan state system had been laid. Independent Greece, of course, had come into existence in 1830. With the exception of Albania, which did not make its appearance until 1913, the major nationalities had established political centers outside of the direct control of Constantinople. Despite the fact that these states often found themselves in conflict, they shared many attributes in their national development. Four—Romania, Serbia, Greece, and Bulgaria—were constitutional monarchies with centralized administrative systems. In each state the real power lay in the police and the army. Political struggles took the form not only of a conflict among political factions, but also between these groups and the monarch. Where the ruler could rely on the armed forces, he kept his throne. Where he lost this support, as Cuza did in 1866 and Othon in 1843 and 1862, his position was either in grave danger or he was forced to abdicate. This pattern was to continue in the future.

In regard to social and economic development each state looked to the West, despite the strong reliance placed at times on Russia as the best source of military assistance against the Ottoman Empire. Western political forms were adopted, and the aim of each state was to attain the general standards of the western European countries. Backward peasant societies sought to accomplish quickly what it had taken their models centuries to achieve.

Despite the obvious desire for political and economic improvement, the prime energies of the new governments were to be channeled in another direction. Having secured national independence or autonomy, each state turned toward national expansion, to gain either ethnic or historic boundaries. No government was content with the *status quo*. After 1878 the Ottoman government still held Thrace, Macedonia, and Albania; Balkan nationals predominated in important areas under Habsburg control such as Transylvania, Dalmatia, and Croatia. The emphasis on the irredenta explains also the importance of the military in Balkan societies. It was recognized that strong armies would be necessary to accomplish national goals and that they would be used not only against the Ottoman and Habsburg empires, but also probably against neighboring Balkan states. Each nation kept a close watch on the military growth of the others.

In this chapter the internal development of each of the Balkan states during the period before the First World War, together with those foreign policy issues that involved only limited areas, will be discusssed. The great international issues of the expulsion of the Ottoman Empire from Europe and the fate of the Romanian and South Slav inhabitants of the Habsburg Empire will be described in subsequent sections.

GREECE

In 1864, it will be remembered, Greece had acquired a new constitution and a Danish dynasty. Thereafter the emphasis remained on national expansion, the one great issue that could rally the nation. Despite constant crises little had been achieved in the subsequent decade. Attention was directed northward toward Macedonia and southward to the island of Crete. In 1881, as a result of the decision reached at the Congress of Berlin, Thessaly and a part of Epirus had been acquired, but in a sense the situation had worsened. The Greek government regarded the Treaty of San Stefano as the worst possible solution of the Macedonian problem. The very establishment of an autonomous Bulgaria, as a future rallying point for Macedonian Slavs, had not been to the Greek interest. The Serbian expansion to the south at this time was also dangerous. In addition, Crete remained under Ottoman control. Since no other power rivaled Greek claims here, however, major attention was still focused on Macedonia. In no case did the Greek government wish to be faced with a situation in which it would be forced to surrender Macedonian lands in return for the possession of the island.

One of the major obstacles to Greek advancement was the nation's poverty, which precluded the acquisition of the military power necessary for an ambitious program of national expansion. In this sense the state was probably in a worse position than her Balkan rivals. A peasant country with less than half of her lands suitable for farming, Greece simply did not have the basis for the strong foreign policy desired by most of her inhabitants. As in the rest of the Balkans agricultural methods remained extremely primitive. The soil could not even supply the grains needed to satisfy national demand. The original kingdom was a land of small units and subsistence farming. With the acquisition of Thessaly the state gained a potentially rich agricultural region, which had previously been predominantly an area of great estates with Muslim landowners. These lands were not divided among the peasants, but fell into the hands of Greek large landowners. As in Romania, the estates were badly managed and run mainly on a sharecropping basis where the peasant tilled the soil and surrendered a third to a half of the produce. There was no incentive for making improvements. Large sections remained in pasture.

In order to pay for imports of wheat and other products, Greece relied at first principally on the export of a single crop, currants. The dangers of dependency on one item in the world market were shown by the fate of this export. Between 1861, with a crop of 42,000 tons, and 1878, when the figure was 100,700 tons, currant exports increased rapidly. In 1878 when French vineyards were hit by phylloxera, French winemakers turned to Greece until their own vines recovered. The French government then moved to protect its agricultural products. In 1892 the tariff adopted by France caused a disastrous collapse of the Greek exports. Thereafter, attempts were made to find a substitute crop. Tobacco gradually assumed an increasingly important position and became the chief item after the First World War.

Economic conditions remained backward throughout this period. In 1870 the only railroad was the nine kilometers of track from Athens to Piraeus. No significant moves toward industrialization were made; in 1875 there were only eighty-nine factories. In addition, the unique problem of the Greek debt remained. As we have seen, the Greek revolution and the first independent governments had been financed by large foreign loans. Succeeding Greek regimes also resorted to borrowing abroad. The bad financial conditions were somewhat eased by the massive emigration which took place at this time. Approximately a half million Greeks left for the United States. From 1905 to the First World War the emigrants sent enough money to Greece to cancel out the large import surpluses that would otherwise have strained the balance of payments.

Greek internal politics reflected accurately the major problems. Expansion remained the national passion, but the real need of the state was internal reform and economic development. The tug between these two directions was shown in the political struggles of the last two decades of the century and in the rivalry between two men, Charilaos Trikoupes and Theodore Deliyannes. As in other Balkan countries, political parties remained groups organized around individuals rather than formal organizations in the Western sense. In 1875 King George agreed that governments would be formed by the party or the individual who had the backing of the majority in parliament. With this measure a kind of two-party system arose. In 1875 Trikoupes organized the first of his seven governments. He was initially opposed by Koumoundouros and his followers, and then, after 1885, by Deliyannes' party.

The Trikoupes party based its reform program on the obvious need to improve the Greek internal conditions. Its main strength came from the professional and commercial classes. During its two long periods of control, from March 1882, to April, 1885, and from May, 1886, to November, 1890, the party did introduce a great deal of legislation. Although Trikoupes did not hesitate to appoint his own adherents to public offices, he did try to improve the civil service and the administrative system of the country. Judges were given tenure, the police reformed. A program of public works was also inaugurated to expand road, railroad, and harbor facilities. In addition, attempts were made to strengthen the armed forces. A French military mission came to advise the army from 1884 to 1887.

Trikoupes encountered considerable opposition. His ambitious plans were costly and involved heavy borrowing. Between 1879 and 1890 Greece received loans totaling 630 million gold francs. Taxes doubled in the two decades after 1875. The Trikoupes government was also vulnerable on questions of foreign policy. This ministry tended to work with Britain and to follow the British recommendations that internal improvements should precede foreign expansion.

Making use of the opposition to the tax measures and foreign policy issues, Deliyannes formed governments in 1885, 1890, and 1895. During his administration many of the reforms were repealed. The Deliyannes program put the chief emphasis on the pursuit of a glorious national policy. The alternation of the two opposing groups in power and the declining economic position of the country was disastrous for state policy. The financial problem became increasingly serious. By 1892 the service on the debt took a third of the budget. In the next year Greece was bankrupt. Trikoupes retired from politics in 1895 after the loss of an election; he died the following year. George Theotokes took over the leadership of his party.

During this period, despite Deliyannes' emphasis on foreign policy issues, this field brought only disappointment. In November, 1885, when Serbia went to war with Bulgaria, Deliyannes was in power. Like the Serbs, the Greeks felt entitled to compensation for the Bulgarian absorption of Eastern Rumelia; they desired the rest of Epirus. In September the army was mobilized. The great powers reacted immediately with an ultimatum, supported by all but France, demanding that Greece demobilize. When the Greek government refused, a blockade was established in May. With the failure of his rival's policies, Trikoupes then returned to power and his regime gave in. The cost of mobilization added to the overburdened state finance.

The chief national goals remained, however, not Epirus, but Macedonia, and to a lesser extent Crete. The Cretan problem played a large part in domestic politics until 1913, when the island became a part of the Greek kingdom. After the revolution of the 1820s Crete remained under Egyptian control until 1840 when the island was returned to the Ottoman Empire. Thereafter, the area became the scene of repeated insurrections. Here the problem was social as well as national and resembled in many respects the situation in Bosnia. About a half of the inhabitants were Greeks who had become Muslims after the Ottoman conquest. They held the best lands and the large estates. The uprisings were against the political and economic dominance of these people. Revolts in 1841 and in 1858 resulted in the introduction of some measures of self-government. From 1866 to 1868 another insurrection took place.

These events put great pressure on George I; his subjects expected him to react forcefully on national issues. In 1867 he had married the Grand Duchess Olga; he could thus hope for some Russian support. In 1868 he named his new born son Constantine, thus referring to the Byzantine emphasis of the Great Idea. Like his predecessor Othon, the king could not, however, act against the combined wishes of the majority of the great powers. Unilateral intervention in Cretan affairs was out of the question regardless of domestic pressures. Although the revolt of the 1860s resulted in the application of the Organic Statute of 1868, the reform measures did not calm the situation. Another insurrection in the period 1875–78 was overshadowed by the more dramatic events on the peninsula. In October, 1878, the Porte accepted the Halepa Pact, an agreement calling for the election of an assembly under rules that guaranteed it would be controlled by the Christians. The sultan also named a Christian as governor and agreed to introduce other reforms. Continued tension resulted in the breaking of this accord. In the 1890s Muslim governors were appointed, and the assemblies did not meet.

The Cretan issue remained, of course, deeply embedded in Greek domestic politics. In November, 1894, the Ethnike Hetairia, or National Society, was formed. Its purpose was to further the Greek cause; three-quarters of the army officers belonged to it. Although primarily interested in Macedonia, this group was to play a major part in Cretan affairs. Its offices became a center for despatching volunteers and arms to the island, and it operated beyond the control of the government.

In 1896, after more disturbances, the Porte agreed to restore the Halepa Pact and to grant measures leading to autonomy. At the same time the Greek government found itself under pressure, on the one hand, from the great powers who wished to stop the flow of men and weapons to the island, and, on the other, from the Greek nationalists who wanted open intervention. In February, 1897, the revolutionary forces in Crete declared their union with Greece. At once a force of fifteen hundred Greeks arrived on the island. In March the Greek government, with Deliyannes at the head, ordered mobilization. In April Greek forces crossed into Turkish territory. The Greek army was now under the command of Prince Constantine, while the navy was under Prince George.

The month-long war showed the Greeks' lack of preparation. The Ottoman forces quickly proved themselves to be immensely superior. Moreover, Greece received no help from her neighbors. Under pressure from the powers, Russia and Austria-Hungary in particular, Serbia and Bulgaria remained neutral. With the Ottoman army driving deep into Thessaly, the powers intervened to secure peace. An armistice was signed in May and a peace treaty, in December. Despite the fact that Greece had lost the war, the country suffered relatively little. Some minor points on the border were surrendered, and an indemnity of a hundred million francs was levied. In the Cretan question, however, the Greeks made notable advances. Pressed by the great powers, the Porte now agreed to an autonomous regime and, most significant, to the appointment of Prince George, the second son of the king, to the post of High Commissioner for Crete.

Despite the advances thus made the war had been a great humiliation for the nation. The dynasty again became the scapegoat. Both the king and Prince Constantine were strongly attacked; the prince was blamed for the poor showing of the army. Moreover, the financial burden of the war and the necessity of paying an indemnity led to the imposition of foreign financial control on the state. An International Commission of Control was now established in Athens with the right to collect certain taxes. Although this supervision stung Greek pride and severely limited the fiscal sovereignty of the nation, the Greek financial situation improved markedly in the next years and the debt was reduced.

Greece, however, entered the new century in an atmosphere of general disappointment and discontent. The need to reform the administration and to improve the armed forces was recognized, but the major problem remained that the country simply did not have the financial basis for either action. Nor was the existing political system favorable to a national resurgence. Between April, 1897, and December, 1905, there were ten changes in the government. Thereafter a ministry was formed by Theotokes, who remained at the head of the former Trikoupes party, which lasted until July, 1909. In March, 1905, Deliyannes was assassinated. His party then divided into two sections, which were under Kyriakoules Mavromichales and Demetrios Ralles. A fourth party was led by

Alexander Zaimes. Greek politics remained much as before. With each change in regime the victorious party put its own followers in the state posts. Strong personal rivalries, bribery, patronage, and a lack of discipline continued to characterize political life. The assembly was paralyzed by obstructionist tactics and filibustering.

Nor were events proceeding smoothly in Crete. Here Prince George soon clashed with Cretan politicians, including Eleutherios Venizelos, soon to become the predominant political figure in Greece. The Cretans continued to seek *enosis,* that is, union with Greece. As before, the Greek government did not oppose this action, but it feared great power interference and it did not wish to be in a position where it would be forced to trade full control of Crete for gains by the Slavic states in Macedonia. In the spring of 1905 the Cretan assembly once more declared the union of the island with Greece; again the great powers intervened. In 1906 Prince George returned to Athens, and his position was taken by Alexander Zaimes.

The defeat by the Ottomans made a complete reform of the Greek army essential. In 1900 the army had over twenty-five thousand men, but neither it nor the navy was in a satisfactory condition. In April, 1900, Constantine was named commander in chief with the authority to reorganize the armed forces. In 1904 a reform program was instituted which set the number of men at twenty-five thousand, but provided for expansion to sixty thousand in time of war. Improvements were also made in the navy. The grave financial conditions blocked further measures; the state could not afford to re-equip these forces. The Greek army was thus weaker than that of either Serbia or Bulgaria. The problem of the prince in command was also to continue to be a political issue.

None of the actions taken in the first years of the new century arrested the increase of discontent with the progress of the state and the slow development of national life. The general desire for change was reflected in the program of the "Japan" party, led by Ion Dragoumes, which took as a model the swift changes occurring within the Oriental nation. This group achieved little and soon disbanded. It is against this background of criticism and uneasiness that the events of 1909 can best be understood.

In 1908 another major Balkan crisis was precipitated by the Young Turk revolt in the Ottoman Empire, an action which was followed by a Bulgarian declaration of independence and the annexation of Bosnia-Hercegovina by the Habsburg Empire. These events, which will be discussed in detail in the next chapter, had repercussions throughout the Ottoman lands. In October, 1908, the Cretans again proclaimed union with Greece, but the Greek government feared to move. A similar Cretan declaration of unity in July, 1909, brought the same response from Athens and produced another intervention by the great powers.

This combination of domestic inaction and continual failures in foreign policy led to another military coup. An organization called the Military League was now formed by patriotic and nationalistic younger officers. On August 28, 1909, Col. N. K. Zorbas led three thousand officers and men of the Athens garrison in a demonstration against the government. As in 1843 and 1862, a military revolt now caused major changes in Greek political life. The ministry of Ralles, which was then in power, resigned and was replaced by a government headed by Kyria- koules Mavromichales, who led a faction with relations with the Military League.

Once in power the league wished to enact a reform program. Its members also opposed the presence of the princes in the army leader- ship. Although in control of the state, the army officers were without po- litical experience and no real political leaders emerged from their ranks. Fully aware of their problem, they now turned to Venizelos. The Cretan statesman came to Athens in January, 1910, as a political adviser to the league. He supported the summoning of a national assembly to change the constitution. Although he worked for the league, he opposed a mili- tary dictatorship. When the king accepted the proposal for the assembly, it was also agreed that the league would dissolve.

In October, 1910, Venizelos formed his first government. From this date until the summer of 1912, he dominated Greek politics. Since he in- sisted that the assembly not be constituent, Venezelos's reforms did not fundamentally alter the constitution of 1864. The king remained in a strong position. The fifty-three amendments aimed at improving the ex- isting structure of government. For instance, civil servants were now to have more secure tenure, a ministry of agriculture was established, ele- mentary education was made compulsory, and the number necessary for a quorum in the assembly was reduced from a half to a third to prevent obstructionist tactics. In regular legislation some social measures were introduced, such as factory laws, a minimum wage for women and chil- dren, and the provision for the distribution of lands from some of the large estates in Thessaly. Venizelos was also deeply interested in military and naval reform; he kept these ministries for himself. The general fi- nancial situation now improved. The popularity of the program was reflected in the elections of March, 1912, when the Venizelos supporters received 150 of the 181 seats in the regular assembly.

The Venizelos measures were in no sense revolutionary. The system was maintained with relatively few changes, and the dynasty was pre- served at a time when increasing numbers of Greeks were coming to at- tack it. Moreover, Venizelos' activities introduced certain new features into Greek political life. His party was organized on mass lines; it had a central leadership and it maintained party discipline. Many of the old abuses remained. The state administrative apparatus was extended in these years, and the posts were given to Venizelos' adherents. Neverthe-less, this government did provide direction and did help prepare the country for the long war; it marked a definite step forward.

ROMANIA

As in the case of Greece, the settlement of 1878 left much dissatis-faction in Romania. Even though part of Dobrudja and the Danube delta were acquired and the state became independent, the three dis-tricts of southern Bessarabia were lost and the settlement of the new boundaries caused further discontent. In Dobrudja the Romanian gov-ernment had wished to acquire Silistria. In this, as in other matters, the Russians gave strong support to the Bulgarian claims. In June, 1880, the disputed lands were awarded to Bulgaria.

Moreover, Romanian independence was not granted without qualifi-cation. Article 44 of the Treaty of Berlin imposed the condition that the state not allow "difference in creed and confessions" to exclude anyone from the "enjoyment of civil and political rights, admission to public employments, functions, and honors, or the exercise of the various pro-fessions and industries in any locality whatsoever." Although this clause referred also to Muslims, its chief effect was on the status of the Jews. This question had become a major national issue by the late 1870s.

After the middle of the nineteenth century, as conditions for Jews worsened in the Russian lands, an increasing number entered the Danu-bian Principalities. In 1859 approximately 118,000 lived in Moldavia and 9,200 in Wallachia. This number rose sharply thereafter, until by 1899 there were 210,000 in Moldavia and 68,000 in Wallachia. The Jews thus formed a group of approximately a quarter of a million out of a total population of 6 million. In 1899 the total urban population was about 1,131,000, of which 215,000, or 19 percent, were Jewish.

The urban concentration of the Jews resulted not so much from choice as from economic necessity. Article 7 of the Constitution of 1866 stated that naturalization would only be given to "foreigners belonging to the Christian faith." Thus, Jews were unable to become Romanian citi-zens. Not only were they deprived of civil rights, but, equally important, they could not purchase or own land. Limited in their choice of occupa-tions, the Jewish population worked where they could; often their em-ployment increased the opportunities for friction with the Romanians. In the cities they were usually small traders and merchants, occupations that native Romanians had traditionally regarded as inferior and had left to foreigners. In the countryside they tended to run inns or act as moneylenders or stewards on the estates of absentee landlords, positions that inevitably led to trouble with the Romanian peasants. Although many Jews were indeed wealthy, the great majority lived in wretched conditions in the larger cities.

The Jewish situation had caused problems in international relations for Romania before the Treaty of Berlin. It had been a major issue in commercial negotiations with countries such as Britain, and it had complicated relations with Germany in the affair of the railroads. The Romanian government had also been the target of attack by European Jewish organizations such as the influential Alliance Israélite. Although accustomed to foreign protests, the Romanian leaders resented Article 44, which they regarded as interference in their internal affairs, in particular since Russia, one of the states requiring acceptance of the clause, did not observe similar rules in relation to its own Jewish population.

Since there was no question, however, that Romanian independence would not be recognized without a change in the regulations, the Romanian assembly did pass some laws in October, 1879. Jews could now become naturalized citizens, but a special act would be required for each case. The provision that only Romanian citizens could own land remained in effect. The measures, which were introduced with reluctance and only after strong German pressure, did not really fulfill the spirit of the Berlin treaty. Nevertheless, the European powers did, after 1880, recognize Romanian independence. The Jewish issue was to remain a sore question in Romanian internal politics. Neither the Romanians nor the Jews desired assimilation, and the religious and cultural split caused repeated conflicts.

The achievement of independence was a personal triumph for Prince Charles. He had long disliked being a Turkish vassal. In March, 1881, with the assent of the assembly he was crowned king of Romania and his country became a kingdom. He then took steps to consolidate the Hohenzollern dynasty. Since it was now apparent that there would be no direct heir, in November, 1880, he named his nephew, Prince Ferdinand of Hohenzollern, as his successor. The prince then came to Romania to become acquainted with the state. In 1893 he married Princess Marie of Edinburgh, a granddaughter of both Queen Victoria and Tsar Alexander II, thus contracting a highly advantageous dynastic alliance.

During most of the 1880s the Liberal Party remained in power. Ion Brătianu held office to April, 1881, when he was temporarily replaced by Dumitru Brătianu. In complete control of the political organization, Brătianu ran the administration along French lines and kept his hold on the country through the prefects and the police. In general, the Liberals continued to represent the city population, the professions, and the bureaucrats as well as the small landowners. The Conservatives remained more the party of the large landowners, although some were in the opposition ranks. During this period the party divided. Catargiu was still the titular head, but a group known as the Junimists, after the literary society Junimea (Youth), split away. Its most prominent members were Peter Carp, Titu Maiorescu, Theodore Rosetti, and Alexander Marghiloman. Educated in Germany rather than France, this group tended to look toward the Central European powers. They also supported a program of moderate peasant reform.

In complete control of the legislature, the Liberal leadership now introduced a change in the electoral law to strengthen further their position. Elections were held for a new constituent assembly. As the government party the Liberals were able to win 134 seats as against 12 for their Conservative opponents, who then boycotted the meetings. The franchise was changed in 1884. The country now had an elaborate electoral system, based on colleges, for the selection of both houses. Two colleges were established for the senate and three for the assembly. The franchise was given to all male citizens paying taxes. The first college was composed of those with landed property bringing an income of 1200 francs; these numbered 15,973 in 1905. The second consisted of those who had completed a primary course of education and those who lived in cities and paid direct taxes of at least 20 francs. This group numbered 37,742. The third college included the rest of the population. The first two voted directly. In contrast, the third voted indirectly, with fifty electors choosing one delegate who would then vote directly. The first college represented 1.5 percent of the voters and chose 41 percent of the 183 delegates; the second college represented 3.5 percent and selected 38 percent; the third, comprising the vast majority of the voting population, elected a mere 21 percent. The franchise for the Senate was even more restrictive. Here the members were chosen by two colleges, one consisting of 10,659 electors and one of 13,912. In June, 1887, a new law on the election of communal councils provided also for a two-college system.

In practice this political organization put the real power in the hands of Charles, who proved to be a capable and clever politician. Since the ministry in office could control the elections through patronage and the police, the king could nominate the government he wished and then dissolve the assembly and be assured of gaining a majority in the ensuing elections. This system also allowed the monarch to play one party off against the other and to balance their influence. Although there were two parties, they represented, at least in their leadership, but a small minority of the population. Both the peasants and the city-workers were effectively excluded from this part of national life. Continual splits within the parties themselves occurred over either issues or personal rivalries. For all the governments until 1914 the major questions debated remained foreign policy, military affairs, and economic advancement.

Although foreign policy predominated in Romanian politics as it did elsewhere in the Balkans, the Romanian position was in some respects unique. The chief irredenta of Greece, Serbia, and Bulgaria were lands under the control of the weak, declining Ottoman Empire. In contrast

the major Romanian goals, Bessarabia and Transylvania, were possessions of the great powers, Russia and the Habsburg Empire respectively.
At the end of the nineteenth century there was no sign that either of
these states was near dissolution; only a major European catastrophe,
which few could envision, could create a situation that would allow the
annexation of these provinces. Thus, of necessity Romanian policy had
to be directed to less important issues, such as the claims against Bulgaria
in Dobrudja and the position of the Vlachs in Macedonia.

The chief impression left with the Romanian leadership from the
crisis of the 1870s had been a feeling of being endangered by Russia.
Participation in the Russo-Turkish War had not only resulted in the loss
of the three districts of southern Bessarabia, but also in fears that the
former protectorate would be re-established. Russian patronage of
Bulgaria was also intensely disliked. This attitude should have led to
close relations with Vienna, but there were obstacles here too. After the
Ausgleich the situation of the Romanians in Transylvania deteriorated
and the whole issue of the position of the nationalities in the Habsburg
Empire began to draw increasing attention. The Romanian government,
in addition, had an interest in limiting the extension of Habsburg control over Danubian river traffic and in avoiding the establishment of an
unfavorable economic relationship. Little could be done on the Danube
question. In 1883 the Dual Monarchy was able to gain its objectives here
and to assure its own predominance over the main course of the river.

Despite the many points of friction with Austria-Hungary, the Romanian government was nevertheless forced by circumstances to enter
into a close political alliance with that state. After the unnerving experiences of the previous years it was felt that Romania needed a foreign alliance to protect herself against Russia. She would have preferred a close
alignment with Germany, but Bismarck insisted that any German-
Romanian relationship be established through Vienna. Therefore, in
October, 1883, Romania and the Habsburg Empire signed a secret defensive treaty directed primarily against Russia. Germany adhered to it
immediately, and Italy did so in 1888. Romania thus became associated
with the Triple Alliance, although indirectly. The terms of the agreement obligated the monarchy to aid Romania against any state; Romania
would have to give assistance only in case of a Russian or Serbian attack
on Austria-Hungary. The alliance, which was renewed periodically and
was in effect in 1914, was kept absolutely secret. It was not submitted to
the assembly, and Charles did not inform all of his ministers of its existence.

Even with this improvement in the political relationship between the
countries, economic ties became strained. The commercial agreement of
1875, described previously, had been disadvantageous to Romania. The
government had originally pressed for its conclusion primarily for politi-

cal rather than for economic reasons. Habsburg products were granted an almost free entrance into Romania, while Romanian agricultural imports into the empire were burdened with a tariff designed to protect Hungarian interests. In practice, Romania had been deluged with Habsburg goods, which hindered the development of or ruined native small industry. As a result, in June, 1885, the Romanian government denounced the commercial convention. This act meant that the protective tariffs of the law of 1874 would apply to Habsburg imports. In May, 1886, a new, protectionist tariff law was adopted. In reply, Austria-Hungary forbade the import of Romanian livestock and placed prohibitive tariffs on goods from Romania. The result was a customs war, which lasted from May, 1886, to December, 1893. In some respects this conflict resembled the later "Pig War" between Serbia and the monarchy. In both cases the Habsburg government used the quarantine, presumably for disease, as a weapon to limit imports of livestock.

The adoption of the protective tariff paralleled a simultaneous attempt by the Romanian government to encourage industry. The Liberals now favored both this type of legislation and subsidies to industry. Laws to this effect were passed in the 1880s, the most significant of which was that of May, 1887, designed to aid in the development of large industry. Advantages were given to those enterprises having at least twenty-five workers. At this time Romania led the Balkan nations in state encouragement of industry. The Romanian endeavors, however, were not truly successful from a national point of view. The new enterprises could not be based on native capital. Some landowners and merchants did invest, but the main support for Romanian industrial development came from abroad, chiefly from Germany and Austria-Hungary. Before the First World War the degree of industrialization remained low, although per capita production was more than double that of Bulgaria, Serbia, or Greece.

In addition, the condition of agriculture declined toward the end of the century as it did in other agrarian states. The competition of wheat from the American prairies, which began to flood the European markets in the 1880s, directly affected the Romanian estates. The tariff war with Austria-Hungary had a disastrous impact on livestock production. An adequate alternate market to the Dual Monarchy could not be readily found, despite the fact that more agricultural exports now went to Belgium and Britain. Although in the next years Romanian economic ties to Germany tightened, that country was not a satisfactory substitute either.

The long period of Liberal predominance came to an end in 1888. In March a Junimist government, headed by Theodore Rosetti with Peter Carp as foreign minister, was chosen. Conservative political control was preserved until 1895, although there were changes of officials reflecting the conflict of the factions within the party. During this period the government passed some reform measures, adopted the gold standard, and nationalized the railroads. A bridge over the Danube at Cernavoda was completed in 1895. Trade conventions were signed with the major European nations, including an agreement with Austria-Hungary in 1893 which ended the trade war. The exploitation of Romanian oil resources also commenced.

The 1890s witnessed the death of the old Liberal leadership, which had been so largely responsible for the establishment of the independent Romanian state. Ion Brătianu and Kogălniceanu both died in 1891. The head of the Liberal Party was now Dimitrie A. Sturdza, who formed a government in 1895. From this time until the outbreak of the First World War the two parties continued to alternate in office. A shift of regimes marked no major change in government policies. Political power was the preserve of but a small minority, and Charles remained in a pivotal controlling position between the rival parties. In the decade prior to 1914 the major problem in internal politics concerned the condition of the peasantry, whose relative position in Romanian society had continued to decline.

The wretched conditions on the land after the reforms of the 1860s have been described. Thereafter Romania remained a country of large estates and an impoverished peasantry. The chief problem from a social and political standpoint continued to lie in the unequal division of the land. The concentration of ownership in the hands of a few, on the one hand, and the continual subdivision of peasant holdings through equal inheritance, on the other, resulted in a situation where the country had no significant number of well-established, prosperous medium-sized peasant holdings. At the beginning of the twentieth century five thousand large estates held half the arable land, while 85 percent of the peasantry had no land or so little that outside employment had to be found.

Concentration of land ownership in large estates had certainly proved of benefit in some nations, notably in Britain and Prussia. There large-scale farming allowed the introduction of modern methods and scientific management, leading to a notable increase in production. This did not happen in Romania. After 1829, as has been shown, a great expansion did indeed take place, but it was due to the fact that more land was brought under cultivation and the raising of livestock curtailed. By 1914 Romania ranked as fourth in the world among cereal exporters and fifth as a wheat exporter. This position, however, had not been won through intelligent exploitation of the land.

The great landowners did not usually run their estates. They preferred instead to lease their property and to live in Bucharest or Paris. Their leaseholders in turn subdivided the land among peasant tenants on a sharecropping or rental basis. By 1900, 72 percent of the estates were handled in this manner. Quite understandably, the leaseholders were primarily interested in a quick profit rather than in the long-term improvement of the estates or the welfare of the peasants. As a group they soon acquired a bad reputation, a situation that contributed to the rise of anti-Semitism, although in fact only 27 percent of the large tenants were Jewish. The lands were thus actually worked by Romanian peasants who provided both labor and draft animals; large landholding did not result in an improvement of methods or the widespread introduction of machinery.

As the population increased during the century, the conditions of peasant life became increasingly difficult. Plots subdivided through inheritance were too small to support families; there was an urgent need of more land. Rent on property naturally rose sharply during this period. Because of the worsening situation peasant unrest became more apparent toward the end of the century. The political parties tried to alleviate the problem by passing measures concerning agricultural contracts and by selling some government lands. The principle of state intervention to protect the peasant was recognized, but little was done in practice.

These conditions finally led to a great peasant revolt in 1907, which began in Moldavia in March and spread throughout the country. It had strong anti-Semitic overtones, but it was also directed against the large tenants and the absentee landlords. The government, which contained few if any real representatives of the peasants, reacted strongly. The army, under the direction of General Alexander Averescu, put down the revolt with extreme violence; about eleven thousand were killed.

Only when the rebellion had been repressed was the need for reform recognized. New laws were passed on agricultural contracts and regulating the relations of the peasants and the landowners. The problem remained that of enforcement in a country where the administration was controlled by persons whose economic and social interests did not coincide with those of the peasantry. Nevertheless, by 1914 the peasant desire for land and the probable necessity of the breakup of the large estates had been recognized. In April, 1908, a law was passed establishing a rural bank to aid the peasants in buying land. Some attempt was also made to control the size of leased estates, but a real reform had to wait until after the war.

Although Romania was potentially the richest Balkan state, she suffered, as we have seen, from many of the same problems as the others. Moreover, the Romanian government, like its neighbors, had to support ever-increasing expenses connected with internal improvements, an expanding civil service, and, most important, the maintenance of a strong army. Like Greece, Romania resorted to foreign loans as the best solution to the financial stresses.

SERBIA

The disillusionment over the results of the events of 1875–78 was perhaps greater in Serbia than in any other Balkan country. Not only had territorial objectives—Bosnia in particular—been handed over to the Habsburg Empire, but Russia, Serbia's former champion, had put the entire weight of its diplomatic influence behind the Bulgarian claims. At the end of the war Jovan Ristić remained in power at the head of a Liberal government. The immediate problems he had to face were the bad financial situation resulting from the years of crisis, and the shape of foreign relations for the future. The latter, of course, were bound to involve primarily Vienna, since Russia had rejected previous Serbian overtures.

In Serbia, as in Romania, the prince occupied a strong position. He named the ministers who in turn could influence the outcome of elections. Milan, however, was not a Charles, who could control the political situation. Nor was he an Alexander of Battenberg, who could unite the country behind him against foreign intervention. Essentially a weak man who was also lazy, corrupt, and petty, Milan made enemies easily. He provided neither a firm rallying point for the national forces nor the strong leadership necessary for a weak and backward country.

This period witnessed the rise of two other groups, the Progressives and the Radicals, who were subsequently to challenge the Liberal Party's predominance. Resembling the Junimists in Romania, the Progressives emerged from the left wing of the Conservative Party. Western-oriented, they wanted to follow the example of the advanced European states and regarded Russia as a backward and primitive state. Their members were usually well educated and had traveled. The Progressives' political program followed the classic pattern of nineteenth-century liberal thought and called for strong civil rights legislation, with provisions for a free press and free assembly, an independent judiciary, and wide local autonomy. In essence the Progressives wanted to duplicate in Serbia the middle-class civilizations of Western Europe.

In contrast, the Radicals had their roots in the populist, Marxist, and anarchist currents of the 1870s. Although they were to modify their program when they attained power, they were at first far to the left of the Progressives. They stood for universal manhood suffrage, the predominance of the legislature in the government, direct and graduated taxes, a strong civil rights program, and virtual autonomy for local government. They were particularly interested in curbing the influence of the police in the elections, a prerequisite for their own victory. Perhaps their most important contribution was their attempt to involve the peasantry for the first time in the political life of the country. Initially, the party did not emphasize this direction, but subsequently the leaders Nikola Pašić and Pera Todorović did work out a program that could attract this mass base.

Meanwhile, Milan and his Liberal ministers attempted to come to an understanding with Austria-Hungary concerning the building of railroads, commercial relations, and, finally, a political treaty. On the first point the Habsburg government wanted to be sure that the Serbian railroad schemes were to its benefit; an extension of the Serbian network southward was sought. In April, 1880, Serbia agreed to continue her line from Belgrade to Vranje through Niš. Unfortunately for Milan, he soon faced a major scandal with effects quite similar to the earlier Strousberg affair in Romania. In March, 1881, Milan signed a contract with a company approved by Vienna, that of E. Bontoux of Paris. Only a short time later, in January, 1882, this firm collapsed, causing not only a financial crisis in Paris, but even severer repercussions in Belgrade. On paper the Serbian state appeared to have lost more than its national income for one year. Moreover, during this incident evidence of widespread bribery and the corruption of Serbian officials, including Milan, was exposed. In the end, thanks to Austrian assistance, Serbia lost only 12 million dinars, but the damage to Milan and his government was extreme.

The negotiation of a commercial convention proved even more difficult than the railroad question. The Serbian government needed a new treaty. At the Congress of Berlin it had been decided that the independent Balkan states should continue to abide by the terms of the agreements negotiated by the Ottoman Empire. The tariffs allowed under these agreements were kept to 3 percent for Serbia, while the monarchy was allowed to increase hers at will. The Habsburg government was willing to make a new arrangement. As in the negotiations with Romania, pressure was applied to Serbia and the excuse of disease was used to limit livestock imports. Again Vienna sought to gain what were in fact quite unequal terms, in particular advantages for their manufactured goods. The conditions offered were not unfavorable to the Serbian peasant, who needed the Habsburg market. Serbia also did not have an industry that needed protection. Nevertheless, Jovan Ristić insisted on equality. He refused to accept the Habsburg proposals and resigned in October, 1880. After twelve years in office the Liberal Party surrendered its position to the Progressives, who were to dominate Serbian political life for the next seven years. The new government, with Milan Piročanac as premier and Čedomil Mijatović as foreign minister and minister of finance, signed the commercial agreement in April, 1881. The terms were advantageous to Serbian agriculture, but they also allowed Habsburg-manufactured goods to enter Serbia on a privileged basis. Serbian trade was now almost exclusively with the Dual Monarchy, with

77 percent of Serbian imports and 82 percent of the exports tied to this market.

The dependence of Serbia on Austria-Hungary, reflected in the commercial treaty, was even more pronounced in the political agreements concluded at this time. With the Habsburg Empire in control of Bosnia-Hercegovina and with the new Bulgaria backed by Russia, Serbia needed some protection for her interests in the only area in which she could hope to expand, Macedonia. Milan, like Charles, also wished to take the title of king. The treaty signed by Austria-Hungary and Serbia on June 28, 1881, contained an assurance of Habsburg support for Serbian expansion southward should future developments allow this action. The elevation of the state to a kingdom was similarly approved. The terms of the agreement contained the assurance that if either state were at war, the other would remain neutral. For its part, the Serbian government made two important promises. First, it agreed that it would not tolerate "political, religious, or other intrigues" against the Dual Monarchy on its territory or in Bosnia-Hercegovina and Novi Pazar. Second, and much more significant, Article 4 stated that "without a previous understanding with Austria-Hungary, Serbia will neither negotiate nor conclude any political treaty with another government, and will not admit to her territory a foreign armed force, regular or irregular, even as volunteers." [1]

These declarations caused an immediate crisis when they became known in Belgrade. Piročanac preferred to resign rather than to accept a statement that reduced Serbia to a position of political subordination to the monarchy. He finally went to Vienna and obtained from the Habsburg government the declaration that the article would not "impair the right of Serbia to negotiate and conclude treaties, even of a political nature, with another government." [2] With this assurance Piročanac stayed in office. Unknown to the premier, however, Milan, in an exchange of letters with Vienna, promised not to "enter into any negotiations whatsoever relative to any kind of political treaty between Serbia and a third state without communication with and previous consent of Austria-Hungary." [3] In this backhanded manner Milan was able to assure for himself the support of the monarchy. In March, 1882, Serbia became a kingdom. Despite the unequal relationship thus established, it must be emphasized that the country really had no alternative. Like Romania, Serbia needed support from a great power in international relations.

1. Alfred Franzis Pribram, *The Secret Treaties of Austria-Hungary, 1879–1914,* tr. by Denys P. Meyers and J. G. D'Arcy Paul (Cambridge: Harvard University Press, 1920), vol. 1, pp. 51–53.

2. *Ibid.,* vol. 1, p. 61.

3. *Ibid.,* vol. 1, p. 59.

With the Russian backing of Bulgaria, no other alliance partner was available.

At the same time the Progressive government had begun to implement its political program. Liberal, not democratic, it proceeded to pass a series of laws resembling those passed by similar parties in the neighboring countries. Measures concerning the freedom of the press, the independence of the judiciary, and compulsory elementary education were put into effect. In 1883 military service was made obligatory. In the same year a national bank was established. The Progressive program reflected middle-class interests, not those of the peasant majority. As in the case of all the neighboring Balkan countries and of previous Serbian administrations, the Progressive Party replaced Liberal Party appointees in the bureaucracy with their own men.

The entire period in which the Progressive government held power was marked by frequent internal scandals and foreign disasters. In addition to the collapse of the Bontoux firm, Milan's dismissal of the popular metropolitan of Serbia, Michael, caused further domestic agitation. A supporter of the Liberal Party and pro-Russian, Michael objected to measures calling for the taxation of church property and to the wholesale dismissal of Liberals from office. To replace him Milan appointed his own candidate, Theodosius. When the Serbian synod would not confirm him, Milan had to turn to the Serbian patriarch in Sremski Karlovci in the Habsburg monarchy. The nomination was finally accepted by the patriarch in Constantinople and by the Greek and Romanian churches, but not by Russia.

Milan and the Progressive Party's declining influence was reflected in the elections of 1883. Despite the Progressive control of the government the Radicals won a two-to-one majority. Refusing to accept this result, Milan called Hristić and the Conservatives back to power. A Progressive government was restored in 1884 following a revolt in the Timok area in November, 1883. The cause of this rebellion was ostensibly the government's demand that the peasant militia store their military weapons in regular arsenals rather than in their homes. Members of the Radical Party were, however, deeply implicated in the action. After the revolt was suppressed by the army, Radical leaders were forced into exile. Nikola Pašić, who had left the country before the event, was condemned to death. A large number of refugees crossed into Bulgaria. Although ninety-four received a death sentence for participation in the rebellion, only twenty were executed.

The presence of the refugees in Bulgaria led to an immediate worsening of relations with that state despite the fact that Milan and Alexander were personal friends. The situation was made worse by an almost comical incident. In the preceding years the Timok River marking the boundary between the two states had changed its course. The shifts in the river bed had resulted in roughly equal losses by both countries, but Serbia now tried to keep the newly won land and to hold on to her former strips. As a result a clash occurred on the border and the Bulgarians ousted a Serbian garrison. The dispute was not settled until 1888.

This growing hostility reached a climax in 1885. This time, as we have seen, the issue was neither minor nor farcical. When it became apparent that Eastern Rumelia would indeed join Bulgaria, Milan at once demanded compensation. In November, 1885, on the mistaken assumption that a Bulgarian army devoid of Russian officers would be weak, Milan launched an attack on the neighboring state. The war was a disaster for Serbia. At the Battle of Slivnitsa the army was defeated, and only the intervention of his Habsburg ally saved Milan from further losses. Peace was restored on a *status quo ante* basis.

From the 1880s to the revolution of 1903 a disproportionate role in the politics of the Serbian state was played by the domestic affairs of the Obrenović dynasty. During this period the Serbian public was presented with a series of scandals which not only disrupted political life but also gave the world an impression of Serbia that damaged the state's prestige. The scandals were a constant danger to the dynasty because of the existence of a possible alternative candidate for the throne in the person of Peter Karadjordjević, who lived in exile but who followed Serbian events closely. In 1883 he strengthened his position by marrying Zorka, the daughter of Prince Nicholas of Montenegro. Despite the dangers of irresponsible public behavior Milan and his wife Natalia proceeded to conduct in public a series of personal and political quarrels. The daughter of a Russian colonel of Romanian extraction, Natalia favored a pro-Russian course in Serbian foreign policy. She also opposed her husband's desire that their son Alexander be educated in Austria. In open and irreconcilable conflict with his wife, Milan sought a divorce; the issue split the government. In 1887 Natalia and Alexander left the country.

By 1888 Milan had sickened of his position. He could not win a clear victory in the elections despite his control of the police. Determined to abdicate, his last act was to summon a constitutional assembly. This body met in December, 1888; five-sixths of its members were from the Radical Party and one-sixth from the Liberals. The Progressives had failed to win a representative. Nevertheless, the draft for the new constitution was drawn up by a committee representing all three parties. The document, which was more democratic than the one it replaced, defined more closely the civil liberties granted, gave more relative power to the parliament, and strengthened local government. It also provided for secret elections and gave the suffrage to all taxpayers. With this task completed, Milan abdicated in March, 1889, in favor of his thirteen-year-old son, Alexander.

The reign of Alexander Obrenović was in many respects a sad interlude in Serbian history. Although not without abilities, he was to see his private life together with that of his mother, his father, and later his mistress become the laughing stock of Europe. He had experienced an extremely lonely childhood coupled with a strict military education. His parents had felt no scruples about using him in their quarrels. Before leaving the country Milan had personally appointed a regency of three, headed by Jovan Ristić. Since the abdication was a victory for the Radicals, this party now took control. General Sava Grujić became premier, and Pašić returned from exile. The Radicals thus had the opportunity to put their program into practice.

Whereas the electoral strength of the party rested on peasant votes, the Radical leadership came from the middle classes and the intellectuals. Once in office the Radicals showed that they shared their predecessors' desire for administrative positions and filled the civil service with Radical candidates. The party did, however, have a program, which it tried to implement at least in part between the years 1889 and 1892. Many Radicals shared a theoretical dislike of the capitalist West. They wished Serbia to be a democratic state based on a union of self-governing communes. The army was to be popularly controlled. In practical legislation, however, they did little more than introduce measures widening the suffrage, strengthening civil rights, and increasing the authority of local government.

These actions could not, obviously, solve the personal problems of young Alexander. His parents, living both within and without the country, continued to quarrel publicly and vie for their son's affection. Milan was perpetually in need of money, and the question of his divorce remained a national issue. At the same time political conditions within the country deteriorated. In June, 1892, the Radical government was replaced by a Liberal regime, which assured itself of a sufficiently strong position in the assembly by using the police and army in the elections. In April, 1893, Alexander, at his father's urging, and with the aid of the army, simply took control of the country. At first the seventeen-year-old king appointed his ministers from the Radical Party; new elections assured a Radical assembly. In 1894 Alexander abolished the constitution of 1888 and restored that of 1869. These actions provoked no real reaction. In fact, in the next years the king was able to control the political system by playing off the parties and controlling the elections. His relatively strong political position was, however, undermined by the popular reaction to his irregular personal life.

Not only did Milan and Natalia continue to struggle openly over the control of Alexander, but the unfortunate king contracted a relationship which deeply offended Serbian sensibilities. At his mother's house Alexander had met a widow, Draga Mašina, who was more than ten years his senior. Her father had died insane and her mother was an alcoholic. It was believed that she could not have children, and she had acquired an extremely bad reputation because of her relationship with other men. Alexander made her his mistress in 1897 and soon announced his intention to marry her. Both the king's parents disapproved. The Russian government, however, used this opportunity to attempt to regain influence at the Serbian court. The tsar acted as best man at the wedding by proxy.

The rest of Alexander's reign was dominated by scandals associated with the new queen and her family. Reports of false pregnancies only served to underline the fact that the Obrenović dynasty was dying out. In April, 1901, Alexander issued another constitution on his own authority. Serbia was now to have a bicameral legislature with an elected chamber and a senate, three-fifths of whose members were to be appointed by the king. Although the government continued to win elections through intimidation, it could not stifle the mounting national discontent.

Alexander's rule came to an end on the night of June 10–11, 1903, with a coup organized by a group of young officers who were humiliated by their ruler and who felt that the country could not advance under his leadership. About 120 were involved in the plot. The conspirators invaded the palace and killed the king, the queen, the premier, the war minister, and both of the queen's brothers. The action horrified Europe. Not only was Alexander shot, but he also received multiple saber wounds.

There was no question who would be the next king; Peter Karadjordjević was the only candidate. The conspirators first organized a provisional government with Jovan Avakumović at the head. The two-house legislature of the constitution of 1901 was then summoned, and it elected Peter, who accepted at once. In 1903 the constitution of 1889 was restored with certain amendments. The new king was almost sixty when he became the ruler of a country about which he knew little. The third son of Alexander Karadjordjević, he had been educated in France and Switzerland. A nationalistic Serb, he had fought in the Bosnian War. His ties were with Russia. His marriage to Princess Zorka had ended with her death in 1890.

The first task facing the new regime was to counter the shocked reaction of the powers to the coup. Although Austria-Hungary and Russia soon recognized the change, Britain and the Netherlands withdrew their ambassadors. None of these countries liked the fact that conspirators occupied high posts in the government after the coup. The removal of these men aided in the resumption of normal foreign relations, but Britain did not recognize the new government until 1906.

Peter was crowned in 1904. With his accession political life became in a sense simplified. The two strongest parties were the Radicals and the Independent Radicals, both offshoots of the original party. After five changes of government between 1904 and 1906, the Radicals held control of the government until 1918.

The Obrenović dynasty had been tied to Austria-Hungary; that link had now been broken. Despite the Russian connections of both Peter and the Radicals, this country was deeply involved in the disastrous war with Japan and could offer little support. Almost immediately conflicts developed with Vienna, chiefly over questions concerning railroads, military purchases, and loans. The Habsburg government wished the Serbs to purchase Škoda guns with money loaned by the monarchy. For their part the Serbs wanted to acquire French weapons similar to those used by Bulgaria, and not restrict themselves to Austrian financing. During the negotiations the Habsburg government learned that Serbia and Bulgaria had signed a customs agreement in June, 1905, which was to go into effect in 1906 and which would result in a virtual economic union by 1917. Regarding this as damaging to the Habsburg position in the Balkans, the monarchy suspended negotiations with Belgrade, including those being carried on over a trade treaty. Pressure was put on Serbia to renounce the Bulgarian agreement, and the Habsburg border was closed to Serbian livestock. Disease was again used as a pretext.

This conflict, known as the "Pig War," in many ways paralleled earlier controversies between the monarchy and Romania. Agreement was only reached in 1911. Although the boycott on Serbian livestock was disastrous for some areas, the action forced the Serbian government to end its close economic dependency on the Dual Monarchy and to look for alternate markets. Commercial treaties were concluded with other states, and the Serbs began to process their own meats. The state also now turned to France for military equipment. The change of dynasties and the consequences of the Pig War effectively broke the former tight political, military, and economic ties between Serbia and the Habsburg monarchy. From this time on the Serbian government looked to St. Petersburg for direction.

Peter's reign was marked by continual crises in foreign policy. Since these events involved deeply the other Balkan states as well as the great powers, they will be discussed elsewhere. It should, however, be mentioned that in the next years the Serbian government entered a period where strong emphasis was placed on national expansion. The Serbian goals continued to involve the annexation of lands still under Ottoman rule, but an increased concern was shown over the fate of the South Slav peoples under Habsburg rule.

BULGARIA

After the resignation of Stambolov Prince Ferdinand appointed the Conservative Constantine Stoilov as his successor. His first task, it will be remembered, had been to effect a reconciliation with Russia. Ferdinand was now determined to be a strong ruler and to control the political process of the state. His goals remained the expansion and strengthening of the nation and, like Charles and Milan, he looked forward to the day when he would win a royal title and rule over an independent state. The prince's desire for power was aided by the evolution of the Bulgarian political system. The former Liberal and Conservative parties soon split into new organizations with competing programs. Ferdinand was thus always able to find a political party or a coalition that would work with him and carry out his policies. Between 1894 and 1913 the government shifted between these groups approximately a dozen times.

Before the First World War nine political parties competed for power. Three were splinter groups from the Liberal Party: the National Liberals led by Dimitur Petkov, Stambolov's successor; the Liberals under Dr. Vasil Radoslavov; and the Young Liberals of Dimitur Tonchev. Their differences centered largely around the personalities of their leaders. All were basically anti-Russian and pro-western in foreign policy, and they found their support in the urban intellectuals and the peasants. Their chief opposition came from the former Conservatives, who were called the National Party after 1894 and were led by Constantine Stoilov. In the political struggles the National Party cooperated with the Progressive Liberal Party led by Dragan Tsankov. This group leaned toward Russia in foreign affairs, and its members came from the middle class and the more prosperous landowners. Between these blocs was the Democratic Party of Petko Karavelov. It preferred a policy of free hands in foreign affairs, but it was rather more pro-western than pro-Russian. The other three parties were the Agrarians and two Social Democratic associations, who were relative newcomers to Bulgarian politics.

The five years of Stoilov's premiership set the direction of Ferdinand's reign. Like Charles, the prince was concerned with internal development and he wished to encourage industrialization. In 1894 a law was passed to protect native industry, and loans were granted to firms that had a capital of over 25,000 leva and at least 20 workers. In 1897 all officials were required to wear domestically produced clothing and shoes. These measures, which encouraged machine production, were harmful to the handicraft industries of the country, but were believed necessary for economic progress.

The prince was also deeply interested in the development of internal communications, particularly in the building of railroads. Like all the Balkan countries, Bulgaria had great difficulties with the foreign concessions granted for this purpose. Prior to 1878 the Ottoman government had contracted with western firms, mainly British and Austrian, for railroad construction. In the Treaty of Berlin the Bulgarian principality was obligated to assume these commitments. During the 1880s the Bul-

garian government found itself under constant pressure from concession hunters, some of whom were now Russian. The foreign entrepre-
neur was, of course, primarily concerned with making a profit for
himself and his stockholders. Some of the lines proposed would have
been of little benefit to Bulgaria. By 1888 the main line through
Bulgaria, which linked Constantinople with Vienna and the other great
European cities, was completed. The country now had 693 kilometers of
track. In order to proceed with the next step, the development of branch
lines, the government obtained loans from Viennese banks, often at high
interest rates. Other problems also arose. Under questionable circumstances the state paid a high price to purchase the railroad of the Oriental Company in Rumelia, which was owned by the Berlin Deutsche Bank.
Stoilov was forced to resign in January, 1899, on this issue. Although
railroads continued to be built—Bulgaria had an impressive 1,931 kilometers of track by 1911—the cost placed a heavy burden on the economy.

Bulgarian agriculture also suffered from many of the same problems
as those found in the neighboring countries. After 1878, with the
breakup of the great estates formerly held by Ottoman proprietors, Bulgaria became a nation of small peasant farmers. The acquisition of land
did not improve the level of peasant life. As elsewhere, the plots were
repeatedly subdivided through inheritance, and farming methods were
not improved. Peasant discontent mounted steadily. This group had certain definite demands; it wanted, for example, loans to be available at
reasonable rates, guaranteed markets for crops, and the assurance of
low prices for staples, such as matches, soap, and sugar. The peasants
particularly disliked the rising costs of consumer goods when their own
incomes were declining. Peasant discontent reached its height when,
after several bad harvests, in 1899 the government imposed a 10 percent
tax in kind. A storm of protest arose. The measure had been introduced
by D. Grekov, the leader of the National Liberal Party, which now dominated the government in coalition with the Liberals. The army was used
to enforce the law, and some peasants were killed. The use of force had
been decided on by Radoslavov, who had replaced Grekov as premier.
This action caused the formation of the Agrarian Union, a new party
devoted to furthering the interests of the peasants, who previously had
largely voted for the Liberals.

Not only did Radoslavov use strong measures against the peasants, but
he also illegally dissolved the communal councils and other local governmental bodies. Ferdinand was aware of his minister's increasing un-
popularity and in 1901 appointed a new coalition government composed
of Democrats and Progressives under the leadership of Karavelov. The
10 percent tax was immediately rescinded. Much of the good-will gained
by this step, however, was dissipated when the government sought to use

a tobacco monopoly to secure a loan from Germany, an action that the assembly would not approve.

Throughout Ferdinand's reign foreign policy was dominated by the Macedonian question. The state not only sponsored the organization of revolutionary societies, but also sought to make advances through negotiations with the Ottoman Empire and Russia. Some success was gained through discussions with the Porte. In 1897 the sultan issued two decrees for new bishoprics to be placed under the jurisdiction of the exarch. Little assistance, however, could be gained from St. Petersburg. Although the Bulgarian crisis of 1885–87 had caused the dissolution of the Three Emperors' Alliance and a period of estrangement between Russia and Austria-Hungary, by the late 1890s the two countries had again developed common interests in Balkan affairs. Russia was more concerned with events in the Far East; the Habsburg Empire had to deal with great internal problems. Therefore, in 1897 the two states agreed to cooperate to prevent any crisis from arising in the Balkans. In the next years they also worked closely together on the Macedonian question. Under these circumstances Bulgaria could not expect Russia to back her aims.

Despite the fact that new territory could not be gained at this time, Ferdinand was soon to achieve another of his goals. In 1908 the Young Turk revolution in the Ottoman Empire brought to power a new leadership, which was determined to maintain the integrity and strength of that nation. Cooperating closely with Austria-Hungary, who was concerned about Bosnia-Hercegovina, Ferdinand prepared to exploit the opportunity presented. He first recalled his representative in Constantinople and then seized the Ottoman railroad in Eastern Rumelia. Finally, in October, 1908, he proclaimed Bulgaria's independence and assumed the title of tsar. The next day the Habsburg monarchy announced the annexation of Bosnia-Hercegovina. Although an international crisis followed, the Bulgarian action was eventually accepted by the Porte in return for an indemnity. This achievement naturally immensely strengthened Ferdinand's personal position, which had been under attack during the period from left-wing groups.

With the achievement of independence the government gave its full attention to Macedonia. By this time it had abandoned hope of acquiring all of this territory. The best solution now seemed a partition with the other Balkan states in agreement with Russia. The obstacle to negotiations with other states was Article 18 of the constitution, which required the approval of the assembly for such agreements. Thus, there could be no secret discussions. The necessity of amending the constitution was clear. In March, 1911, a coalition government of the National Party and the Progressives was formed under the premiership of E. Geshov. The mood of the nation and the importance attached to the solution of the Macedonian question was expressed when the newly convened Grand

National Assembly unanimously approved the constitutional change. Ferdinand could now enter into secret treaties with the neighboring states.

Despite the numerous domestic problems Bulgaria did progress in many areas in the years before 1913. As noted previously, the railroad network almost tripled from 693 kilometers in 1887 to 1,931 in 1911. During the same period roads increased from 3,727 kilometers to 8,945. Telegraph lines extended from 3,548 kilometers to 6,517, and telephone lines from 195 kilometers to 2,231. In addition, the Turnovo constitution had guaranteed free, compulsory education for all. At first this program could not be implemented because of the shortage of trained teachers and schools. Yet by 1910 a system of education had been developed; administered by local school boards, it provided for four years of primary education, three years of pregymnasium, and five years of gymnasium. In 1888 the so-called Higher School was established in Sofia, which in 1904 became the University of Sofia.

ECONOMIC AND SOCIAL PROBLEMS: THE INTERVENTION OF THE GREAT POWERS

In previous chapters economic and social problems have been discussed as part of either the domestic political life or the foreign relations of a state. Before continuing to the complicated international situation, which led ultimately to the great war of 1914, it might be well to summarize these developments, particularly for the period after 1878, and to consider briefly the standard of life achieved by the Balkan people in the century of national liberation. Emphasis will also be placed on the role of the great powers in this sphere of Balkan activity.

The Congress of Berlin marked an historical break in Balkan and to an extent general European development. The achievement of separate national existences by the majority of the Balkan people at this time coincided with a new epoch of imperial expansion on the part of the European great powers. The western industrial states now turned with increasing interest to the rest of the world in search of new markets, sources of raw materials, and opportunities for investment. The old imperial countries of Britain and France were now joined by Germany, Italy, and the United States as the leaders in the movement. Although Russia was to be an imperial power in the Far East and Central Asia, she could not offer direct economic competition with these western states. In fact, in her relations with the West Russia was to share with the colonial lands the attribute of being an exporter of raw materials and an importer of industrial goods and capital.

As we have seen, once the Balkan states had achieved some measure of independence they desired the characteristics of a modern state—in particular a large bureaucratic establishment and an efficient army. They also needed internal improvements, especially better means of communication. All of these items were expensive and none of the states had an adequate tax base or sufficient accumulation of wealth to meet the immediate new expenses. Greece, for example, had been forced to go deeply into debt simply to pay for the national revolution. As a result the Balkan states sought capital and industrial goods from the great imperial powers, who were willing to make loans to win political allies and who regarded the Ottoman Empire and the successor states as areas of imperial exploitation. The relationship could not be equal. The Balkan nations and the Ottoman Empire did not have the power to resist the encroachment of the strong empires. Moreover, the large states were themselves in a period of intense economic and national rivalry. By entering the Balkan conflicts they not only became involved in the Balkan disputes, but in turn drew the small states into the major powers' quarrels.

Perhaps the question of the railroads provides the best example of the differences between the great powers' interests and the problems associated with European investment. In the middle of the nineteenth century all nations had a passion for railroad building. The Balkan governments, on achieving a measure of political independence, were no exception, but for them the question of payment was not easy. The desires of the Balkan states were seconded strongly by the powers because the lines would facilitate their trade. The West wanted a direct link with the Ottoman Empire for both economic and strategic reasons. Because of these considerations, the Balkan railroads were generally built more to meet the needs of the powers than those of the Balkan states. The first lines built, the Constanța-Cernavoda and the Varna-Ruse routes, served Austrian and British interests by connecting the Black Sea and the Danube River. In 1868 the most ambitious plan for a Balkan railroad network was drawn up. At this time the Ottoman government gave the Austrian concern of Baron Hirsch a concession for a line to run from Constantinople through Adrianople, Plovdiv, Sofia, Niš, and Belgrade to the Habsburg border. Construction began in 1872, but was interrupted by the wars of the second half of that decade. Constantinople and Vienna were joined only in 1888.

The issues connected with railroad building were a constant source of conflict between the states, as has been shown in the case of Romania and Germany in the 1870s and Austria-Hungary and Serbia in 1882. Similar friction developed between the Habsburg monarchy and Russia in 1908 over the desire of Russia and Serbia to construct a line running east to west from the Danube to the Adriatic, a plan in conflict with Vienna's desire for a north-south route through Ottoman territory from the Austrian border to Thessaloniki.

The completed Balkan railroad network did run counter to some of the economic interests of the states through whose territory the lines ran and who in fact paid for the construction. Certainly, the first effects were not favorable. The increased penetration of European manufactured goods served to drive out local products, and native handicraft industries were often wiped out. The financing of the railroads also brought the Balkan governments a great deal of trouble, including the above-mentioned association of members of both the Romanian and Serbian governments with obviously corrupt financial practices.

Nevertheless, despite these disadvantages the Balkan countries did acquire a railroad system.[4] The first Greek line was the nine-kilometer stretch from Athens to Piraeus constructed in 1867–69; by 1914 the state had 2,196 kilometers of track. The initial Romanian railroad ran from Bucharest to the Danube port of Giurgiu; by 1914 the network had increased to 3,754 kilometers. By this date Serbia had 1,567 kilometers of railroad and Bulgaria 2,227. The chief Bulgarian line was the stretch of the Constantinople-Vienna route that ran through the state. This railroad was a national luxury; it did not support itself and it was of limited aid in the economic development of the country. It should also be noted that all of these railroads, although built by foreign private enterprise, became state owned—in Romania in 1888, in Serbia between 1889 and 1892, in Bulgaria in 1885, and in Greece from the beginning.

Construction of a better system of roads and improvements on rivers and ports in all of the Balkan countries closely paralleled the building of railroads. Particularly notable were the completion of the Cernavoda bridge across the Danube and the cutting of the Corinth Canal between the Peloponnesus and Greece proper, both of which occurred during the 1890s. By the outbreak of the First World War, the transportation facilities in the peninsula were much superior to those in the days of Ottoman rule.

These internal improvements were made largely with borrowed money. Loans also paid for military equipment and for regular state expenses. By the end of the century all of the Balkan governments faced real difficulties because of this policy. Not only had much of the money gone into noneconomic expenditures, but the service of the debts had come to absorb an entirely disproportionate percentage of the state budget. Greece was forced to accept an international commission with control over most of her state finances; Serbia and Bulgaria had to allow similar arrangements for the state monopolies only at the beginning of the new century. In each case foreign advisers gained control of the rev-

---

4. The statistics on the following pages come principally from Nicolas Spulber, *The State and Economic Development in Eastern Europe* (New York: Random House, 1966) and Ivan T. Berend and Gyorgy Ranki, *Economic Development in East-Central Europe in the Nineteenth and Twentieth Centuries* (New York: Columbia University Press, 1974). See also appropriate statistical handbooks.

enues from certain taxes. Romania, because of her grain exports and her developing oil industry, was in the best economic position, but she, too, borrowed heavily for military and railroad expenditures, with 52 percent of the debt owed to German investors. By 1914 the new states had acquired a large public debt burden: Bulgaria owed 850 million francs; Serbia, 903 million; Greece, 1.25 billion; and Romania, 1.7 billion.

Closely allied with the desire of the Balkan governments to acquire modern armies, bureaucracies, and public works was their natural wish to follow in the path of the western states towards an industrial economy. With a poor basis for such a development, little advancement was achieved in this direction in any Balkan state during the nineteenth century. In the beginning of the twentieth century changes did commence, but the outbreak of the First World War found the area still overwhelmingly agrarian in character. Of the states the most notable achievements were in Romania, chiefly because of the development of the oil resources, but even here the place of industry in the total economy remained very small. In 1863 Romania had 565 plants employing 5 or more workers for a total of 5,500 workers. The main enterprises were food processing, construction materials, and textiles. In 1902 the country had 625 large works with 40,000 workers. By 1912 the Ploeşti oil fields and the related chemical industry became important. Here foreign capital dominated, the Romanian share in the oil exploitation being only 8 percent.

In Greece a similar pattern can be found. In 1877 the state had 136 industries with 7,350 workers; by 1917 the number had increased to over 2,000 plants with 36,000 workers, with food processing and textiles predominating. In addition, Greece had strong handicraft industries. Foreign capital was also important here. The Greeks themselves traditionally preferred to invest in small enterprises and in trade. In one area, the historic occupation of shipbuilding, Greece was unique in the Balkans. The introduction of steamships resulted in a momentary setback for Greek builders, but this was later recovered. Unfortunately for the state, the later rise of large shipping concerns under the direction of Greek nationals did not profit the nation. For tax and other reasons these ships were often not registered in the Greek kingdom.

Both Serbia and Bulgaria were slow in industrial development; both were markets for Habsburg and British products. Nevertheless, after the turn of the century some progress was made. In 1910 Serbia had 16,000 workers employed in 470 industrial plants, of which half were mills. The mining of coal and some copper was also developed. Small enterprises characterized Serbian economic development.

In Bulgaria national liberation resulted in an economic decline because of the loss of the Ottoman market. The emigration of Turkish craftsmen after 1878 and the building of railroads, which brought in competing foreign goods, similarly was a blow to local production. In the 1870s some industry did exist, particularly in textiles and food processing. In 1910 there were 110 mills with 1,400 workers and 76 textile enterprises with 4,400 workers. There were also breweries, ceramics enterprises, alcohol distilleries, and a match factory. By 1911 the country had 345 industries with 16,000 workers.

Despite these slow beginnings the Balkan governments did encourage industrial development, although not to the extent of offering direct subsidies as in the Hungarian half of the Dual Monarchy. Assistance was given instead through protective tariffs on manufactured imports and measures that exempted industrial firms from taxes, and through import tariffs on raw material and machinery. Although there were discussions in the various assemblies about a concerted effort to foster industrial and general economic development, the level and indeed the type of aid was not sufficient to achieve the desired results. In addition to the very obvious problem of poverty, the governments were restricted because of the determination of the great powers to maintain essentially unequal economic relationships with the Balkan states and the Ottoman Empire.

As we have seen, Serbia, Bulgaria, and Romania shared the problem that at first their tariff limits were determined by the Treaty of Berlin which provided that the former Ottoman commercial treaties should remain in effect. It was not until the new century that the results of this provision could be fully set aside. International considerations thus hindered the introduction of a truly protective tariff. Moreover, each state had to consider the interests of its people; there were in fact few infant industries to protect. If the governments raised tariffs to stimulate such development, other states might retaliate to the detriment of the agrarian interests. Serbian and Romanian peasants did, for instance, need an export market for grain and livestock. The commercial treaties between the states and the Dual Monarchy, which allowed an almost free import of Habsburg manufactured goods, did no direct harm to the majority of the population. Only later, when tariffs were raised and customs wars resulted, did the peasants and merchants suffer. Nevertheless, all the Balkan states raised their tariffs when they could. Bulgarian rates were increased in 1905; the Serbian during the Pig War; and the Greek in 1910.

In addition to these commercial policies the Balkan governments also gave their industrial enterprises certain direct aid through legislative measures. Such assistance took, in general, the form of tax exemptions, duty-free imports of machinery and raw materials, preferential rates on railroads, free land for factories, and the assurance of government contracts. The Romanian law of 1887, as we have seen, gave special favors to industries with more than twenty-five workers; Serbia passed similar laws in 1898. Here factories with more than fifty workers received privileges. Bulgaria introduced comparable measures in 1894 and 1897.

Along with this assistance, the governments sought to encourage industrial development by creating an atmosphere favorable to foreign investment. Since this source of capital was believed essential, official approval helped attract outside money. And indeed foreign investment did play a major role in the initial exploitation of the natural resources of the area. This condition was particularly apparent in Romania, the most advanced of the nations under consideration. In that country the major part of the industry rested on foreign investment. In the oil industry by 1914 only 8 percent of the capital was from Romanian sources, while 27.5 percent was German, 23.7 percent British, and 20 percent Dutch. A similar domination of outside investment could be found in the gas, electric, sugar, and timber industries. Foreign capital was also heavily involved in the exploitation of Serbian mineral resources, in particular of coal, iron, copper, lead, chromium, and zinc. European investors naturally developed the fields that would yield the highest profits; their activities usually did not contribute to the real economic development of the countries in which they operated because there were few links between these extractive operations and the native economy. The fact that members of the Balkan governments benefited from participation in certain of these activities did, of course, introduce the issue of political corruption into the entire relationship.

Despite the efforts to industrialize the Balkan nations were hampered by the two-fold problem of an agrarian economy and an extremely backward agriculture. Important regional differences did exist, but the states shared certain parallel disabilities. In every area, regardless of whether small peasant farming or estates dominated the picture, agricultural methods were too primitive to produce a crop that could compete in the world of the late nineteenth and early twentieth centuries. In Serbia, Bulgaria, and Romania agriculture had developed along a roughly similar line: the peasant producer had shifted by the second half of the nineteenth century from livestock to grains. During this period the amount of land under cultivation had risen resulting in a great increase in production. The primary goal of farming itself also shifted from self-sufficiency to the cultivation of cash crops. In the 1880s American and Australian wheat began to enter and then flood the European markets to the detriment of the Balkan products. At the same time both Serbian and Romanian agricultural interests were harmed by the Hungarian desire to protect the Habsburg market for its own grains and livestock.

As the competitive value of Balkan agriculture declined, the population rose. In 1878 Serbia had a population of 1.7 million; by 1910 she had 2.9 million. Together Bulgaria and Eastern Rumelia had 1.5 million people in 1881, but 4.3 million in 1910. In 1815 the Romanian Principalities had 1.5 million inhabitants, but 6.9 million in 1910. The Greek figures rose from 750,000 in 1829 to 2.7 million in 1911. The Greek increases, of course, reflect the annexation of Thessaly, the Ionian Islands, and part of Epirus in 1882.

This rise in population was not accompanied by an improvement in land use. During the first part of the century the increase could be absorbed by the development of unexploited lands. For instance, the great Serbian forests gradually disappeared. Once the unused land had been claimed, the difficulties began. Balkan agriculture did not benefit from the experience of other countries, which had shown that the cheapest and most efficient manner by which export crops could be produced was on large estates managed along capitalist lines and worked by hired labor. On such estates modern techniques, advanced farm machinery, and the new chemical fertilizers brought vastly increased yields. Instead, Balkan agriculture went in precisely the opposite direction. Even the large estates, such as those in the Principalities and Thessaly, were cultivated chiefly by sharecropping peasants using their own primitive implements. Although some machinery was introduced, the majority of the peasants continued to use wooden plows and oxen for transport. In Bulgaria, for example, only 10 percent of the peasants had iron plows in 1900; in 1910 the figure had risen to 20 percent. Backward methods resulting in low yields meant that the Balkan peasant could not compete with the American farmer, let alone assure himself of anything but the most primitive standard of living.

By 1914 the situation had become critical: there was simply not enough land to support adequately the population, given the level of agricultural activity. The problem of underemployment was acute; so many people were not needed for the tasks they fulfilled. Unfortunately, what changes were made went in the wrong direction largely because the individual peasant saw the solution to his problem mainly in the acquisition of more land; he wanted the division of the large estates. He also continued to support inheritance laws, such as one passed in Bulgaria in 1890, that maintained the equal division of property among all the children of a family. This system, together with the increase in population, led to a proliferation of dwarf plots on which the majority of Balkan peasants attempted to support themselves. The peasants sought to remedy their situation by acquiring more land, not by improving farming methods.

In addition to the basic economic problems connected with Balkan landholding, the peasant majority carried the chief weight of supporting the national bureaucracies and the armies. Taxes, which had often been negligible under Ottoman rule, became extremely burdensome and their collection was more efficient. Thus between 1879 and 1911 it has been estimated that the Bulgarian peasant paid between 15 and 20 percent of his earnings to the state in taxes. Moreover, the peasant had to make high payments on the land he was able to acquire. For example, although Turkish landowners in Bulgaria were forced to leave after 1878, the Bulgarian peasant had to compensate them for their losses. When state lands were sold or when private lands came on the market, the prices were high. Rents on agricultural property also rose steeply. This had been one of the main causes of the Romanian peasant revolt of 1907.

As a result of these circumstances the peasant was constantly in need of money. He often had to borrow just to survive. The problem of peasant loans remained constant in the century before 1914. Usurious charges were commonplace in the countryside throughout the Balkans. The governments did little to protect the peasant from the money-lender, although some laws were passed such as the Serbian Homestead Act of 1836. It should also be mentioned that the Balkan peasant had learned to enjoy many products, such as tea, coffee, sugar, manufactured cloth and thread, and other industrial products, which usually came from outside of the country, were costly, and required cash. More products that he wanted were available to him, while his ability to purchase them declined.

The impoverished condition of the masses affected the entire structure of each of the Balkan states. Obviously, a poor people could not pay enough taxes to keep the Balkan governments out of financial difficulties. Nor could it form a satisfactory market for an increase of local industry; nor could it provide capital for industrial or commercial development. The failure of the states to develop an industrial base, of course, deprived the rural population of alternative employment.

In this account little attention has been given to the condition of the workers, largely because of the overwhelmingly agrarian character of the Balkan states and the fact that industrialization commenced late and remained weak. Nevertheless, because of their enormous future importance mention must be made of the Social Democratic parties, in particular in Romania and Bulgaria.

The beginnings of industrialization in the Balkans were accompanied by all the abuses so familiar in other parts of the world. The workers were employed for long hours, sometimes twelve to sixteen hours a day, at low wages and in bad conditions. The housing and food available in the cities was deplorable. Like their western equivalents, Balkan workers also formed unions, conducted strikes, and established political organizations to protect their interests. They sought state intervention to control the activities of their employers and to improve their working conditions. The Social Democratic parties, usually with a workers' base but with an intellectual, middle-class leadership, represented their political goals.

In Romania workers' organizations of importance first appeared in the 1880s. The most influential Marxist writer and organizer in this period was Constantine Dobrogeanu-Gherea, a major figure in world socialism. In 1893 fifty-four delegates from various Romanian cities met in Bucharest and formed the Social Democratic Party. In 1899 it dissolved with many of its members joining the Liberal Party. Meanwhile, the trade union movement made headway. In 1906 the first conference was held and a general commission was set up. In the following year the Socialist Union was organized, and it became the basis for the revival of the Social Democratic Party in 1910. This organization, under the direction of Christian Racovski, was militant and revolutionary in its attitude. Its political program called for universal suffrage and social reforms. It should be noted that Romanian socialist programs also advocated agrarian reform, and support was given to the peasants in the revolution of 1907.

Similar developments occurred in Bulgaria. It is interesting to note that this country, with the weakest industrial development, produced perhaps the most vigorous and controversial Socialist movement. Like Romania, Bulgaria had a socialist leader of international stature in Dimitur Blagoev. In 1891 he and twenty others founded the Social Democratic Party of Bulgaria. Almost at once a conflict developed between Blagoev and Ianko Sakazov, who believed that the party should concentrate on bettering the condition of the workers by shortening the working day and obtaining higher wages rather than on revolutionary activity. He also welcomed the support of the peasantry with whose help he was elected to the assembly in 1894. Blagoev, in contrast, did not trust the peasants. He concentrated on the industrial workers, despite their infinitesmal numbers, and his program was radical. He insisted that all private property be confiscated, "from the biggest machine to the tailor's needle, from the large tracts of land to the last inch of land." [5] Because of his interpretation of Marxism his followers were called the Narrows, while Sakazov's, with their less dogmatic views, were referred to as the Broads.

The fortunes of the party and the two factions fluctuated from election to election. For example, there were six Socialists in the assembly in 1899 and eight in 1902. They were elected mainly with peasant votes. After the formation of the Agrarian Union this support was lost so the Socialists had no representatives between 1903 and 1912. In 1913, however, twenty-one Broads and sixteen Narrows were elected, reflecting the dissatisfaction of the voters with the defeat in the Balkan Wars rather than the appeal of the socialist program.

5. Joseph Rothschild, *The Communist Party of Bulgaria: Origins and Development, 1883–1936* (New York: Columbia University Press, 1959), p. 25.

Despite their poor political showing the Socialists did lead in the labor movement and the organization of strikes. In the 1890s there were strikes among textile workers, printers, tobacco processors, and wood-workers, and there was a large railroad strike in 1907. In 1904 the Narrows organized the General Workers Trade Union Federation and the Broads countered with their own Free Trade Union Federation. By 1914 these organizations together had less than ten thousand members, the majority of whom were teachers, civil servants, and others in that category, and not industrial workers. Despite these limitations the basis for a future strong Socialist movement had been laid.

The Social Democratic Party in Serbia was organized in 1903. In 1905 it had 300 members, and by 1911 it had grown to 2,889. As in Romania and Bulgaria, unions were formed and strikes were organized. One of the longest occurred in the Čukarica sugar factory in Belgrade in 1907. In Greece socialist parties were not organized until after the First World War, but worker's organizations were formed in the 1880s and strikes held. Prior to 1910 many of these unions had representatives of the employers; in that year a law forbade this, and the workers' position was improved.

The strikes and political agitation in the Balkan cities for an improvement in the miserable working and living conditions served to emphasize the fact that national liberation, that is, the establishment of independent and autonomous governments, had not in fact been accompanied by a rise in the condition of the majority of the population. This situation, of course, was the result of general economic as well as political circumstances. Improvements in life had come to the minority of the population—to the landowners, the merchants, the industrialists, the bureaucrats, the army officers, and the professional classes, who usually lived in the cities and adopted Western European manners and customs.

In the period before 1914 the governments attempted to pass social legislation aiding the peasants and workers. They accepted the principle that the state should intervene to protect the mass of the population. The main focus in national life, however, was not in this direction. In the twentieth century, as before, the leaders continued to emphasize foreign affairs, each state concentrating on the acquisition of lands still under foreign control. The real financial support went to the army. These efforts were not in vain; the opportunity to act was soon to arise. Although the great powers during the nineteenth century had been usually able to restrain the national controversies and maintain something like a balance on the peninsula, these controls broke down for the decade from 1912 to 1922. In these years the Balkan nations were involved in a continuous period of war or in postwar conditions that were equally perilous. The prizes at stake were primarily lands still under Ottoman control, but also the territories in the Habsburg Empire inhabited by South Slavs and Romanians. The first decade of the twentieth century was to see the beginning of the expulsion of Ottoman rule from the peninsula, with the exception of the city of Constantinople and its hinterland; the second was to witness the completion of that process and the dissolution of the Dual Monarchy.

CHAPTER 13

The Expulsion of the Ottoman Empire from Europe

AFTER 1878, despite severe losses, the Ottoman Empire still held extensive lands. Direct control was exercised over Macedonian and Albanian territories. Although the Habsburg Empire controlled Bosnia-Hercegovina and the Sanjak of Novi Pazar, that state was in theory only "administering" the areas, which were under Ottoman suzerainty. In the next years the situation remained much as before. The Porte was determined not to surrender its possessions; the Balkan states were equally set on their partition. Moreover, the Habsburg desire eventually to annex Bosnia-Hercegovina was shown in subsequent negotiations which were carried on between the partners of the Three Emperors' Alliance. Until 1914 the peninsula remained a major center of conflict between both the Balkan states and the powers. The great prize to be won was Macedonia.

THE MACEDONIAN QUESTION

Macedonia is generally defined as the area that is bounded on the north by the Šar Mountains, on the east by the Rhodope Mountains, on the south by the Aegean Sea, Mt. Olympus, and the Pindus Range, and on the west by Lake Ohrid. The region includes the Vardar and Struma rivers and the cities of Thessaloniki (Salonika, Solun), Kastoria, Florina, Serres, Petrich, Skopje (Üsküb), Ohrid, and Bitola (Monastir). In the nineteenth century this region was not prosperous. Its main crops were cereal, tobacco, and opium poppies; livestock, mainly sheep, were also raised. The population of less than two million within a 25,000 square-mile area was divided into nine distinct groups: Turks, Bulgars, Greeks, Serbs, Macedonians, Albanians, Vlachs or Kutzo-Vlachs, Jews, and Gypsies. Since the population was intermixed, a clear line could not be drawn separating the nationalities. The cities usually had strong Turkish, Greek and Jewish elements. In the villages and rural areas different nationalities existed side by side. Nor was it possible to determine accurately the precise numerical strength of any of the groups. Census reports were almost meaningless because the results usually reflected the interest of the census-taker. There were school, language, and religious censuses, but any of these could be misleading. For example, it is known that the Slavic peoples of Orthodox faith attended Greek churches when a Slavic service was not available. Serbs and Bulgars also went to each other's churches if the only other alternative was a Greek service. In other words, expediency and politics as well as nationality could determine church membership.

When the struggle over Macedonia became more heated after the Congress of Berlin, anthropologists, linguists, and physiologists from the Balkan countries all used their specialty to claim the area for their own particular nationality. The Bulgarians used linguistic arguments to demonstrate that the Macedonian Slavs were indeed their brothers. Serbian linguists countered with claims of the closeness of their grammar to the language spoken in the area. Serbian anthropologists argued that their *slava* festival, found also among the Macedonians, made them Serbs. The Greeks sought to demonstrate that anyone in Macedonia under the authority of the ecumenical patriarch was Greek. Thus, each nation used every conceivable argument to back its claims, and each could be effectively challenged.

The real significance of the region, the geographic-strategic, involved both the Balkan states and the great powers. Bulgaria, Greece, and Serbia all wished to acquire Macedonia or a major portion of it for three main reasons. First, it would enlarge the state and incorporate more nationals within it. Second, the acquisition of the Vardar and Struma river valleys and the railroads through them would have great economic advantages. Third, and perhaps most significant, whoever controlled Macedonia would be the strongest power on the peninsula. For the great powers this last concern was certainly the most important. They also recognized that possession of Macedonia gave the owner a strong strategic outpost in relation to Constantinople and the Turkish Straits. Britain had violently opposed the creation of San Stefano Bulgaria, a state that would have been under Russian control, because of these military considerations. Austria-Hungary shared Britain's concern, but the monarchy had an additional reason. She was interested in developing economic links with Thessaloniki and in extending her influence southward toward the Aegean.

Until the creation of the Bulgarian exarchate in 1870 the influence of Greece was paramount. She had assets that at first seemed unassailable. Certainly Philhellene sentiment in the first part of the century assured her important European support. Many Europeans sincerely believed in the Greek nationality of the area. Travelers stayed in towns and cities where there was indeed a large Greek population; the inns were almost always run by Greeks. Moreover, the ecumenical partriarchate, as we have seen, did serve to strengthen Greek national interests throughout the Balkans. In Macedonia it strongly resisted any challenge by the Bulgarians and the Serbs. Before 1870 even Russia was not ready to undermine the patriarch's authority in the interest of the other Balkan peoples. The Greek church also controlled the education available in the area. Many non-Greeks who attended Greek schools learned the language and simply passed over into the Greek cultural sphere. They were then willing to accept Greek political control.

Against these advantages Greece had liabilities. For most of the nineteenth century attention had to be directed first to the acquisition of Thessaly and Epirus, lands that separated the kingdom from Macedonia. Thereafter, the Cretan problem absorbed much Greek energy. Any Greek attempt to expand was also bound to meet with British disapproval since that empire usually favored the maintenance of Ottoman rule. With the British fleet predominant in the Mediterranean, Greece could not move northward without danger. In addition, as the century progressed, the Greek position weakened. The creation of the Bulgarian exarchate was a real blow. Because of this erosion of its strength, toward the end of the century the Greek government came to stand more for the preservation of the status quo until a situation arose that would allow it to advance. Ottoman sovereignty was certainly preferred to either Bulgarian or Serbian possession of Macedonia.

Unlike Greece, the position of Bulgaria improved with the years. In the Treaty of San Stefano that state had received what it considered its ideal boundaries. Even though these were lost, hope of their eventual attainment remained high. In this period, therefore, the Bulgarian government wished to precipitate an immediate solution to the problem. As we have seen, at first Russia supported the Bulgarian position. When that aid was lost, Britain and Austria-Hungary became more sympathetic toward Bulgarian aspirations. Along with this strong outside assistance, the exarchate also proved a useful means of extending Bulgarian influence. If two-thirds of the inhabitants of any district expressed a desire to join the exarchate, they could do so. It was relatively easy to convince the Slavic people of the region that they should choose the "Slavic" exarchate rather than the "Greek" patriarchate. The Ottoman government usually aided in these endeavors.

Notwithstanding these favorable aspects, Bulgaria had numerous problems to face. Most serious was the fact that after San Stefano both the Greeks and the Serbs saw Bulgaria, backed by Russia, as their chief adversary. With their vital interests threatened, both states mobilized their educational, religious, and political resources. Romania also joined with them at the turn of the century. In addition, although Bulgaria was at times aided by the great powers, this assistance was never certain. The Balkan policy of all of the great states was determined by their world interests which could and did shift frequently.

Of the three powers Serbia was in the weakest position. In fact her initial task was simply to convince the great powers that she did indeed have a rightful claim in the area. The Greek and Bulgarian interests were recognized, but not those of Belgrade. In the 1880s the Serbian disadvantages seemed many. First, since 1804 Serbia had sought to expand principally in the west, toward Bosnia, Hercegovina, and the Adriatic. In addition, she was concerned about the Serbs to the north, in Srem, Bačka, and the Banat of the Vojvodina. The shift to an emphasis on the south, which occurred principally after the Habsburg monarchy occupied Bosnia-Hercegovina and thus made the provinces for the time unattainable, was not easy to make. Second, the Serbian government did not have religious institutions comparable to the exarchate and the patriarchate. Nor did it, of course, enjoy the support of Russia until the accession of Peter Karadjordjević, a patronage that might have offset some of the advantages of its rivals. Third, the Obrenović dynasty and the Habsburg alliance of 1881 were an impossible basis for a strong and aggressive national policy. Milan and Alexander were not rulers who could rally their people behind them. Although the monarchy did give some assistance at the Congress of Berlin, it was unlikely that this state would allow a real strengthening of Serbia in view of the South Slav problem within its own state.

In addition to Greece, Bulgaria, and Serbia, Romania also put forward claims to Macedonia. In this heterogeneous population there were a large number of Vlachs who were mainly traders and shepherds. Related to the Romanians, their exact numbers are not known. Despite the weakness of the relationship, by 1900 the Romanian government was subsidizing Vlach schools and by 1912 it is estimated that one million francs had been spent for this purpose. In 1905 the sultan was persuaded to recognize a Vlach millet separate from the ecumenical patriarch. The Romanian intentions were clear; the state could make no realistic claims to Macedonia or hope to annex any land there. The chief purpose was to block Bulgaria and to make impossible the re-creation of the San Stefano boundaries. It was also hoped that Romanian claims in Macedonia could be used as a bargaining point to gain additional territory in Dobrudja.

At this time also there was the beginning of a Slavic Macedonian national movement. Its premise was that the Slavs in Macedonia were neither Bulgars nor Serbs, but another distinct and separate branch of the Slavic race with a unique national language. Initially overshadowed and overwhelmed by the Bulgarian and Serbian forces, this idea was to acquire major importance only in the future and outside of the framework of this narrative.

Although the struggle for Macedonia primarily involved the Christian people, it must not be forgotten that the region had large numbers of Muslims. Most of these were Turkish or Albanian, but some were Slavs who had converted earlier. This population naturally strongly favored the maintenance of Ottoman rule and looked to Abdul Hamid II for protection. The Porte, in turn, made every effort to defend its position.

Despite the existence of other nationalities, the chief contestants remained the three neighboring states: Bulgaria, Greece, and Serbia. In the last two decades of the nineteenth century they entered into a regular battle for predominance. Their weapons were the competing churches, educational establishments and national societies. The ecclesiastical warfare continued on previous lines. The Bulgars sought to gain the approval of the sultan for more bishoprics; the Greeks worked through the patriarchate to try to block the requests. The Serbs, too, now sought a separate organization, but it was not until 1902 that they were allowed a bishopric in Skopje. By the end of the century each nation had also established a large number of schools, which became instruments of state policy. Primers, grammars, history books, and propaganda tracts were disseminated, each of which argued for one or another national cause.

The organization of competing national societies, however, was to cause the greatest difficulties. Although some were primarily cultural in intent, others were dedicated to achieving a solution through violence. The first, the Cyril and Methodius Society, was founded in 1884. Its purpose was to educate, indoctrinate, and convert the Slavs in Macedonia to the Bulgarian cause. Two years later the Serbs responded with the creation of the Society of St. Sava, named after their patron saint, with the same goals to be achieved in behalf of Serbia. In 1894 the Greeks formed the Ethnike Hetairia, which was also effective in Crete.

Although most of the societies were for cultural and propaganda purposes and did not participate in outrages, some did. The best known of the extremist organizations were both Bulgarian. The Internal Macedonian Revolutionary Organization, or IMRO, appeared in 1893. Its purpose was to overthrow Ottoman rule and establish an autonomous Macedonian state; hence its motto was Macedonia for the Macedonians. Its sympathies were nevertheless Bulgarian. Its rival was the Macedonian Supreme Committee, known both as the Supremists and the External Organization. It was located in Sofia and its membership came chiefly from refugees from Macedonia. It enjoyed the support, although not openly, of the Bulgarian government. Its goal was the annexation of the area to Bulgaria. Whereas IMRO initially devoted its energies to the preparation of a carefully planned uprising to be carried out in the future, the Supremists did not hesitate to send raiding parties into Macedonia to terrorize villages or even to assassinate Turks with the hope that reprisals would force the population to revolt.

The Greeks and Serbs responded with their own acts of violence and terror. The diplomatic reports of European consular officials and correspondents attest to the atrocities committed by all sides. Not only did the local population suffer from the action of their more fanatical members, but the Ottoman authorities also were caught in a dilemma. They were responsible for maintaining order, yet if they acted to apprehend and punish the guilty, they could find themselves pillored in the European press as barbaric and oppressive even when the charges were not deserved.

Both the governments of the Balkan States and the great powers recognized that the danger in these disturbances was that they might force another major crisis in international affairs such as that of 1875–78. All conducted negotiations on the question. In 1892–93 Serbia and Greece attempted to reconcile their differences at the expense of the Bulgarians, but they could not agree on spheres of influence. In 1897 the Macedonian problem was an important part of the Cretan crisis and the Greek-Turkish War. The most significant discussions, however, were those conducted between Franz Joseph and Nicholas II in April, 1897. Since neither wished a Balkan upheaval at this time, the two powers reached an understanding of far-reaching significance. Once again the rulers of Russia and the Habsburg monarchy agreed upon the partition of Turkish lands. In these negotiations the annexation of Bosnia, Hercegovina, and the Sanjak of Novi Pazar by the Habsburg Empire was foreseen, as was the eventual creation of an independent Albania. The remainder of the Ottoman territory in Europe was to be divided equitably between the Balkan states. This decision signified that Serbian claims would also be taken into account. These plans were not, however, to be implemented until the distant future. Both governments were determined that for the present the Balkan governments should be kept from bringing about a European crisis or upsetting the status quo.

Notwithstanding the intentions of the great powers, the Bulgars, Greeks, and Serbs intensified rather than curtailed their activities. The height of these endeavors was reached in August, 1903, when IMRO precipitated the Ilinden Uprising. Its goal was to seize the vilayet of Monastir as the prelude to the complete liberation of Macedonia from Ottoman control. It was another of the scores of ill-conceived and poorly prepared revolts that had plagued the Balkans in the nineteenth century. The Ottoman forces responded with unusual vigor. It is estimated that about nine thousand homes were destroyed.

While this event was unsuccessful in its wider aims, it did force Russian and Habsburg intervention. In 1903 Franz Joseph and Nicholas met at

Mürzsteg and sponsored a new program of reform. The Ottoman gendarmerie in Macedonia was now to be placed under the control of foreign officers, and the victims of the Ilinden Uprising were to receive financial compensation for their losses. The impossible task of defining ethnic boundaries in the region was also attempted. In 1905 the Porte accepted the international supervision of the collection of taxes. In the next years further reform proposals were offered by the powers. In 1908, however, the Macedonian question was temporarily overshadowed by more dramatic events in Constantinople. In that year a revolution occurred, which was again to bring into question the status of all of the sultan's domains.

THE YOUNG TURK REVOLUTION

Not only was the Ottoman government faced with Christian rebellion, but dissatisfaction was again growing within the Muslim society. Although Abdul Hamid II ruled autocratically, he did believe in reform. During his reign elementary and secondary education was expanded, medical schools were founded, and the University of Istanbul established. The army was greatly improved. Means of communication, such as railroads and telegraphs, were expanded. Keenly aware of the losses that his empire had suffered previously, the sultan was convinced that the cause had been primarily the political and economic exploitation by the European powers. Adopting an antiwestern attitude, he sought to strengthen his position by emphasizing his role as caliph, that is as the temporal and spiritual head of the Islamic faith, and by attempting to unite the 300 million Muslims of the world against these alien influences. His actions were popular with his religious leaders and with many of his Turkish Muslim subjects, but among the intellectuals and many in the military there was a rising sense of frustration and dissatisfaction. These men shared the sultan's alarm about the condition of the empire, but they did not believe that autocratic rule was the answer.

Three basic concepts were advanced as means by which the empire could be revived and saved. The first was Pan-Islamism, which Abdul Hamid favored. A state based on the unity of the Muslims would, however, presuppose the abandonment of the Christian Balkan lands. The second program, Ottomanism, has been discussed before. This plan favored the attempt to create a common citizenship, which would embrace Muslims and Christians alike. It ran directly counter to the nationalist movements not only among the Christians, but also among the Arabs. The third idea, Pan-Turanianism, or the unity of the Turkic people including those in Russia, more closely resembled contemporary national concepts elsewhere. Its obvious weakness lay in the disproportion between the Ottoman and Russian military power.

These proposals together with the practical problems of the Ottoman state had been analyzed, debated, and discussed in the empire for three decades before 1908. Those who were most outspoken in their demand for a change in the political structure of the state were exiled to remote provinces of the empire. The more fortunate fled to Europe, principally to Switzerland and France. There they published newspapers and held meetings. Most of these men supported the restoration of the constitution of 1876. They emphasized the need to assure the equality of all Ottoman subjects, and they stressed the preservation of the empire. Links were also established with the Ottoman army, in particular with the Third Army Corps, whose headquarters were in Thessaloniki in Macedonia.

The army officers were practical and realistic in their outlook. Alarmed by the continuing decline of the empire, they were determined to restore its strength and prestige. At the same time they were disturbed by conditions in Macedonia. They were bitter that the government could not control the Bulgarian insurgents, and they resented the fact that European officers were in charge of the gendarmerie after the Mürzsteg reforms. Many were angry because they were not being paid regularly. By 1908 some had joined secret cells where plans for the future were discussed. Their leaders were also in touch with their compatriots living abroad. These people formed the most important part of the membership of the Committee of Union and Progress (C. U. P.) which had been formed in the 1890s. By 1908 it is estimated that this organization had over fifteen thousand members. The goal became the restoration of the constitution of 1876 and the removal of Abdul Hamid, but not of the royal dynasty.

Through his secret service the sultan learned of the conspiracies, but he did not appreciate the strength of the movement. When he began to investigate, spontaneous revolts erupted throughout the Third Army Corps area in June and July, 1908. The loyal troops could not suppress an uprising led by army officers. On July 23 the Committee of Union and Progress demanded that Abdul Hamid restore the constitution. The next day he capitulated to the demands of his best military unit, the Third Army Corps.

The Committee of Union and Progress had as its motto Liberty, Justice, Equality, and Fraternity. Jubilant in their victory and fervent in their belief that they could save the empire, the rebel leaders placed their faith in the constitution and in the appeal of their promise of equality to all citizens. They could not proceed with the removal of the sultan because the soldiers who supported them revered the ruler as the "sultan-caliph" despite the desire for constitutional government. The country then prepared for elections for an assembly.

On October 5 and 6 the revolutionary movement suffered a severe blow. In a coordinated move first Bulgaria proclaimed her independence and then the Habsburg Empire announced the annexation of Bosnia-Hercegovina. The actions did immense harm to the Young Turk movement. Its leaders had come to power determined to save the empire, but within less than three months they had lost important European territories. The crisis also gave courage to the conservative elements. In April, 1909, they were able to stage a brief counterrevolution. Although the army quickly crushed the revolt and proceeded with the deposition of Abdul Hamid, with the concurrence of the Sheik-ul-Islam, the highest religious authority of the empire, it was obvious that the new government would continue to face serious opposition. Moreover, the Austrian and Bulgarian actions had caused an international crisis and reopened the eastern question. The consequences could further endanger Ottoman interests.

THE BOSNIAN CRISIS

Under the terms of the Treaty of Berlin, it will be remembered, Bosnia and Hercegovina, despite the Habsburg occupation, remained an integral part of the Ottoman Empire. Therefore the assembly that was called to convene in Constantinople by the Young Turk regime was to include representatives from this region as well as from autonomous Bulgaria. Naturally neither the Habsburg nor the Bulgarian governments could allow this development. Prince Ferdinand had long determined that he would proclaim Bulgarian independence when possible. The Habsburg monarchy saw the control of Bosnia-Hercegovina as absolutely essential, particularly after the accession of King Peter Karadjordjević, which placed a pro-Russian regime in power in Belgrade. Not only did the control of the provinces provide a military-strategic hinterland to Dalmatia, but the spread of Serbian influence could be better curbed. The monarchy had also devoted considerable attention to the area and had contributed to its material prosperity.

Preparations for the Habsburg annexation were made not only in cooperation with Bulgaria, but also with Russia. In September the Austrian foreign minister, Alois von Aehrenthal, met with the Russian minister, A. P. Isvolsky, in Buchlau in Moravia. No official record was kept of the meeting, about which there was considerable controversy later, but it can be assumed that the Habsburg desire to annex the provinces was accepted. In return, Aehrenthal agreed to support the Russian plan for a change in the Straits settlement, which would open the waterway exclusively to the warships of the Black Sea states. Later disagreement arose on the question of timing. Isvolsky evidently expected that the monarchy would not act at once. Instead, he read in the newspapers on his way to Paris of both the annexation and the Bulgarian declaration of independence.

An immediate diplomatic crisis followed. The most violent reaction came from Belgrade. Despite the Habsburg occupation, nationalist Serbs had still numbered Bosnia and Hercegovina among their irredenta. So long as the provinces were technically still under the sovereignty of the weak Ottoman Empire, there was hope that sometime they would join with Serbia. As an integral part of the strong Dual Monarchy, they now seemed lost. The Serbian press and some of the political leaders urged that a defiant attitude be maintained and that the Habsburg action not be accepted. There was also hope of Russian assistance. For five months Serbia remained adamant. The government was forced to yield only when the Russians accepted the annexation after receiving a virtual ultimatum from Berlin.

The immediate questions, that is, the annexation and the establishment of Bulgarian independence, were settled finally on the basis of negotiations between Constantinople, Sofia, and Vienna. In return for its acceptance of the changes, the Porte received an indemnity and the return of the Sanjak of Novi Pazar to its full control. For the Balkan states and the European powers the main significance of the crisis was that it ended the period of cooperation between the monarchy and Russia which had commenced in 1897. The results of this incident were deeply humiliating for both Serbia and Russia. With strong German support the Habsburg Empire had forced the Russian government to retreat. Russia's goal became to reverse this situation and to organize the Balkan states in a front against the monarchy. The nations were to prove willing, but they wished to set their own diplomatic objectives.

THE BALKAN WARS: 1912, 1913

The Balkan League, which was to initiate the conflict aimed at expelling the Ottoman Empire from Europe, was formed under the initial prodding of Russia. After the Bosnian debacle the Russian government again gave its Balkan policy priority. In October, 1909, an agreement was made at Racconigi with Italy, signifying that these two powers would cooperate on Balkan affairs. In 1911 Italy launched a war against the Ottoman Empire to seize Tripoli. The Ottoman defeat in this conflict and the continuation of internal unrest in the empire, as well as the general international situation, encouraged the Balkan states to hope that Macedonia would soon be partitioned.

Bulgaria and Serbia were the first states to start negotiations. Between 1904–7 the two nations had developed closer cultural, economic, and even political ties. In the discussions after the Bosnian crisis each had entirely different objectives. The Bulgarian government wished any agreement to be directed primarily against the Porte and to have as its chief aim the establishment of an autonomous Macedonia, which would later, it was assumed, either voluntarily join or be annexed to Bulgaria. Serbia, in contrast, rejected the idea of autonomy and asked for a partition agreement. Considering itself primarily endangered by the Habsburg government, the Serbian government wanted any pact to cover also an attack on its territories from the north. Finally, on March 13, 1912, an alliance of mutual defense was signed. It was agreed, in addition, that both powers would take common action against any state that threatened to seize Ottoman lands. The core of the pact, however, was the secret annex in which concrete arrangements were made for the partition of Macedonia.

The secret clauses stated that in the division of the region the lands north of the Šar Mountains would fall to Serbia, whereas those east of the Struma River and the Rhodope Mountains would become Bulgarian. This understanding left the overwhelming bulk of the Macedonian territory unallocated. In this unassigned area, nevertheless, the Serbian government agreed that its maximum claims would only extend to a line running roughly from Kriva Palanka near the Bulgarian frontier in northeastern Macedonia, then southwest, north of the city of Veles, and ending just north of Ohrid. Should the two allies not be able to agree, the disposition of this contested territory, that is, the area between the Šar Mountains to the north and Kriva Palanka-Veles-Ohrid line to the south, would be made by the tsar, whose decision both parties promised to accept. In other words, the maximum Serbian demands at this time represented at most about a third of Macedonian lands inhabited by Slavs. The remainder would thus be divided between Bulgaria and Greece. It should be noted that it was the question of the control of precisely this area that was to become the center of the Serbo-Bulgarian dispute which led to the Second Balkan War. This agreement was followed by a military accord in which Bulgaria agreed to provide 200,000 troops and Serbia 150,000. Of these each was to send 100,000 to the Vardar, i.e., Macedonian, front.

The next understanding was between Bulgaria and Greece. In the previous years relations had gradually improved. In 1911–12 there was more cooperation between the exarchate and the patriarchate, the mutual acts of terror in Macedonia abated, and some students were exchanged. The common enemy was now the Ottoman Empire. Unlike the previous treaty, the Greek-Bulgarian agreement was a simple defensive alliance. The Bulgarian government was not able to obtain Greek approval of an autonomous Macedonia, and both states wanted Thessaloniki. With rival claims that could not be compromised, the states signed a document that did not contain the word Macedonia.

The final agreements were made by Serbia and Bulgaria with Montenegro. Their aim was simply to prepare the stage so that small country could start a conflict with the Porte. The other Balkan states would then be able to join in on an assault on Ottoman territories.

These negotiations extended well over a year. It soon became appar-

Map 8. The Macedonian Contested Zone, 1913

ent to the Russian government that its interest in the Balkan League, that is, that it block Austria-Hungary, had now become a secondary issue for the Balkan states. In addition, the territorial provisions, which included a Bulgarian claim to Adrianople, a city close to Constantinople and the Straits, caused real concern in St. Petersburg. Russia was at the time in no position to face a crisis in which the fate of that area would come before the great powers. Therefore, in cooperation with other European states, the Russian government now tried to pacify the Balkan nations by proposing a new reform program for the Ottoman Empire. On October 8, 1912, Russia and Austria-Hungary, the two adversaries, cooperated to warn the Balkan states in behalf of the powers that modifications in the territorial integrity of the Ottoman Empire would not be recognized. It was, however, too late. On that same day Montenegro had commenced hostilities, to be enthusiastically joined by her allies.

The military operations progressed relatively smoothly. While the Greek navy prevented the Ottoman army from receiving reinforcements, the combined allied armies of over 700,000 men attacked the

320,000 Ottoman defenders. The main Bulgarian thrust was toward Constantinople, whose outskirts were quickly reached. With the aid of some Serbian forces the Bulgarian army laid siege to Adrianople. Although the Bulgars raced to Thessaloniki, they found that the Greeks had occupied this prize the previous day, November 8. Meanwhile, Serbian troops advanced far beyond their assigned sphere of influence and took Prilep, Bitola, and Ohrid, cities south of the Kriva Palanka-Veles-Ohrid line.

The hostilities involved more than the Macedonian lands. After its experiences in the Pig War the Serbian government was determined to acquire an outlet to the sea. The best port available was Durrës (Durazzo) in northern Albania. Although the territory was Albanian, the Serbs justified their claim on strategic and economic grounds. Other Albanian lands were also the objective of the Balkan allies. Serbian and Montenegrin forces besieged the city of Shkodër (Scutari); the Greeks attacked Janina. These actions again brought the fate of the Albanian population of the peninsula to the attention of the great powers.

The military successes of the Balkan states meant that at the beginning of 1913 the Ottoman Empire in Europe had been reduced essentially to the four besieged cities of Constantinople and Adrianople in the east and Shkodër and Janina in the west. At this point the great powers intervened to halt the hostilities. In May, 1913, they imposed the Treaty of London, which set the Enos-Media line as the boundary of the Ottoman Empire, thus excluding Adrianople and leaving Constantinople with only a small hinterland. Crete was finally assigned to Greece. The great problem of the disposition of Macedonia, Albania, and the Aegean Islands remained, but it was now clear that the great powers rather than the Balkan allies would determine the final fate of these territories.

The Macedonian issue was tied directly with the Albanian. Both Austria-Hungary and Italy were determined to exclude Serbia from the Adriatic. The establishment of an independent Albania would accomplish this purpose. In addition, Italy was interested in such a state as her sphere of influence in the Balkans. After Italy was unified she, too, began to vie with the Habsburg Empire and Russia for a share in the political domination of the peninsula. The strong support of Italy and the Dual Monarchy assured that an Albania would come into existence. This decision, of course, affected the settlement drawn up between the Balkan states. Thus, Serbia in the north and Greece, with her claims to southern Albania,[1] were thwarted in their plans to annex Albanian territories. Both demanded compensation elsewhere.

For the Serbian government the only alternate lands were those origi-

1. It should be mentioned that in Greek terminology Epirus includes a large part of present-day southern Albania, an area referred to in much Greek writing as northern Epirus.

nally assigned to Bulgaria. Arguing that the outlet to the Adriatic had been denied and that Serbian troops had carried the main weight of the fighting in Macedonia, Serbia now demanded that her share of Macedonia extend beyond the Kriva Palanka-Veles-Ohrid line. The question was not whether the inhabitants were Serbian or Bulgarian; some Serbian scholars referred to them as Macedo-Slavs. The question was rather of the balance of power among the Balkan states. Bulgaria had now extended her control to the shores of the Aegean; this, along with the Macedonian territory assigned to her, would make her the predominant power in the peninsula. The Greek government, which did not like the presence of Bulgarian forces just a few miles north of Thessaloniki, shared the Serbian apprehensions about this situation. The Serbian government refused to yield the lands in Macedonia that they had occupied even though those lands extended beyond the previous maximum claims. The Bulgarian position, in contrast, was that the terms of the original treaty of alliance should be enforced.

As explained earlier, it was less difficult for the Serbian and Greek governments to reach an agreement than for either to come to an understanding with Bulgaria. Athens and Belgrade could simply divide Macedonia, with Greece taking the southern and Serbia the northern part. The Bulgarian interests stretched across the area to Albania, thus cutting across the lands claimed by the two other states. As relations between the nations over the peace terms became strained, it was thus natural that Greece and Serbia should cooperate. They now made a secret agreement that they would seek a common frontier in Macedonia west of the Vardar River. This division still left an eastern section for Bulgaria. The two signatories further promised to aid each other if war broke out. They were also able to gain the support of Montenegro and even Romania, who had designs on the Dobrudjan territory in Bulgarian hands. Discussions were further initiated with the Ottoman Empire.

Meanwhile, the Bulgarian civilian and military leaders were becoming convinced that a solution by force might be necessary. The diplomatic scene was also more complicated. Russia proposed that the tsar mediate the differences between the Balkan states and invited the premiers of Bulgaria, Serbia, and Greece to St. Petersburg. The Bulgarian government agreed to take part only on the condition that arbitration be concluded within seven days, a step necessary to placate the army, which was urging military action. This condition was interpreted in St. Petersburg as an ultimatum and was categorically rejected. Thereafter Russian support was given to Serbia. The Habsburg monarchy also attempted at this time to disrupt the Balkan League through negotiations with Greece and Romania. As a result of these discussions Bulgaria was left without allies among the Balkan states and real supporters among the great powers. Her adversaries, in contrast, had concluded firm mutual defense pacts among themselves. Evidently, Sofia failed to understand the seriousness of this predicament.

Convinced of its military superiority, the Bulgarian government, on the night of June 29–30, 1913, mounted a surprise attack on Serbia and Greece, thereby starting the Second Balkan War. Montenegro, Romania, and the Ottoman Empire subsequently entered the conflict against Sofia. Bulgaria did not have a chance against this combination; on July 31 she signed an armistice.

The Treaty of Bucharest, concluded on August 10, settled the contest over the division of the Albanian and Macedonian territories. The terms were, as could be expected, extremely damaging to Bulgaria. Adrianople and most of Eastern Thrace reverted to Ottoman control; Romania took southern Dobrudja; Greece extended her border to about fifty miles north of Thessaloniki and eastward beyond the port of Kavalla. In the west Greece annexed Epirus including Janina. Serbia almost doubled her size with the acquisition of the major portion of Slavic Macedonia, including areas that she had earlier agreed were not within her maximum claims. The Sanjak of Novi Pazar was divided between Serbia and Montenegro, giving the two states a common frontier. Bulgaria was awarded only a small part of eastern Macedonia in the Struma valley, but she did obtain an eighty-mile stretch along the Aegean coastline, including the port of Dedeagatch. The treaty also provided for an independent Albania.

The Treaty of Bucharest is of great significance for the Balkan states because, with minor adjutments, the boundaries set at this time remained fixed. In addition, the agreement marked the expulsion of the Ottoman Empire from Europe with, of course, the exception of the city of Constantinople and a small section of Thrace. The Balkan Wars thus brought about the final realization of the goal set by most of the Balkan leaders throughout the nineteenth century. Until the last part of the century the chief objective of each government had been the acquisition of lands occupied principally by members of their own nationality. In 1912 and 1913 these considerations proved secondary to concerns about maintaining the balance of power on the peninsula, or to desires to obtain more territory for strategic or economic reasons. No state had been in the least hesitant about claiming lands with Albanian inhabitants. Each state had shown itself primarily interested in advancing its own interests rather than in protecting the national principle as such. Finally, this period resulted in the appearance on the map of the last of Balkan national states, Albania.

CHAPTER 14

The Establishment of Albania

THE Albanian national movement was unique in comparison with those previously discussed in that the leaders, at least before 1912, did not wish the Ottoman Empire dismembered, nor did they seek an independent state. Instead, they feared that should the empire fall their lands would be divided among their neighbors. Autonomy within the Ottoman state appeared to be the best guarantee of their national safety.

The Albanian attitude can perhaps be best understood when the complexity of the Albanians' situation is considered. The Albanians were one nationality and spoke dialects of the same language. They were, however, divided into two main groups, the Gegs and the Tosks, and had three religions: Muslim, Orthodox, and Catholic. The Gegs, comprising the majority of the population, lived in the northern half of the country, where those who lived in the mountains had a strong tribal organization, were very conservative, and had little contact with the outside world. The Tosks, in contrast, were concentrated in the south and had more opportunities to associate with other peoples or to migrate. Most Tosks were peasants, many of whom worked on estates for large landowners who were generally Albanian.

After the Turkish conquest a majority of the population had accepted the Muslim faith. In 1914, 70 percent of the population was of that religion while 20 percent were Orthodox and 10 percent Catholic. The Catholics, who lived predominantly in the northern coastal areas, had contact with neighboring Italy and Austria-Hungary. The Orthodox, concentrated in the south, naturally were more closely associated with the patriarchate and were more under Greek cultural influence. The Muslim majority held the strongest position in the country. Conversions here had followed to some extent the pattern of those in Bosnia-Hercegovina. The landed aristocracy had accepted Islam to preserve their political and economic position, but in Albania the peasantry also be-

222

came Muslim. Most of the Muslim Gegs belonged to the conservative Sunni sect, whereas the Tosks were both Sunni and Bektashi. The Sunni stood strongly for the maintenance of Ottoman traditions, for loyalty to the sultan, and they were less susceptible to ideas of political reform. They preferred the established tribal rule and adherence to local customs and laws. In the empire at least thirty of the grand vezirs had come from these Muslim Albanians. Some of the finest and bravest Ottoman soldiers were born in this region. Throughout the previous centuries the Albanian population as a whole had been an element of strength in the empire.

Despite the loyalty of the people, Albania had remained one of the most backward areas of the empire. An improverished country whose population supported itself by livestock raising and subsistence agriculture, its political system mirrored its state of development. The people lived in remote communities under local leaders. Until late in the nineteenth century the country lacked most of the bases for the development of national self-consciousness which existed in the other states. Physical communication within the country was extremely difficult; by 1912 there were only about 200 kilometers of paved roads. What schools existed, except for the Catholic institutions in Shkodër, were taught in either Turkish or Greek. Here religion, which had been a strong unifying force in the other Balkan countries, was a divisive element. The great common bond was language, but it was not taught in the schools nor had a standard alphabet been devised. Books in Albanian were almost nonexistent.

Largely because of these negative considerations an Albanian national movement did not make an appearance until 1878, and even then it came about largely as a reaction to external threats. Before that time neither the historical background of the area nor the fact that prominent rebels of Albanian background had challenged Ottoman rule had produced a national ideology or leadership. The ancestors of the people, the ancient Illyrians, had settled in the Balkan peninsula before the Slavs. Although Mohammed Ali of Egypt and Ali Pasha of Janina were Albanians, both worked for their own power and not the interests of their countrymen. After 1830 there had indeed been numerous instances of local revolts against Ottoman rule, but most of these were in protest against high taxation, reforms in the army, or changes in the central administration. By and large the Albanians were satisfied with the status quo and local autonomy. Their privileged position in the empire outweighed the liabilities of membership in a rapidly weakening political entity.

The Albanian leaders first sensed the growing danger to their position when the terms of the Treaty of San Stefano were announced in March, 1878. Under the provisions of this agreement Greater Bulgaria included parts of present-day eastern Albania, while Montenegro was awarded lands in the north primarily inhabited by Albanians. National territories were thus assigned to two Slavic Orthodox states, neither of whom could be expected to deal leniently with Muslims. It was to save themselves from their neighbors, not from the Ottoman government, that the Albanians were forced to act.

Protests were immediately organized against the treaty and committees were formed throughout the land. The center of resistance became Prizren, a city in the Kosovo region of present-day Yugoslavia. Here northern Muslim conservative landlords and local notables, joined by some representatives from the south, particularly Abdul Frashëri, the driving nationalistic force of the time, met in June, 1878, and established the League of Prizren, or the Albanian League. The goal was simply to defend the integrity of the Albanian lands. It was decided that committees would be set up in other cities, most notably in Shkodër, to counter Montenegrin encroachments. In addition, the Albanian leaders agreed on two practical steps: first, that they would support the maintenance of the integrity of the Ottoman Empire at the Congress of Berlin, and, second, that they would petition the sultan to unite the four vilayets of Janina, Monastir, Üskub, and Shkodër and to grant this area autonomy. In other words, they wished to unite the Albanian population in one political and administrative unit.

At the Congress of Berlin the Albanian lands were left largely intact, principally because of the conflict of the great powers and not because of the Albanian protests. Greater Bulgaria was divided, and the Albanian sections returned to Ottoman control. In response to their demands for Epirus, including Janina, the Greeks received only a small section. Some territory claimed by the Albanians was given to Montenegro, but not all that this small nation desired. The Albanian actions at this time, which were not limited to words but in some places involved fierce fighting, also made the European states aware of the existence of these people and their wish not to be partitioned by their neighbors.

Although the Albanians had cooperated with the Ottoman government in resisting the Bulgar, Greek, Montenegrin, and Serbian demands, the sultan refused to unite the four vilayets. The attainment of this objective was, however, crucial for Albania's national interests. Moreover, Article 23 of the Treaty of Berlin sanctioned administrative changes in the region, although it indicated no specific direction. In November, 1878, the southern Albanian leaders met in Frashër under the direction of Abdul Frashëri and formally adopted the program of the union of the vilayets. Subsequently, the northern Albanian organization accepted the principle of territorial unity and autonomy, but the two groups could not agree on details of timing and implementation. The radical faction believed that immediate steps should be taken to achieve autonomy. The conservative group, led by the feudal *begs,* preferred a moderate, cautious approach and were ready to cooperate with the Ottoman authorities.

There followed much political maneuvering, but by 1880 the autonomist element in Prizren and Frashër was able to gain control of the Albanian League. They were strongly opposed by the large landowners who remained staunchly loyal to the sultan-caliph. In April, 1881, the sultan ordered his army, under Dervish Pasha, to move against Prizren and crush the autonomist movement. Despite this setback the previous three years had produced significant achievements for the national movement. First, many Albanian leaders had come to recognize that the Ottoman Empire was near collapse and that they had to plan for the future. Second, the initial steps had been taken to affect a common policy in both the north and the south, areas that hitherto had not been in communication. Third, and most important, the spirit and basic program of the Albanian League had been accepted by the various factions who now differed chiefly on how the common aims should be achieved. The first concrete moves towards the creation of an Albanian state had thus been taken.

As elsewhere, the Albanian national movement was accompanied by a period of cultural awakening. With the lack of a common religion or geographic center, language remained the main bond between the people. There was not, however, any standard literary language, nor was there common agreement on the alphabet. In the mid-nineteenth century the area had attracted the interest of foreign scholars, most notably F. Bopp, who first affirmed that Albanian was an Indo-European language, and the Austrian J. G. von Hahn, generally regarded as the father of Albanology, who produced a grammar, a vocabulary, and a collection of folklore. By the end of the century it was established that "the Albanians were descendants of a great and ancient Indo-European people in the Balkans." [1] This heritage played the same role in boosting national pride among Albanian intellectuals as did the similar links to the classical past among the Greeks and Romanians. Subsequently, the study of Albanian history, language, and folklore became popular, particularly among the Albanians in Italy.

A major aid to the literary movement occurred in 1879 with the founding of the Society for the Printing of Albanian Writings in Constantinople. The goal of the organization was to establish a standard language which would lead to the publication of books, journals, and newspapers to be used and understood by all. The translation of important foreign works into Albanian was also an objective. The spirit of the organization was well expressed in the preamble to its constitution: "All en-

1. Stavro Skendi, *The Albanian National Awakening, 1878–1912* (Princeton, New Jersey: Princeton University Press, 1967), p. 115.

lightened nations have been . . . civilized by writings in their own language. Every nation that does not write its own language and has no works in it is in darkness and is barbarian. And the Albanians, not writing their own language and having no [present] works in their own language, are in the same state." [2]

The question of a standard literary language involved not only the question of the choice of a basic dialect, but also of a common alphabet. At this time foreign and native scholars vied with one another to produce a standard form. Usually, each preferred the alphabet employed in the region of Albania with which he was most familiar. After much discussion and controversy a congress was held in Bitola in November, 1908, where the Latin alphabet was adopted. There was much opposition to this decision, particularly among the Muslims of the north who still preferred the "script of the Koran." Even the Young Turk regime reacted strongly against the preference shown for the Latin alphabet. In March, 1910, the Grand Vezir stated that: "The government considers the desire to adopt the Latin characters [on the part of the Albanians] as the first step to be detached from Turkey. . . . The government must do everything, and will do everything, to prevent the adoption of the Latin alphabet." [3] Nevertheless, this form was accepted as standard. A common literary language, however, was not adopted in this period.

Education also was a major problem. There were only a few Albanian schools or institutions that taught Albanian. As in other Balkan countries at the beginning of the century, the instruction available was ecclesiastical—here Muslim, Orthodox, or Catholic. The schools that the Ottoman government supported for the Muslim population were not only religious in direction, but Turkish in language. The basic purpose was to unite the Muslim people against their Christian neighbors and to make them loyal subjects of the Ottoman state. The Orthodox schools had other objectives. They were Greek in language and thus vehicles of Hellenization. Both the Ottoman government and the patriarchate opposed the establishment of secular Albanian schools. The Ottoman officials saw them as the basis for future claims for autonomy or independence. The patriarchate, after the recent bitter experience with the Bulgarian exarchate, feared that they would be the prelude for the demand for a separate Albanian Orthodox church.

In contrast to the Muslim and Orthodox establishments the Catholic schools were conducted in the native language. The Habsburg government had certain privileges in the empire, one of which was to maintain Catholic schools and churches. The Franciscans and Jesuits played a prominent role in their development. Italian Catholics also had their in-

2. *Ibid.*, p. 120.
3. *Ibid.*, pp. 387–88.

stitutions. Both the Habsburg and Italian schools naturally had political as well as religious aims. Like the Ottoman government and the Greek patriarchate, the two Catholic nations used their educational weapons to advance their causes and to counteract Slavic influences.

Under these conditions there was an obvious need for secular schools under Albanian control. Some were, in fact, run secretly in defiance of Ottoman and Orthodox disapproval. Others were opened when influential Albanians gained the assent of sympathetic local Ottoman administrators. Thus, the first Albanian boys' school was opened in Korçë (Koritsa) in 1885, followed by an institution for girls in 1891. These and similar schools functioned only a short time before Constantinople ordered them closed. The situation remained difficult in view of the continued opposition from the chief civil and ecclesiastical authorities. The Greek Orthodox church excommunicated students who attended the new schools. The Ottoman government became if anything more severe in its restrictions on Albanian education. In 1902, for instance, it was forbidden to possess books in Albanian and to use the language in correspondence. A change for the better did not occur until after the Young Turk Revolution. This new regime did approve at first the teaching of the language in primary and secondary schools and the opening of new institutions.

The educational activity described above was enthusiastically supported by the Albanians living in Italy, Egypt, Constantinople, Romania, Bulgaria, and the United States. Although these groups differed on plans and strategy, they were united in their desire to encourage the development of Albanian national feeling. These Albanian colonies published books, journals, and newspapers, and they championed the national cause abroad. Ultimately, they were able to rally influential segments of European public opinion behind Albanian interests.

For the Albanian nationalist these cultural activities were, of course, not enough. Although quiet generally prevailed after the dissolution of the Albanian League in 1881, there were sporadic outbreaks with nationalist overtones in the next years. The most serious situation occurred in 1897 during the Cretan revolt when the Ottoman government used Albanian troops against the Greeks. Once armed, the Albanian forces naturally considered making political demands for themselves, and they were reluctant to surrender their weapons at the end of the fighting. More disturbances thus took place.

The Macedonian problem, however, caused the most difficulty. As mentioned earlier, the Bulgarian, Greek, and Serbian governments had largely ignored the existence of the Albanians and Turks who in many regions of Macedonia comprised an absolute ethnic majority. These two people thus had a common interest in resisting the Christian Balkan states, and the Porte sought to exploit this situation. Although usually supporting Constantinople, the Albanian leaders were constantly aware of their own interests. Thus, in the anarchical conditions prevailing in the area in the decade before the Young Turk rebellion, Albanians sometimes fought for the empire, but when conditions were favorable they also came into conflict with the government over their objectives of further autonomy. They did not, however, form a common front with the Christian nationalities against Constantinople.

The success of the Young Turk Revolution aroused great hopes among the Albanian nationalists. Many Albanians, including Ismail Kemal, took an active part in the organization of the revolt, and Bitola was one of its main centers. The Young Turk program, with its emphasis on the re-establishment of the constitution of 1876, decentralization, the rights of non-Turkish people and the opening of Albanian schools, was naturally welcomed. National associations were quickly formed, and twenty-six Albanians were elected to the Turkish parliament. The only serious opposition to the new regime came from the northern Kosovo area where the conservative beys remained loyal to the sultan and defended their historic rights and privileges. This favorable attitude changed sharply when after the loss of Bulgaria and Bosnia-Hercegovina the Young Turk regime reversed its former policy and instead attempted to impose a centralized, Turkish-national administration. Albanian schools were closed, and national associations and newspapers were prohibited. The government also attempted to convey the impression abroad that the Albanian people did not really want autonomy.

Both the nationalists and the conservative northerners strongly opposed the new policies. The main center of resistance was the Kosovo region where the inhabitants organized to protect their traditional rights and privileges and to oppose the tax and military recruitment measures. In March, 1910, the Porte dispatched a military force to the region. The best indication of the bitterness that now developed between the Albanians and the government is the fact that about ten thousand refugees fled into Christian Slavic Montenegro, a state that had been heartily detested in the past. The fighting was strongest in the north, but there was also resistance in the south. The aim of the Albanians remained the achievement of autonomy within the empire. When it became evident that the movement could not be suppressed by force, the Young Turk government once again changed direction. In March, 1911, it was decided that Albanian schools could reopen and the Latin alphabet was accepted. The government, however, insisted that the Koran be studied in Arabic script as decreed in 1869. Thus, after three decades of effort the Albanians finally had their own schools and the right to use their language. Although the north and south had acted together against Constantinople to achieve certain limited goals, they had not agreed on a common national policy nor had they chosen a mutually acceptable leader.

The final resolution of the Albanian question came as a result of the long period of warfare which began for the Ottoman Empire in 1911. In September of that year the war with Italy commenced and the Balkan states opened negotiations toward the formation of the Balkan League. To consolidate their internal position and to meet the threat from abroad better, the Young Turk regime held new elections for the Ottoman parliament and won 215 of the 222 seats. This vote, clearly the product of fraud and intimidation, precipitated the conclusive break between the Young Turks and their Albanian supporters. By August, 1912, the entire country was in open revolt. Despite the fact that they soon gained military control, the Albanian leaders remained divided on their ultimate objectives. Some preferred to seek the restoration of Abdul Hamid II and the prerevolutionary regime; others wished to have the stipulations of the constitution of 1876 enforced. The majority, however, continued to pursue the elusive goal of autonomy, including the specific conditions of a union of the four vilayets, the creation of a separate national administration, control of local taxes and expenditures, the official use of the Albanian language, and the right of the populace to remain armed. In September, 1912, Constantinople accepted the basic demands, but before all of the issues could be resolved, the First Balkan War broke out in October. With this event all of the rival factions in Albania realized that the very survival of the nation was at stake. The danger now existed that the lands would be partitioned by their Slavic and Greek neighbors.

At first the Albanian leaders stood by their previous goal: autonomy within the empire. When the initial success of the Balkan states in the fighting opened the possibility that the Porte might well lose all its European lands, the objective shifted to the gaining of absolute independence. Instead of defending the empire, the Albanians now joined those who stood for dismemberment. On November 28, 1912, a national assembly of eighty-three Muslim and Christian delegates met at Vlorë (Valona) and proclaimed Albanian independence. Ismail Kemal was elected president, and a cabinet of Muslims and Christians appointed. This action would have been little more than a futile gesture in face of the threatening Bulgarian, Greek, Serbian, and Montenegrin armies had not the state been able to gain the support of at least some of the great powers.

Of the outside nations Italy and Austria-Hungary had the most direct interest in the survival of Albania. Each wished to add the area to its own sphere of interest and to check the expansion of the neighboring Slavic states. If Italy could dominate the land and thus control both sides of the Straits of Otranto, which are only fifty miles wide, the Adriatic would indeed become an Italian sea. If, conversely, Austrian influence prevailed, the safe passage of the Habsburg navy through the straits could be assured. Recognizing the importance of the region, the two powers started a struggle for predominance after the Congress of Berlin. The Italian government attempted to use the large Albanian colonies on its territory for this purpose. Because the latter were predominantly Catholic or Uniate, however, they were not completely trusted by the Muslim and Orthodox Albanians. The Habsburg government appealed more to the native intellectuals and was even able to gain the sympathy of some Muslims despite the connection with the Catholic church. In fact, for a brief period after the First Balkan War began a few prominent Albanians called for an Austro-Hungarian protectorate over their country should the Ottoman Empire collapse. Pursuing their individual aims, the Italian and Habsburg governments were most active in opening schools, hospitals, and orphanages. Their scholars were diligent in the study of Albanian subjects, and their public was instructed in the strategic importance of the area.

The chief issues in the territorial settlement after the Balkan wars have been discussed previously. As we have seen, Serbia sought a port on the Adriatic Sea in order to escape the Austrian hold over her economy. Durrës, in northern Albania, was the chief objective. If this city with its hinterland were lost, a future Albanian state would be badly crippled. The Habsburg monarchy, however, was determined to keep Serbia a landlocked state; Montenegro's attempt to acquire Shkodër and other Albanian lands was also opposed. The Italian position was similar; this government too wished to check the expansion of the Slavic states. In addition, it was concerned about the Greek designs on Southern Albania and the threat to the port of Vlorë and the Island of Saseno, that is, to the eastern shore of the Straits of Otranto. Vienna and Rome thus joined in a solid front against the claims of the Balkan states in favor of the creation of an independent Albania with ethnic frontiers.

Of the other great powers, only Russia expressed a serious interest in the question. The Russian government was sympathetic to the claims of the Slavic states, especially to the Serbian desire for an Adriatic port. France in general backed the Russian position; Britain and Germany pursued essentially a neutral course. During the ambassadorial conferences in London, which decided the question, the Italian and Habsburg point of view eventually prevailed. In December, 1912, the great powers agreed to recognize an independent Albania. Thus, the last Balkan state was established in 1913.

As a final act the great powers assumed the task that they had previously undertaken in the other Balkan states, namely, to draw the boundaries of the new nation, to determine its form of government, and to choose its ruler. The frontier issue was particularly complex. The Al-

MONTENEGRO

SERBIA

•Cetinje

•Peć

•Djakovica

Drin R.

Shkodër•

•Prizren

Skopje•

•Debar

•Tirana

Durrës•
(Durazzo)

Shukumbî R.

Ohrid

Bitola•
(Monastir)

•**Lushnjë**

Saseno Is.

Frashër

Kastoria•

•Vlorë

Tepelene•

Vijosë R.

Gjirokastër•

GREECE

CORFU

•Janina

0 _____ 100
Miles

Map 9. Albania, 1913

banian leaders naturally sought ethnic boundaries, a goal supported by Austria-Hungary and Italy. Russia, in contrast, wished to allow Serbia and Montenegro at least some of their territorial objectives, even though they included lands that were ethnically Albanian. The Serbian government remained determined to gain its Adriatic outlet; the Montenegrins were similarly desirous of obtaining Shkodër. The negotiations were protracted and delicate. There was also a problem in that Serbian and Montenegrin troops were in possession of the regions in dispute; they retreated only before an Austrian threat of war. In return, however, Austria reluctantly agreed that districts including the cities of Peć (Ipek), Prizren, Djakovica (Gjakovë), and Debar (Dibër) should be ceded to the Slavic states. Thus, many Albanians were excluded from the national state.

Whereas the northern and eastern borders were drawn at the expense of Albanian interests, the frontier with Greece was more equitable. The Greek government sought to annex Southern Albania (which was called Northern Epirus in Greek terminology) with the districts of Gjirokastër (Argyrokastro) and Korçë. This territory comprised about 2,800 square miles and had a mixed population of Muslims and Orthodox Christians. Since the great powers decided that the line should be drawn on the basis of nationality, the responsible commission assigned most of the contested area to Albania, an act that left about thirty-five thousand Greeks under foreign rule and an equal number of Albanians under Greek control. Despite the fact that Greece, Serbia, Montenegro, and Albania were not satisfied with the final settlement, the boundaries established in 1913 were to remain essentially unchanged.

The next problem, the form of the government to be introduced, did not cause as much international controversy despite its enormous importance to the Albanian people. Ismail Kemal headed the provisional government, which was formed in November, 1912, for over a year, but not without encountering strong opposition from rival political leaders. One of the most important of these, Esad Pasha Toptani, was a member of a distinguished family of Tirana. He and his followers defied the central government from their headquarters in Durrës. In the southern Korçë area Greek-supported Albanian dissidents also resisted the provisional regime. In addition, throughout the land many of the feudal landlords would not surrender the rights and privileges that they had enjoyed for centuries to any regime, be it Ottoman or Albanian. These divisions made the conduct of orderly administration almost impossible. The situation led the great powers in October, 1913, to create an International Control Commission to direct the national administration; Ismail Kemal resigned in January, 1914.

In April, 1914, the commission, to which one Albanian member had been added, completed the draft of a constitution. The state was to be a sovereign principality whose neutrality would be guaranteed by the great powers. The national assembly was to be composed of three representatives from each of the seven administrative divisions, to be elected by direct suffrage, and ten delegates nominated by the prince. Certain notables, the heads of the Muslim, Orthodox, and Catholic faiths, and the commissioner for the national bank were to be ex-officio members. The legislature was to have a four-year term. The prince had the power to appoint the Council of Ministers, which was responsible to him. Thus, once more the great powers determined the form of government for a new Balkan state.

In the selection of the prince the choice again fell on a German, as had been the case in Greece, Romania, and Bulgaria. William of Wied, a thirty-five-year-old captain in the German army, who was also a nephew of Queen Elizabeth of Romania, arrived in Albania in March, 1914. Six months later, shortly after the outbreak of the First World War, he left the principality, never to return. The difficulties in governing the new state had proved insurmountable. The prince lacked administrative experience and he proved a weak leader, but even the most gifted ruler could not have accomplished much in the six months before Albania was engulfed by war. William also suffered from the grave disadvantage that he was regarded as an Austrian protégé, particularly in Italy. The Italian government openly intrigued against him and found ready collaborators among the Albanians who aspired themselves to the throne. The prince's cabinet proved another source of weakness. It was headed by the ambitious Esad Toptani, a potential rival, who held the position of both Minister of Interior and Minister of Defense, two key posts. Instead of appeasing him, his offices gave him a better opportunity to intrigue and foster dissension throughout the country. The prince also included in his government representatives of the feudal landowning class. This action alienated many of the young intellectuals who had championed first the autonomist movement and then independence. In the north the traditional conflicts between the Muslim and Catholic factions were renewed. Had William been granted a number of years of peace, many of these problems might have been resolved. As it was, the establishment of a stable government and the final recognition of the borders had to await the end of the great conflict in Europe.

Despite the collapse of the first government, the thirty-six years since the Congress of Berlin had produced great changes in the Albanian lands. Previously, Albanian history had been characterized by regional loyalty and rivalry between different religions and political groups. These antagonisms had been at least for the moment buried in face of the grave danger of partition. In the process local interests, which had been paramount for centuries, began to yield to larger considerations encompassing the entire Albanian population. Because of the necessity of cooperating for national defense, Albanians from different geographic areas came to know each other. The leadership of the national movement came from every region, from different social and economic groups, and from all three religious communities. Although much was left to be done, the Albanian efforts had resulted in the establishment of an independent state and had laid the basis for the postwar developments.

CHAPTER 15

Balkan Nationalities in the Habsburg Empire

WITH the weakening of the Ottoman Empire and the growing strength of the national idea in Eastern Europe, it was natural that the fate of the other great multinational state should come into question. At the beginning of the nineteenth century the Habsburg Empire was an assemblage of territories differing widely in size, tradition, culture, economy, and language. These lands had been gathered together under the Habsburg dynasty over many years through inheritance, marriage, diplomacy, or war. The boundaries had fluctuated strongly from century to century and had at one time even embraced the great Spanish empire of the new world. The symbol of unity was the imperial family. Its position had been immeasurably strengthened by the great wars of the sixteenth, seventeenth, and eighteenth centuries against the Ottoman Empire, when the monarchy stood as the outpost of Christendom against the Turk. Before the eighteenth century the weight of the central government, the court, was, with a few exceptions, little felt in the outlying provinces. The monarchy concerned itself with the army and foreign policy; the local nobility had free sway in the countryside. In the eighteenth century, during the reigns of Maria Theresa and Joseph II, an attempt was made to introduce a uniform administrative system and German as the language of government. These efforts met the same resistance encountered in the Ottoman Empire when the Porte attempted similar reforms.

In the nineteenth century eleven distinct national groups lived in the monarchy. Among these there were great differences in power and historic tradition. In the first position were the Germans, whose language had been that of politics and literature and who had consistently provided governmental and military leadership throughout most of the

235

previous history of the state. Next in influence were the Magyars, who possessed a strong sense of national pride and self-consciousness and were usually able to maintain control over their historic territories, known as the lands of the Crown of St. Stephen. These territories contained large Romanian, Slovak, and South Slav populations. Below the two dominant nationalities were the Czechs, Poles, Croats, and Italians, each with an important place in the structure of the empire. On the bottom of the scale were to be found the Slovaks, Serbs, Slovenes, Romanians, and Ruthenians. The national ranking of each people was also reflected in its social composition. Thus among the nationalities with Balkan connections, the Croats, occupying a middle position, had a middle class and an aristocracy, while the Serbs, Romanians, and Slovenes were primarily peasants.

Within the empire the peoples most influenced by the events in the Ottoman Empire were naturally those with close ethnic ties—the Romanians and the South Slav Slovenes, Serbs, and Croats. The Romanians lived principally in Transylvania, but also in Bukovina and the Banat. In language and nationality they were identical with the inhabitants of Wallachia and Moldavia. The South Slav situation was more complex. The Slovenes lived chiefly in Carniola and Styria. They were a Catholic, peasant people with a western Slavic language not readily intelligible to most Serbs and Croats. The Croats of the empire were to be found principally in Dalmatia, Croatia, and Slavonia and in Bosnia-Hercegovina which was occupied in 1878. They were Catholic in religion and spoke a language almost identical to that of the Serbs except that the Latin alphabet was used. In Dalmatia, a land acquired from Venice only in 1797, the peasant population was primarily Croatian, but the cities had a large Italian middle class. In Croatia and Slavonia there was a Croatian nobility, middle class, and peasantry. The Serbs of the monarchy were concentrated primarily in the Vojvodina, in the Croatian Military Frontier region and in Bosnia-Hercegovina. Like their conationals of Serbia, they were Orthodox in religion and they used the Cyrillic alphabet in their writing.

In their political ties Slovenia, Dalmatia, and Bukovina remained close to Vienna and the imperial government. Although some political controversy existed here in the nineteenth century, the true centers of the local national movements were in Transylvania and Croatia-Slavonia. During modern times these provinces were closely tied with Hungary and were included in the lands of the crown of St. Stephen. The political struggles here were not so much over the relationship with Vienna and the court as with Budapest and the Hungarian administration. As in the Balkans, where the Slavic and Romanian people had first to overthrow Greek cultural and political dominance, in the Habsburg Empire the major conflict through most of the period under consideration was with Hungary and the force of Hungarian nationalism. Given the fact that in the nineteenth century the Hungarian leaders were principally interested in gaining almost complete rights of self-government from Vienna, a three-cornered conflict was actually in progress among the Habsburg central government, the Hungarians, and the other nationalities that were part of the historic Hungarian realm. In the next pages the emphasis will be placed on the national movements in the three provinces of Transylvania, Croatia, and Slavonia. No attempt will be made to discuss the evolution of the empire as a whole or subjects outside of the framework of the national question as it relates to the formation of the Balkan states.

TRANSYLVANIA

The political history of Transylvania, in many ways as complex as that of Macedonia, has in recent times involved primarily a contest for supremacy between the Romanian and the Hungarian inhabitants. Most of the basic problems of this relationship find their origins in the Middle Ages. At the end of the ninth century the Hungarians appeared in Europe and conquered their present homeland; in the following century they also took Transylvania. Thereafter, they invited the so-called Saxons, Germans from the Rhineland, to settle there as frontier guards, merchants, and prosperous peasants. Another group, the Szeklers, who were related to the Hungarians and spoke the same language, also inhabited the territory. The Saxons and the Szeklers received charters from the king of Hungary which made each a medieval "natio" or nation, with the right of self-government in their districts. They elected their own count, who was responsible to the Hungarian king, and the land was administered through the Transylvanian diet. By the fifteenth century the province under the domination of these three people had become a state semi-independent of Hungary proper. After 1526 Transylvania and Hungary fell under Ottoman rule, but the region was still able to maintain its separate status. The religious conflicts of the Reformation also left their imprint here. During this period the Saxons became Lutheran, the Magyars were Catholic and Calvinist, the Szeklers, Catholic, Lutheran, and Unitarian. At the end of the sixteenth century there were thus three recognized nations and four religions: Catholic, Calvinist, Lutheran, and Unitarian. Each nation had its own nobility and clergy and, from a political point of view, constituted the only people with a recognized status.

In these arrangements no place was allotted to the Orthodox church or to the Romanian people, although this population was obviously large. By the eighteenth century it has been estimated that it constituted the absolute majority in the province. Hungarian and Romanian historians have hotly debated the question of the origin of the Romanian settlements here for two centuries. Without entering into the merits of the arguments, it can be said that the Romanians claim to be descended from the Dacians and Roman colonists, that they have lived continuously in Transylvania since ancient times, and that their settlements thus precede those of the Hungarians by centuries. The Magyars, in opposition, argue that the Romanians only arrived during the thirteenth and fourteenth centuries from south of the Danube, and that since they came as shepherds and poor peasants they could not be regarded as equal to the three privileged nations. No matter which version is accepted, the fact remains that in the eighteenth century the majority of the Transylvanian people, the Romanians, had no political rights and their church was not recognized.

In the Treaty of Karlowitz (Sremski Karlovci) of 1699 the Habsburg Empire received back Transylvania from the Porte. Already in 1691 Emperor Leopold had issued a diploma defining the status of the province, a regulation that was to remain in force until 1848. In this document he confirmed the rights of the three nations and the four religions, and he acknowledged the autonomy of the area. In 1722 Transylvania was recognized as part of the Hungarian crownlands, but the province kept its own diet and administrative system. The emperor and the court retained ultimate political control. A governor was regularly appointed, and the diet was chosen from the upper classes of the recognized nations and religions.

In this political framework the Romanians had little opportunity for advancement. It should be emphasized that socially and economically they formed the lowest strata of society. Most of the peasants lived on the estates of large landowners where they worked under the same burdens of taxation and labor dues that have been seen elsewhere. They were illiterate and politically passive. In no section and among no national group in the empire did this level of society enjoy political rights. In other words, the subservient Romanian position in Transylvania was due to the social composition of the population as well as to its national and religious attributes.

As among other Balkan peoples, the Orthodox church in Transylvania played a major role in the first steps of the national movement. The clergy here was the single educated group among the Romanian population. Its members suffered from the fact that their church was not recognized and that the empire was predominantly Catholic. At the beginning of the eighteenth century, hoping to better their position, the Orthodox officials signed the Act of Union with the Catholics, creating the Uniate church. Although the Romanian expectations that this action would improve their position were disappointed, this institution henceforth played a leading role in Romanian national development. The first major spokesman for Romanian rights in Transylvania was Ion Inochentie Clain, a bishop of the Uniate church from 1729 to 1751. Since he could gain nothing from the Transylvanian diet, he repeatedly appealed to Vienna. He requested in particular that the Romanians should join the Hungarians, Saxons, and Szeklers as a fourth nation, and he protested against the exploitation of the peasantry. He was finally forced into exile. In 1761, however, discontent in Transylvania led the monarchy to allow an organization for the Orthodox church to be formed, although on a stage lower than that for the four privileged religions. Under Joseph II some attempt was also made to improve the status of the peasants.

Both the Uniate and the Orthodox churches remained the center of Romanian intellectual life. The three major names in the early national movement, George Şincai, Peter Maior and Samuel Clain (Micu), were all educated in Uniate establishments. They became the founders of the so-called Transylvanian School, which sought to establish the fact that the Romanians were indeed the descendents of the ancient Dacians and Romans, and that they were the original inhabitants of the province, while the Hungarians were recent arrivals of the Middle Ages. The work of George Şincai and Samuel Clain for the Romanian language was also extremely important. In 1780 they published the first Romanian grammar, *Elements of the Daco-Roman or Wallach Language*. They also secured the replacement of the former Slavonic alphabet with the Latin, and they worked to remove non-Latin words from the language. Their efforts thus paralleled those of Obradović and Karadžić in Serbia. In 1812 Maior completed the highly significant *History of the Origins of the Romanians in Dacia*. The influence of these men extended into Wallachia and Moldavia, where their works greatly stimulated the national movement there.

The major political document for the Romanian movement in the eighteenth century was the *Supplex libellus Valachorum* of 1791, a petition that was sent to the Transylvanian diet. It was drawn up by Samuel Clain and other leading Romanians. The Supplex stated the Romanian version of their history and made definite demands. These included the recognition of the Romanians as a fourth nation and proportional national representation at all levels of administration in Transylvania. The signators also desired that a national congress be convened and that Romanian place names be used where the majority of the population was of that nationality. The diet summarily rejected these proposals. The time was not favorable for such actions; the entire empire was in a period of reaction against the reform measures of Joseph II and to the events of the French Revolution. Nevertheless, the Supplex represented a national program, which was supported by Romanian intellectual and religious leaders.

In the next years the Romanian movement not only failed to make progress, but it faced increasing dangers. At the beginning of the nineteenth century Hungary went through a period of intense national revival. The goals were two in number. First, the attempt was to be made to create a unitary, centralized state out of the lands of the Hungarian crown, and, second, complete independence from Vienna was to be sought. The first policy signified that the effort would be made to assimilate, or magyarize, the Slav, Romanian, and Saxon inhabitants under the jurisdiction of an Hungarian administration. The initial step in this direction would be the substitution of Hungarian as the sole official language of the country for Latin.

This policy, which was to be the base of all the subsequent nationality conflicts, was not without logic from the Magyar point of view. It represented essentially the policy of Louis Kossuth, the great Magyar national leader of the mid-century. If the Hungarian nationalists limited their program to the establishment of an ethnic state, the great crown lands with a primarily non-Hungarian population, such as Transylvania, Croatia-Slavonia, Vojvodina, and Slovakia, would have to be surrendered. Without these territories Hungary would be a poor and weak nation. If, however, all of the territories of the crown of St. Stephen were to be held, some political arrangement would have to be made for the other nationalities, who represented more than 50 percent of the population. They could not be given autonomy, since this concept was in contradiction to the basic idea of a Hungarian national state. The only alternative appeared to be a policy of magyarization. The chief means would be the imposition of the language and its exclusive use in the administrative, judicial, and educational systems as well as in commerce and business. In essence this remained the Hungarian policy until 1914, notwithstanding certain periods when compromise and moderation appeared to prevail as, for example, in 1860–66. For the Romanians and the Slavs the defeat of this policy was essential for their national survival.

The crucial year for the Hungarian movement came in 1848. As the Habsburg central authority collapsed before the revolutionary movements which swept the empire, the Hungarians too established their own separate government. In accordance with the liberal ideas then prevailing they set up a constitutional regime, which promised civil liberties to the entire population. The occasion was also used to integrate Transylvania into Hungary. The Romanian leaders welcomed the liberal reforms, but not the union of Transylvania with Hungary. At a meeting attended by forty thousand people in Blaj in May, 1848, on the so-called

"Field of Liberty," resolutions were adopted which again called for the recognition of the Romanians as a nation and of the Orthodox church as an equal religious institution. Proportional representation in the diet and the administration was also sought. Most important, the meeting rejected the idea of a union of Transylvania with Hungary without the assent of population of the province.

The Hungarian revolutionary government under the leadership of Kossuth not only rejected these demands, but similar declarations from the Saxons, Serbs, and Croats. Faced with this refusal and the adamant Hungarian attitude, the Romanian leaders next turned to Vienna. Although the court was at this time faced with great difficulties, it nevertheless listened to the Romanian representations. Since their demands had at least not been rejected, the Romanians, like the South Slavs, gave their support to the government in Vienna against the Hungarian revolution. When in 1849 the Austrian army entered the Hungarian lands, non-Magyar nationalities cooperated with it. The Russian troops, who joined in the conflict in June, 1849, to assist the imperial forces, received similar assistance.

Much to the disappointment of both the Romanian and the South Slav leaders, their political position did not improve with the restoration of Habsburg power and the suppression of the Hungarian revolutionary government. Instead, the Habsburg government attempted to impose a centralized administration, known as the Bach system, upon the entire country. Transylvania lost her autonomous rights and came under direct imperial administration. The delegations and petitions that were repeatedly sent to Vienna to protest this condition were disregarded. The Romanian goals remained the same: acceptance as one of the recognized nations, and an autonomous government for Transylvania in which Romanians would enjoy a position proportionate to their numerical strength.

During this period the outstanding Romanian leader was undoubtedly the Orthodox Bishop Andreiu Şaguna. He devoted his efforts both to improving the position of the Orthodox church and to the education of the Romanian population. The main obstacle for the church remained the Catholic fear that a strong Orthodox establishment would damage their proselytizing efforts through the Uniate church. In addition, opposition came from the Serbian patriarchate of Sremski Karlovci, under whose jurisdiction the Romanian Orthodox fell. In the educational field Şaguna attempted to improve the training of the clergy so that they would be more effective teachers in the schools. These institutions were considerably expanded at this time. Approximately a decade later about five hundred new elementary schools had been added to the previous hundred. Şaguna was also responsible for the establishment of a new printing press and a newspaper. At this time he supported imperial rule from Vienna, recognizing that it was preferable to a system that placed Transylvania under Magyar control.

The greatest Romanian success came in 1863. After its defeat in Italy in 1859 the Habsburg government abandoned the Bach system and attempted to return the state to some form of constitutional rule. For Transylvania the changes meant that the diet would be restored. Moreover, each national group, including the Romanians, was now to be consulted concerning future reforms. The new measures met strong Hungarian opposition. The Magyar argument was that the union of Hungary and Transylvania proclaimed in 1848 should be regarded as still valid, and that there should be no separate diet for the province. The Romanians, supported by many Saxon leaders, replied that the union had been invalidated by the Hungarian defeat in 1849 and by the Bach system. They further demanded and succeeded in introducing a new electoral law to replace that of 1848, which had resulted in the choice of only three Romanians in a diet of three hundred delegates. The Hungarian reaction was simply to refuse to participate when the next diet was chosen.

With the Hungarian abstention, the Romanian and Saxon delegates were free to enact far-reaching changes in the administration of the province. The Romanians were declared a nation equal to the Magyars, Szeklers, and Saxons; the Uniate and Orthodox churches were placed on the same level with the other four. Largely through Şaguna's efforts, the emperor also agreed to the separation of the Romanian Orthodox church from the Serbian patriarchate. A metropolitanate was created at Sibiu and bishoprics at Arad and Caransebeş. The Romanian language was also recognized to be on the same level with German and Hungarian. For the first time in modern history the Romanians were legally equal to the other inhabitants of Transylvania.

These reforms did not last long. Within the empire the Hungarian position was too strong and that of the central government too weak. The abstention of the Magyars from cooperation with the imperial authorities forced Franz Joseph finally to surrender to many of their demands. In 1865 the former franchise for election to the Transylvanian diet was reintroduced. As a result the Hungarians, who were only 29 percent of the population, elected eighty-nine delegates while the Romanians, the majority of the people, had only thirteen. This diet then proceeded to vote the union of Transylvania and Hungary, a decision that was accepted by the emperor. Thus, the province which, although a part of Hungary, had previously had its own administration and diet, was directly incorporated into the kingdom of Hungary. Whereas in 1863 the Romanians were a majority in Transylvania and had achieved a status of equality with the other nationalities, they were now to be transformed into a minority of 15 percent within the Hungarian kingdom. Moreover, the future was to be bleak in other respects. A new generation of Hungarian statesmen was now to carry on the tradition of Kossuth and to inaugurate a determined policy of magyarization.

After the defeat by Prussia the Habsburg government, as has already been described, was completely reorganized in the Ausgleich (Compromise) of 1867. This event was to have unfortunate repercussions for both the Romanians and the South Slavs. Henceforth, Austria-Hungary or the Dual Monarchy, as the state was now designated, was divided into two distinct entities, united chiefly in the person of the common ruler, who was emperor of Austria and King of Hungary. There was, in addition, to be a common foreign policy and one army. Delegations from the two halves were to meet periodically to resolve common problems. With respect to their internal administrations, the governments of Austria and Hungary were free to pursue their own policies. The Romanians and South Slavs under the Hungarian crown could thus no longer appeal to Vienna for redress against measures decided upon in Budapest.

Initially, the Ausgleich did not appear to be an unfavorable development. In 1868 the Hungarian parliament proclaimed the equality of all Hungarian citizens and the abolition of special privileges to any nationality. At the same time the Law of Nationalities was passed. One of the most progressive pieces of legislation ever enacted in a multinational state, it basically guaranteed the right of each nationality to use its own language in all phases of its cultural and political life. For example, primary and secondary schools were to be taught in the mother tongues of the students; the local language was to be used in district courts of justice; each member of a county assembly could use his native language; district administrators were to know the language of the area; and non-Hungarians would be employed in administrative and judicial positions. As similar reforms in the Ottoman Empire, however, its provisions were never put into practice.

Unfortunately, the generation of Hungarians who brought their nation from the defeat of 1849 to the political triumph of 1867, men such as Francis Deák and Joseph Eötvös, were not able to carry through their programs. Their policy had been based on the conviction that accommodations would have to be made with the nationalities. Their adversaries, whose chief spokesman was Koloman Tisza, were determined to make Hungary a unitary, Magyar state. In 1875 Tisza became Minister President of Hungary, and for the next thirty years the Liberal Party controlled the Hungarian government. During this time every means was used to assure Magyar predominance. Elections were arranged to produce Magyar majorities. With a safe parliament the Liberals were able to pass laws affecting the educational system, which was regarded as the key to the success of magyarization. As Bela Grunwald, Tisza's collaborator, so vividly described it: "The secondary school is like a huge machine, at one end of which Slovak youths are thrown in by the hundreds and at the other end of which they come out as Magyars." [1] In 1879 all elementary school teachers were required to know Hungarian, even those in Romanian or Slovak villages. Later measures for the establishment of secondary schools provided chiefly for Hungarian institutions. Soon all public notices, street, postal, and railroad signs were in Hungarian. Families were pressed to magyarize their names. The courts and administration were put in safe Magyar hands. In addition, Hungarian peasants were encouraged to colonize Transylvania, and Hungarian entrepreneurs received inducements to develop industries there.

The policy of magyarization produced the expected reaction. The measures brought the entire population together and made all classes more aware of their national identity. The first Romanian political party, the National Party, was founded in Sibiu in 1881. Its program called for the restoration of Transylvanian authority, the use of Romanian in the administration and the courts, and the appointment of officials who knew the language. The Romanian leaders further adopted the policy of "passivism" to meet the Magyar threat. They boycotted the parliament and refused to take part in any governmental activities. At the same time a new generation of students, resembling those of Moldavia and Wallachia in 1848, came to stand for a program calling for the union of all Romanians in a single kingdom, a goal that would, of course, mean the dismemberment of the Hungarian crown lands. The National Party in 1890 also used similar references in speaking of a great Romanian nation of eleven million people.

Throughout the nineteenth century events in Transylvania had been followed closely in the Principalities. The issue of the treatment of the Romanians in Transylvania had long been a sensitive point in Romanian-Habsburg relations. As the pressure on the Romanians in the empire increased, a reaction in the Romanian kingdom was bound to come. In 1891 the Romanian Cultural League was founded in Bucharest by university teachers and students. This group drafted a "memorandum" in five languages to call the Romanian grievances in Transylvania to the attention of European opinion. This declaration drew a reply from the Hungarian students in Budapest, which in turn solicited a rebuttal from Romanian students in Transylvania. The author of the Transylvanian answer, Aurel Popovici, who in 1906 was to produce a famous plan for the reorganization of the monarchy, was sentenced to prison, but he succeeded in escaping to Romania. The cause of the students was taken up by the National Party, which drafted its own memorandum and sent a delegation to Vienna to appeal to Franz Joseph.

1. R. W. Seton-Watson, *A History of the Roumanians from Roman Times to the Completion of Unity* (Cambridge: Cambridge University Press, 1934), p. 400.

The document, which called again for the restoration of Transylvanian autonomy, was not accepted by the emperor. The leaders of the National Party were subsequently arrested and brought to court by the Hungarian government. The Memorandum Trial, as it was called, proved to be an excellent opportunity for the Romanians to bring their cause to the attention of a wider public. Although the trial damaged the position of the National Party and the defendents were jailed, the episode had the same propaganda value for the Romanians as similar court proceedings were later to have for the South Slavs. In addition to these actions, the Romanians began to cooperate more with the Slavic nationalities. In 1895 a Congress of Nationalities was held with the Serbs and Slovaks in Budapest; there it was stressed that Hungary was a multinational and not a national state.

The protests of the other nationalities did not affect Hungarian policy. In fact, the Hungarian government now extended its national aims in another direction and came again into direct conflict with Vienna. In 1905 the attempt was made to create a separate army at the expense of the common force established by the Ausgleich. Here, however, a point was raised on which Franz Joseph was extremely sensitive and on which he would not yield. Because the Hungarians were forced to retreat, the Romanians were encouraged to abandon their policy of passivism, which had not, in any case, been a success, and to participate again in the government.

When the Romanian delegates returned to the parliament, they were faced with further severe measures. Count Albert Apponyi, the minister of education, introduced new school laws in 1907. Teachers were henceforth to be required to have a fluent command of Hungarian; Magyar patriotism was to be taught in all schools. If at the end of four years the students did not know Magyar, the teachers were to be dismissed. In addition, the state now took over the Romanian church school system. In order to weaken it the salaries of the teachers were set so high that some church institutions could not afford to pay them. In 1909 further regulations required that religious instruction in Romanian middle schools should be in Hungarian. Additional moves against the church occurred in 1912 when the Vatican approved the Hungarian request that eighty-three parishes be removed from the control of the Romanian Uniate church. These districts were placed under the newly created Hungarian Greek-Catholic bishopric of Hajdudorog. The liturgical language was to be Byzantine Greek, but until the clergy learned it, Magyar was to be used. This action was thus a further attempt at magyarization. Although some efforts were made before 1914 to calm national discontent, the Romanian demand that Transylvanian autonomy be restored was an issue that Budapest would not even consider.

By 1914 it can thus be seen that the Romanians of Transylvania had developed strong feelings of national self-consciousness, made particularly intense by increasing Magyar pressure. The goals of the Romanian opposition remained the restoration of Transylvanian autonomy and the assurance that the nationalities would enjoy a political position proportionate with their numbers. In 1910 the Romanians were 55 percent of the population; the Hungarians, 34 percent. Although on many issues the Saxons sided with the Romanians against Budapest, it was unlikely that they would support the dissolution of the empire at this time. Since the Romanians held only a small majority in the province and were faced with what appeared to be a stable European situation, the aim of the Romanian nationalists had of necessity to be the reform of the monarchy, not its dissolution. Moreover, although there was considerable Romanian political activity in Transylvania, it did not compare with that in the South Slav lands where throughout the nineteenth century we find a profusion of political programs and parties and where the lands in dispute were usually overwhelmingly historically and ethnically dominated by the non-Magyar nationalities.

Although the Transylvanian question did receive a great deal of attention from the Romanian government, acquisition of the province was not at this time a part of the official policy of the nation. On the eve of the First World War, however, it is undoubtedly true that the question had come to play a greater role in relations between Bucharest and Vienna than previously, and that those Romanians with political influence had become even more sensitive to the national issue. Throughout the previous century the Habsburg government had consistently been aware of the possible attraction that the Romanian state could offer to its minorities in Transylvania. Liberal Party oratory had repeatedly spoken of historical Romanian lands, which included Transylvania along with Bukovina and Bessarabia, as irredenta to be acquired in the future.

Before 1914, however, severe limitations restricted the actions of Romanian leaders in Bucharest. First, Romania was part of the Triple Alliance system. The Habsburg Empire was in fact an ally. Second, King Charles, although a conscientious and devoted ruler, remained basically a German prince in sympathy and background. Unlike King Peter in Serbia, he could not be expected to lead a national movement against countries to which he had a sincere personal attachment. Third, it must be emphasized that the primary Romanian problems at this time were economic, not political. Of first importance was the fact that the kingdom had experienced in 1907 what was one of the greatest peasant revolts of the entire period with which this narrative deals. The status of the Romanian peasant and that of land distribution was the first national priority. Equally important, Romania, more than the other Balkan countries, was proceeding toward an economic transformation and a development of her natural resources and industrial capacity. Members of the government were involved in this process. The possibility of acquiring Transylvania became a matter of immediate national concern only after the outbreak of the war when an entirely unforeseen situation arose.

Before 1914 the immediate problem in Romanian foreign policy was not the Transylvanian irredenta, but relations with Bulgaria. The Romanian leaders, like those in Greece and Serbia, strongly opposed the Bulgarian determination to restore the San Stefano boundaries and thus gain a position of preponderance in the Balkans. In addition, Southern Dobrudja remained a Romanian territorial objective. In 1913 this policy brought Romania into conflict with the monarchy, which sought to protect Bulgarian interests, but it did not break the alliance. The Romanian actions in the Balkan Wars had, as we have seen, resulted in close cooperation with Serbia. By 1914 Serbia, in turn, was also deeply involved in the national controversies in the Habsburg Empire and had, particularly in Bosnia-Hercegovina, an irredenta that she would claim should a favorable occasion arise.

The South Slav Question

In Transylvania the national question had centered on the relatively straightforward issue of the conflict of the Romanian majority with the Hungarian authorities. In the South Slav lands of Dalmatia, Croatia, and Slavonia the problem was far more complex since it involved not only the relations of the Croatian majority with the Magyar-dominated administration, but also with the Serbian minority in these areas. Like Serbia, Croatia had been a medieval kingdom whose territory included roughly the present-day regions of Croatia, Slavonia, Dalmatia, and much of Bosnia. In 1102, with the death of their own king and after a defeat by the Hungarians, the Croatians elected the ruler of Hungary as their monarch. The two countries, nevertheless, remained as separate kingdoms united through the crown. This relationship existed until 1527 when, after the defeat of Hungary by the Turks, Croatia elected the Habsburg emperor as her king.

Unlike Serbia, where the native aristocracy was wiped out after the Ottoman invasion, Croatia did have a nobility which in the past had preserved the identity and protected the interests of the nation. In Croatia proper the aristocracy was largely Croatian, but most of its members belonged to the lesser nobility and some were so poor that they were scarcely to be distinguished from the peasantry. In Slavonia, although a Croatian aristocracy existed, the large estates of the region were primarily in the hands of landowners of German or Hungarian origin who spoke Latin, not Croatian, as their common language. In Dalmatia, the predominant class was more closely associated with commercial and maritime pursuits, and it spoke Italian. The peasantry was Croatian. In these lands the church shared the privilege of land ownership with the nobility, and the upper clergy had the same social, economic, and political interests as the aristocracy. A small urban middle class was to prove extremely active politically. In all three areas the overwhelming majority of the population were peasants. Until shortly before the outbreak of the First World War this group sought economic reforms and was not a serious political force.

In the Croatian lands there was also a strong minority of Serbs, particularly in Croatia-Slavonia where, according to the 1910 census, there were 62.5 percent Croats and 24.6 percent Serbs—or 1 Serb for every 2.5 Croats. The two people had an essentially identical language, written in different alphabets, and they were both South Slavs, but the Serbs were Orthodox and the Croats, Catholic. Most of the Serbs in Croatia-Slavonia lived in an area called the Military Frontier, a buffer zone established by the Habsburg Empire during the sixteenth century as a barrier against the Ottoman Empire. In order to attract settlers who would garrison and defend the area, the monarchy had offered favorable economic, social, and political conditions. Large numbers of Serbs, refugees from Ottoman-occupied Serbian lands, took advantage of the opportunity. The Military Frontier began on the Adriatic Sea, south of the city of Rijeka (Fiume), and extended well beyond Belgrade in the east. It was a stretch of land, varying in width, but averaging over twenty kilometers, with the Sava River as its southern border. It was completely contained within the historic Croatian lands. It should be noted that Serbs also lived in Bačka and Banat, part of the Vojvodina, but this area never became a point of conflict with the Croats.

The distribution of population set the pattern for the basic conflicts of the nineteenth century. With the development of the national movements at that time, both the Serbs and the Croats had two choices. They could follow a separate road and look to the re-establishment of their medieval kingdoms on an independent basis, or they could emphasize their South Slav, or Yugoslav, bonds and work for the formation of a common state. A similar dilemma faced the Serbian kingdom. This state could seek to form a greater Serbia on a strictly national basis or it could assume the leadership in a movement to unite all of the South Slav lands. The chief obstacle to the creation of an autonomous or independent Croatia was to be the existence of the large Serbian minority; the great hindrance to a Yugoslavia was the inability of the Serbian leaders in Belgrade to submerge their individual nationality into the larger framework. Thus, until 1914, throughout the South Slav lands of the monarchy there was the double national conflict of the Hungarians against the Slavic inhabitants, and the struggle among these people for their political future. The question of the relationship with Vienna was also present.

During the late eighteenth century the Croatian and Hungarian nobil-

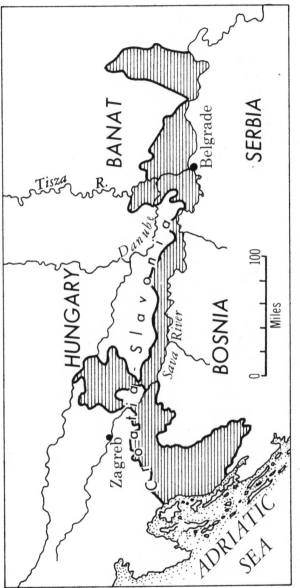

Map 10. The Habsburg Military Frontier

ity shared a common dislike for the reform plans of Joseph II. They both stood for tradition, custom, and the established order against a "revolutionary" emperor. In particular, they defended the use of Latin, which had been their means of communication for centuries, against the threatened introduction of German as the language of administration. When the Hungarians soon thereafter attempted to impose Hungarian, the Croatian nobility remained the strong supporters of Latin. Although there was opposition to Magyar control on this question, by 1828 the social and economic interest of the Croatian aristocracy prevailed over any national sentiments. In that year they agreed that Hungarian could be taught in Croatian schools; the first step in magyarization.

As in other central European nations the true nationalists, whether Croatian or Yugoslav, were to be found among students, intellectuals, and the small but active middle class. The first national idea of real significance to emerge from this group was the Illyrian movement, which has been closely associated with the name of Ljudevit Gaj. A close adherent of the romantic national currents so strong in Europe at this time, Gaj was influenced by the Slavic scholars and writers P. J. Šafařik, Jan Kollár, and J. Dobrovský. The turning point in Gaj's career came in 1835 when he obtained permission from the Habsburg authorities to publish a Croatian newspaper, *Danica* (Morning Star). The Austrian government was now well aware of the dangers of the growing Magyar nationalism to the empire so they approved the expression of Croatian opposition to Hungarian control. During this period the Croats, like the Transylvanians, could thus appeal to Vienna against the Hungarians.

Gaj's principal contribution was, however, his advocacy of the linguistic, cultural, and political unity of the empire's South Slavs. The Illyrian movement aimed at bridging the historical differences which had separated these people through the centuries and in bringing them together to resist Magyar influence. For a period of eight years, from 1835 to 1843, there was a veritable explosion of literary activity and of publication in this direction. As part of this program Gaj was also able to persuade the Croatian writers to use not the kajkavian dialect of Zagreb, but the štokavian of Bosnia-Hercegovina, Dalmatia, and Serbia. He saw the importance of a common literary language and realized that this unity could lead to political cooperation.

Although the Illyrian movement enjoyed great popularity among Croatian intellectuals, it did not receive similar acclaim among the Slovenes and Serbs. The Slovenes, closely associated with Vienna, did not feel threatened by the Magyars. Moreover, the Slovenian language was distinct, and their history set them apart from both the Serbs and the Croats. For their part the Serbs did not like the implications of the Illyrian idea. Most Serbian leaders at this time adhered to the views expressed in the Načertanije of Ilija Garašanin and preferred to work for a united ethnic Serbian state. Vuk Karadžić, the greatest Serbian scholar of the period, was unsympathetic to the idea. He felt that anyone who used the standard štokavian dialect was a Serb. In the same manner most of the Serbian intellectuals in the Vojvodina reacted negatively to the movement.

Despite the lack of success among the Serbs and Slovenes, the program upset the Magyar leaders. In 1841 they succeeded in forming the first Croatian political party, the Croatian-Hungarian Party, whose members, called Magyarones, strongly rejected the Illyrian idea and favored the maintenance of close ties with the Hungarians. Efforts were also made to persuade the imperial authorities that the movement was dangerous. The argument was advanced that Illyrianism was an ally of Panslavism and a threat to the empire. In 1843 Vienna took measures to suppress it and to control Gaj's newspaper. Nevertheless, the impact of Illyrianism was profound. It became the basis for the later Yugoslav movement, which also had its center in Croatia.

The first practical test of possible South Slav unity occurred during the revolutions of 1848–49. At the time of the Hungarian revolution the supporters of Illyrianism were in control in Zagreb. Josip Jelačić, a colonel in the Habsburg army and the *ban* (governor) of Croatia, became their leader and spokesman. When Kossuth and his government demanded that the Hungarians have the right of self-government in the empire, the Croatians asked for the same conditions from the Magyars. They wanted freedom from Hungarian administrative control, a separate parliament, the abolition of serfdom, and the restoration of the Triune Kingdom, that is, the union of Croatia, Dalmatia, and Slavonia. Of these historical lands, Austria ruled Dalmatia, while Hungary controlled Croatia and Slavonia. When Kossuth rejected these demands outright, the Croatians, like the Transylvanians, turned to Vienna.

At this time the Croatian leaders found an ally in the Serbs of the Vojvodina, who also sought local self-government and were willing to unite with the Croats in a common state. This cooperation was solemnly proclaimed when Josip Rajačić, the Serbian Orthodox Patriarch of Sremski Karlovci in the Vojvodina, bestowed his blessings in Zagreb on Jelačić, the Catholic governor. Both Serbs and Croats, joined by Serbian volunteers from the principality, now fought together against the Hungarians. In addition, the government of Prince Alexander Karadjordjević in Belgrade clandestinely encouraged its Serbian conationals with arms, supplies, and men.

Although both the Serbs and Croatians were strongly anti-Magyar, neither at this time opposed the Habsburg government. In 1848 their ideas were best expressed in the Austro-Slav program, whose purpose was to gain political equality for the Slavs within a federalized empire. In 1849 Serbian and Croatian military units joined Austrian, Russian, and

Romanian soldiers in crushing the Hungarian revolution. Jelačić led his troops loyally even though by this time he knew that the Habsburg government would not grant the type of local autonomy that both the Slavic peoples and the Romanians sought.

The revolutions of 1848–49 meant the end of the Illyrian movement. Within a decade two opposing political currents emerged. The first emphasized Croatian nationalism, while the second was an expansion of the Illyrian idea. In 1861 Ante Starčević and Eugen Kvaternik founded the Party of Rights (i.e., state's rights). Its program, which was in the tradition of nineteenth-century nationalism, called for the formation of an independent Croatia. As for Illyrianism, Starčević not only scorned it, but he even denied the existence of the Serbs and the Slovenes as a separate people. The former he regarded as Croats who had become Orthodox; the latter, as "mountain Croats." He could thus plan to incorporate these people in the future greater Croatia. This program, which was the strongest expression of Croatian separatism to date, repudiated the beliefs of both the Magyarones and those who wished to cooperate with Vienna. Hungarians and Germans alike were seen as enemies. More important, the party rejected any accommodation with the Serbs or Slovenes. Ultimately, *Pravaštvo,* as the program was called, played a major role in dividing the South Slavs of the empire. The Serbs of Serbia could understand its implications because it was the Croatian counterpart of their own greater Serbian national ideas.

The Illyrian tradition was carried on by the Catholic clerics Josip Juraj Strossmayer and Franjo Rački. The two were to be an inseparable partnership. Strossmayer, the bishop of Djakovo and Croatia's leading ecclesiastical spokesman, was an astute politician with great influence and authority among his own people and abroad. Canon Rački, more the intellectual, developed the basic ideas of Yugoslavism as their program came to be called. Whereas Starčević had rejected the Illyrian movement, Strossmayer and Rački developed it further. The immediate goal of Illyrianism had been the unification of the South Slavs of the empire; the aim of Yugoslavism was to join together all South Slavs both within and without the monarchy. Illyrianism had been oriented more toward Central Europe. It had stressed linguistic and cultural unity and it had attempted to overlook religious issues. Yugoslavism was directed towards the Balkans, and its leaders sought to bridge the religious differences between the Serbs and the Croats. In contrast to Starčević, who wished an independent Croatia, Strossmayer and Rački saw the country as part of a South Slav federation. To further their goals they established in Zagreb a "Yugoslav" rather than a "Croatian" Academy of Arts and Sciences to provide, among other things, an outlet for all South Slavic scholarly publications.

In line with his beliefs Strossmayer attempted to establish contacts with the Serbian government. At this time, it will be recalled, Prince Michael and his foreign minister Garašanin were pursuing an active foreign policy aimed at uniting Montenegro, Greece, and Romania against the Ottoman Empire. They entered into correspondence with Strossmayer with the aim of using him for their goals rather than working toward a union with the Habsburg South Slavs. The Ottoman lands were their target, not the Habsburg Empire. In fact, in 1866 when Strossmayer believed that he had reached an understanding with Belgrade, the Serbian government was negotiating an accord with the Magyars at the expense of the Croats.

In addition to these two groups two other Croatian parties were in existence, one pro-Magyar and the other pro-Habsburg. The Magyarones still supported the idea that the Croats should join with the Hungarians in a common front against Vienna. They wished the restoral of rights and privileges enjoyed before 1848, and they sought the abolition of the Bach system. At this time also Ivan Mažuranić, a well-known Croatian author, formed the Independent National Party. Its goal was to restore the Triune Kingdom through cooperation with the Habsburg government. Since Dalmatia was under Vienna, Mažuranić thought that his objectives could only be obtained by a pro-Habsburg policy. The existence of these parties demonstrated the divisions among politically conscious Croatians. It will be noted, however, that of the four parties, three were based on cooperation with other national groups.

The Ausgleich was a blow to all of the parties except the Magyarones, who, of course, approved it. In 1868 the Hungarians and the Croatians signed another agreement, the Nagodba (Compromise), which allowed Croatia-Slavonia a large degree of self-government. Croatia was to have its own Sabor (assembly); the official language was to be Croatian, and the Croatian flag was to fly beside the Hungarian. In addition, a delegation of Croatian representatives was to take part in the common parliament in Budapest. The *ban*, however, was still appointed by the Hungarian government, which also maintained considerable control over Croatian finances.

For different reasons Strossmayer, Rački, Starčević, Kvaternik, and Mažuranić all rejected the agreement. The new *ban*, Levin Rauch, was able to manipulate the elections to the Croatian assembly to bring about an overwhelming victory for the Magyarones. With the failure of his program Kvaternik organized a revolt at Rakovica to liberate Croatia by force. It was immediately crushed by the army and its leader was killed. Strossmayer became disillusioned with the new developments and withdrew from active politics. He continued nevertheless to support the Yugoslav idea in his writings and speeches until his death in 1905.

The real test of Serbo-Croatian relations and the Yugoslav idea was to come during the crisis of the 1870s and particularly after the Habsburg occupation of Bosnia-Hercegovina in 1878. Here issues arose in which the Croatian and Serbian national ideas were in direct conflict. The Habsburg administration of these lands, which Serbia regarded as ethnically hers, was a tremendous blow to the Serbian nationalist. In Croatia, however, the reaction was different. It was felt that since the provinces were now under Habsburg control it would be easier for the Croatians to assert their claims to the lands than if they had remained a part of the Ottoman Empire, or, worse, if they were to fall to Serbia. The issue concerned both those who favored a Yugoslavia and those who were for an independent Croatia. Because of their central location, whoever held this territory would dominate a South Slav state; without this area a separate Croatia was impossible.

The geopolitical importance of Bosnia-Hercegovina to Croatia is best understood in the context of the Triune Kingdom. These three lands—Dalmatia, Croatia, and Slavonia—are shaped like a crude boomerang. In this form they are militarily indefensible. With Bosnia-Hercegovina the Triune Kingdom would be transformed into a quadrilateral, and thus it would become a viable state. While the area was indispensable to a Croatian state, its annexation by Serbia would be disastrous for the Croatian position in their historic lands. Because of the Military Frontier, with its high concentration of Serbs, the danger existed that should Serbia ever succeed in carrying through the greater Serbian program of uniting all her people, Croatia would lose her claims to Bosnia-Hercegovina and much of her southern lands in the Military Frontier. In fact by seizing the Lika region in southwestern Croatia, which had a large Serbian population, Serbia could drive a wedge between Croatia and Dalmatia. Should this happen it would be inevitable that the rest of the Croatian territories would eventually be absorbed by the neighboring states. In this contest the Croatians had the disability that only 20 percent of the population of Bosnia-Hercegovina could be classified as Croatian, while 43 percent were Orthodox Serbs. The third of the population that was Muslim was to be courted by both sides.

The disputes over Bosnia-Hercegovina were a prelude to a quarter century, 1878–1903, of strong antagonism between the Serbs and the Croats. At the same time, in Serbia, as has been shown, Milan and his son Alexander worked closely with Vienna. In Croatia Ban Charles Khuen-Hédervary, who was in office from 1883 to 1903, successfully increased hostility between the Serbs and the Croats by using a divide and rule policy. Favoring the Serbian minority in educational, economic, and political matters, he thus won the support of the Serbian middle class, some intellectuals, and the clergy. Understandably, the Croats responded by giving strong support to Starčević's Party of Rights. In the 1880s this group, with its strident Croatian nationalism and its anti-Serbian tone, clearly dominated the Croatian political scene. In the 1890s relations were so bad that bloody clashes took place between Croats and Serbs in Zagreb and other cities. These incidents in turn elicited an angry response from Belgrade, where some went so far as to demand a war of extermination between the two South Slav peoples.

In these years Yugoslavism as a political program practically disappeared. In 1903, however, an abrupt change took place. In that year, it will be remembered, Peter Karadjordjević became king of Serbia. At the same time Khuen-Héderváry was replaced as *ban* of Croatia, and Benjamin Kallay, who had been governor of Bosnia-Hercegovina in the preceding two decades, was removed. Although the provinces had benefited materially during Kallay's tenure, the political situation had worsened. Attempts had even been made by the Habsburg authorities to foster a separate Bosnian nationalism. The principal changes were, however, those in Belgrade and Zagreb. Relations between the Croatians and the Magyars now improved, but those between the Serbian kingdom and the Habsburg monarchy declined precipitously. With a new regime in power in Belgrade, the Serbian government could better contemplate the possibility of exploiting the Habsburg national problems to its own benefit.

During King Peter's reign, as we have seen, Serbia was almost constantly in conflict with her northern neighbor. It was thus natural that Belgrade should become a cultural and intellectual center for South Slav activities. There were congresses of students, teachers, and physicians as well as art exhibits and concerts. In 1904 some students and intellectuals formed a society called *Slovenski Jug* (the Slavic South), whose purpose was to bring about the unity of not only the Serbs, Croats, and Slovenes, but also the Bulgars. The events in Belgrade and the obvious improvement in economic and political relations between Serbia and Bulgaria were observed by the South Slavs of the monarchy. Serbia under the Karadjordjević dynasty was now a point of attraction.

Changes were also taking place in Croatia. Hitherto the Hungarian pressure against the Croatians had led them to emphasize their own national idea and not Yugoslavism. After 1895, following serious student disorders in Zagreb, many South Slav students left to study in Prague. There they came under the influence of Professor Thomas G. Masaryk, who, along with Strossmayer, became a foremost advocate of the Yugoslav idea. A keen observer of Habsburg politics and an outstanding scholar and persuasive teacher, Masaryk emphasized to his students how Austrian and Magyar policy aimed at dividing the Serbs and Croats in the interest of maintaining the dual system. By 1903 a new generation of young Serbs and Croats existed who were determined to work together. They held meetings and attended congresses in Belgrade.

Equally significant was the reconciliation that now took place between the majority of the Croatian and Serbian political parties in the empire.

Impetus for cooperation came from Dalmatia where for the preceding forty years Croatian and Serbian parties had usually collaborated, except when they had directly opposing interests, such as in Bosnia-Hercegovina. In 1905 the Hungarians were again in conflict with Vienna over the question of the army. The Croatian leaders in Dalmatia decided to exploit the differences between these two centers of state power. Since they now felt that Austria was the major danger, they backed cooperation with not only the Serbs, but also the Magyars and even the Italians. They hoped in return for their stand to win Magyar support for the restoration of the Triune Kingdom. These considerations were the basis of the Rijeka (Fiume) Resolution of October, 1905, passed by a meeting of the Croatian parties of Dalmatia. Two weeks later at Zadar (Zara) the Serbian parties of the entire empire endorsed this plan in return for Croatian recognition of the Serbian nationality in the Triune Lands. These events in turn led to the formation of the Croatian-Serbian Coalition of 1905, whose program was based on the Rijeka and Zadar resolutions and whose membership was drawn from Croatian and Serbian parties from both parts of the monarchy. The goal of the coalition was to achieve South Slav unity within the empire to be followed in the future by a union of all the Yugoslavs. The coalition, reflecting the complex political situation in the Croatian lands, was composed of the Croatian Party of Rights, the Croatian Progressive Party, the Serbian Independent Party, the Serbian Radical Party, the Social Democrats, and prominent figures not associated with specific factions. The leadership lay in the hands of Frano Supilo, Ante Trumbić, Josip Smodlaka, and Svetozar Pribičević, all of whom were to play major roles in future South Slav politics.

Efforts to reach a reconciliation with the Magyars soon collapsed. The Hungarian leaders again abandoned their demand for a separate army and temporarily settled their differences with Vienna. Although attempts to magyarize Croatia continued and an effort was made to break the coalition, the core remained intact until 1918. The chief result of Hungarian policy was to drive the coalition closer to Belgrade. Many of the ties with Serbia remained secret, but the coalition did not conceal its desire for South Slav unity. Moreover, it was able to win a position of leadership in the Croatian Sabor after the elections of 1906 and 1908. In three years, therefore, major Serbian and Croatian political parties had been able to reconcile many of their differences and to form a common front which became the single most influential political organization among the South Slavs of the empire, even though it did not represent a majority of the electorate.

Meanwhile, the problem of Bosnia-Hercegovina had again arisen. After the occupation of 1878 the monarchy had invested a great deal of money in the provinces and had attempted to appease the population, particularly during the governorship of Kallay in the two decades between 1883 and 1903. Roads, schools and public buildings were constructed, and attempts were made to modernize the backward area. The Bosnian population had also taken steps to improve its own position. The annexation of the provinces in 1908 had, as we have seen, produced a great national reaction in Serbia. Many were ready to go to war on the issue. In December, 1908, the Narodna Odbrana (National Defense) society, a civilian organization, was formed to rally the nation behind the Bosnian cause and to send volunteers to fight the Habsburg occupation troops. Within the monarchy adherents of South Slav unity held public meetings, issued proclamations, and appealed for support through the European press. Their cause was aided by the inept conduct by Habsburg officials in two political court proceedings—the Zagreb (Agram) and Friedjung trials—which were connected with the annexation and the Croatian-Serbian Coalition.

The Zagreb trial resulted from charges of treason brought against some members of the Croatian-Serbian Coalition. The accused were primarily Serbs, and the purpose of the trial was to destroy the organization by turning its members against each other. The trial began in March, 1909, and lasted six months. The contention was that the coalition was a tool of the Serbian state. The evidence produced, much of it forged, was of such a weak nature that even after the defendents were all found guilty, the Budapest newspaper, *Pester Lloyd,* declared that "all and everything [in the trial] was politics." [2] In 1910 Franz Joseph pardoned the imprisoned men.

The Friedjung trial was more serious because its objective was to provide a justification for war with Serbia at a time when it appeared that Belgrade would not accept the annexation. Again, the target was the coalition and some of its members, all of whom were accused of being in the pay of the Serbian government. Again, forgeries were used by the Habsburg authorities, some of which appeared to have been constructed with the knowledge of the foreign minister, Count Aehrenthal. When the nature of the proceedings became clear, the charges were dropped and the accused exonerated. Both trials provided fine material for South Slav propaganda, and they received a great deal of attention in the European press.

The primary target during the Friedjung trial was Frano Supilo, the head of the coalition. Although not convicted, he resigned to protect the coalition. The members then elected Svetozar Pribičević, the leader of the Serbian Independent Party. Whereas Supilo, a Croat from Dalmatia, had believed that Croatia should lead Yugoslav unification, Pribičević, a Serb from Croatia, saw Serbia in this role. The fact that a Serb led the co-

2. Henry Wickham Steed, *Through Thirty Years, 1892–1922: A Personal Narrative* (New York: Doubleday & Page, 1924), vol. 1, p. 307.

alition was another example of the success of the attempts to reconcile the two Slavic peoples since 1903. Equally important, as a Serb, Pribičević could serve as an effective link to Belgrade.

Despite the achievements of the coalition, the popularity of the Yugoslav idea among a greater circle of people, and the continued mistakes made by chauvinistic Hungarian and Habsburg officials, the majority of Croatians on the eve of the World War wished reform within the empire, not its dissolution and the formation of a South Slav state with Serbia. The former fears and hesitations remained. Thus the Pure Party of Rights, which broke off from the Party of Rights in the 1890s, strongly championed an autonomous Greater Croatia, which would include Bosnia-Hercegovina and remain part of the empire. It was actively hostile to Serbia. The Peasant Party of Stjepan Radić, which was to be the strongest Croatian party after the war, supported only the union of the South Slavs of the monarchy. This viewpoint was now shared by the Social Democrats, who wished a "national-cultural" union, but without leaving the state. In addition, the program of Trialism associated with the name of the heir to the throne, Franz Ferdinand, who in fact did not espouse the idea, had wide appeal. In this plan the South Slavs of the empire were to be united in a political unit equal to the two already in existence. Throughout the programs of most of the Croatian parties the awareness of the religious difference with Belgrade was apparent, but, even more important, their members did not want to be drawn into the Balkans, an area which they felt was culturally inferior, by a union with Serbia.

After the turn of the century another element entered Croatian politics. Hitherto the Croatians had used legal and peaceful means to achieve their goals. Now, however, a group of young students appeared who, impatient with both the supporters of the coalition and those who opposed it, resorted to violence. Thus, in 1912 two efforts were made to assassinate the *ban* of Croatia, Slavko Cuvaj, and in 1913 and 1914 attempts were made on the life of his successor, Ivo Skerlecz.

Although the emphasis in this account has been on the events in Croatia-Slavonia, a brief comment should be made on developments in Slovenia. Of the South Slavs the Slovenes remained most loyal to the monarchy, and their strongest party, the Clerical Party, supported Trialism, not Yugoslavism. Both factions of the Slovene Liberal Party were interested in gaining more autonomy for Slovenia, but within the empire and not at its expense. In the same manner the Social Democrats stressed national autonomy in cultural affairs, not the breakup of the monarchy. Only some students of the Preporod (Renaissance) group, founded during the Balkan Wars, believed that the Slovene national question could be solved within the framework of a larger South Slav state. Yugoslavism was thus not a vital force among the Slovenes before 1914.

The reaction to the Yugoslav idea in the kingdom of Serbia was, everything considered, even less sympathetic than among the Slavs of the Dual Monarchy. It is true that to some King Peter had become a symbol of South Slav unity; his statements appealed to many Serbian students and intellectuals, within both his kingdom and the Habsburg Empire, and caused much apprehension among officials of the monarchy. Yet the dominant political forces in Serbia, the army officers and the politicians, were not so concerned about the fate of the Slovenes and the Croats. Their attention had for over a century been directed toward the formation of a great Serbian state embracing lands that were historically and ethnically Serbian. Serbs under Habsburg rule, particularly in Bosnia-Hercegovina, were naturally objects of their interest. Although their aims were similar, the civilian officials and the military officers disagreed on the means to be used. The politicians were realistic and cautious; they saw the dangers of a reckless expansionist foreign policy. The army, in contrast, with considerable support from the Orthodox clergy, was willing to risk war with either the Ottoman Empire or the Dual Monarchy for national goals. Understandably, the government wished to determine state policy, but King Peter equivocated. The army, which had brought him to power in 1903, retained considerable autonomy. Hence, in the decade before 1914 he was faced with pressures from the Serbian statesmen and the military, each of which had their own plans for their state's future.

The loss of Bosnia-Hercegovina in 1909 was a bitter blow to all. The government recognized that it had to back down on the issue; it even curbed the activities of the Narodna Odbrana, which was a civilian and not a military organization. This attitude was not understood in the army, which came to feel that at best the state was led by weaklings and at worst by traitors. In face of what seemed to be a situation of national peril, some of the army officers now determined to organize to prepare to meet any further international crises and to exploit them in order to bring the Serbs of the Ottoman and Habsburg empires into Serbia.

In 1911 the secret society Ujedinjenje ili Smrt (Union or Death), also know as the Crna Ruka or Black Hand, was formed under the leadership of Colonel Dragutin Dimitrijević, pseudonym Apis. One of the conspirators in the 1903 assassination, Dimitrijević was a strong patriot and in many ways an outstanding man, but he was reluctant to entrust Serbia's fate to her civilian rulers. Army officers were the nucleus of his group, but there were also other members who were intrigued by the conspiratorial aspects or who strongly championed pan-Serbian programs. The objective of the Black Hand was affirmed in the first article of its constitution: "to achieve the ideal of the unification of Serbdom." The second article stated that this aim was to be attained through "revolutionary action, rather than cultural, and is, therefore [to be] kept secret from the general public." [3] By 1913 Dimitrijević had become Chief of Intelligence of the Serbian General Staff, a position of obvious major importance. The army had its own network of agents among the Serbs of the Ottoman and Habsburg empires. Through them Colonel Dimitrijević worked for the unification of the Serbs, not the South Slavs.

The task of the control of the military was, of course, the duty of the Serbian government, headed by Nikola Pašić, who was also the leader of the Serbian Radical Party. A brilliant and astute politician, he was well aware of the limitations of his country's power. His handling of relations with Austria and his diplomatic success during the Balkan Wars attest to his skill. He was now faced with two alternative roads—whether Serbia should concentrate on the establishment of a greater Serbia or seek a united South Slav state. There was no doubt that the Serbian idea had the overwhelming support of the Serbian people—the politicians, professional men, soldiers, clergy, peasants, and even most of the students and intellectuals. Pašić himself adhered to this view. Furthermore, Serbian nationalism was in the tradition of the past, while Yugoslavism was at best a nebulous concept. Moreover, Pašić could not ignore the army. Its political role in 1903 and the military victories in 1912 and 1913 had enhanced its power and prestige. It could, on certain issues, effectively defy the government.

At the same time Pašić recognized that he could not rebuff the supporters of the Yugoslav idea. He expected the state of enmity with the Dual Monarchy to continue in the future. Unredeemed Serbian lands lay within that state. Consequently, any individual or group that could aid in the Serbian objectives should obviously be encouraged. The Serbian government thus surreptitiously maintained relations not only with the Serbs, but also with the Yugoslav sympathizers in Bosnia-Hercegovina, Vojvodina, and Croatia, lands with large Serbian populations. Perhaps the best evidence of Pašić's restricted interest in Yugoslavism was his lack of concern for the Slovenes, who were regarded as essential members of the Yugoslav movement by its sponsors. The minister was also well aware that the advocates of Yugoslavism needed Serbia more than Serbia needed them.

By 1914 the Yugoslav idea had won adherents in all the South Slav lands. Although it promised a better future for all of the South Slavs, it was primarily a Croatian concept and lacked mass Serbian and Slovenian support. Even in Croatia the Croatian-Serbian Coalition did not represent the majority of the country. The inhabitants of the empire

3. Vladimir Dedijer, *The Road to Sarajevo* (New York: Simon and Schuster, 1966), p. 374.

preferred programs advocating the unity of the South Slavs within the existing political boundaries. In Serbia too, as we have seen, there was strong agreement that the future goal of the state should be a strong Serbia containing all of the Serbian lands.[4]

SARAJEVO

The immediate causes of the First World War stem directly from the complex situation arising from the force of Serbian nationalism, the Habsburg annexation of Bosnia-Hercegovina, and the implications of the Yugoslav movement for the monarchy. The incident that led to the war is well known. On June 28, 1914, Franz Ferdinand was in Sarajevo after attending army maneuvers in Bosnia. The day for the visit was badly chosen; it was the anniversary of the Battle of Kosovo, the Serbian national holiday. Security was inexcusably lax. Six young Bosnians armed with pistols and bombs were stationed along the streets where the archduke was expected to drive. The first attempt to assassinate him failed when the bomb rolled off the automobile, exploded, and injured some officials. This episode caused the plans for the procession to be altered. When it was resumed, the archduke's chauffeur, who was not informed of the changes, was forced at one point to stop, back up, and then proceed at an intersection. By chance another conspirator, Gavrilo Princip, was on the street corner. He stepped to the car, fired at the archduke and General Potiorek, the military commander of Bosnia. He missed the general, but killed both the archduke and his wife.

The conspirators, all but one of whom were under twenty-one, were Bosnian revolutionaries in the romantic tradition. Gavrilo Princip had been fourteen years old when Austria-Hungary annexed Bosnia. In the six years that followed he and his companions were caught up in the underground activities of the province. The young men, who came from one of the poorest districts of the Balkans, read extensively in the revolutionary literature of the day—Chernyshevsky, Bakunin, Dostoevsky and Gorki as well as Western writers such as Ibsen, Wilde, Poe, Dumas, and

---

4. Since this subject is controversial, it might be well to quote the views of three well-known scholars concerning the acceptance of the Yugoslav idea in the South Slav lands. Professor Michael B. Petrovich, University of Wisconsin, writes that "in Serbia itself, while the Yugoslav ideology was nurtured with sincere enthusiasm, especially by the intelligentsia, the idea of the unification of all Serbs offered a more immediate attraction" to Serbia than did the Yugoslav concept. Michael B. Petrovich, *A History of Modern Serbia, 1804–1918* (New York: Harcourt, Brace, Jovanovich, 1976), vol. 2, p. 607. Professor Bogdan Krizman, University of Zagreb, states that "on the eve of the First World War there were . . . not many movements in Croatia that were openly anti-Austrian or threatened the existence of the Austro-Hungarian Monarchy." Bogdan Krizman, "The Croatians in the Habsburg Monarchy in the Nineteenth Century," *Austrian History Yearbook*, 3, pt. 2 (1967), p. 144. Professor Fran Zwitter, University of Ljubljana, comments that "on the eve of the First World War the anti-Austrian movement was only in its incipient stage in the Slovenian areas of the monarchy." Fran Zwitter, "The Slovenes and the Habsburg Monarchy," *Ibid.,* pp. 182–83.

Map 11. The Balkan States, 1914

Scott. They particularly admired the activities of another young Bosnian, Bogdan Žerajić, who in 1910 had committed suicide after trying to assassinate a government official. The aim of the conspirators was to eliminate Franz Ferdinand whom they saw as a major obstacle to their principal political objective, which was the union of Bosnia-Hercegovina to Serbia. They feared that the program of Trialism, which they incorrectly associated with the archduke, would be introduced and that the provinces would become an integral part of a reorganized Habsburg Empire.

Two main aspects of the assassination need concern us here: first, the responsibility of the Serbian government, and second, the degree to which fears concerning Yugoslav activities led the Habsburg government to declare war on Serbia. The answer to the first question is complex. The archives of the Serbian government on this problem have not been opened to historians, but there are certain generally accepted conclusions. On the question of complicity the activities of two men, Pašić and Dimitrijević, are crucial. In late May or early June Pašić learned that some young Bosnians who were students in Belgrade were planning an unspecified action against the archduke during his visit to Sarajevo. The Serbian premier also ascertained that Serbian officials had assisted them in crossing the frontier into Bosnia illegally. With this knowledge the Serbian government through its representative in Vienna attempted to warn the Habsburg authorities on June 5. Since this advice was not given in a direct or forthright manner, its seriousness was not appreciated in Vienna. Neither Pašić nor members of his government knew of the exact plans, nor did they assist directly in illegal activities.

Although the civilian authorities can be exonerated of the charge of direct involvement, the Chief of Intelligence of the army, Colonel Dimitrijević, cannot be cleared. At the head of the Serbian secret service, he did have agents in Bosnia. Since he was also the leader of the Black Hand, he could have recruited the disaffected youth for action against the monarchy. It is, however, almost certain that the plot was initiated by the young men themselves and that the Black Hand merely assisted at their request. Whatever interpretation is accepted, the fact is that members of the conspiracy did meet with Dimitrijević in Belgrade in May. Through his offices they were provided with pistols and bombs from an official army arsenal. Arrangements were also made to smuggle them back into Bosnia. When the Central Committee of the Black Hand learned what had taken place, it ordered Dimitrijević to halt the plans, but it was too late.

The question of Serbian complicity thus becomes the issue of whether the Serbian government was responsible for the actions of its army officers. The Black Hand was at this time a state within the state; it could not be controlled. In June it was even able to defy the government on a

Macedonian issue and to force King Peter to yield his authority to his son, Prince Alexander. The chief of army intelligence did provide the assassins with the weapons used to kill the archduke, and his associates did send the conspirators back to Bosnia illegally. The Habsburg government, in these circumstances, clearly had ample reason to take strong action.

The second question, that concerning the Habsburg opinion of the Yugoslav danger, can be clearly answered. It had certainly been a major subject of discussion among the Habsburg authorities in the past. The implications of the program of South Slav unity for the integrity of the state and the role of Serbia in such an action were apparent to everyone. Two alternate solutions were suggested, one associated with the name of the Chief of Staff of the army, Conrad von Hötzendorf, and the other with Franz Ferdinand. Hötzendorf favored force. Since he regarded Serbia as the greatest threat to the monarchy, he consistently advocated, after 1906, a preventative war. Without Serbian support a Yugoslav movement could not succeed. Ideally he would have liked to partition Serbia between the monarchy and Bulgaria. In contrast, Franz Ferdinand, who also had army support, preferred to reach an understanding with the Slavic peoples and the Romanians. Regarding the Hungarians as the major menace, he wished to grant more autonomy to the other ethnic groups.

The assassination presented the imperial leaders with the apparent necessity of making a clear choice, since they were convinced that Serbia was implicated in the plot. They could either destroy the Serbian state, which had been the center of continual anti-Habsburg activities since 1903, or they could await the slow dissolution of the monarchy. The decision was reached over the long period between June 28 and July 28. Foreign Minister Count Leopold von Berchtold and Hötzendorf were the first to be convinced of the advisability of war; they then set out to convince the emperor and Count Stephen Tisza, the Hungarian premier. They also had to consult their German ally. It must be stressed that none of these men expected the dispute to end in a general European war, although the possibility was considered. Franz Joseph was persuaded to accept a strong solution without too much difficulty, but Tisza proved obdurate. He only agreed to action on the condition that Serbian territory not be annexed to the empire. The Hungarians wanted no more Slavs. With internal agreement and with the support of Germany the Habsburg government then delivered a forty-eight hour ultimatum to Belgrade. It will be noted that no attempt was made to reach an understanding with Russia, despite the close association of that power with Serbia. This action violated a two-century-old tradition of close consultation between the courts.

The ultimatum to Serbia was designed to be rejected. It called for the suppression of anti-Habsburg publications in Serbia, the dismissial of anti-Habsburg teachers and officers, the participation of Austrian officials in the investigation in Serbia of the assassination, the arrest and dismissal of men implicated in the event, and similar provisions. The Serbian government agreed to everything except Habsburg participation in inquiries concerning the assassination in Serbia proper. The apparent capitulation brought relief to the diplomats of Europe. The German emperor, William II, called the answer "a brilliant performance for a time-limit of only 48 hours. This is more than one could have expected! A great moral success for Vienna; but with it every reason for war drops away . . ." [5] The Habsburg government, unfortunately, did not agree with this last opinion. Since the ultimatum had not been completely accepted, the reply was rejected and the war commenced.

By early August Austria-Hungary and Germany were at war with France, Russia, Serbia, and Britain. Italy and Romania, both a part of the Triple Alliance system, remained neutral. Once again as in the Crimean War, the great powers found themselves pulled into war over problems associated with the Eastern Question and the rise of the national movements in the Balkans. In contrast to the earlier conflict, however, the First World War was to be a catastrophe for all of the participants. Not only did the Balkan states suffer devastating losses, but the political repercussions were to bring down the Habsburg and Ottoman empires as well as the government of tsarist Russia and imperial Germany.

Before proceeding to an account of this disastrous period, Balkan cultural developments in the preceding century will be discussed. The accomplishments of the peoples in the Habsburg monarchy, the Ottoman Empire, and its successor states will be included.

5. Sidney Bradshaw Fay, *The Origins of the World War* (New York: Macmillan, 1928), vol. 2, p. 348.

CHAPTER 16

Balkan Cultural Developments

DURING the period under discussion Balkan culture evolved in close association with the political events. Books, educational systems, and art works reflected, with few exceptions, the great central issues of the establishment of the national state and the social tensions arising from the political and economic changes. For this reason the preceding pages have often dealt with literary figures and have mentioned the opening of universities, libraries, and similar institutions. It is impossible to avoid some repetition in this section. In fact, a discussion of cultural trends will serve admirably to sum up the more than one century of Balkan history. Chief attention here will be given to literature because of its primary position in Balkan life, but some comment on art, architecture and music will be included.

In general, Balkan cultural developments can best be followed on two levels: first, that of the peasant and the village, which included the majority of the people, and second, that of the educated and politically aware minority, a group ranging in composition from the village priest and the schoolmaster to the Romanian boyar and Phanariote merchant prince. Toward the end of the nineteenth century a small urban industrial working class joined the first category. Although the main stress will be placed on the activities of the second literate group, it will be seen that both sections of the population were joined by common participation in the national movements, by the intense interest which many Balkan intellectuals often devoted to peasant problems, and by the fact that folk poetry and art underlay many of the products of Balkan high culture.

The primary characteristic of the cultural life of the Balkan peoples was the strong national direction, including the aim of the establishment of the independent, nationally based state. Once this goal had been achieved writers and artists continued to give active support to their nation and any measures leading to its expansion and strengthening. Al-

266

though they often criticized its political and social organization, they remained basically nationalistic in outlook. Controversies did arise, however, concerning the direction which national life should take and whether foreign, that is, West European, examples should be followed rather than purely native forms. In this atmosphere it was inevitable that writers and artists would be deeply involved in political activities, either as participants in rebellions, or as teachers and holders of state offices. The emotional attraction of the national idea and the dramatic events of the century inspired fine artistic accomplishments, but also the production of what can best be termed blatant political or social propaganda.

In discussing literature, the central theme here, three divisions will be made, each reflecting the major events previously recounted. The first section will cover the role of Balkan literary developments during the revolutions and the establishment of the first autonomous or independent governments. The second will include the early history of these administrations. The third will discuss the movements characterizing the final years of the century to the outbreak of the First World War. The shift from romanticism to realism to the modern currents of impressionism, symbolism, and decadence of the pre-war era paralleled, with some unique local variations, comparable movements in general European cultural life. The relationship was to become a major point of dispute.

The evolution toward a modern national culture began in the eighteenth century before the chronological limits of this study. All Balkan peoples entered the new era with two major foundations for further development. Of first importance was the basic peasant culture, which showed both common characteristics over the whole geographic area and unique local qualities. The majority also shared in the Orthodox religion with its formal literature and music, its popular accounts of saints and martyrs, and the world of art and architecture associated with the Byzantine tradition. Catholic peoples maintained a similar relationship with their church. In addition, some nationalities had a secular literature of long standing. For instance, Greek writers, chiefly in Crete and the Ionian Islands, and their Croatian counterparts, in Dalmatia in particular, produced major works during the Ottoman period.

Because of the almost universal illiteracy and the paucity of printing presses in the Ottoman Empire, cultural life for the majority of the people centered in deeply rooted folk art and oral literature. This heritage can be divided into three general categories. First, poetry dealing with nature, the emotions, and problems that the peasants encountered in their daily lives, in particular, love, marriage, and death; second, stories and folk tales, including those about local heroes, *klephts*, and *haiduks*; and, third, epic poetry based on historical events. The latter were usually sung or chanted, often by professional singers, to the accompaniment of simple instruments like the one-stringed *gusla*. Such songs and poems continued to be composed to record major events throughout the nineteenth century, but with rapidly diminishing frequency.

For the national movements the epic poetry assumed a prime significance. The earliest in this group were the Greek Acritic songs, which described the exploits of Byzantine border fighters against the Arabs in the tenth century. The most famous was *Diogenes Akritas*. For the Greeks the fall of Constantinople was also the subject of narrative poetry. By far the most significant cycle of songs for the South Slavs concerned the Battle of Kosovo, the event symbolizing the crushing of the Christian medieval states by the Muslim empire. Bulgarians and Serbs alike had a hero in Prince Marko (Marko Kraljević in Serbian, Krali Marko in Bulgarian). The Catholic Slavs had similar poems concerning the struggle with the Ottoman forces which date from the fifteenth century. Albanian Muslim songs concerned the struggle with the Christian Slavs. In these epics the emphasis was on the activities of the individual hero and the attraction of the fighter's free life. In the nineteenth century the national aspects came to the fore. Thus the Battle of Kosovo came to stand not for the acts of the individual heroes or Christianity, but for the fate of the Serbian nation.

This body of peasant oral literature was to play an active role in the national revivals and in the subsequent development of modern literatures. The first enthusiasm for the study and collection of this material came from Europe, particularly from Germany. The romantic school found such writings the best source for the expression of the "folk spirit." Writers from many countries, including Goethe, Pushkin, Mickiewicz, and Scott, were interested in and translated folk epics. Balkan scholars soon showed a similar concern over the collection and publication of these works and made them a part of the national revival movements.

All of the nations exhibited certain common characteristics during the first period in the development of secular literatures. Many aspects of European romanticism, such as the emphasis on history, on the basic values of peasant societies, and on the emotions and the imagination, fit well with the spirit of early Balkan liberation efforts. The interest in history held a particular attraction since all of the Balkan people could look back to a more heroic era when they were free of foreign control. For the Balkan scholars the revival of the past was to have more than an academic appeal. It was regarded as an educational tool to inform and enlighten a nation on its historic importance and to instill pride in its previous achievements as a spur to political action. The attention paid to language and its "pure" and "national" character had similar objectives. In most instances this direction of intellectual activity was in opposition to the church and to religious education, which was usually conducted in a language not generally spoken by the community in its everyday life. The rise of secular education thus involved a sharp break with an ecclesiastical past.

The preeminent position of the Greeks among the Orthodox Balkan peoples in the eighteenth century has been discussed previously. Not only did they have political power through the church and the position of the Phanariotes in the Ottoman administration, but they came into close touch with general European developments through their rich commercial enterprises. With centers of influence in Constantinople, Bucharest, and Jassy and with large colonies in Vienna, Paris, and other western cities, they were best qualified to inaugurate first a period of national cultural revival. Because of the conditions in the Ottoman Empire, Vienna became the center of the first significant activities. Books and periodicals appeared here when after 1783 Joseph II allowed publications in Greek to be printed. Paris and the Ionian Islands were also important for the new movement.

The two great Greek names of this era were Rhigas Pheraios and Adamantios Koraes. Of the two the works of Koraes held the greater significance for future writing. Koraes emphasized political education and believed that the Greek people should be instructed through a knowledge of the classics. His major effort was thus directed towards the production of new editions with long introductions. His main undertaking was the Library of Greek Literature, which appeared between 1805 and 1826 and included seventeen volumes of classical texts. Koraes' activities had an enormous influence on future Greek literary development. In a nationalist effort to "purify" spoken and written Greek of words of Venetian, Slavic, and Turkish origin and to reintroduce into current usage many forgotten classical words, he devised a new form, *katharevousa*, the purist language, to replace demotic Greek, the natural heir of Byzantine Greek. As we have seen, *katharevousa* became the official language of the independent state despite the fact that most subsequent writers did not use it.

In the Romanian lands the impetus toward cultural change came from two directions. Never under direct Ottoman rule, the Principalities had always been more open to outside ideas than had their immediate neighbors within the empire. Through the Orthodox church these lands had been under a strong Slavic influence and the language was first written in Cyrillic. The Phanariote rule of the eighteenth century represented another foreign element, one that had both positive and negative effects. The Greek princes brought into the country not only Greek culture, but that of the West. The Phanariote educational institutions of Bucharest and Jassy taught mathematics and science. Through Greek circles the ideas of the Enlightenment were also disseminated among the Romanian boyars. European classical literature, including the works of writers such as Molière, Corneille, Schiller, and Shakespeare, was similarly introduced, often through Greek versions.

The second, and for the national movement more significant, impulse came from Transylvania. The activities of George Şincai, Peter Maior, and Samuel Clain (Micu) of the Transylvanian School have already been discussed. Of prime importance were their efforts to trace the history of the Romanian people in an unbroken line back to the Romans. Their publication of grammars and historical works was to have a major impact on the Principalities. The views of the Transylvanian School were brought across the Carpathians chiefly through the endeavors of two men, George Lazăr in Bucharest and George Asachi in Jassy, in the second decade of the nineteenth century. The ideology of the adherents of this school also involved the form of the written language. Like their Greek counterparts, they wished to emphasize the ancient nature of their speech and thus endeavored to eliminate where possible non-Latin based words from the literary language.

This direction naturally tended to strengthen Romanian associations with the other Latin countries, France and Italy. Particularly influential in this regard was the work of Ion Eliade Rădulescu. The central organizer of two cultural groups, the Literary Society of 1826 and the Philharmonic Society of 1833, Eliade not only wrote prolifically himself, but he was also responsible for the translation and publication of many French works. French political concepts naturally penetrated through these channels. After 1821, when Greek power waned with the beginning of the revolt, French cultural influence became predominant.

As we have seen, the generation that led the revolution of 1848 was largely French educated. Although the French imprint was strongest, some of these men had also traveled widely, in particular in the German states, the Habsburg Empire, and Italy, and they were aware of international cultural developments. Living in an era of romantic nationalism, which involved a union of intense patriotism with an urge to take direct action, these young men also placed a high value on literary endeavors. Nicholas Bălcescu and Michael Kogălniceanu both influenced future Romanian prose writing. Bălcescu is best known for his work on the national hero Michael the Brave; Kogălniceanu, for his publication of medieval manuscripts. The major poet of this period was Vasile Alecsandri, whose career was to span the century. The historical fiction of Constantine Negruzzi, the poetry of Iancu Văcărescu and his brothers, as well as the writings of Dimitrie Bolintineanu and Gregory Alexandrescu belong also to this epoch.

Similar developments occurred in the South Slav lands. Here, too, the question of past historical glory and the form of the literary language became major issues. Because of conditions in the Belgrade pashalik, the

Serbian revival came from the communities in the Vojvodina established principally in the late seventeenth century. As with the Greeks, the first Serbian newspaper and journal were published in the Habsburg monarchy in 1790s. By the beginning of the nineteenth century the Serbs of the Habsburg Empire had available to them institutions of higher education, libraries, and printing presses. Serbian students received the type of education common to the other citizens of the monarchy. A language problem, however, existed here too. The Serbian Orthodox church, with its center in Sremski Karlovci, was closely tied to Russia. Theological students went to Kiev for their training. As a result the literary language became not Serbian or Church Slavic, but the so-called Russo-Slavic with its high proportion of Russian words. This form was used by the church and the educated Serbs of the Habsburg Empire.

A counterinfluence to this artificial usage came from the two most influential Serbian writers of this period, Dositej Obradović and Vuk Karadžić, both of whom wrote in the form of the spoken language. For the development of the Serbo-Croatian literary language Karadžić was to be the most influential scholar of the century. Working both in Vienna and Belgrade, he involved himself in a wide range of activities in the national interest, including the publication of a grammar and a dictionary, and the collection of folk songs and poetry. Through his efforts the Kosovo cycle and the *haiduk* songs became part of the literature of the national movement.

Like the Serbs, the Croatian writers were faced with a choice of languages. At the beginning of the century Latin was still used to communicate with the Magyars. There was also a national literature, which had developed first in Dubrovnik and in the nineteenth century in Zagreb, but which was written in the two separate dialects of these areas. As has been previously shown, the chief influence in the final choice came from the Illyrian movement, associated closely with the name of Ljudevit Gaj. Following the ideas of the Czech scholar Jan Kollár, that the Slavs were one people speaking four dialects (Russian, Czech, Polish, and Illyrian), he gave his preference to the štokavian dialect, which was also that chosen by Karadžić.

The Slovenian intellectuals faced more difficult problems. German held a strong attraction for the educated classes. Equally complicated were the issues raised by the Illyrian movement. The political implications and the advantages of sharing a common literary language with the Serbs and Croats were obvious. Nevertheless, awareness of the distinct Slovenian national existence remained alive. Two writers initiated modern Slovene literature: Anton Linhart, who published a history of Carinthia in German, and the poet Valentin Vodnik. A journal, the *Carinthian Bee* (Kranjska Cbelica), was founded in 1830. Although issued only until 1834, it published the work of the greatest Slovenian poet,

France Prešeren. Unhappy in his own life, Prešeren's outlook was pessimistic; his main work, *A Wreath of Sonnets* (Sonetni venec), concerns a disappointed love affair, a theme which received a nationalistic interpretation. After Prešeren the principal literary figure was Fran Levstik. Both a poet and a prose writer, he was active in the Slovenian national movement.

Because of the double restraint of Ottoman rule and Greek political and ecclesiastical domination, Bulgarian literary development lagged behind that of the neighboring lands. In the early part of the nineteenth century, however, particularly after the revolution removed Greek influence, the Bulgarian lands went through a period of economic and cultural revival known as the Bulgarian renaissance. Again as in other nations the first interest was in history and the language. The initial endeavors of Father Paisii and Bishop Sofronii of Vratsa and the educational activities of Vasil Aprilov were important. Mention should be made also of the publication of Dr. Peter Beron's schoolbook, called the Fish Primer because of its illustrations, in 1824 and Neofit Rilski's grammar in 1835. Although the first Bulgarian newspaper, the *Bulgarian Eagle* (Bulgarski orel), appeared in Leipzig in 1846, the most successful was the *Constantinople Herald* (Tsarigradski vestnik) published in the Ottoman capital between 1848 and 1862.

Because of the political conditions within the Bulgarian lands, the initial cultural centers were outside of the country. The question of the literary language was settled with the adoption of the eastern Bulgarian dialect. This was the language of the first major poet, Naiden Gerov. His principal work, the poem *Staian and Rada,* was published in Odessa in 1842. Modern Bulgarian literature dates from the middle of the century. Among the first important writers was Petko R. Slaveikov, a poet and journalist. A strong nationalist, he favored the gaining of Bulgarian independence by evolutionary and not revolutionary means.

In contrast, three literary figures appeared, George Rakovski, Liuben Karavelov, and Khristo Botev, whose revolutionary exploits have already been described. These men were deeply involved in political activity and revolutionary exploits. Their literary talents were at the service of the national idea and they were closely associated with the conspiracies of the time. The first, George Rakovski, it will be remembered, moved to Belgrade in 1860 where his periodical *Danube Swan* (Dunavski lebed) was published; he later lived in Bucharest. His major work was the narrative poem, *The Forest Traveler* (Gorski putnik), published in 1857 in Novi Sad. The second, Liuben Karavelov, was a leading poet, journalist, and prose writer. Both he and Rakovski were interested in the collection and publication of folk poems. Of the three, the major talent belonged to Botev. His reputation as the greatest Bulgarian poet rests on some twenty lyric poems written between 1867 and 1873. A radical national and social revolutionary, Botev became a national martyr and hero after his death in the ill-fated action in 1876.

The common cultural characteristics, such as emphasis on education, national history, language, and participation in political activities, which linked the Balkan nations in the first revolutionary period, continued after the establishment of independent or autonomous regimes. At first the new governments followed in the tradition of romantic nationalism and patronized national educational systems, the foundation of libraries and academies, and the publication of works that would be supportive of the political order in existence and the national aims. A reaction soon set in, however, to overstated chauvinistic literature and to reliance on foreign models for national development. Most important, as economic change took place interest began to shift to social problems, first to the life of the peasant and then to the city-dweller. Awareness of and concern over the problems of peasant life in an age of declining prosperity and the breaking of traditional patterns of life increased. Realism and naturalism gradually replaced romanticism as the primary characteristic of the national literatures.

After 1835 Athens became the center of Greek cultural life. The Phanariotes, expelled from positions of power in the Ottoman capital, now transferred their activities to the new kingdom. The deeply Philhellene Bavarian administration favored the classical over the Byzantine and Orthodox past. Athens was rebuilt in the neoclassical style on the model of Munich. This emphasis naturally gave support to continued use of the archaic form of the language. Greek writing was also strongly influenced by French romanticism, which, with its attention to the past and its emotional content, coincided ideally with Greek feelings in the post revolutionary epoch. The foremost writer of the period was the poet Achilles Paraschos, who composed highly patriotic verse in *katharevousa*. Also of importance was the poetry of Alexander Soutsos, the prose and poetry of Alexander Rizos Rangaves, and the prose of Emmanuel Roides.

In the years immediately after the revolution many participants published their memoirs. The best of these was written by the military leader, S. Makriyannes, in the vernacular. Constantine Paparregopoulos wrote the first major historical work, entitled *History of the Greek Nation* (Historia tou hellenikou ethnous) and published between 1860 and 1872. His objective was to show the links of the modern state with ancient Greece.

Parallel with Athens, the Ionian Islands, under Britain until 1864, became a center of Greek cultural development. The greatest modern Greek poet, Dionysios Solomos, was born in Zante. Influenced by his Italian education, he wrote first in that language and then in demotic. He did not finish his major undertakings, and only fragments of his work remain. Among his most popular poems are the Greek national anthem, *Hymn to Liberty* (Hymnos es ten Eleutherian), *The Free Besieged* (Oi Eleutheroi Poliorkemene), *The Poisoned Girl* (He Farmakomene) and *The Woman of Zakynthos* (He Gynaika les Zakynthos). A second Ionian poet, Andreas Kalvos, wrote in the archaic language.

The poetry of Solomos was to achieve great importance later in the century when a group of poets joined together to challenge the romantic writers of the older generation and to write in demotic. Expressing the extreme frustration felt at the time with the development of the Greek state, they attacked both the style and the language of their predecessors. The battle for linguistic reform was launched in 1888 with the publication of John Psychares' book, *My Journey* (To taxidi mou), a travel account in demotic. The foremost writer and main figure of the New School of Athens was, however, the poet Kostes Palamas. Dominating Greek cultural life for sixty years, he is best known for his two poetic works, *Dodecalogue of the Gypsy* (Didecalogos tou Gyftou) and *The Flute of the King* (I flogera tou Vasilia). Nicholas Polites' folklore studies were also an inspiration to this group. The bitter conflict between the supporters of the vernacular and those who preferred *katharevousa* was never finally settled. In practice, demotic now came to be used in poetry and in most fiction.

In Romania a similar reaction against the older ideas occurred. As we have seen, the first writers had drawn their ideas largely from French sources. Extremely active politically, this group, the men of 1848, had led the movement that resulted in the unification of the Principalities in 1859 and 1861. They then formed the basis of the Liberal Party. In the 1860s a rival circle was formed around Titu Maiorescu. The German-educated Maiorescu was influenced by idealist philosophers such as Kant, Hegel, and Schopenhauer. He and his followers formed in 1864 the group known as Junimea (Youth). In 1867 they founded a journal, *Literary Discussions* (Convorbiri Literare) which continued publication, with minor interruptions, until 1944. Almost all of the important writers of this period were associated at one time or another with this circle. Its program stressed reliance on native rather than foreign sources for political and cultural inspiration. The political activism of the earlier generation was also condemned. Conservative in its political stance, its members reproached the Liberal Party for having a program based on foreign principles.

The most famous writer of this group, Michael Eminescu, was also the greatest Romanian poet. Born in 1850 in Moldavia, he led an extremely unsettled youth. In 1870 he attended the University of Vienna, and in 1872 the Junimea group gave him the funds to spend two years in Berlin. He was later employed in lower educational offices in Jassy, and in 1877 he became a journalist in Bucharest. He became mentally disturbed in 1883 and died in 1889. Despite his short life, he wrote a great deal. His lyric poetry remains the base of his reputation; *Evening Star* (Luceafărul) is perhaps the best example of his work. Often pessimistic in outlook, he was attracted to the magical, dreamlike, and changing. Concerned also with political and national issues, he believed that each nation should follow its own spirit, and that it was the task of those in political life to find the institutions which would best express this unique attribute.

Two other outstanding writers were associated with the Junimea circle. Ion Creangă, who published almost all of his work in *Literary Discussions* between 1875 and 1881, is known for his descriptions of peasant life, particularly for his memoirs of his youth, *Recollections of Childhood* (Amintiri din copilărie). His literary versions of folk tales have remained extremely popular. The leading dramatist, Ion Luca Caragiale, had a satirical style and was interested in portraying urban life. Other authors closely associated with Junimea were Alexander Odobescu, Ion Slavici and Duiliu Zamfirescu.

The stand of Junimea on the subject of outside influence and, more important, its members' belief that art should stand apart from political controversy were bound to arouse opposition. Criticism came from two divergent directions: socialist and populist writers who expected social engagement in literature, and nationalists who did not like the group's cosmopolitan attitude on certain questions of literary standards. Among the latter were the most prominent Romanian historians. Historical writing on a modern basis, as we have seen, had commenced with Bălcescu and Kogălniceanu and the generation of 1848. Now three authors, Bogdan Hașdeu, Alexander Xenopol, and Nicholas Iorga, opposed the Junimea stand and continued the nationalist emphasis. Xenopol, the first major Romanian historian, taught at the University of Jassy. Like Paparregopoulos in Greece, he traced the history of his people back to their ancient origins. His major work was the six volume *History of the Romanians of Trajan Dacia* (Istoria Romînilor din Dacia Traiană) published in Jassy from 1888 to 1893. The greatest Romanian, in fact the foremost Balkan historian, was his pupil Nicholas Iorga. A man of formidable energy, Iorga wrote some 1,200 books and pamphlets and 23,000 articles and reviews, while at the same time conducting an active and controversial political life. He is best known for his two syntheses of Romanian history, *Geschichte des rumänischen Volkes im Rahmen seiner Staatsbildungen* (1905) and the ten volume *History of the Romanians* (Istoria romînilor) (1936–44) which also appeared in a French edition.

In the South Slav lands the romantic current, which included the work of Karadžić, remained predominant in Serbia. The greatest Serbian poet was not, however, from the principality, but from Montenegro. There the poet prince Peter Petrović Njegoš wrote three major works which rank among the masterpieces of Balkan culture. The best known, the dramatic poem *The Mountain Wreath* (Gorski vijenac), was published in 1847 and concerned Montenegro's struggle with the Ottoman Empire. The two others were *Light of the Microcosm* (Luča mikrokosma), 1815, and *The False Tsar Stephen the Small* (Lažni car Šćepan Mali), 1851. The latter dealt with the life of an adventurer who became ruler of Montenegro in the eighteenth century.

Other noteworthy Serbian writers of the romantic school were the poet Branko Radičević, the novelist and dramatist Jovan Sterija Popović, and three outstanding poets of the latter part of the century, Jovan Jovanović-Zmaj, Djura Jakšić, and Laza Kostić. By this time the cultural center of Serbian life had shifted from the Habsburg Empire to the principality. The question of language had been decisively settled in favor of the popular form with the emphasis in writing on poetry and themes connected with patriotism, human emotions, and the natural world.

In Serbia, as in the other Balkan countries, the years after the Congress of Berlin were marked by a growing concern over the problems of the changing economy and the difficulties associated with the organization of a modern state. Interest shifted from national to social problems and to the life of the common man, in particular the peasant. Instead of the romantic attention to poetry, the new realism was best expressed in the short story. As previously, contemporary European writing remained influential. The works of such authors as Turgenev, Hugo, Zola, and Daudet were translated. Great interest was shown in the Russian Populist movement and in the writings of Dobroliubov, Herzen, and Gogol. A major literary critic of this time was Svetozar Marković, who was also the founder of Serbian socialism. In contrast to previous trends, he believed that literature should actively serve the needs of the majority of the people and deal with the basic problems of everyday life. Among the authors of the realistic short story and novel were Jakov Ignjatović, Milovan Glišić, Lazar Lazarević, and Simo Matavulj.

Croatian romanticism, as we have seen, had found expression in the Illyrian movement. After Gaj, the next eminent writer was Ivan Mažuranić, who was best known for his epic poem, *The Death of Smail Aga Čengić* (Smrt Smail-age Čengića). As in Serbia, the last decades of the century brought a turn for the worse for the South Slav people of the Habsburg monarchy, a change which was also reflected in Croatian literature. The economic developments, as previously noted, led to the ruin of the small nobility. After the Ausgleich the major positions in the state went to other nationalities, particularly to Hungarians. Emigration increased rapidly. Reflecting the new concerns, the novel became the principal literary form, and urban predominated over rural themes. Almost without exception the writers belonged to the Party of Rights and were politically active.

The foremost Croatian writer in this period was undoubtedly August Šenoa. He believed that literature should have a social and national purpose, and that it should be written for the people. As a poet, editor, dramatist, critic, and novelist, he exerted a major influence on his era. Other Croatian realist writers were Evgenij Kumičić, Ksaver Šandor Djalski, Ante Kovačić, and Vjenceslav Novak. A similar development occurred among the Slovenes, whose authors included the poets Ivan Tavčar and Anton Askerc and the novelist Janko Kersnik.

Historical writing progressed in both Zagreb and Belgrade. In Croatia the central figure in the development of modern historiography was Franjo Rački, the close associate of Strossmayer, who was responsible for the publication of medieval source collections. Important also was the work of Tadija Smičiklas and Ferdo Šišić. Šišić, the outstanding Croatian historian, published a three volume *History of Croatia* (Hrvatska povijest) between 1906 and 1913. The major Serbian historians were Stojan Novaković, Stanoje Stanojević, Jovan Radonić and Slobodan Jovanović.

In Bulgaria the establishment of the autonomous regime created a different atmosphere. Botev and Liuben Karavelov had died. Many who had previously been engaged in literary activities found themselves drawn into state service as officials or teachers. Most writers, including Slaveikov and also the now prominent Ivan Vazov and Constantine Velichkov, worked for the government. Of the latter two, Vazov was undoubtedly the best known and dominates the period to the 1920s. His most famous novel, *Under the Yoke* (Pod igoto), was started in Odessa where the author was in political exile during the Stambolov regime. This book, highly emotional and patriotic in tone, dealt with the last period of Ottoman rule including the April uprising of 1876. In 1896 Vazov published a second novel, *New Land* (Nova zemia), which was more critical in tone. Like others, he had become disillusioned by his experiences under the autonomous regime. Velichkov and Aleko Konstantinov, both novelists, shared this outlook. Konstantinov's best work is his account of his visit to the United States in 1893, entitled *To Chicago and Back* (Do Chikago i nazad), and his satirical *Bai Ganuo* in which he presented a major character who was the "embodiment of all that was crude, unintelligent, blundering and bourgeois in the Bulgarian spirit." [1] While these writers described urban as well as rural conditions, another group, chiefly influenced by the Russian narodnik movement, dealt primarily with the crisis in peasant and country life. Returning often as teachers to the villages, they met at first hand the disintegration and destitution on the land. In this number were Todor Vlaikov, Tsanko Tserkovski, and Mihalaki Georgiev.

1. Charles A. Moser, *A History of Bulgarian Literature, 865–1944* (Hague: Mouton, 1972), p. 111.

In the third period of this survey, covering the turn of the century to the outbreak of the First World War, many of the earlier currents continued. There was still concern with social and economic problems and with the life of the peasant and the urban middle class. The idea was held that literature and art should teach and serve with the emphasis on the social rather than the national aspects of state life. At the same time some authors believed that the cultural life of their country should join with the main stream of European thought, which had become increasingly dominated by impressionism, neoromanticism, and symbolism. They argued that national and peasant themes had either been exhausted or represented a backward cultural emphasis.

In Greece the continuance of the poetic tradition brought to the fore two major writers. Angelos Sikelianos carried on the tradition of the New School of Athens. In contrast, Constantine Cavafy, who lived and worked in Alexandria, wrote in the demotic, but used some *katharevousa* words. His poetry was, on the one hand, intensely personal and sensual, and, on the other hand, historical. His historical poems are largely set in the Hellenistic period of Greco-Roman culture. Since his experiences were with those of the Greek community in Egypt, his work was more nationalistic in content. In prose writing both the demotic emphasis and the interest in the life of the common people continued. Greece's foremost short story writer, Alexander Papadiamantes, dealt with themes concerning peasants and fishermen. Andreas Karkavitsas continued in the same realistic line. City problems now received attention in the novels of such authors as Gregory Xenopoulos, Kosmas Polites, and Constantine Theotakes.

Romanian literature continued to reflect a reaction to the Junimea standpoint. Both the new socialist left and those who continued to emphasize traditional nationalism urged the return to an attitude of political engagement. In addition, a smaller group adopted the modernist stand of contemporary western and central Europe. In general, however, attention remained focused on the great problems of national life and the peasant dilemma, which reached a climax in the revolt of 1907.

Like his Serbian counterpart Svetozar Marković, the first major Romanian socialist writer, Constantine Dobrogeanu-Gherea, favored a politically involved literature. He directed his attention primarily to the problems of the victims of the social and economic developments of the new age. His most important work, *Neoserfdom* (Neoiobăgia), was published in 1910 after the peasant rebellion. Of greater influence at the time, however, were the works of writers who gave their full attention to rural problems. In 1901 a new journal, *The Sower* (Sămănătorul) began publication under the initial direction of George Coșbuc and Alexander Vlahuță. The review and the circle around it stressed national and traditional views. From 1903 to 1906 Iorga took over the editorship. A conservative, he opposed both socialist and populist as well as modern currents. Early in his career the great novelist of the interwar period, Michael Sadoveanu, was associated with this group.

In addition to this circle another was formed to represent the populist view, or *Poporanism.* Its journal, *Romanian Life* (Viaţa Românească), appeared in 1906 and was edited by G. Ibrăileanu in close association with Constantine Stere. Like the Russian narodniks, these writers believed that intellectuals should involve themselves in political questions and work for peasant reform.

Although the modernist school was first represented in Romania by the poet Alexander Macedonski, its major exponent was Ovid Densusianu. Influenced by his studies in Paris, he became convinced that symbolism was the true expression of the Latin spirit. In contrast to the populist authors, he contended that literature should entertain and inspire rather than teach.

A similar dual development was discernable in the South Slav lands. Here, however, the modernist trends were more important than in Romania or Greece. Although realism had been the prevailing mode, by the end of the century a new direction was apparent. Since most Serbian intellectuals had either had a French education or felt ties with Paris, their models became French writers, in particular the symbolists. Social themes were replaced by a highly individualistic and subjective literature, which emphasized artistic value and style. The leading figures were the poets Jovan Dučić and Milan Rakić.

In the Croatian lands a parallel change took place. Although realist prose emphasizing patriotism and the life of the people continued to be written, Croatian *moderna* drew its primary influence from the new current. The principal writers of this group were the dramatist, poet, and novelist Ivo Vojnović, the essayist and critic Antun Gustav Matoš, and the poet Vladimir Nazor. Slovenian literature followed in the same direction.

In Bulgaria the modernist writers, known as "Europeans," had their center in the journal *Thought* (Misal) founded by Krastiu Krastev. Like their counterparts elsewhere, they wanted to remove their writing from social and political involvement and from what they regarded as parochial influences. They wished to introduce instead permanent and universal standards. The poet Pencho Slaveikov and the novelist Petko Todorov were among this group. The realist novel continued, however, to appear. The early writing of the two outstanding postwar writers, Elin Pelin and Iordan Iovkov, belongs to this period. In 1904 and 1911 Pelin published collections of short stories based on conditions in the countryside and on peasant life.

Art, architecture, and music showed the same basic lines of development. Again, the foundation for the nineteenth century lay in the two sources: the peasant world and the church. Under Ottoman rule a great wealth of artistic activity existed on the village level with the emphasis on textiles, pottery, and the ornamentation of homes, clothes, and persons. Church exteriors had to remain unobtrusive because of Ottoman restrictions on Christian buildings, but the interiors could be richly decorated with ikons, frescoes, and wood carving. With the founding and the development of the modern state this aspect of national cultural creativity gradually died. With industrialization, machine-made textiles rapidly replaced homemade fabrics. Other village handicrafts followed a like path to extinction. Ecclesiastical art was similarly affected. The new age was secular; the leadership of the revolutionary movement was unlikely to favor the investment of large sums in church building or decoration.

As in literature and politics, Balkan art and architecture were to be closely tied to European models. Paris, Vienna, and Munich held at different times an attraction for the artists of the different nations. As could be expected, France was the main source of inspiration for the Romanian artist. The first great modern painter, Theodore Aman, studied in Paris and became known for his historical scenes, portraits, and portrayals of village life. Nicholas Grigorescu and Ion Andrescu followed in the same pattern. At the end of the century the new trends were reflected in the work of Stefan Luchain. Known for his use of color, he took themes from village and urban life. Jean Al. Steriadi, Stefan Dimitrescu, and Camil Ressu also belong to this period. The foremost painter of the interwar period, George Petraşcu, commenced his work at this time.

Serbian and Croatian artists were influenced by both French and German examples. In Serbia the classical school, which emphasized the painting of portraits, historical scenes, and mythological subjects, dominated until the middle of the century. The outstanding painter of the succeeding romantic school was Djura Jakšić; Novak Rakonić, and Stevan Todorović were known for their landscapes. Among the realists of the last decades of the century, the most popular was Uroš Predić. Miloš Tenković, George Krstić, and Paja Jovanović were also of importance. The leading Croatian painter of the middle of the century, Vjekoslav Karas, was connected with the Illyrian movement. As in Serbia, realism then dominated until the end of the century. The new impressionist trend was introduced by Joseph Račić and Miroslav Kraljević; both studied in Paris and together with Vladimir Bečić rank as the greatest Croatian painters.

Bulgarian art developed more slowly. Although some artists studied abroad before the establishment of the autonomous administration, it was not until the 1890s that the country had an organized and active group of painters. The first artists of importance were both of Czech origin: Ivan Mrkvichka and Iaroslav Vesin. The landscape painting of

Nicholas Petkov and the work of Vladimir Dimitrov the Master marked the height of Bulgarian prewar accomplishments.

As could be expected, modern Greek artists first studied in Munich where they were primarily influenced by German examples. The main painters of the romantic school were Nicephoros Lystras, Nicholas Gyzes, and Constantine Volonakes. At the end of the century French impressionism became of chief importance. Constantine Parthenes, one of the greatest Greek artists, belongs to this period.

Although Balkan painters in general did not enjoy general European popularity, two sculptors received world recognition; Constantine Brancuşi and Ivan Meštrović. Brancuşi was born in Oltenia in 1876 and subsequently studied in Paris where he was greatly influenced by Rodin. Abstract in form, his work also took themes from Romanian folklore. Meštrović, born in Dalmatia in 1883, received his early training in Vienna and with Rodin in Paris. Although modern in style, his sculpture before 1914 had a predominantly nationalistic imprint. Later he became interested in religious and other subjects.

In architecture the new Balkan nations were similarly under central and west European influences. Only in Romania and Greece was any real attempt made to build on national foundations. After the establishment of the modern states the chief large-scale building naturally involved the construction of offices for the new bureaucracy, schools, and libraries. Architects were imported, and the Paris of Napoleon III and the Vienna of Franz Joseph were greatly admired. Existing Balkan styles were often rejected as "Turkish." Only much later were attempts made to preserve historical buildings and appreciation shown for native construction.

Perhaps the greatest adjustment from Ottoman life had to be made in the field of music. There had been no equivalent of the opera or the symphony orchestra in the empire. Although the new states early acquired opera houses, in imitation of the other European capitals, and showed a great interest in contemporary composition, no outstanding national composers arose. The one composer of European stature, the Romanian George Enescu, belongs properly to the next era.

In the preceding pages the cultural evolution of the Turkish and Albanian-speaking people has been omitted. In general in this account Ottoman developments have been limited to those directly affecting Balkan life. Although in the preceding centuries certain facets of Ottoman culture such as architecture, language, and attitudes toward life had deeply influenced all of the inhabitants of the empire, this condition changed sharply in the period under discussion. Like the Balkan nations, the modern Turkish writers were strongly attracted by western, in particular by French, literature. After the middle of the century, at the time of the reform movement, standard French authors such as Racine,

Fénélon, Voltaire, and Lamartine were translated. The drama and the novel were introduced as new literary forms. The Young Turk Revolution accelerated this trend. Turkish writers used themes from their own historical past and dealt with their own people, but in the spirit of western European writing. The question of language, which was unusually complicated, was not settled until after the First World War.

The general cultural background to the Albanian national movement has been covered in a previous chapter. Mention should be made, however, of several outstanding writers of this period. The national literature originated in the middle of the nineteenth century among the Albanians in Italy. The first prominent writers were Demetrio Camarda and Girolamo de Rada. Camarda, a linguist, studied the language for the purpose of demonstrating its ancient origin. De Rada, a poet, took themes from pre-Ottoman Albanian life; his *The Hapless Skenderbeg* (Skanderbeku i pafanë) described the struggle of the Albanians under their great leader against the Ottoman invaders in the fifteenth century. Other poets with this background were Giuseppe Serembe and Giuseppe Schirò.

Increased agitation for autonomy within the empire marked the period after the Congress of Berlin. Two authors, one Muslim and one Catholic, were particularly important for the national cause. Naim Frashëri, a member of the Bektashi sect, was a romantic nationalist poet of a strongly religious temperament. His best known works are *Cattle and Land* (Bagëti e Bujqësi), *Spring Flowers* (Lulet i Verës), and *History of Skenderbeg* (Istorí e Skënderbeut). Of greater importance, however, was Father Gjergj Fishta, a Catholic priest from northern Albania. His great epic *The Lute of the Mountains* (Lahuta e Malsisë) was published in three parts between 1905 and 1931. Its main theme was the struggle of the Albanians against the Slavs.

By the eve of the First World War the political evolution of the states had thus been paralleled by developing Balkan cultures that mirrored the change from the previous ecclesiatic, Ottoman-dominated societies to the modern secular national states. With few exceptions, as we have seen, writers and artists supported national objectives and provided an ideology to back expansionist programs. These same men participated in the life of the state and often held official positions. The audience for their work was drawn almost solely from the same social groups that dominated the new regimes. Toward the end of the period more interest was shown in peasant life and in urban problems, but few writers were revolutionaries in a social or political sense. A different situation, of course, existed in the Habsburg Empire, particularly in those lands under Hungarian control.

Extreme patriotism did not prevent the wholesale importation of foreign ideas. Paris remained the primary point of attraction. The assumption was made that western European culture represented progress and provided a pattern that civilized nations must follow. Both tsarist Russia and the Ottoman Empire were regarded as backward. Abandonment of Muslim and Byzantine examples was usually considered a step forward. Where there was a reaction against imitation, it proved difficult to formulate concrete alternative styles. Of course, the greatest creative artists, such as Eminescu and Solomos, did not follow the pattern. By August, 1914, however, when the great powers became involved in a war over what was initially a Balkan issue, the leadership of the new national states was fully determined to emulate in their political, economic, and cultural life the prosperous and apparently successful great powers.

CHAPTER 17

The First World War

THE First World War began in the Balkans, and the first indication of its conclusion appeared here when Bulgaria surrendered on September 29, 1918. During the four-year interval the peninsula was a secondary theater of operations. For the great powers the main battlefields were in northern France and in the vast and fluid eastern front. The fate of the small states was also linked to the outcome of the conflicts in these areas rather than to local campaigns. After the beginning of the war both the Allies and the Central Powers sought the support of the Balkan states to strengthen the military position of their own alignment. The Balkan nations, in contrast, desired to complete the process of national unity. There was no one great adversary blocking this objective. Instead, depending on the state, the enemy could be Austria-Hungary, the Ottoman Empire, Russia, Italy, or even a Balkan neighbor. Thus, the governments committed themselves militarily and politically only when they received assurances that they would attain concrete objectives. They also did not want to be on the losing side.

The first Balkan state to feel the full effects of the war was, of course, Serbia. A nation of 4.5 million now found itself in conflict with a great power of 50 million. When it received the ultimatum the government tried to avoid a war and accepted all but one of the conditions, including those that, like the censorship of publications, would have required an amendment to the constitution. The Serbian leaders had also wished to continue negotiations and had asked that Vienna "not hurry in deciding this matter." [1] Nevertheless, on July 28 Belgrade was bombarded from across the Sava and Danube rivers.

Despite the fact that Serbia could mobilize about 350,000 men, most military experts expected that the monarchy would win a quick victory.

1. G. P. Gooch and Harold Temperley, eds., *British Documents on the Origins of the War, 1898–1914* (London: H. M. Stationery Office, 1926), vol. 11, p. 371.

As expected, the Habsburg forces crossed the Sava and Drina rivers and entered Serbian territory. In mid-August the two armies met in a bloody four-day battle, which ended in a major victory for Serbia, most of whose troops were veterans of the Balkan Wars. The Habsburg army was forced to retreat to its own territory. By this time Russia had entered the war and some Habsburg units had to be transferred to other fronts. With their morale high, the Serbs then went on the offensive and carried the war into the Habsburg lands. The situation changed early in December when a new Austrian offensive resulted in the capture of Belgrade. It was soon obvious that a major obstacle for the Serbs would be a lack of supplies and replacements; only a limited amount of material was sent by the Allies through Thessaloniki.

In mid-December the Serbian army scored another major military victory by defeating the Habsburg forces at the Kolubara River. The invading army again withdrew from Serbia and Belgrade was retaken. The battle cost the Serbs about 100,000 men, and it became obvious that Serbia could not win a war of attrition or hold out in a prolonged struggle. This victory was the last great Serbian military achievement. The country was further weakened by a disastrous typhus epidemic, which hit both the army and the civilian population. Notwithstanding the fact that the Allies sent medical supplies, it is estimated that by the summer of 1915 Serbia had lost another 150,000 people.

During the course of these and other deadly campaigns both sides were engaged in intense negotiations to involve other Balkan nations. The next state to enter the war was the Ottoman Empire. This government signed a secret alliance with Germany, directed against Russia, on August 2, a day before Berlin declared war on France and two days before Britain entered the conflict. The treaty was the work of Enver Pasha, the pro-German minister of war. Thereafter, although the empire was not at war, it did aid the German effort. Eight days after the agreement was signed, two German warships, the Goeben and the Breslau, sailed into the Straits to avoid capture by the Allied fleets. This action violated the international conventions that closed the Straits to warships when the Ottoman Empire was at peace. The Ottoman government argued that it had purchased the warships, which nevertheless continued to be manned by German officers and sailors wearing Turkish fezzes. After two months of intense pressure from Germany, the Ottoman fleet, including the two warships, attacked the Russian navy in the Black Sea. The Ottoman Empire was now committed to the Central Powers; in November the state was formally at war with the Allies.

The Ottoman entrance had the profound effect of breaking the only adequate lines of communication between the western Allies and Russia, which were through the Straits. Because of the significance of this action, the British government adopted a controversial plan of Winston Churchill, designed to open the Straits and defeat the Ottoman Empire. The Dardanelles and Gallipoli campaigns were organized with these goals in mind. The first began in February, 1915. The major action occurred in the middle of March when eighteen British warships attempted to force their way through the Dardanelles. After four ships had been lost, the commander ordered a withdrawal. Had the attack been pressed, it would have succeeded. It is now known that the Ottoman troops, because of the shortage of munitions, could not have withstood another day of bombardment.

Despite the failure at the Dardanelles, the Allies continued with their plans to take the Gallipoli Peninsula, whence they hoped to base a major campaign against the Porte. Although the Allied troops, who came chiefly from New Zealand and Australia, fought stubbornly, the Turkish soldiers were well entrenched on the heights above the landing sites. Unable to break out of the tight area, the Allied forces remained there from April, 1915, to January, 1916. Finally casualties, disease, combat fatigue, and low morale led to their evacuation.

The entrance of the Ottoman Empire into the war, the weakening of Serbia, and the failure of the Dardanelles campaign gave the apparent advantage in the Balkans to the Central Powers. These gains were to a degree offset when Italy joined the Allies in April, 1915. Italian unification had occurred late and was, at least in the eyes of the intense patriots, still incomplete. Like the Balkan states, this government had claims on ethnically Italian territory, but more important, it also laid claim to other lands whose acquisition could be justified only on strategic and military lines or for reasons of glory and prestige. The territories chiefly coveted by Italy were the South Tyrol, Trentino, Istria, and Dalmatia— all of which belonged to the Habsburg monarchy, and Albania—which was in theory an independent state. Although a member of the Triple Alliance, Italy had not gone to war with Germany and Austria-Hungary, because the alliance was defensive and the action of the monarchy against Serbia had been clearly offensive. Instead, the government remained neutral and immediately commenced sharp bargaining with both sides. In these negotiations the Central Powers had less to offer. The Habsburg monarchy was willing to surrender only Trentino in return for continued Italian neutrality. The Allies were in a theoretically better position because they could use Habsburg territory as an inducement, but even they were caught in a difficult position. Ostensibly, the war had started over Serbia, but if Dalmatia and Istria were surrendered to Rome, 700,000 South Slavs would be placed under Italian rule. Not only would the creation of a Yugoslav state be made impossible, but Serbia would be deprived of the outlet to the Adriatic that she had sought over the past decades.

The Serbian war aims, which were involved in these negotiations with

Italy, had in fact not yet been clearly defined. At the beginning of the war the Serbian government was chiefly concerned with the fate of the Serbs in Bosnia-Hercegovina and in securing an outlet on the Adriatic. As we have seen, the Serbian government under Nikola Pašić was not an ardent champion of South Slav unity, but it did wish to acquire the lands that it regarded as ethnically Serbian. Moreover, tsarist Russia, on whom Serbia depended for diplomatic support, was not for a Yugoslav policy. In 1915 Serge Sazonov, the Russian foreign minister, stated that: "if it would be necessary for the Russian people to fight under arms only half a day in order that the Slovenes be liberated, I would not consent to it." [2] Despite this attitude, Pašić was soon forced to deal with the question in his relations with the Allied powers.

As soon as the war began a number of South Slav leaders from the monarchy, including Ante Trumbić and Frano Supilo, left for Italy where they formed the Yugoslav Committee. From the beginning the organization was committed to the union of Serbs, Croats, and Slovenes in a single state. Learning that negotiations detrimental to their cause were taking place, the committee left Rome and went to Paris and London where it vigorously lobbied. At first no power would commit itself to a plan that involved the dismemberment of the Habsburg Empire. Nevertheless, the committee's intensive and vigorous propaganda campaign did have its effects on opinion in the United States, France, and Britain. Its major weakness was the failure to come to an early understanding with Serbia. Quite understandably, so long as the Serbian state was intact Pašić and his government did not treat the committee as an equal body. They regarded themselves as spokesmen for all of the South Slavs. It was not until the kingdom fell and its leaders moved to Corfu that an agreement could be made.

Regardless of whether the Belgrade government chose to follow the path to a greater Serbia or to a Yugoslavia, the Italian demands were in direct contradiction to Serbian national interests. The Allies themselves were divided on the issue. Russia was, of course, more closely involved with Serbia than was Britain or France. Yet in August, 1914, she was prepared to grant Italy a dominant position in the Adriatic as well as control of Trentino, Trieste, and Vlorë in Albania in return for prompt military aid. At this time Britain and France did not share this view. However, by spring, 1915, the military situation on all fronts made Italian assistance even more necessary. Russia now proved reluctant to make an agreement at the expense of Serbia, but her hesitation was overcome by the British assurance that Constantinople and the Straits would be Russian after the war.

The Allies and Italy signed the Treaty of London on April 26, 1915.

2. Milada Paulova, *Jugoslavenski Odbor* (The Yugoslav Committee) (Zagreb: Prosvjetna Nakladna Zadruga, 1925), p. 54.

In return for its entrance into the war within thirty days, the Italian government was awarded the South Tyrol, Trentino, Trieste, Istria, much of Dalmatia, the strategic island of Saseno, and the port of Vlorë in Albania. The Greek-inhabited islands of the Dodecanese archipelago in the Aegean together with a promise in a share of any Ottoman territory that might be partitioned completed the bargain. The Allies thus gave Croatian, Serbian, Slovenian, Albanian, and Greek national territory to Italy in return for her services as an ally. On May 23, 1915, Italy declared war on Austria-Hungary and then waited fifteen months, until August, 1916, to enter into conflict with Germany. This agreement was to have immense consequences in the future for the South Slavs and the Albanians.

The next state to enter the war was Bulgaria. Throughout all of the negotiations that government had only one aim: to gain what it regarded as its legitimate share of Macedonia, including important areas under Serbian control, and territories recently acquired by Greece, in particular the port of Kavalla. It also wanted to regain the part of southern Dobrudja that the Romanians had taken in 1913. In return for her support Bulgaria had much to offer both sides because of her central strategic position in regard both to the Straits and to Serbia. Should the state join the Central Powers, they would then have a solid front from Germany to the Ottoman Empire, unless, of course, the Gallipoli campaign succeeded. At the same time the position of Serbia would be made impossible because that state could not withstand the opening of another front in the south. These developments in turn would affect the attitude of the yet uncommitted Romania and Greece. If the Allies, on the other hand, could gain the support of Sofia, the situation would be reversed. Bulgaria could be an effective military asset in the Gallipoli campaign to seize the Straits and to open the supply route to Russia. The Central Powers would then face a dangerous situation.

In this bargaining the Allies were in the weaker position. Once again, as in the case of Italy, they had to bargain with Serbian interests. This time, however, Serbia would be expected to yield territory, not like Dalmatia on which she only had claims, but lands in Macedonia which her armies had conquered in the Balkan Wars and which were under her administration. So long as her forces were holding the Habsburg invader back, the Serbian government would not make real concessions. Later it would only agree to relinquishing territory east of the Vardar River; in no case was the common border with Greece to be surrendered. The Central Powers, of course, did not have to worry about Serbian sensibilities; they could agree to partition the country. However, both the Central Powers and the Allies were in the same difficult position in regard to the Bulgarian claims against Greece and Romania.

Under the leadership of King Ferdinand and Premier Vasil Radoslavov the Bulgarian government was still suffering from the shock of the Second Balkan War when all of its neighbors had been allied against it, and of the Treaty of Bucharest, which deprived the country of Macedonian lands considered Bulgarian. Both the king and the premier were sympathetic to the Central Powers. Moreover, relations were now cool with St. Petersburg. In early 1914 the new Russian minister in Sofia, A. A. Savinskii, had told Ferdinand that Bulgaria would have to demonstrate that she deserved Russian support. At a subsequent meeting Savinskii advised: "You must not forget that Russia has her own political tasks, which exceed all others in importance; that is what the Bulgarians have so often overlooked." [3] It was clear that the situation of 1878 was now reversed. Russian assistance would go to Belgrade and not to Sofia. San Stefano Bulgaria was not a Russian goal. Despite this fact, once the war broke out the Russian diplomats did endeavor to win Bulgaria, and they were ready to offer more Macedonian territory than Serbia was willing to concede.

Whereas Ferdinand and Radoslavov tended to lean toward the Central Powers, the country was in fact divided. There was almost universal support for the acquisition of Macedonia, but the nation was not anxious to enter another war. The two Balkan wars had cost 58,000 dead and over 100,000 wounded. Both the Socialists and the Peasant Union opposed further fighting. Yet the appeal of Macedonia finally overcame most opposition. It was soon apparent that Bulgaria would join the alignment that would best assure the acquisition of what were considered just territorial concessions.

In the negotiations with the Allies Sofia soon found that the terms offered were closely tied to successes or failures on the battlefield. In May, 1915, when the Allied position appeared favorable and Italy had joined the war, they were willing to concede to Bulgaria the Macedonian lands south of the 1912 Kriva Palanka-Veles-Ohrid line, but on the condition that Serbia gained Bosnia-Hercegovina and an outlet on the Adriatic. The Allies also agreed that Bulgaria's southern boundary could stretch to the Enos-Midia line, within easy striking distance of Constantinople, and that Bulgarian claims to Kavalla and Dobrudja would be considered. The Serbian government, however, refused to agree to the surrender of Macedonian lands until September, 1915, when its military situation had worsened, but even then it would give up only half of the territory under consideration.

None of these concessions could compete with those that came from the Central Powers. Germany and the Habsburg Empire now offered the boundaries of San Stefano together with all of the lands east of the Morava River to the Danube. This solution meant the dismemberment

3. James M. Potts, "The Loss of Bulgaria," in Alexander Dallin, et al., *Russian Diplomacy and Eastern Europe, 1914–1917* (New York: King's Crown Press, 1963), p. 200.

of Serbia. In addition, Bulgaria was to receive Dobrudja and Thrace should Romania and Greece join the Allies. An alliance to this effect was concluded in September, 1915. In October a major Austro-German offensive was commenced against Serbia. On October 14, as stipulated in the treaty, Bulgaria entered the war and attacked Serbia from the east. At the same time the Allies landed four divisions in Thessaloniki in the hope of aiding the Serbs. Unsuccessful efforts were also made to bring Greece into the conflict.

Caught between two invading forces, the Serbian army, which had fought stubbornly for a year, proved unable to withstand the combined assault. Within six weeks the country was overrun. As the army retreated in the dead of winter across the rugged mountains of northern Albania, many died from enemy action, cold, or disease. Eventually thirty thousand soldiers reached the Adriatic and were evacuated in January, 1916, in Allied ships to the island of Corfu. There a Serbian government-in-exile was established under the leadership of Pašić and the prince regent Alexander, who, it will be remembered, took control from King Peter in 1914.

In early 1916 the Central Powers were thus in control in the Balkans. In January the Allied troops withdrew from Gallipoli, and in the same month the last remnants of the Serbian army arrived in Corfu. The Central Powers now held a bloc of territory running from Germany through central Europe to the Persian Gulf. For this reason the alignment of the two uncommitted Balkan states, Romania and Greece, became of particular importance to the antagonists. Both of these nations had respectable armies and occupied strategic positions.

Unlike Bulgaria, which had one principal irredenta, Romania had two major areas of concern, Transylvania and Bessarabia, and two minor regions, Bukovina and the Banat. Three of these were under the control of Austria-Hungary and one of Russia. For both the Allies and the Central Powers Romanian allegiance was important for economic and military reasons. Romanian oil and wheat were needed by all the belligerents, and the Romanian army, although not as effective as the Serbian, was an asset to any ally. In the preceding decades the chief Romanian diplomatic ties had been with the Habsburg monarchy and Germany. The defensive alliance of 1883 had been renewed five times, most recently in 1913, and was in effect when the war began. The agreement had been made, it will be remembered, because of the Romanian fears of Russia and, to an extent, of her Slavic neighbors, Bulgaria and Serbia. In the years immediately preceding the war relations with Vienna had become strained over the Transylvanian question and also Romania's actions in the Second Balkan War. When the fighting commenced in 1914, the Hohenzollern king Charles believed that his honor and the treaty of 1883 obligated the country to stand with the German nations. However, he did not have the authority to carry through his desires. The real power lay in the hands of his prime minister, Ion I. C. Brătianu, the son of the great Liberal Party leader.

Whereas King Charles was pro-German, Brătianu was pro-Entente. Brătianu's goal was to unite all of the Romanians in one state, almost half of whom lived outside of the kingdom in 1914. In addition, he sought to preserve the balance of power that had emerged among the Balkan states after 1913. Because of his amazing success in finally achieving these aims he has been variously described as shrewd, Byzantine, deceptive, and untrustworthy. Although these descriptions may not be wholly justified, Brătianu must be credited with a remarkable ability to exploit diplomatic situations to make gains for his country.

Before the war Romanian relations with the Habsburg Empire had cooled while those with Russia had definitely improved. The Bessarabian issue still rankled, but the problem of Transylvania now received more emphasis. In June, 1914, on the eve of the assassination, Nicholas II paid a highly successful official state visit to Romania. Brătianu and S. D. Sazanov, the Russian foreign minister, established a close relationship. Thus, by the opening of the war Russian-Romanian relations were basically amicable. At this time Brătianu seized upon a diplomatic blunder committed by Sazonov which was to cause the Allies great difficulties in the future.

Apprehensive over the prospects of war and desirous of influencing the Romanian position, the Russian government on July 30–31, without consulting Britain or France, offered Transylvania to Romania in return for neutrality. At the same time Germany assured Bucharest that it could have Bessarabia on the same terms. In other words, by remaining neutral Romania would receive either Transylvania or Bessarabia, depending on who won the war. When these alternatives were presented to the crown council meeting on August 3, only the king and the pro-German minister Peter Carp urged that the nation commit itself to the cause of the Central Powers. The others agreed with Brătianu, who urged a policy of neutrality.

In the next months Brătianu exploited Sazonov's blunder. When the Russian government sought to persuade the Romanians to join the Allies, it had no real leverage. Romania would receive Transylvania for simply being neutral. When the Allies suggested that Russia make concessions in Bessarabia, that state turned down the idea, just as the Dual Monarchy had rejected similar suggestions by Germany in regard to Transylvania. The Allies did receive, however, the assurance of Romanian neutrality in a secret treaty signed between Bucharest and St. Petersburg on October 1, 1914. In this Romania received the guarantee that she would acquire all of Transylvania and those portions of Bukovina that had a predominantly Romanian population. In return, the Romanian government agreed that it would permit Russian supplies to cross its territory to Serbia, but that German matériel destined for the Ottoman empire would not be allowed transit rights. Thus, technically the state was not neutral; it was obvious which side was now favored.

Between the signature of this treaty and Romania's entrance into the war in August, 1916, negotiations were carried on concerning the exact terms and conditions under which Romania would join the Allies. Brătianu concentrated on gaining a written statement on the territories to be received. The Allies in turn pressed Romania for concessions such as yielding southern Dobrudja to Bulgaria in order to entice that power into the Allied camp. The discussions and terms closely reflected the fortunes of the battlefield. When Serbia was fighting desperately in the fall of 1915, Sazonov appealed to Brătianu to aid the country, to whom Romania was still bound by the treaty that joined the two states against Bulgaria in 1913. The Romanian minister, however, observed that Germany had captured Warsaw, that the Austrians had retaken Galicia and Bukovina, and that the Gallipoli campaign was stalled. Therefore, before he would consider such an action he demanded a British and French invasion of Bulgaria, a more vigorous Gallipoli operation, a new Russian offensive, and the delivery of more war matériel to Romania. These conditions were clearly designed to preclude Romanian participation. Moreover, at the same time Romania continued to sell oil and grain to the Central Powers, thus keeping that option open. For these actions Brătianu was denounced in the Romanian chamber for "trafficking with one side and with the other, deceiving both, lying in wait watching for the best opportunity." [4] Yet he continued to enjoy the support of the majority of the chamber and King Ferdinand, who had succeeded to the throne after the death of Charles in October, 1914.

The year 1916 found the Allies in a bad situation on all fronts. A stalemate existed in the west; Russia was losing ground in the east. In the Balkans Bulgaria had joined the Central Powers, Serbia was defeated, and Gallipoli abandoned. Nevertheless, when in June, 1916, the Brusilov offensive was launched by the Russians, Brătianu concluded that the moment had come to fight. In the campaign, which lasted three months, the Russian army advanced about a hundred miles; it seized such important cities as Czernowitz and it captured about half a million prisoners. This action coincided with the Somme offensive in the west. Brătianu was now obsessed with the fear that Russia would take Transylvania without Romanian assistance and that the province might be lost. He was also afraid that a general or separate peace might be made in which Transylvania would remain under Habsburg rule. The Russian government did not disabuse him of this suspicion.

4. Sherman David Spector, *Rumania at the Paris Peace Conference: A Study of the Diplomacy of Ioan I. C. Brătianu* (New York: Bookman Associates, 1962), p. 30.

Romania now negotiated with Britain, France, and Italy and not with Russia alone. Brătianu was determined to extract the maximum benefit from the discussions, which lasted almost two months. He was successful largely because the Russian military offensive was meeting stiffer resistance with each day, and so the Allies needed Romania's active participation. He finally obtained everything he wished. Romania was promised Transylvania and the Banat up to the Tisza (Theiss) River as far as Szeged. The boundary would then follow a slightly northeasterly direction passing Debrecen to the Someş River, giving a good portion of what is present-day eastern Hungary to Bucharest. In addition, Romania was to extend her boundary in the Bukovina to the Pruth River and to enjoy an equal status with the other powers at the postwar peace conference. There was no provision for a coordinated Russo-Romanian military effort; Romanian forces alone were to operate in Transylvania. When these terms were presented to the crown council, they were enthusiastically received. On August 26, 1916, the nation went to war against the Dual Monarchy.

Romania had waited too long. By the time the country entered the war, the Brusilov offensive had lost its momentum. Germany now transferred fifteen divisions from the western front, and the tide turned. Within a month the Romanian armies in Transylvania were halted by General Erich von Falkenhayn; next a concerted German-Bulgarian attack under Field Marshal August von Mackensen was launched in Dobrudja. Bucharest fell in December, and the Romanian army and government retreated into Moldavia where a capital was established at Jassy. The Central Powers now controlled two-thirds of the kingdom, including crucial oil wells and grain supplies. In the next eighteen months the situation became even worse. The Allies, including the United States after her entrance into the war in 1917, made it clear that the dismemberment of the Dual Monarchy was not one of the war objectives. At the time these governments were negotiating with Vienna for a separate peace. For Romania this decision meant the repudiation of the agreement that had brought her into the war. The revolutions in Russia in March and November, 1917, also weakened the Romanian position.

The military defeats and the general diplomatic situation led the Romanian government to sign an armistice with the Central Powers in December, 1917. This act was done against the advice of the Allies who had wished the Romanian government and army to withdraw into southern Russia. In February, 1918, Brătianu was replaced as premier first by General Alexander Averescu and then by Alexander Marghiloman, a known Germanophile. This action was taken on Brătianu's advice. Should the Allies win, the onus for the German orientation would be on another's back. In May, 1918, the new Romanian ministry signed the Treaty of Bucharest with the Central Powers. This agreement awarded Romania Bessarabia, but it assigned all of Dobrudja to the Central Powers collectively, and a number of strategic areas in the Carpathians to the Dual Monarchy. Germany also acquired control over the Romanian oil fields for ninety years.

The last Balkan state to enter the war was Greece, who joined in 1917. Her entrance was delayed by internal developments in Greece, which differed sharply from those in other Balkan states. Although there had been substantial disagreement on foreign policy in all of the countries, finally one course of action had been accepted by both the monarch and his ministers. Moreover, the policy adopted did not arouse enough internal opposition to impede its implementation. In contrast, in Greece the nation simply split into two opposing camps with King Constantine at the head of one faction and Prime Minister Venizelos leading the other. For the three years that this stalemate prevailed, the state could not join either the Allies or the Central Powers.

As we have seen, the national program in Greece was expressed by the Great Idea, which called for the unification of all Greeks; for some it also meant a revival of the Byzantine Empire and the acquisition of Constantinople. By 1914 Greece had most of the Greek-inhabited territories, including Crete and lands in Macedonia and Epirus. Nevertheless, a Greek population remained under Bulgarian rule in Thrace, under Ottoman control in western Anatolia, under British administration in Cyprus, and in the Italian-ruled Dodecanese Islands. The first two areas, Thrace and western Anatolia, now became the immediate national objectives with the acquisition of Constantinople only a remote dream. Negotiations toward gaining these areas were precluded, however, by the conflict that developed between the king and his minister.

King Constantine was the brother-in-law of the German emperor. He concealed neither his sympathy for the Central Powers nor his hope that they would triumph. Many Greeks, some of whom had studied at German universities, shared his feelings. Realizing that Greece was exposed to Allied naval reprisals, and that he could not gain direct assistance from the Central Powers, the king favored a policy of neutrality. In contrast, from the beginning of the war Venizelos supported the Allies and was convinced that they would win. He wished to commit the Greek army to their cause because he believed that this was the best means of completing Greek unification. Although Constantine disagreed, he could not dismiss this popular and powerful minister. Venizelos, on his side, was unwilling to work for the deposition of the king. The government was thus deadlocked on the basic issue of participation in the conflict.

Although Greece did not take a decided stand, negotiations were carried on throughout the entire three-year period. When the war began, the country was technically obligated by the alliance of 1913 to aid Serbia against an unprovoked attack by any power, including the Dual Monarchy. The Greek government justified its inaction by arguing that Serbia had provoked the attack. Instead, neutrality was proclaimed, a policy that not only the king but also Venizelos approved under the existing circumstances. Thereafter, the two men went their separate ways. Once the Ottoman Empire entered the war and with the intensification of pressure on Serbia, the Allies naturally became increasingly interested in gaining Greek support. Later, during the Allied attempts to win Bulgaria, Greece was asked to yield lands on the Aegean in return for unspecified territories in Asia Minor. Venizelos was willing to give up the Drama-Kavalla area and 30,000 Greek inhabitants, but only in return for the Smyrna region of Anatolia with its 800,000 Greeks. This acquisition would turn the Aegean into a "Greek lake." Venizelos further conditioned the Greek entrance into the war on the simultaneous action by both Bulgaria and Romania, an impossible achievement.

The Dardanelles and Gallipoli campaigns produced a major governmental crisis. When the action was being planned, Venizelos was ready to join it. Both the king and the chief of staff disagreed, arguing that participation would expose the country to a Bulgarian attack. They would also not surrender any territory to appease Bulgaria. When his plan was refused, Venizelos resigned in March, 1915. New elections were then held, which returned the popular minister to power. Another clash between the two sides soon came. In September, 1915, when Bulgaria mobilized in preparation for an attack on Serbia, the Allies urged Greece to honor the 1913 commitment. Venizelos again approved, and Constantine consented to mobilize the army. The General Staff, however, construed this as a defensive measure only. It contended that the treaty obligated Serbia to put 150,000 troops on the Bulgarian front, an impossible condition to fulfill under the circumstances. The Allies then agreed to meet this commitment with some of their own forces. Venizelos and the assembly accepted this solution. Between October 3 and 5, 1915, one British and one French division landed at Thessaloniki to be supplemented later by more French troops. On October 5, however, Constantine repudiated his minister's policy; Venizelos again resigned.

The two camps in Greek politics were now irreconcilably set. New elections were held in which Venizelos's Liberal Party refused to participate. Instead, his supporters formed a "semigovernment" in opposition to the king and his adherents. The royal government in turn blamed the nation's problems on the Allies, whose actions it regarded as a violation of the sovereignty of the state. The Allied troops in Thessaloniki were harassed, and permission was refused to Serbian forces on Corfu to cross Greece to join this encampment. Finally, in May, 1916, no resistance was placed in the way of a German and Bulgarian occupation of Fort Rupel, which commanded the Struma Valley.

The Allies now moved against the king in what was indeed a flagrant intervention in the affairs of the state. In June, 1916, they demanded that Constantine dissolve parliament, demobilize the army, and form a new government. The king consented only to nominate another prime minister. The final crisis came in October, 1916, when Venizelos transferred his separatist government from Crete, where it had been formed in August, to Thessaloniki. In December Britain recognized this regime as the government of Greece. In the same month Allied fleets again appeared at Piraeus, where they stayed for more than three months. Finally, in June, 1917, Constantine, without a formal abdication, surrendered his throne to his second son, Alexander. Venizelos then returned to Athens, and in June, 1917, Greece joined the Allies.

Whereas Italy and Romania on their entrance into the war had received concrete commitments on what they would receive in the future, Greece had asked for no similar assurances. The country would thus have to depend on the good will of the Allies for the acquisition of territory. Not only was Greece assured of no concrete rewards, but the nation remained bitterly divided even after the departure of Constantine. Nevertheless, the Greek army joined its allies in Thessaloniki and took part in the last battles in the Balkans.

The offensive from Thessaloniki was not launched until September, 1918. By this time it was clear that the Allies would win the war. The withdrawal of Russia had been more than balanced by the entrance of the United States. The final German offensives in northern France had failed; the initiative was on the opposing side. Of the twenty-eight Allied divisions under French command in Thessaloniki, nine were Greek and six Serbian. They were faced with German and Bulgarian forces of about equal strength. Whereas the Allied army had a high morale, the Bulgarian troops showed little spirit for the battle. The war had become a terrible burden on the nation. In addition to the losses in the Balkan Wars, it had suffered an additional 101,000 killed and over 300,000 wounded. In other words, between 1912 and 1918 about 160,000 had been killed and 400,000 wounded from a total population of about 5 million. The country had also experienced several bad harvests. Much of the available grain had been bought up by the German and Austrian authorities, an act that antagonized the urban population although the peasants temporarily seemed to profit. Popular disaffection soon infected the army, which had to contend with extensive desertions. In other words, Bulgaria was not prepared to face further warfare.

Under these conditions, on September 29, two weeks after the Allied offensive began, the Bulgarians surrendered in the hope that their country might be spared an invasion. The German and Habsburg forces continued fighting, but were rapidly forced northward. By November 1 Belgrade had been taken and Serbia was freed from foreign occupation. The Serbian army then crossed into former Habsburg territory and took the South Slav lands of Bosnia-Hercegovina and the Vojvodina. Serbia was thus in effective occupation of much of the lands which the proponents of a Yugoslavia wished included in such a state.

Meanwhile, Romania re-entered the war on November 10 and immediately set out to take the lands that she had been promised by the Allies in 1916. This advance was aided by simultaneous Serbian moves and by Czech actions in the north. The Dual Monarchy now simply dissolved into its national components. An Austrian republic was proclaimed on November 13, and an independent Hungary on November 16. On December 1, 1918, the Kingdom of the Serbs, Croats, and Slovenes was officially proclaimed. On the same day a national assembly of Romanians from Transylvania and the Banat met in Alba Iulia and announced their union with Romania. Notwithstanding these developments, the crucial question of the settlement of the boundaries of these states and their international recognition had still to be met. The dangerous issue of the conflicting claims of the nationalities, even among the victors, had now arisen.

Simultaneously, the other great multinational empire was meeting a fate similar to that of the Dual Monarchy. On October 31 the Ottoman Empire, largely as a result of a successful British campaign in the Arabian lands, was also forced to surrender. The disposition of the Ottoman possessions in Asia Minor was to cause conflicts among the nations as bitter as those in Europe. In fact, the settlements in the two areas were soon to become intertwined.

Before continuing to the peace negotiations, brief mention should be made of Albania's involvement in the war. After the departure of William of Wied in 1914, the central government of the new state collapsed, and the Albanian lands again became the victim of their neighbor's policies. First Greece, Serbia, and Montenegro occupied parts of the land; then France and Italy seized territories. When Serbia fell in 1915, Austria-Hungary took over most of central and northern Albania, while the southern sections remained in Italian and French hands. After the Bulgarian and Habsburg troops withdrew, the Greek, Serbian, and Italian armies took possession of the lands they claimed. Of all the Balkan states Albania was obviously in the most vulnerable position at the conclusion of the hostilities. The fate of this nation, as well as the distribution of other Balkan territories in dispute, thus would be determined at the peace table.

CHAPTER 18

The Postwar Settlements

THE conclusion of the armistice agreements in mid-November, 1918, did not mark the introduction of a period of either peace or stability in the Balkans. Greece and Turkey were not to settle their differences until 1922. Romania invaded Hungary in 1919, and Yugoslav troops on a number of occasions entered Austrian territory until 1921. Moreover, in the immediate postwar years drastic changes, which forced the peoples to adjust to entirely new political relationships, occurred in most of the areas under study. The major events were the formation of a South Slav state, the establishment of a greater Romania, the expulsion of the Greeks from Asia Minor, the revolution in the Ottoman Empire, and the final formation of a stable Albanian government. This section will concentrate on these questions rather than on a discussion of the peace treaties themselves. Some mention, however, must first be made of the basis on which the treaties were concluded.

As throughout the entire century of Balkan history covered in this volume, the final agreements were chiefly the work of the great powers, with relatively less influence being exerted by the small states at the conferences. Nevertheless, there were severe limitations on the actions of the strong nations. These states, too, were divided among themselves and they had to face realistically the conditions in Europe at the time, many of which had been created by the policies of the small countries. Three former great powers were not at the peace tables. Germany was excluded as a defeated state, a situation unique in European diplomacy. Austria-Hungary had dissolved into its national components during the last weeks of the war. Russia under Bolshevik control was considered a dangerous revolutionary element; Allied forces were operating on her territories. The settlements were thus to be the primary responsibility of Britain, France, Italy, and the United States, the latter a new major participant in European affairs.

In the making of the treaties the statesmen were bound by certain prior agreements, most importantly the secret treaties, many of which were to prove most embarrassing to their signatories. There was also the necessity of restoring the European balance of power, which was in fluctuation after the elimination of the Central Powers and the Russian revolution. In addition, further considerations had arisen towards the end of the war, which had to be taken into account. Post-war Europe was in a state of revolution; Russia already had a communist regime and that state had become a center of revolutionary propaganda. Upon gaining power the Bolshevik regime had promptly renounced and then published the secret treaties. It came to stand for a "people's peace" and one without "annexations or indemnities," as did the strong Social Democratic parties of Europe. In January, 1918, Woodrow Wilson repeated some of these principles in his Fourteen Points and declared American support for self-determination. These idealistic declarations were, of course, in sharp contrast to the terms of the secret treaties, which bartered territories and peoples quite freely. The makers of the peace agreements repeatedly had to decide whether they would abide by their wartime pacts or stand by their publicly declared principles.

In the peace negotiations, therefore, two contradictory bases for negotiation existed: the secret treaties and the principle of the self-determination of peoples. Each state tended to support the stand that was in its best interest. The victor small nations thus tended to favor the secret treaties and a policy of maximum territorial aggrandizement. The defeated powers and sometimes Woodrow Wilson defended self-determination and the concept of justice. Serbia, although a victor, naturally denounced the secret Treaty of London. The western great powers, France and Britain, were equally concerned about the restoration of the balance of power, but they wished to go about it by different means. In the treaties France endeavored to build up a front of victorious powers in Eastern Europe to replace the former Russian alliance and to check Germany. Romania and the South Slav state were to have important positions in the new French alignment. Britain, in contrast, wished to restore the balance through a more equitable settlement and a return to normal conditions, although many compromises were made in her policy. The British statesmen, well aware of past history, had also no desire to see France emerge as the clearly predominant power on the continent.

In the final agreements two Balkan states, the future Yugoslavia and Romania, emerged as enormous winners; Bulgaria and the new Turkish Republic were losers, as was Greece ultimately. Albania was restored to her prewar condition. The fate of these states will be discussed in that order.

The Formation of the Kingdom of the Serbs, Croats and Slovenes

The proclamation of the establishment of the Kingdom of the Serbs, Croats, and Slovenes in December, 1918, marked the culmination of protracted negotiations that had been carried on during the war, and of the evolution of Serbian policy. The initial lack of enthusiasm felt by Pašić, backed by the Prince Regent, for a Yugoslav state has been recorded previously. However, the government-in-exile on Corfu was open to outside influence. After the fall of tsarist Russia, which had been the major Serbian supporter, Pašić found that the domestic and foreign pressure for an understanding with the Yugoslav Committee was too strong to resist. In July, 1917, in the Declaration of Corfu the Serbian government was, for the first time, formally committed to work for the unification of the Serbs, Croats, and Slovenes in one state. The political form was to be that of a constitutional monarchy with the Karadjordjević dynasty at the head. A constitution for the new state was to be drafted by an assembly elected by direct, secret suffrage. All religions were to be recognized, and both the Cyrillic and Latin alphabets were to have equal status. Local autonomy was to be granted. This document was also endorsed by the Montenegrin Committee in Paris, a group of refugee politicians similar to that formed by the Habsburg South Slavs. It will be noted that the great question for the future, whether the state was to be unitary or federal, was not settled at this time.

At first little progress was made toward the implementation of this common program. It will be recalled that in early 1918 Britain, France, and the United States, who were trying to negotiate a separate peace with the Dual Monarchy, made it clear that they were not seeking the destruction of that nation. Determined to save what he could, Pašić instructed his minister in Washington to find out if Serbia could at least receive Bosnia-Hercegovina. When the Yugoslav Committee heard of this move, there was a crisis within the South Slav ranks. By April, 1918, however, when it became clear that a separate peace would not be made, the Allies again shifted their policy. Very significant also was an apparent change in the Italian attitude.

In April, 1918, the Congress of Oppressed Nationalities was held in Rome which ended by calling for the breakup of the monarchy. At this time Dr. Andrea Torre, the chairman of the Italian parliamentary delegation to the meeting, signed the Pact of Rome with Ante Trumbić, the president of the Yugoslav Committee. This agreement, which recognized the legitimacy of the Yugoslav goals, was concluded with the knowledge of the Italian prime minister, V. E. Orlando, but against the wishes of the foreign minister, Baron Sidney Sonnino. In the next months Sonnino continued his opposition to the Yugoslav concept and he attempted to block Allied recognition. Finally, by September he, too, had to admit that South Slav unification could not be stopped, but he was nevertheless determined to secure for Italy the terms of the Treaty of London.

Meanwhile, as the hostilities were coming to an end, parallel developments were occurring in the lands of the monarchy. At the end of October, 1918, the political leaders of the Croats and Slovenes who had remained in the country during the war created a revolutionary government, the Narodno Vijeće (National Council) of Zagreb and proclaimed the union of the Serbs, Croats, and Slovenes of the Dual Monarchy. This body was a third organization, distinct from the Serbian government and the Yugoslav Committee abroad. It quickly won popular support, and for one month it became the government of the South Slav lands of the empire. It then voted to join Serbia and Montenegro to form a new South Slav kingdom. In a solemn ceremony on December 1, 1918, in Belgrade the representatives of this group invited Prince Regent Alexander to proclaim the union. The action also involved the participation of Montenegro. A similar committee had been formed in Cetinje and, against the strong opposition of Nicholas who had taken the title of king in 1910, had likewise voted to join a South Slav state.

In the excitement of the moment and under the pressure of outside events, the Yugoslav statesmen of all nationalities had concentrated on the basic issue of union and of gaining the recognition of the powers. The question of the exact form of the association was thus not settled before the unification was actually accomplished. In fact, the issue of the frontiers was to take precedence over that of the future internal political order. The new Yugoslav state of December, 1918, had no settled frontiers. Once the unification was proclaimed this matter held the highest priority in Belgrade. Here the most acute controversies were to arise with Italy which now wished to implement the Treaty of London and to win a predominant position on the Adriatic.

The Yugoslav conflict with Italy centered on three areas: Dalmatia; Istria, with its port city of Trieste; and the port of Fiume (Rijeka). The first two regions had been promised to Italy in the Treaty of London, but Fiume had not. Both Dalmatia and Istria were predominantly Slavic; Dalmatia and its islands had a population that was 95 percent South Slav. The Italians had a majority in only one city, Zara. In Istria the Slavic inhabitants numbered 58 percent, but the vital port of Trieste was overwhelmingly Italian. In fact, the bulk of the Italian population in Istria was concentrated in the two cities of Trieste and Pola (Pula) while the countryside was Slavic. Fiume, the only other natural port in the area, was historically Croatian, but it also had an Italian and Hungarian majority.

In the debates on the fate of these lands, Italy based her arguments on the Treaty of London. Although the United States stood for ethnic boundaries here, neither France nor Britain was prepared to repudiate the secret treaties, from which they too benefited, and they sought instead a compromise. The Yugoslav case rested completely on the national principle and the clear preponderance of the Slavic population in the areas claimed. The principal support for Belgrade came from President Woodrow Wilson. In the peace conference he had already gone against his convictions in allowing Italy to take all of Trentino and the South Tyrol with their strong German minority of 250,000. In return for this concession Wilson expected Italy to yield on the Yugoslav frontier. Most observers felt that the so-called Wilson Line was a fair solution. This boundary would have granted Italy approximately three-fourths of Istria with about 370,000 Yugoslavs. Belgrade accepted this settlement, but Italy would not. When Wilson went back to the United States, the Yugoslav position was considerably weakened. The fate of Fiume took up a great part of the discussions. In a dramatic move the Italian poet, Gabriel D'Annunzio, seized the city and proclaimed himself dictator on September 12, 1919.

The final settlement reflected more the Italian than the Yugoslav demands. In September, 1920, Italy agreed to renounce her claims to Dalmatia and to support an independent Albania within the 1913 boundaries in return for all of Istria, an independent Fiume, the city of Zara, and some Dalmatian islands. Although the Istrian settlement meant abandoning a large number of Yugoslavs to Italian rule, the terms were reluctantly accepted by Belgrade. By this time also the Kingdom of the Serbs, Croats, and Slovenes, as the Yugoslav state was officially called until 1929, had been recognized by the major powers, including Italy.

The second controversy over frontiers involved the new state of Austria and centered on the Klagenfurt region, north of the Karawanken Mountains. Finally a plebiscite was held which was won by Austria, but the Maribor and Medjumurje districts of Styria were awarded to Belgrade. Similar conflicts developed with Hungary over parts of Baranja, Bačka and the Banat, areas where the Serbs had a plurality of the population. The fact that the Serbian army was occupying these territories assisted the Yugoslavs in gaining the majority of their demands. In the Banat, however, they met not only Hungarian opposition, but also Romanian. The Romanian government wished to annex the entire Banat up to the Tisza River, which had been promised in the Treaty of Bucharest of 1916. The Romanians also argued that the province was an indivisible economic and political entity. The Yugoslav position, which was finally accepted, involved the partition of the region along ethnic lines. A frontier was thus drawn leaving Romania with a minority of only 65,000 Yugoslavs, and Belgrade with a similar group of 75,000 Romanians.

The Yugoslav government wished to make similar gains on their Bulgarian frontier. Here the basis for the claims was military and strategic,

Map 12. The Formation of the Kingdom of the Serbs, Croats, and Slovenes, 1920

not ethnic. The attempt was made to acquire the Struma River as the boundary, to secure control of the Dragoman Pass and to take the city of Vidin. In other words, Belgrade sought territories east of and well beyond the natural watershed that had been the previous frontier and where the population was indisputably Bulgarian. None of the other powers would allow these extravagant demands, but the Yugoslavs did receive four strategic salients—Negotin, Tsaribrod, Vranje and the Strumica Valley. The Greek and Albanian frontiers remained the same as those of 1913.

The battle at the peace table was paralleled by the conflict that developed on the form of government to be established in the new state. Two major national groups, the Croats and the Serbs, were now brought together; each had undergone an entirely different historical experience in its political development. Serbia, as we have seen, in the accomplishment of its national program had fought first against the Ottoman Empire and then against the Habsburg monarchy. A unitary state on the French model had been established early in the century. To the Serbian leaders the new South Slav state was simply the culmination of the long line of events leading to national unity. They saw no need to adapt their institutions and their political convictions to their new partners. The Croatians, in contrast, throughout their history had lived usually in a federal relationship with other peoples or within a larger political framework. The union with Hungary in the Middle Ages and the subsequent Habsburg rule had safeguarded the maintenance of a separate and autonomous Croatia right up to 1914. The Croatian leaders insisted on the continuance of this tradition. They stood for the establishment of a federal system in which they would be equal partners not only with the Serbs but also with the Slovenes, who had a similar opinion on the question.

In the Declaration of Corfu it had been agreed that a constituent assembly would be summoned. Because of the crisis with Italy this body could not be called at once. In December, 1918, a cabinet was formed representing all the political groups and the regions. A transitional government was thus in power while the preparations were made for the elections. Fifteen political groups participated in the voting, which was held in November, 1920, to choose 419 delegates. The two winning parties were the Radicals, who elected ninety-one delegates, and the Democrats with ninety-two. The Radical Party was the continuation of the prewar ruling party in Serbia, which was now supported by some of the former Habsburg Serbs. The Democratic Party had been founded in 1919 and was composed of members of the Croatian-Serbian Coalition, some former Serbian Radicals, Slovenian Liberals, and others. It was the only Yugoslav party and it supported a centralist regime. Two parties that emerged with surprising strength were the Croatian Peasant Party, with fifty seats, and the Communist Party, with fifty-eight. The Peasant

Party under Stjepan Radić won the overwhelming support of the Croatian peasants, and it stood strongly for Croatian autonomy. Some of its leaders even favored total independence. The Communists, representing all sections of the country, received a strong protest vote in the desparately poor areas of Montenegro and Macedonia.

Before the assembly met the Peasant Party withdrew in protest against the regulations drawn up for voting in the body. The government took measures against the Communists after a conflict over a number of political and economic issues. Thus, only 342 of the 419 members of the assembly took part in the deliberations. Many drafts for a constitution were presented. The government's version was based on that of Serbia, the only changes being in matters such as religion. The state was to be a centralized, constitutional monarchy, with universal male suffrage and a secret ballot, and the country was to be divided into departments. The drafts presented by the other parties differed widely. The chief influence in the assembly was that exerted by Svetozar Pribičević, a Serb and a former leader of the Croatian-Serbian Coalition, now in the Democratic Party. A strong believer in the Yugoslav idea, he wished to end the historic divisions. He was backed by Pašić, who not only preferred this form but wanted to form a stable government as soon as possible. The Radical and Democratic parties, the strongest in the assembly, also stood for this goal. In June, 1921, only 258 delegates participated in the final voting. Not only the Peasant Party, but other Croatian groups, Slovene clericals, and the Communists had withdrawn. The constitution was accepted by 223 of the delegates, who represented mainly the Democrats, the Radicals, and representatives of the Bosnian Muslims. The new state thus received a highly centralized government, which was in fact a continuation of the Serbian system. The troubled history of the nation during the next years in great part stemmed from the nature of this document.

GREATER ROMANIA

Although the debates over the Yugoslav border had been protracted and difficult, the question of the Romanian boundaries caused perhaps even greater controversy. It will be remembered that Romania had joined the Allies in 1916 with the promise of Transylvania and the Banat. After its defeat the country had signed a separate peace with the Central Powers. Romania then re-entered the war on November 10, 1918, a week after Austria-Hungary had surrendered and one day before the German capitulation. At this time King Ferdinand dismissed the pro-German premier Marghiloman and on December 12 recalled Brătianu, who was determined to secure the terms of the 1916 agreement despite the fact that Romania had violated its provisions in making the separate peace. Brătianu not only intended to get Transylvania, Bukovina, and the Banat, but he had hopes for Bessarabia and most of

Dobrudja. He also expected the Allies to treat his country as an equal at the peace negotiations.

Brătianu had certain definite advantages. His armies were in occupation of many of the territories claimed. The Allies were divided on their attitude toward the Romanian demands. Most important, the Russian Revolution had introduced a new element into the East European picture. Not only had a Bolshevik regime come to power in Russia, but in March, 1919, a similar government was set up in Budapest under Bela Kun. Allied fears of the new revolutionary menace were to aid the Romanian cause in both Hungary and Bessarabia. In addition, as in the case of the Yugoslav lands national committees in some regions had voted for unification with the original kingdom. Most impressive was the meeting at Alba Iulia on December 1, 1918, where a hundred thousand Transylvanian Romanians declared their desire to join with Bucharest. Similar votes took place in Bukovina on November 28 and in Bessarabia on December 10. In January, 1919, the Saxon-Germans made the same decision. The Romanian army was in occupation in all of these areas.

For Brătianu the major prizes were the Banat and Transylvania. The Romanian position in the first region has already been discussed; the Banat had about 1,500,000 inhabitants of whom, according to Romanian statistics, 600,000 were Romanian, 385,000 were German, 358,000 Serbian, and 240,000 Hungarian. The Romanian government wished to preserve the unity of the province and argued that the German population would prefer Romanian to Yugoslav rule. Brătianu thus proposed a plebiscite. The Allies, however, did not want to expose the capital city of Belgrade, which would happen should Romania gain the entire Banat. Serbian troops also occupied the Torontal district, which was Serbian in population, and it would be difficult to dislodge them. The partition plan was thus finally adopted.

Such an equitable solution was not to be found for the Transylvanian problem. The final terms of the Treaty of Trianon left almost two million Hungarians in Romania. This result was to a large measure due to the fact that the Hungarian population was concentrated in east central Transylvania, surrounded by the eastern and southern Carpathian Mountains and the Bihor range. To the west the inhabitants were predominantly Romanian. The main group of Hungarians was thus cut off from Hungary proper. Although the Hungarian government did not wish to surrender even these nationals, the most heated controversy developed over the lands in the west where Romanians and Hungarians lived together along the line of cities Arad, Oradea (Nagyvárad), Carei (Nagykároly) and Satu Mare (Szatmárnémeti). An important railroad connected these cities; whoever controlled it had a decided economic advantage. In general, the cities were primarily Hungarian and the countryside Romanian. A true ethnic boundary would bisect the rail line in several places.

Brătianu's plans, however, went far beyond the achievement of an ethnic boundary. He sought, instead, the border of the Tisza River, which would have awarded Romania the eastern portion of Hungary. These demands, together with his other proposals, were too much for the Allied statesmen.[1] Brătianu for his part felt that he was not appreciated and that Romania should be rewarded for "having saved Salonika, decongested Verdun, and stopped Bolshevism."[2]

Despite such criticisms, the Romanian government had an immense advantage at the peace negotiations because of the Allied attitude toward the apparent communist threat. In March, 1919, when Bela Kun's revolutionary government was established in Budapest, Brătianu sent the Romanian army into Hungary and occupied Budapest on August 4. The Romanian minister then announced that his army had "protected European civilization against the destructive wave of Bolshevism."[3] The Allies approved the suppression of the Kun regime, but not subsequent Romanian actions. As reparations the Romanians demanded that Hungary surrender half of her river boats and railroad cars, about a third of her cattle and industrial machinery, and 35,000 wagon loads of grain. The Allies protested sharply; the American representative at the peace negotiations went so far as to suggest that an Allied fleet be sent to restrain the Romanians.

For Brătianu personally the issue of the Hungarian boundary became intertwined with a second question, that of the minorities treaties. Since it was obvious that the new boundaries would include many minorities in each state, the Allies wanted the East European nations to sign treaties pledging that they would respect the political and personal rights of these people. Both the Yugoslav and the Romanian governments resented these agreements as being infringements of their sovereignty, in particular because the great powers would not accept similar provisions. Brătianu led the opposition in Romania and used this as a campaign issue. In September, rather than agreeing to a treaty, he resigned to be replaced by General Arthur Văitoianu, who was one of his close supporters. In November elections were held in which the Liberal Party was defeated by the Transylvanian Nationalists, a new party, and by the peasant parties of the original kingdom. In the same month the Allies sent an ultimatum to Bucharest to evacuate Hungary to a prescribed frontier, to sign the minorities treaty, and to submit the issue of reparations to an Allied commission. If these terms were not accepted, relations would be severed. Despite the harsh tone, the Allies did not immediately act. In December, 1919, King Ferdinand appointed Alexander Vaida-

---

1. Spector, *Rumania at the Paris Peace Conference,* pp. 144, 145.
2. *Ibid.,* p. 137.
3. *Ibid.,* p. 167.

Voievod, a Transylvanian, as premier. The Allies then tried to smooth the path for the new and apparently more conciliatory minister.

Although he reluctantly agreed on the minorities treaty, Vaida-Voievod, for internal political reasons, hesitated to withdraw from Hungary. Finally, Lloyd George broke the deadlock by proposing that the Allies recognize the Romanian acquisition of Bessarabia after her troops had withdrawn from Hungary. This action was taken in March, 1920, under the new government of Alexander Averescu. The Romanian government thus abandoned the claim to the lands to the Tisza River, but it did obtain the Arad-Oradea-Satu Mare boundary and the railroad. At the same time Romania divided the Maramureş region with Czechoslovakia and received roughly the southern third, which had a Romanian population, and the city of Satu Mare.

Romania gained a favorable settlement in two other areas, Bukovina and Bessarabia. In the Treaty of Bucharest of 1916 the state had been promised about two-thirds of Bukovina, which was predominantly Romanian; the other third, with a Ruthenian population, was expected to go to Russia. After the Bolshevik Revolution, Romania claimed the whole province and her armies occupied it. Despite strong American objections, most of the province was allotted to Bucharest, although Poland received a portion in the north.

Bessarabia, as we have seen, had been a hotly disputed region between Russia and Romania. Like Transylvania, this province was a major Romanian irredenta. In the negotiations with the Central Powers, this was the one prize that those states could offer. The area had been thrown into a condition of chaos by the Bolshevik Revolution of November, 1917. Subsequently the Romanian nationalists in Bessarabia, through their governing body, the Sfat Ţării (Council of the Land) appealed to the Romanian government for protection against both Bolshevik and Ukrainian intervention. Romanian troops then occupied the province. At the same time the Romanian government had made an armistice with the Central Powers. In the negotiations for a peace, the question of Bessarabia was most important. The Treaty of Bucharest, signed in March, 1918, however, only gave the Romanians permission to occupy the area. In December, 1918, the Sfat voted for union with Romania. Despite this action the Allies, in particular the United States, were not eager to hand over the territory. Suspicions were expressed about the truly representative nature of the Sfat and about the role of the Romanian army in the decision. There was also some reluctance to hand over former Russian territory until the fate of the Bolshevik regime was finally decided, despite the fact that the population was at least 60 percent Romanian. Finally, as has been shown, the question was linked with that of Hungary, and in January, 1920, the Allies agreed to award this disputed land to Bucharest.

Thus, by clever diplomacy and by exploiting the fears of Bolshevism, the Romanian diplomats were able to achieve their maximum program. Both Translyvania and Bessarabia were acquired, an event that would have been considered highly improbably in 1912 and almost impossible in the preceding century. Minorities now constituted 30 percent of the state's population, but that was to be a problem for the future. Like Serbia after the war, the officials of the kingdom had to determine what their relationship would be to the new provinces, all of which had their own distinct histories and traditions. Similar to their counterparts in Belgrade, they could think of no alternative but to extend their political system over the entire country. The worst reaction was to come from Transylvania. In voting for union in December, 1918, at Alba Iulia the Transylvanian leaders had not considered this an unconditional action. They hoped to gain from Bucharest what they had not obtained from Budapest. At this time they demanded strong guarantees for all nationalities and religions in Transylvania and civil rights such as freedom of the press and of association, and the use of native languages in administration, education, and justice. They also requested that local autonomy be allowed until a constituent assembly could be called. The assembly chose a Directing Council and a cabinet of fifteen under Julius Maniu, who was now to emerge as the strongest Transylvanian politician. A telegram announcing the union was sent to Bucharest. In the same month some Transylvanians, like Vaida-Voievod, were taken into the Romanian government.

In November, 1919, what were perhaps the first really free elections in Romania were held. The result was a shock to Brătianu's Liberal Party, which won only 93 out of 244 seats for the assembly. The victors were the National Party of Maniu and Vaida-Voievod, which was to ally with the peasant parties of the original kingdom. Despite Ferdinand's dislike of parting with Brătianu, as we have seen, he did appoint Vaida as premier. However, he was replaced in March, 1920, by General Averescu. New elections were held in May in which it was soon apparent that Romanian politics had gone back to their former condition. The Liberal Party, returning to the tradition that the group in power wins the elections, gained 209 of the 369 seats in the chamber. At this time the Transylvanian Directing Council was abolished. In December, 1921, Averescu left office and was followed in January, 1922, by Brătianu. The Liberal Party was to dominate Romanian politics until 1928.

In the elections, which were held in March, 1922, the Liberals increased their hold to 260 seats. This assembly than proceeded to draft a new constitution. Completely under Liberal control, this body produced a document that was little more than a continuation of that of 1866. The centralist direction was shown in the statement that Romania was "a unitary and indivisible state." The organization of the government remained much the same, with the monarch retaining extensive powers.

By this time the strong reaction of the provinces, in particular Transylvania, had been expressed. The government at Bucharest had over-run the new territories with officials from the old kingdom. The army, the high administrative positions, and the foreign service remained the stronghold of the Wallachians and Moldavians. The strength of feeling was shown when Ferdinand was crowned in October, 1922, at Alba Iulia. Not only was the National Party, the strongest in Transylvania, not present, but the ceremony was attended by none of the leaders from the new territories, who had been chiefly responsible for the union. As in Yugoslavia, the future pattern of Romanian politics was largely to be determined by the insensitive treatment by the central government of their new, and often more highly developed, provinces.

BULGARIA

Of the states that have been previously discussed, two, Bulgaria and the Ottoman Empire, found themselves on the losing side. Of these Bulgaria had to submit to the harshest terms. As mentioned before, the Bulgarian leaders had been divided on the question of entrance into the war. In June, 1918, popular pressure forced King Ferdinand to dismiss Radoslavov. In September the agrarian leader, Alexander Stambolisky, was freed from prison. Within a week of his release, he was at the head of a revolutionary movement which declared Bulgaria a republic. The army easily crushed this revolt, but, nevertheless, Ferdinand on October 4, 1918, felt compelled to abdicate in favor of his son, Boris III. Ferdinand and Radoslavov then went into exile in Germany. For about eight months a coalition government of Democrats, Agrarians, Socialists, Liberals, and Conservatives ruled, and in August, 1919, elections were held, which produced a plurality for the Agrarians. The king then entrusted the government to Stambolisky who signed the extremely punitive peace terms.

The Bulgarian loss of four strategic points to Yugoslavia, areas that were ethnically Bulgarian, has already been discussed. The Allied decision to give Western Thrace to Greece and to deny Bulgaria an outlet on the Aegean was based on similar strategic considerations, chiefly the desire to keep a former enemy nation away from the Turkish Straits. The area had a mixed population of Turks, Bulgars, and Greeks, none of which had an absolute majority. However, the outlet at Dedeagatch was much more important for the Bulgarian economy than for the Greeks, who already had Kavalla and Thessaloniki. To soften the judgement, the Greek government agreed to let Bulgaria use a duty-free port on the Aegean, but the offer was refused. The Bulgarian government preferred to keep the issue open, and they did not accept the loss of the area.

Equally drastic were other provisions of the final treaty. Bulgaria was required to pay an indemnity of $450 million over 38 years. The poorest nation in the Balkans, aside from Albania, the state was placed under an impossible burden. Her army, gendarmes and border guards were limited to 33,000, but this provision could be easily circumvented. It should be noted that all aspects of this harsh peace did not receive general approval. For instance, in the preliminary deliberations the American representatives suggested that Romania might cede to Bulgaria the areas in southern Dobrudja where the Bulgarians had a plurality. Brătianu, needless to say, was not a statesman to yield land. For the next years the Bulgarians in general remained bitter about the results of both the Second Balkan War and the First World War. They would accept any opportunity in international affairs for revision.

GREECE AND THE OTTOMAN EMPIRE: THE TURKISH REPUBLIC

Despite the differences in their positions, the post-war fate of Greece and the Ottoman Empire was to be closely intertwined. At first the Ottoman government appeared to face a hopeless future. Not only were the Ottoman armies defeated in the Arab lands, but in November, 1918, an Allied fleet passed through the Dardanelles and anchored before Constantinople. The final humiliation occurred in February, 1919, when the commanding French general rode into Constantinople on a white horse provided by the Greek community. In May, 1919, Greek troops began disembarking in Anatolia.

In drafting the terms for a peace with the Ottoman government, the Allies had to consider four secret treaties in which Britain, France, Italy and Russia had previously partitioned the empire among themselves. In 1915 Britain and France agreed that Russia should gain Constantinople and the northern shores of the Bosphorus and the Dardanelles at the end of the war. At the same time the Treaty of London promised Italy Adalia, the southwestern portion of the Anatolian peninsula. In 1916, in the Sykes-Picot agreements, Britain and France divided the Arab lands between themselves. Russia was now to take Armenia. Finally, the St. Jean de Maurienne accord of 1917 reaffirmed Italy's right to Adalia and also further assigned her the district of Smyrna which was predominantly Greek in population. If these agreements had been carried out, the Ottoman government would have been left with only the northwestern and north central section of the peninsula. Lands inhabited exclusively by Muslim Turks were assigned to European states.

The agreements, like similar ones concerning other areas, were to prove difficult to implement. With the collapse of the tsarist government and the Bolshevik publication and denunciation of the pacts, the Allies could disregard their commitments to Russia. There remained, however, the problem of the contradictory arrangements. Italy was determined to take both Adalia and Smyrna, despite the fact that the latter and its surrounding area contained a Greek population of over a million and that Greece was an ally. Venizelos was equally convinced that the time had come to realize the maximum program of the Great Idea and to gain control of the eastern shores of the Mediterranean in Anatolia. Capitalizing on his obvious loyalty to the Allied cause in the war, Venizelos obtained the approval of Britain, France, and the United States to land Greek troops in Smyrna in May, 1919. The western powers not only wished to back the Greek position, but they also needed the Greek forces to use against the rising Turkish opposition in Anatolia. In other words, since they did not have troops of their own because their electorates demanded demobilization, they expected the Greeks to enforce the stringent peace terms on the Ottoman government. At this time there were also French and Italian troops in occupation of other parts of Anatolia and an independent Armenian state had been proclaimed.

In August, 1920, Sultan Mohammed VI was forced to sign the Treaty of Sèvres. The stipulations were severe. All of the Arab lands were taken by France and Britain; Armenia was to become independent. Greece was awarded Eastern Thrace, that is, lands north of the Dardanelles, the Sea of Marmora, and Constantinople. In addition, Greece was to administer Smyrna and its hinterland for five years. A plebiscite, whose result anyone could foretell, would then be held. Greece was also awarded the strategic islands of Tenedos and Imbros. The Italian control of the Dodecanese Islands was reaffirmed and the Straits were to be internationalized. The Ottoman Empire kept Constantinople and the remainder of Anatolia. This settlement involved not only the dismemberment of the empire, but the partition of ethnically Turkish lands. The surrender of the Arabic territories was accepted reluctantly, but the other losses, in particular those to Greece, aroused a violent national reaction. If the treaty were put into effect the Turkish state would be cut off from the Aegean and Greek-held lands would surround Constantinople. The Treaty of Sèvres and the Greek occupation thus led to a new revolutionary current, which was to result in the final overthrow of the Ottoman government and the establishment of the Turkish republic.

The Turkish national movement was fortunate to have as its leader one of the most gifted statesmen of the period, Mustafa Kemal. In the war he had displayed great military ability, and he emerged as the only victorious Ottoman general with successful campaigns at the Dardanelles and against the Russians to his credit. After the war, realizing the impotence of the Imperial government, he began secretly to organize a resistance to both the sultan and the occupying powers. At first, he did not find much support because the average Turk was still loyal to the sultan-caliph. This attitude shifted as a result of sporadic Greek resistance activities, especially in Thrace, but mainly because of the Greek landing in Smyrna in May, 1919. The Greek troops not only occupied the areas assigned to them, but they began to advance inland into Turkish territory. Although the Turkish soldiers were fatigued, the country had been at war almost continuously since 1911, large numbers now rallied to the side of Mustafa Kemal. He established a center of operations not at Constantinople but at Ankara in Central Anatolia. His movement was political as well as military, and his followers won control of the Ottoman parliament in the elections of 1919. Since the sultan still commanded much support, Kemal did not immediately challenge his position. When the terms of the Treaty of Sèvres were announced, there was an immediate outcry from the entire country. In order to compel the sultan to accept the terms and to silence Kemal's followers, the British government encouraged the Greeks to advance. In July they took the city of Brusa in Anatolia and reached the Sea of Marmora; they also occupied Adrianople, north of Constantinople. On August 10 the sultan surrendered and accepted the peace terms. By then, however, the real leader of the country was Mustafa Kemal.

The Greek decision to undertake these operations in Antolia had come about due to a complicated political situation in Athens and a continuation of many of the same conflicts that had existed throughout the war. When the hostilities were concluded, Greece seemed at first in a good position. The country had been on the winning side; the two principal enemies of the past, Bulgaria and the Ottoman Empire, had been defeated. It was expected that the country would receive rewards, including perhaps southern Albania. To guarantee the success of his policies Venizelos went to the peace conference at Paris and remained there for two years. Although he succeeded in influencing the Allies, his electoral strength at home virtually vanished. At the same time he allowed his country to be drawn into the dangerous Anatolian campaigns. At first both he and the Greek staff officers opposed any action in the area, particularly an operation without the participation of other Allied troops. Finally, however, Venizelos went against his own judgement and the best military advice. The possibilities of gaining large territories in Asia Minor appealed too strongly to this nationalistic leader, and he responded to the British call for military assistance.

In Greece Venizelos's military ventures were not fully understood. The Greek population supported the occupation of the Smyrna area, but not the further campaigns. Weary of war, the people wanted the three hundred thousand troops demobilized. The royalists also kept up a constant criticism of Venizelos and his policies. From Paris the Greek statesman could do little to influence the electorate or explain his objectives. Then, suddenly, in October, 1920, the nation was thrown into a constitutional crisis when King Alexander died of a bite from a pet monkey. The crown was offered to his younger brother, Prince Paul, who refused saying that his father, ex-King Constantine, had not formally abdicated. Consequently, the parliamentary elections held in December, 1920, became in effect a plebiscite on the return of Constantine, Venizelos's adversary.

The supporters of the former king conducted a clever campaign. A stunning defeat was inflicted on Venizelos. He lost his seat in the assembly, and his Liberal Party held only 120 seats in the parliament of 370, although his adherents did win 52 percent of the total vote. A proud man, Venizelos was deeply humiliated by this result and left Greece three days after the election. A month later Constantine returned in triumph to Athens. The change in government, however, did not mean an abandonment of Venizelos's Turkish policy. Although the royalists had strongly criticized it, they, too, were caught up in a wave of enthusiasm and hoped to fulfill the Great Idea by a final, crushing defeat of the Ottoman adversary.

In 1921 the Greek forces in Anatolia launched another campaign. The Turkish troops gradually retreated inland, thereby drawing the Greek army deep into Anatolia, into hostile territory, with a single-line railroad and extended lines of communication. On August 24 Mustafa Kemal, in charge of the Turkish operations, decided to make a stand along the east bank of the Sakaria River in Central Anatolia. For two weeks the Greeks assaulted the Turkish fortifications. The battle was fierce; it is estimated that both sides lost half of their men. By September 16 the Greek troops were forced to withdraw.

The victory of the Turkish army over the invader made Mustafa Kemal a great military hero and unquestionably the most important political figure in the country. The real power rested not with the sultan in Constantinople, but with Kemal and his followers in Ankara, which was now the nationalist capital. Not only had Kemal won military honors, but in the preceding months he had conducted a skillful diplomatic campaign that had split the great powers and had left Britain and Greece alone in their attempts to enforce the Treaty of Sèvres. He also had come to terms with the Bolshevik regime, and in April, 1920, he made a military agreement with that government. In October he was able to suppress the independent Armenian state that had been set up. He then proceeded to conclude a peace treaty with the Soviet government in which he returned Batum, but kept Kars and Ardahan, which had been taken by Russia in 1878. With this agreement Kemal's eastern flank was secured. Next, in March, 1921, he persuaded Italy to evacuate southwestern Anatolia in return for economic concessions.

The diplomatic successes continued after the victory at Sakaria. In October, 1921, the French evacuated the Cilician region also in return for economic advantages. Thus by October, 1921, Italy, France, and the Soviet Union had made agreements with Mustafa Kemal and not with the sultan. The latter's sole supporters were Britain and Greece. Since British troops were only in the Constantinople area, the Greek army in Anatolia was Kemal's last major obstacle.

In August, 1922, the Turkish leader launched a well-organized and coordinated campaign against the Greek troops. Exhausted and dispirited, these forces collapsed and on September 9 the Turkish army entered Smyrna. By September 14 fire had destroyed this once rich city. Attention was next turned to Eastern Thrace. Although Britain called upon Italy and France to help defend this territory, both refused. With the failure of the Allies to enforce their settlement, in October Eastern Thrace, Constantinople, and the Straits returned to the full control of the Turkish forces. On November 1, 1922, the Turkish assembly declared that the sultanate had ceased to exist; Mohammed VI fled on a British warship. The Treaty of Sèvres was now dead. A new agreement had to be drawn up, but with Turkish delegates who now represented a victorious cause.

The negotiations commenced in Switzerland in November, 1922, and resulted in the Treaty of Lausanne of July, 1923. The Turks retained possession of all of Anatolia, Eastern Thrace, the Straits, and the islands of Tenedos and Imbros. No reparations were assessed, and the capitulations, which had previously caused so many problems for the Ottoman Empire, were abolished. The most serious discussions concerned the Straits. Despite Soviet and Turkish efforts, Britain succeeded in securing a settlement favorable to her interests. The Straits were to be demilitarized and open to all ships unless Turkey were at war. No single nation was to be allowed to send into the Black Sea naval tonnage in excess of that of the largest Black Sea power, Russia. This provision thus allowed two nations, for instance Britain and France, to bring in twice the tonnage of Russia.

On October 29, 1923, the Turkish Republic was proclaimed, and Kemal was elected president. The capital was now changed permanently to Ankara. In April, 1924, a constitution was adopted. The chief power in the state was placed in the hands of the assembly, which was elected by universal male suffrage. This body elected the president, who in turn chose a cabinet. In the next years Mustafa Kemal dominated the Turkish political scene.

The real loser in the Anatolian struggle was clearly Greece. Lands that had been inhabited by Greeks for 2,500 years were evacuated. The burning of Smyrna and the stream of refugees from Anatolia caused a strong reaction in Athens. A Revolutionary Committee composed of army officers and politicians was organized to determine who was responsible for the national disaster. When it demanded that the king abdicate, Constantine withdrew in favor of his son, who came to the throne as George II in September, 1922. Another commission was appointed to investigate the Anatolian calamity. It quickly returned indictments against eight ministers and military advisers. A court martial found them guilty, and on November 28 the commander in chief of the army and five ministers were executed by a firing squad. The brutality of the action shocked both Greeks and Europeans.

The military defeat and the domestic turmoil placed the Greeks in a weak position at the Lausanne negotiations. In addition to the territorial losses the country had to sign an agreement for the exchange of populations. With the exception of those in Constantinople, all of the Greeks were to be expelled from Turkey; Muslims in Greece, except those in Western Thrace, were likewise to be forced to migrate to Turkey. It is estimated that about one and a half million Greeks and four hundred thousand Muslims, mostly Turkish but some of Greek or other ethnic origin, were affected. It was a harsh and radical solution and the first of its kind in the modern era. For Greece it provided one advantage. Many of the Anatolian Greeks were settled in the newly acquired Macedonian lands, some of which only now acquired an overwhelmingly Greek character.

Although Greece thus lost her ethnic hold on western Anatolia, it will be remembered that the country did acquire Western Thrace from Bulgaria. This was to be the single positive gain from the First World War. The Greek government was unable to secure its claims in southern Albania because of the negative attitude of the Allied great powers. These states were now determined to restore an independent Albanian state with its prewar boundaries.

ALBANIA

Of the Balkan nations Albania held the most difficult position at the end of the war. Threatened with partition by her neighbors, the state depended completely on the decisions of the great powers. It will be remembered that an independent Albania had been established only in 1913. Internal political dissentions had caused the breakdown of the central government and the expulsion of the first ruler, William of Wied, in 1914. Thereafter the country reverted to the condition that had existed for centuries. Each region, group, and clan sought to protect its own interests. No united opposition could be put up against foreign intervention. Greece, Serbia, and Montenegro took advantage of the situation to seize those lands that had been denied them in 1913. Greece immediately occupied southern Albania. Although this action was taken with Allied approval and the understanding that the lands would be evacuated later, the Greek government soon showed that it had no intention of abiding by this agreement. In 1916 deputies from the area were elected to the Greek assembly, and the region was formally annexed. The Greeks insisted that the lands were ethnically theirs. These claims were based on the fact that there was an indigenous Greek population, but more important, those Albanians were counted as Greeks who went to Greek schools, who were Orthodox, or who knew the Greek language—a policy the Greeks had followed in Macedonia.

Serbia and Montenegro acted in the same manner; both powers still desired an outlet on the Adriatic and thus seized lands north of the Drim

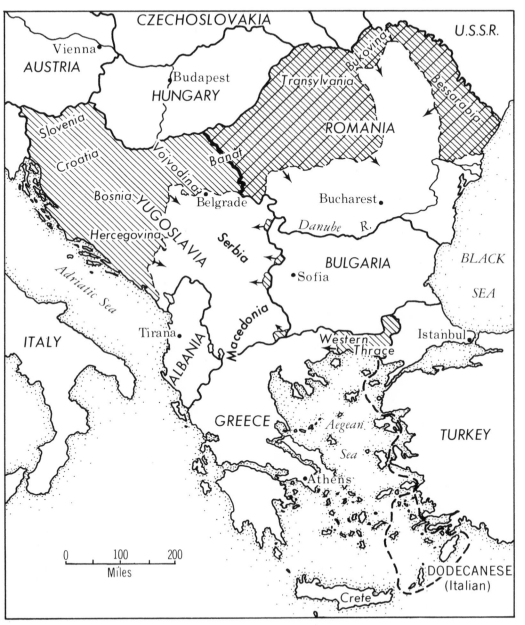

Map 13. The Balkans after World War I

River in 1914–15. Meanwhile, Italy, too, moved to take possession of her claims. In October and December, 1914, the island of Saseno and the port of Vlorë were occupied. Although the areas seized by the Serbs and Montenegrins had to be evacuated later after the victories by the Central Powers, both states hoped to annex the territories should the Allies finally win the war.

The dismemberment of Albania was recognized by the western Allies in the Treaty of London of 1915. In this pact Italy received full control of Saseno and Vlorë with its hinterland. In addition it was agreed that if Italy acquired Trentino, Istria, and Dalmatia, as stipulated in the pact, then Greece was to take southern Albania, and Serbia and Montenegro could partition northern Albania. Greece and Serbia were also to establish a common frontier west of Lake Ohrid through the annexation of Albanian territory. The central portion was to be set up as an autonomous, not independent, state, which would be represented in foreign affairs by Italy.

The fate of Albania was decided at the peace conference during the prolonged negotiations over the Italian-Yugoslav boundary. Here the Italian government, as we have seen, agreed to surrender its claims on Albanian territory, except Saseno and Vlorë, in return for the city of Fiume. In other words, this port, with its population of 46,391 of whom only 24,212 were Italian, was more important to Rome than the control of Albania with its 800,000 inhabitants. In the complicated negotiations that followed Wilson alone fought against the application of the Treaty of London, which, of course, the United States had not signed. Greece and Serbia followed their traditional policies with the exception that Athens could work with Italy, while the Serbian government strongly opposed the creation of an Albanian state under Italian control.

The obvious danger to their national lands led the Albanians finally to take political action. In January, 1920, a group of prominent Albanian leaders convened a National Congress, which was followed in March by the summoning of a National Legislative Assembly in Tirana. Here a regency was established and an army set up. At the same time, Albanian emigrants living in Europe and the United States had organized. Their representatives went to Paris to argue for the restoration of their nation. Again, the American representatives were the most sympathetic.

The final decision of the powers to recreate Albania came as a result of the previously discussed bargain involving the exchange of Fiume for Italian concessions on the Albanian question. In August, 1920, the Italian foreign minister, Count Carlo Sforza, called for the restoration of Albania with her 1913 boundaries; Saseno and Vlorë were also surrendered. Italy immediately evacuated the country, but both Greece and Serbia, despite their formal acceptance of the solution, were reluctant to abandon their influence in the area. In 1921 Belgrade supported the

Mirdite revolt in northern Albania and was only forced to abandon this effort when pressured by the great powers. The loss of Anatolia so weakened Greece that the state was compelled to yield finally on southern Albania. By 1922 the country was thus clear of foreign influence, a condition that was to last only until 1925, when Italian predominance was established.

Meanwhile, within Albania the organization of the government proceeded. Instead of adopting the provisions of 1914, the Albanian leaders drafted a new constitution at the Congress of Lushnjë in January, 1920. This assembly of fifty-six delegates decided that the state should be a constitutional monarchy. Until a ruler was chosen, his functions were to be fulfilled by the High Council of State, which was composed of four regents. Two of these were Muslims, one each from the Bektashi and Sunni sects; the others were Orthodox and Catholic. To assist the regency the congress appointed a cabinet responsible not to the regency but to a thirty-seven man senate, which was given the principal power in the state. A national assembly was also proposed, but its membership and functions were not defined until 1922. In April, 1921, elections were held. In 1922 the Lushnjë Constitution was amended and the number of the representatives to the assembly was set at seventy-eight to be elected for four-year terms by the vote of all male citizens. Further measures were taken to strengthen the power of the legislative branch at the expense of the regency. An independent judiciary was also created.

During the constitutional period factions, or crude political parties, were formed. The Congress of Lishnjë was dominated by Suleiman Bey Delvina. His supporters, called the Liberals, sought to exclude from office those Albanians who had been part of the Ottoman administration. These officials had close ties with and represented the interests chiefly of the large conservative landowners. After the 1921 elections other parties emerged. Among these were the Democratic Party of Bishop Fan Noli and Luigj Gurakuqi and the Popular Party of Sefi Vlamashi and Eshref Frashëri. All of these men favored economic, social, and political reform and the introduction of western institutions. Their chief opposition came from the Progressives, led by Shefqet Vërlaci and Ahmet Zogu. This group stood for the interests of the large landowners and the upper clergy, and it rejected agrarian reform.

The lack of political experience in the country was soon in evidence. It proved impossible to maintain a stable government. In June, 1924, Bishop Noli led a revolt, which was in turn suppressed by a conservative counterrevolution led by Ahmet Zogu, assisted by Yugoslavia. In 1925 Zogu became president and a new constitution was promulgated. In 1928 he became king. The country was now a royal dictatorship and an Italian protectorate.

CHAPTER 19

Conclusion

In 1922 with the formal establishment of the Turkish Republic the last vestiges of the Ottoman Empire disappeared. Already in October and November, 1918, the Habsburg Empire had divided into its national components. The demise of the two great imperial powers of central and southeastern Europe marked the final victory of the national principle for the organization of the political life of the area. The change had thus been made from the concept of a state in which many nationalities with differing languages, cultures, and religions occupied the same geographic space, although not in an equal relationship, to the more modern idea that one people with one language should have the virtually exclusive possession of a given area. As we have seen, the basis for the right of control was principally that of historic claims and national composition of the population. Most national programs, as enunciated by intellectuals and politicians, emphasized the historical arguments and referred back to the medieval kingdoms, or, for the Greeks, the Byzantine Empire. The right of self-determination played a lesser, although significant role, in particular as a weapon to influence public opinion among the great powers. In practice each state concentrated on asserting its prerogatives and not in forwarding the national idea in general. Certainly, Bulgaria, Greece, Montenegro, and Serbia showed not the slightest hesitation or moral qualm in planning the partition of Albanian lands.

With this exclusive concept of national possession the dominant people in each region looked on the others as interlopers or invaders. The Christian people without exception regarded the Muslim Turk in this light, despite the five centuries of occupation. The expulsion of thousands of Muslims as a result of the national movements has not been regarded as an injustice. The great dispute between Romanian and Hungarian historians over Transylvania has been over who was there

320

first, the apparent assumption being that the solution of this question has direct relevance to its present ownership. After national liberation no state felt comfortable with its minorities; in the postwar period all resisted laws guaranteeing the civil rights of these people, who were uniformly regarded as a source of national weakness and subversion, which indeed they often were. Despite centuries of humiliation and debasement at the hands of an alien conquering power, the victorious nationalities too often found no better way to treat those under their control than simply to apply the same methods to which they themselves had been subjected in their period of weakness.

The problems of exclusive national control were most clearly shown in areas where the dominant nation was in a minority, as in Transylvania before 1914, or merely held a weak plurality. The great tragedy of modern Balkan history has been the struggle over Macedonia. No practical program was advanced which, given the intensity of national feeling, could realistically solve the problem of how an area with a complex ethnic structure could be governed without one state assuming control. The culmination of the national idea was the exchange of populations between Greece and Turkey in the 1920s. Here Greeks, whose families had inhabited Anatolia for literally thousands of years, were returned to mainland Greece while Muslims, sometimes of Greek ethnic origin, were expelled from Crete to Anatolia, an area with which they had absolutely no previous connection.

With the acceptance of the national concept the Balkan people, except those under Habsburg authority, experienced also a transfer from ecclesiastical to secular control. In the Ottoman Empire the church and state had been virtually inseparable. The shift from the millet to the national governments involved a change in the legal as well as in the political framework of Balkan life. The church was now reduced from being the principal governing body on the higher level to that of a department in a secular administration.

Along with these changes all of the Balkan states either adopted or were endowed by the protecting powers with similar patterns of government. They thus became constitutional monarchies with highly centralized administrative systems. The concentration of power in the capital city often meant the destruction of systems of autonomous local government that had functioned throughout the Turkish period. In practice this shift also created a situation in which politics was in fact in the hands of a small percentage of the population and one that became increasingly separated from the mass of the people. As we have seen, in the internal politics of the new states the primary political issue was the struggle between the prince and groups of notables or prominent men. Organized into informal groupings or political parties, these politicians fought for control of the government. Victory in political struggles carried with it the ability to restaff the administrative system and to use political influence for private profit. Throughout the nineteenth century the peasant masses of the Balkans played no significant political role in the actual functioning of the new state apparatuses. It was only on the eve of the First World War that the organization of peasant parties and the increasing dissatisfaction over the land situation brought the interests of the majority of the population into the center of the political stage.

This evolution of Balkan politics paralleled the events in the European states, which were, after all, the Balkan models. In no country did the workers or peasants run the state. In all men of property and education dominated the government. The contrast with the Balkan countries was a matter of numbers. Lacking the highly developed industrial, commercial, and professional middle classes of the West, a much smaller percentage of the Balkan population played a determining political role. Moreover, although corruption was indeed an attribute of all political systems, the heritage of the Balkan states in this direction was far deeper. Separation from the Ottoman administrative system in no way assured that the malpractices of that government would not be repeated in the successor states. The relative poverty of these nations made such actions more serious in their general effects on the country.

In accepting western political ideas, the Balkan leaders, like their European counterparts, appeared to assume that the adoption of progressive political institutions would automatically remedy most economic and social ills. Undoubtedly, the major problem of the new Balkan nations was economic, not political, a fact that was neither clearly defined nor even recognized. From their establishment the states were not truly economically viable units on a modern level. The autonomous and independent regimes were from the beginning faced with enormous financial burdens. They had to find the resources to pay for their wars of national liberation, for establishing their administrative systems, for internal improvements, and, most important, for national defense. No nation wished to remain an oriental backwater; all wished modern improvements, like railroads, and the attributes of an advanced culture, such as libraries, universities, opera houses, and theaters. National pride and prestige demanded an impressive capital city. Similar feelings together with real fears for national safety called for the organization of as large an army as possible, equipped with advanced weapons.

To meet these national tasks the governments had few of the necessary resources. Taxation of the basically impoverished population could not yield the needed revenue. As we have seen, all of the states, including the Ottoman Empire, resorted to foreign loans. Inexperienced in the handling of state finances and without the means of repayment, the governments either carried heavy debts or were in fact bankrupt by the end of the century. The Ottoman Empire, Bulgaria, Greece, and Serbia were all forced to accept a degree of foreign control over their internal finances because of this condition.

The basic economic weakness of all of the nations was, of course, simply a reflection of the poverty of the people. The condition of the peasant has been discussed in detail previously. Even where the peasant families enjoyed the free use of a plot of land, the quick rise in the population in the century had resulted in repeated subdivisions so that too many people were forced to exist on entirely inadequate acreage. The lack of technical knowledge and of capital to invest in land resulted in backward methods and low yields. In many areas the peasants were deeply in debt because they had been forced to borrow continually to exist from year to year. The entire land problem was complicated by the fact that the peasant himself preferred traditional methods and solutions. His answer was simply the acquisition of more land without meeting the problems of increased production or the inevitable consequences of repeated subdivision.

Although in the postwar years it has been estimated that half of the peasant population was simply not needed on the land, there was no alternative employment for this surplus labor. Steps toward industrialization were taken before the war, but these actions in no way met the basic economic problem. Like agriculture, industrial development in the Balkans was severely hampered by historical conditions. A backward area, the peninsula was not prepared to make good use of the domestic capital available for industrial development nor to attract sufficient foreign capital for investment. The previous historical experience had deprived the area of a skilled and disciplined working force for the factories. In the same manner, the prosperous classes lacked experience in management and organization. Nor did this group feel any particular attraction to industrial or commercial pursuits. The majority of students in the universities took law degrees as a preparation for government employment.

These conditions necessitated reliance on foreign capital and expertise, and this meant, as we have seen, that sectors of the economy that enriched the investors and not necessarily the country itself were developed. Foreign entrepreneurs were primarily interested in the Balkans as a source of raw materials and semifinished products, such as Romanian oil and Serbian nonferrous minerals. The governments of the great powers similarly wished to maintain the region as a market for their own goods. The Austrian tariff controversies with Serbia and Romania, involving protection for Hungarian agriculture, and the British endeavors to keep the Ottoman tariff schedules are all examples of these powers acting in the interests of their own citizens.

Economic intervention on the part of the great powers was, as we have seen, closely paralleled by similar actions in the diplomatic field. Every step in the establishment of the Balkan national states was accompanied by European interference and supervision. This condition arose chiefly from the fact that in the nineteenth century the peninsula was one of the crossroads of the world. The Eastern Question was the single dominant source of great power conflict from 1815 to 1914. It was the subject of the one major conflict during that period, the Crimean War, and the direct cause of the outbreak of the First World War. No power could afford to allow a rival to dominate either the decaying Ottoman Empire or a significant number of the new states. Because of the vital concern of Europe in the fate of the peninsula, most crises were initiated by the Balkan states, but were resolved by the powers. The major treaties regulating Balkan affairs—Adrianople, Paris, and Berlin—represented exclusively great power decisions. Minor matters were usually disposed of in ambassadorial conferences, held, in general, in London, Paris, or Constantinople, and in which Balkan representatives were seldom present. This condition continued through the First World War. The postwar settlements were the result of discussions between France, Britain, Italy, and the United States. At no time in this narrative did members of Balkan foreign ministries negotiate on an equal basis with representatives of the powers.

Not only did the dominant states determine the territorial boundaries of the Balkan nations and their relationship to the Ottoman Empire, but they also established the first governments and, except in the case of Serbia, named the first ruler. The states became constitutional monarchies because the great powers approved this form of government. These regimes represented a middle way between the desires of the Habsburg and Russian empires for conservative regimes and that of France and Britain for more liberal forms. Before 1878 European control was formal and determined by treaty. The Russian protectorate of Serbia and the Principalities was the result of the Akkerman convention; the three power protectorship of Greece was part of the Treaty of London. In contrast, the Russian domination in Bulgaria and the Austrian hold over Serbia after 1878 were not spelled out in an agreement, but were clearly understood in the negotiations carried out between the two powers.

Balkan subordination to foreign dictation resulted primarily from geography rather than from choice, and the effects were unfortunate for the new states. The temptation for each Balkan government to cooperate with a great power against a neighbor and the necessity of maintaining a high level of armament were the direct results of the fact that the peninsula was a prime area of world tension. The percentage of national income devoted by each nation to war was extremely high. In fact, these states spent more on arms on a per capita basis than did the great powers. The price paid in deaths and the destruction of property due both to the wars of national liberation and to the resulting diplomatic situation was tragic.

Although European tutelage was largely imposed, all of the Balkan national leaders absorbed willingly the current western political doctrines. In the first part of the century liberalism and nationalism were regarded in the East as in the West as the progressive ideas of the epoch. Democratic, populist, and socialist programs became a significant element in the political scene only at the turn of the century. Although the political and revolutionary ideology was much the same, the applicability of these principles in the Balkans could not be the same as in Western or Central Europe. The national idea obviously worked differently in a nation such as Britain, with her vast colonial empire, and France and Germany, with their extensive territories and adequate resources for an industrial economy, than in a state such as Greece or Albania. In the same manner, nineteenth-century liberal thought, at least in the first part of the period, was tied to laissez-faire economic policy and with the general idea that the state should not meddle in the personal concerns of its citizens. Although the economic doctrines were modified when protective tariffs and assistance to industry were introduced, Balkan governments did not devote sufficient efforts to matters such as health, rural education, or the general problems of extreme poverty and indebtedness in the countryside. No governments in the nineteenth century, with the possible exception of Bismarck's Germany, were directed toward social service, but the Balkan countries might have fared better had they had more conservative regimes with wider social programs. The great pride of liberal achievement in the West—constitutions providing for secret ballots and universal manhood suffrage and containing bills of rights assuring freedom of speech, press, and association—was only seldom effective in practice in the Balkans and had less value for a population that was largely illiterate and whose view of contemporary politics was parochial.

In studying the history of any country, no matter how powerful or fortunate, hindsight and a wide historical perspective make it easy to point out the errors and failures in national development. In regard to the Balkan states the great accomplishments of the century and the positive gains from national unification should, in the final analysis, take precedence over any reservations or negative judgments. Criticism has been made of the results of applying the national solution to the peninsula, but it must be strongly emphasized that no other practical alternative existed at the time. From a purely theoretical standpoint it can be regretted that no political evolution was possible that would have allowed an adoption of a system by which different nationalities could live peacefully under the same government, but the fact is that in modern times no such organization has been developed. All *advanced* states are national in character.

In the nineteenth century two successful models of political evolution existed. The first, the European, was based on the subdivision of the continent into an ever-increasing number of unitary national states. Like the Balkan nations, the governments of the great powers, France, Germany, Italy, and Britain, did not give equal treatment to their considerable minorities. The second example was the United States, a nation that became a haven for emigrants from over-crowded Europe, who upon arrival in their new home immediately were virtually compelled to drop their national language and heritage and accept that of the Anglo-Saxon privileged strata. In the educational system Shakespeare became the principal figure in the literary heritage of children from Italian, Greek, German, French, Chinese, Japanese, and other such divergent backgrounds. "Self-determination" was never invoked in American immigrant centers. In fact the bloodiest civil war of the nineteenth century was fought to prevent the principle from being applied by the southern states. It is impossible to imagine Woodrow Wilson suggesting that Mexican-dominated cities along the southern border of the United States should be allowed plebiscites to determine if the population would prefer to join Mexico or to have their schools conducted in Spanish.

It is certainly also to be doubted if any program of reform could have preserved the Ottoman Empire as a multinational state whose citizens would have been content to remain within its control. Repeated efforts were made, as we have seen, to strengthen the state and appease the dissident population. Throughout the century, however, the basic problem remained: the majority of the Balkan peoples, of every nationality and social level, simply wished to leave the state. The national idea was not merely a program of intellectuals and politicians; it had, by the end of the century, become a passionate conviction, a secular religion, for the majority of the inhabitants of each state. The Muslim Turks themselves finally accepted this solution for their own political future.

The economic and political weaknesses of the new states have also received much emphasis in this study. Here too, however, it must be emphasized that despite their extreme backwardness and the increasing economic burdens, the individual states did achieve a great deal. Thrown into a competitive world system, in a difficult geographic position and with few resources, the new governments nevertheless made real efforts to lift themselves to the standards of the most advanced European states. Conditions in the new nations at the end of the century were certainly greatly superior to those in the area at the beginning of that epoch. At that time the Ottoman government was unable to assure the basic conditions of civil peace in its lands. Not only were the local governors unrestrained, but bandits, groups of soldiers, and local warlords with armed retainers made life impossible for the peasant population, Christian and Muslim alike, in many areas. The national governments not only assured the establishment of an orderly system of administration, but they initiated measures directed toward the improvement of general conditions in the country. Educational systems were established, internal improvements were made commensurate with the economic resources of the individual states, and by the beginning of the First World War some social welfare legislation had been introduced. The great question of land distribution had become a matter of direct political concern in every state. Much remained to be done, but a beginning had been made.

Finally, although the territorial settlement in the peninsula, which had been the result largely of war and great power bargains, was far from ideal, it at least was to prove stable. After the great war of 1939 to 1945, only three territorial changes occurred: the Soviet acquisition of Bessarabia, the Bulgarian regaining of southern Dobrudja, and the Yugoslav annexation of the Istrian peninsula, but without Trieste. Many problems have remained as causes of friction and conflict. The Macedonian, Transylvanian, and Bessarabian questions, among others, remain under discussion, but they have not led to disastrous wars. The years after 1945 have witnessed repeated crises among the Balkan nations, including Turkey, and among the great powers. However, in contrast to the nineteenth century, these disputes have been settled by negotiation and not on the battlefield.

Bibliographic Essay

THIS essay is restricted to a discussion of works in English, which the authors believe the reader might wish to consult for further information on specific topics. In no sense does it cover all of the material on which this account is based, nor does it attempt to cite all of the excellent books and articles in English on Balkan history. Volume XI of this series will contain a comprehensive bibliography in all languages.

BIBLIOGRAPHIES AND JOURNALS

The standard bibliographic guide for the Balkans is Paul L. Horecky, ed., *Southeastern Europe: A Guide to Basic Publications* (Chicago: University of Chicago Press, 1969). Fifty American and European scholars collaborated with Dr. Horecky in compiling this annotated listing of over three thousand books in the Balkan, Russian, and western languages, which is indispensable for any student of the area. A work of similar significance is *Südosteuropa-Bibliographie* (Munich: R. Oldenbourg). Published every five years since 1956, this guide contains all books and articles in the relevant languages. In addition, under the auspices of the Slavic Division of the Library of Congress, the United States Government Printing Office has published three valuable works: Stephen Fischer-Galati, *Rumania: A Bibliographic Guide* (1963); Michael B. Petrovich, *Yugoslavia: A Bibliographic Guide* (1974); and Marin V. Pundeff, *Bulgaria: A Bibliographic Guide* (1965). Another helpful reference is the *American Bibliography of Russian and East European Studies*, an annual publication presenting books and articles in the social sciences and the humanities. The volumes for 1956 to 1967 were published by Indiana University; those that appeared thereafter, by Ohio State University. Shirley Howard Weber, *Voyages and Travels in the Near East made during the XIX Century* (Princeton: American School of Classical Studies at Athens, 1952) is an annotated, chronological bibliography of over twelve hundred travel accounts, many of which deal with the Balkans.

The major journals for the area are: *Balkan Studies* (Thessaloniki, Greece, 1960–), *Canadian-American Slavic Studies* (Pittsburg, 1967–), *East European Quarterly* (Boulder, Colorado, 1967–), *Journal of Central European Affairs* (Boulder,

1941–1964), *Rumanian Studies* (Champaign-Urbana, Illinois, 1970–), *Slavonic and East European Review* (London, 1922–), *Slavic Review* (Seattle, 1940–), and *Southeastern Europe* (Pittsburgh, 1974–). In addition, the following European language journals often contain significant articles in English: *Études balkaniques* (Sofia, 1965–), *Österreichische Osthefte* (Vienna, 1959–), *Revue des études sud-est européenes* (Bucharest, 1963–), *Südost-Forschungen* (Munich, 1936–), *Balcanica* (Belgrade, 1970–), and *Byzantine and Modern Greek Studies* (Oxford, 1975–).

GENERAL WORKS ON BALKAN HISTORY

The outstanding survey is Leften S. Stavrianos, *The Balkans since 1453* (New York: Holt, Rinehart, and Winston, 1958). Beginning with the fall of Constantinople, the author presents a broad sweep of Balkan history through the Second World War, concluding with a detailed, annotated bibliography of seventy-five pages covering the major books and articles published through 1957. Still useful are the earlier works of Ferdinand Schevill, *The History of the Balkan Peninsula and the Near East* (1922; reprint ed., New York Arno Press, 1971), and of William Miller, *The Ottoman Empire and its Successors, 1801–1927* (Cambridge: Cambridge University Press, 1936). In 1950 René Ristelhueber, a French diplomat who served in the Balkans, wrote a survey that has recently been translated by Sherman David Spector, *A History of the Balkan Peoples* (New York: Twayne Publishers, 1971). Shorter similar accounts are L. S. Stavrianos, *The Balkans, 1815–1914* (New York: Holt, Rinehart, and Winston, 1963), and Charles and Barbara Jelavich, *The Balkans* (Englewood Cliffs, N.J.: Prentice-Hall, 1965).

Another survey of a different nature is Traian Stoianovich, *A Study in Balkan Civilization* (New York: A. A. Knopf, 1967), a provocative and stimulating work in which the author shows his keen appreciation of anthropological, economic, and sociological factors. In 1960 a conference was held at the University of California, Berkeley, at which thirteen experts on the Balkans analysed the geopolitical, religious, literary, social, economic, and political problems of the area in the nineteenth and twentieth centuries. These studies are published in Charles and Barbara Jelavich, eds., *The Balkans in Transition: Essays on the Development of Balkan Life and Politics since the Eighteenth Century* (1963; reprint ed., Hamden, Conn.: Archon, 1974).

On the national question, the central issue in Eastern Europe in the nineteenth century, the early work by Robert W. Seton-Watson, *The Rise of Nationality in the Balkans* (London: Constable, 1917) should still be consulted. The best recent studies are to be found in Peter F. Sugar and Ivo J. Lederer, eds., *Nationalism in Eastern Europe* (Seattle: University of Washington Press, 1969), which has chapters on Albania by T. Zavalani, on Bulgaria by Marin V. Pundeff, on Greece by Stephen G. Xydis, on Romania by Stephen Fischer-Galati, and on Yugoslavia by Ivo J. Lederer, together with an introduction by Peter F. Sugar on nationalism in Eastern Europe. The Balkan nationalities in the Habsburg Empire are discussed in three standard works: Robert A. Kann, *The Multinational Empire: Nationalism and National Reform in the Habsburg Monarchy, 1848–1918* (New York: Columbia University Press, 1950), 2 vols; C. A. Macartney, *The Habsburg Empire, 1790–1918* (London: Weidenfeld and Nicolson, 1968); and Arthur J. May, *The Habsburg Monarchy, 1867–1914* (Cambridge, Mass.: Harvard University Press, 1968). A stimulating article on the same subject is Peter F. Sugar, "The Nature of the Non-Germanic Societies under Habsburg Rule," *Slavic Review,* 22 (March, 1963) 1:1–30, in which the author deals with the Romanians, Serbs, Croats, and Slovenes. It is accompanied by comments by Stephen Fischer-Galati, "Nationalism and Kaisertreue," *Ibid.,* pp. 31–36 and Hans Kohn, "The Viability of the Habsburg Monarchy," *Ibid.,* pp. 37–42. The national question in the empire was also the theme of a conference held at Indiana University in 1966. The papers were published under the title "The Nationality Problem in the Habsburg Empire in the Nineteenth Century" in volume 3 of *Austrian History Yearbook,* 3 parts (1967). Those of particular importance for this study are in part 2 and include essays on the Romanians by Andrei Oţetea and Stephen Fischer-Galati, on the Serbs by Wayne S. Vucinich and Dimitrije Djordjević, on the Croats by Charles Jelavich and Bogdan Krizman, and on the Slovenes by Fran Zwitter.

THE OTTOMAN EMPIRE

Up until twenty years ago scholarly treatments of Ottoman history in the western languages were relatively rare; since that time a number of excellent works have appeared. A fine introductory survey is to be found in Roderic H. Davison, *Turkey* (Englewood Cliffs, N.J.: Prentice-Hall, 1968) in which the author gives a broad sweep of Turkish history from the beginning to the mid-1960s. This may be supplemented by Wayne S. Vucinich, *The Ottoman Empire: Its Record and Legacy* (Princeton: Van Nostrand, 1965), which also contains a documentary supplement. For the nineteenth and twentieth century the standard work is Bernard Lewis, *The Emergence of Modern Turkey* (London: Oxford University Press, 1967). The nineteenth century British attitude toward the area is reflected in Sir Charles Eliot, *Turkey in Europe* (London: Edward Arnold, 1908). Stanford J. Shaw's latest contribution, *History of the Ottoman Empire: Empire of the Gazi's—The Rise and Decline of the Ottoman Empire, 1280–1808* (Cambridge: Cambridge University Press, 1976), vol. 1, is a much needed work. The second volume, covering the last two centuries, will appear in 1977.

For the eighteenth century background the reader should consult H. A. R. Gibb and H. Bowen, *Islamic Society and the West: A Study of the Impact of Western Civilization on Moslem Culture in the Near East* (London: Oxford University Press, 1950, 1957), one volume, 2 parts. The first reform movement is covered in Stanford J. Shaw, *Between the Old and New: the Ottoman Empire under Sultan Selim III, 1789–1809* (Cambridge, Mass.: Harvard University Press, 1971). The reorganization of the army is discussed in two articles by the same author: "The Origins of the Ottoman Military Reform: The Nizam-i Cedid Army of Selim III," *Journal of Modern History,* 37 (September, 1965) 3:291–306, and "The Established Army Corps under Selim III, 1789–1807," *Der Islam,* 2 (1965):142–84. The article by Deena R. Sadat, "Rumeli Ayanlari: The Eighteenth Century" *Journal of Modern History,* 44 (September, 1972) 3:346–63, concerns the problem of Muslim opposition to the central government.

The great majority of the books on the nineteenth century emphasize either the changes in Ottoman society in the century or the reforms. Of great significance are the works of three Turkish scholars. The evolution of Ottoman attitudes is discussed in Şerif Mardin, *The Genesis of Young Ottoman Thought: A Study in the Modernization of Turkish Political Ideas* (Princeton: Princeton University Press, 1962) and Niyazi Berkes, *The Development of Secularism in Turkey* (Montreal:

McGill University Press, 1964). Social and economic aspects are covered in the work of Kemal Karpat, in *An Inquiry into the Social Foundations of Nationalism in the Ottoman State: From Social Estates to Classes, From Millet to Nationalism*, Research Monograph No. 39 (Princeton: Center for International Studies, 1973); "Structural Change, Historical Stages of Modernization and the Role of Social Groups in Turkish Politics" which was published in a volume, edited by Karpat, entitled *Social Change and Politics in Turkey: A Structural-Historical Analysis* (Leiden: E. J. Brill, 1973), pp. 11–92; and "The Transformation of the Ottoman State, 1789–1908," *International Journal of Middle East Studies*, 3 (1972):243–81. Similar issues are discussed in the five articles by Stanford Shaw, Albert Hourani, Kemal Karpat, Roderic Davison, and Ercumend Kuran in William R. Polk and Richard L. Chambers, eds., *Beginnings of Modernization in the Middle East: The Nineteenth Century* (Chicago: University of Chicago Press, 1968).

Among the other books to be recommended Roderic H. Davison, *Reform in the Ottoman Empire, 1856–1876* (Princeton: Princeton University Press, 1963) is an excellent analysis of the complexity of political and administrative problems facing the empire. The problem of reform is also covered in F. E. Bailey, *British Policy and the Turkish Reform Movement: A Study in Anglo-Turkish Relations, 1826–1853* (Cambridge, Mass.: Harvard University Press, 1942). In addition, Robert Devereux, *The First Ottoman Constitutional Period: A Study of the Midhat Constitution and Parliament* (Baltimore: Johns Hopkins Press, 1963) is a detailed study of the 1876 constitution. The origins, beliefs, and leadership of the Young Turks is ably treated in Ernest E. Ramsaur, *The Young Turks; Prelude to the Revolution of 1908* (Princeton: Princeton University Press, 1957). This story is carried to the World War in Feroz Ahmad, *The Young Turks: The Committee of Union and Progress in Turkish Politics, 1908–1914* (Oxford, Clarendon Press, 1969).

The effects of Ottoman rule in the Balkans are the subject of Wayne S. Vucinich, "The Nature of Balkan Society under Ottoman Rule," *Slavic Review*, 4 (1962):597–616; Stanford Shaw, "The Aims and Achievement of Ottoman Rule in the Balkans," *Ibid.*, pp. 617–22; and Traian Stoianovich, "Factors in the Decline of Ottoman Society in the Balkans," *Ibid.*, pp. 623–32. These articles should be supplemented by K. Abu-Jaber, "The Millet System in the Nineteenth Century Ottoman Empire," *Muslim World*, 57 (1967):212–23, in which the author shows the discord and disunity engendered by the millet system, and Roderic H. Davison, "Turkish Attitudes concerning Christian-Muslim Equality in the Nineteenth Century," *American Historical Review*, 59 (July, 1954) 4:844–64. The significance of travel books for a study of the Balkans is shown in Barbara Jelavich, "The British Traveller in the Balkans: The Abuses of Ottoman Administration in the Slavonic Provinces," *Slavonic and East European Review*, 33 (1955) 81:396–413.

THE SOUTH SLAVS

The South Slavs, or Yugoslavs, are yet to have an adequate history in English. The two most recent works, Phyllis Auty, *Yugoslavia* (New York: Walker and Co., 1965) and Stephen Clissold, ed., *A Short History of Yugoslavia from Early Times to 1966* (Cambridge: Cambridge University Press, 1966), are brief general surveys. The latter consists mainly of selected portions of the British Naval Intelligence Handbook on Yugoslavia prepared during the Second World War. The best general work on the area is Jozo Tomasevich, *Peasants, Politics, and Economic Change in Jugoslavia* (Stanford: Stanford University Press, 1955). Although the economic developments are stressed, information on the politics of the South Slav peoples is also included. A work that has caused a major controversy in Yugoslavia is Vladimir Dedijer, Ivan Božić, Sima Ćirković, and Milorad Ekmečić, *History of Yugoslavia* (New York: McGraw-Hill, 1974), which is a translation of *Istorija Jugoslavije* (Belgrade: Prosveta, 1972). The criticism centers on Ekmečić's interpretation of the nineteenth century and on the fact that he displays a better understanding of Serbian history than that of the other nationalities, in particular the Croats and Bosnians.

Instead of writing general histories of the Yugoslav lands as a unit, most authors have concentrated on one of the three primary component parts of the present state—Serbia, Croatia, or Slovenia. Of these, the Serbs have attracted the most attention since a separate Serbian state did exist in the nineteenth century. Hitherto the basic work has been H. W. V. Temperley, *History of Serbia* (London: G. Bell and Sons, 1917). This work is superceded by Michael B. Petrovich, *A History of Modern Serbia, 1804–1918* (New York: Harcourt Brace and Jovanovich, 1976). The author dovers all phases of Serbian history; there is nothing comparable to it even in the Serbian language.

On specific subjects the only book in English on the Serbian revolution is Leopold von Ranke, *A History of Servia and the Servian Revolution*, translated by Mrs. Alexander Kerr (London: Bohn, 1853). It is still of value. Roger Viers Paxton, "Nationalism and Revolution: A Reexamination of the Origins of the First Serbian Insurrection, 1804–1807," *East European Quarterly*, 6 (September, 1972) 3:337–62 describes the factors that impeded immediate demands for independence by the Serbs. A fine source for the background and course of the revolution from the viewpoint of a participant is *The Memoirs of Prota Matija Nenadović*, tr. and ed. by Lovett F. Edwards (Oxford: Clarendon Press, 1969). The contributions of the two Serbian scholars who principally influenced the early national movement, Obradović and Karadžić, are to be found in George R. Noyes, *The Life and Adventures of Dimitrije Obradović* (Berkeley: University of California Press, 1953), a fine translation of Obradović's autobiography, and in the biography by the former British ambassador to Belgrade, Duncan Wilson, *The Life and Times of Vuk Stefanović Karadžić, 1784–1864; Literacy, Literature and National Independence in Serbia* (Oxford: Clarendon Press, 1970).

For the reign of Miloš Stevan K. Pavlowitch, *Anglo-Russian Rivalry in Serbia, 1837–1839: The Mission of Colonel Hodges* (Paris: Mouton, 1961) provides a good description of general internal conditions in the country in the 1830s. Some of the issues he raises are further analysed in the excellent article by Traian Stoianovich, "The Pattern of Serbian Intellectual Evolution, 1830–1880," *Comparative Studies in Society and History*, 1 (1959) 3:242–72. For the second half of the century, the first prominent Balkan socialist is the subject of Woodford D. McClellan, *Svetozar Marković and the Origins of Balkan Socialism* (Princeton: Princeton University Press, 1964), which is based on Serbian and Russian sources. The difficult position of a Serbia caught in the center of the Russian-Habsburg rivalry in the Balkans is the subject of Wayne S. Vucinich, *Serbia between East and West: The Events of 1903–1908* (Stanford: Stanford University Press, 1954). John C. Adams, *Flight in Winter* (Princeton: Princeton University Press, 1942) is an account of the hardships endured by the Serbian army as it retreated across northern Albania to Corfu in the winter of 1915–16.

For the Croats and Slovenes the reader is first referred to the works on the Habsburg Empire mentioned previously. In addition, although somewhat outdated, Robert W. Seton-Watson, *The Southern Slav Question and the Habsburg Monarchy* (London: Constable, 1911) is still useful. On particular topics Gunther E. Rothenburg, *The Military Border in Croatia, 1740–1881: A Study of an Imperial Institution* (Chicago: University of Chicago Press, 1966) deals with a unique organization in both Habsburg and Croatian history. Its affect on the nationality problem is analyzed by the same author in "The Croatian Military Border and the Rise of Yugoslav Nationalism," *Slavonic and East European Review*, 43 (December, 1964) 100:34–45. The Napoleonic occupation of South Slav lands is treated in George J. Prpić, "French Rule in Croatia, 1806–1813," *Balkan Studies*, 5 (1964) 2:221–76. Elinor Murray Despalatović, *Ludovit Gaj and the Illyrian Movement* (New York: Columbia University Press, 1975) is a much needed contribution on this vital subject in Croatian and Yugoslav affairs.

For Slovenia R. Auty, "The Formation of the Slovene Literary Language against the Background of the Slavonic National Revival," *Slavonic and East European Review*, 41 (June, 1963) 97:391–402 concerns an important aspect of national development. Two articles by Carole Rogel, "The Slovenes and Cultural Yugoslavism on the Eve of World War I", *Canadian Slavic Studies*, 2 (Spring, 1968) 1:46–67, and "Preporodovci: Slovene Students for an Independent Yugoslavia, 1912–1914," *Ibid.*, 5 (Summer, 1971), 2:196–212, show the limited and restricted response within the Slovene nation to the appeal of the Yugoslav movement.

GREECE

Of the Balkan peoples the Greeks have received the most attention in the West. Of the numerous surveys of modern Greek history, the three most recent are by English scholars: John Campbell and Philip Sherrard, *Modern Greece* (London: Ernest Benn, 1968), C. M. Woodhouse, *The Story of Modern Greece* (London: Faber and Faber, 1968), and Douglas Dakin, *The Unification of Greece, 1770–1923* (London: Ernest Benn, 1972). Although somewhat out of date, William Miller, *Greece* (London: Ernest Benn, 1928) can be recommended because of the author's close acquaintance with the country. In the same sense the work of the nineteenth-century British scholar George Finlay, *A History of Greece from its Conquest by the Romans to the Present Time, 146 BC to 1864AD* (Oxford: Clarendon Press, 1877) should be consulted, especially volumes 6 and 7.

By far the greatest amount of attention paid to a particular period has been on the Greek Revolution. Among the many accounts, the newest is Douglas Dakin, *The Greek Struggle for Independence, 1821–1833* (London: B. T. Batsford, 1973). Christopher Woodhouse, *The Greek War of Independence: Its Historical Setting* (London: Hutchinson, 1952) is an effective, brief account. The diplomacy of the period is well analyzed in C. W. Crawley, *The Question of Greek Independence: A Study of British Policy in the Near East, 1821–1833* (Cambridge: Cambridge University Press, 1930). Biographies or memoirs are available concerning the careers of four of the Greeks most prominent in the revolutionary movement. Stephen G. Chaconas, *Adamatios Korais: A Study in Greek Nationalism* (New York: Columbia

University Press, 1941) stresses the cultural importance of Koraes as a factor in the background of the revolution. On Capodistrias C. M. Woodhouse, *Capodistria: The Founder of Greek Independence* (London: Oxford University Press, 1973) covers the statesman's entire career, while William P. Kaldis, *John Capodistrias and the Modern Greek State* (Madison: State Historical Society of Wisconsin, 1963) focuses on his years as president in Greece. Two memoirs, Theodore Kolokotrones, *Memoirs from the Greek War of Independence, 1821–1833* (Chicago: Argonaut Publishers, 1969) and Ioannes Makriyannes, *The Memoirs of General Makriyannis*, translated and edited by H. A. Lidderdale (London: Oxford University Press, 1966) are indispensable for the study of the revolution.

For the reign of King Othon one of the best books written for any aspect of Balkan affairs is John Anthony Petropulos, *Politics and Statecraft in the Kingdom of Greece, 1833–1834* (Princeton: Princeton University Press, 1968), which covers thoroughly the political and social development of the first decade of the modern Greek state. The role of Greece in Russian policy is the subject of Barbara Jelavich, *Russia and Greece during the Regency of King Othon, 1832–1835* (Thessaloniki: Institute for Balkan Studies, 1962) and *Russia and the Greek Revolution of 1843* (Munich: Oldenbourg, 1966). The establishment of the Greek national Orthodox church, independent of the ecumenical patriarchate, is described in Charles A. Frazee, *The Orthodox Church and Independent Greece, 1821–1852* (Cambridge: Cambridge University Press, 1969). The overthrow of the Bavarian dynasty and the establishment of the Glücksberg ruler, George I, is the subject of a well-documented study of Eleutherios Prevelakis, *British Policy towards the Change in Dynasty in Greece* (Athens, 1953); Domna N. Dontas, *Greece and the Great Powers, 1863–1875* (Thessaloniki: Institute of Balkan Studies, 1966) continues the subject for the next decade. The Macedonian question from a largely Greek point of view is presented in Douglas Dakin, *The Greek Struggle in Macedonia, 1897–1913* (Thessaloniki: Institute for Balkan Studies, 1966). The Greek entrance into the war and the conflict between Venizelos and the king is discussed in George B. Leon, *Greece and the Great Powers, 1914–1917* (Thessaloniki: Institute for Balkan Studies, 1974) and Christos Theodoulou, *Greece and the Entente, August 1, 1914– September 25, 1916* (Thessaloniki: Institute for Balkan Studies, 1971). Although Venizelos is generally regarded as Greece's greatest modern statesman, there is only one reliable study of his career: Doros Vlastos, *Venizelos: Patriot, Statesman, Revolutionary* (London: Lund Humphries, 1942).

On other general topics two books should be mentioned: John A. Levandis, *The Greek Foreign Debt and the Great Powers, 1821–1898* (New York: Columbia University Press, 1944) and Nicholas S. Kaltchas, *Introduction to the Constitutional History of Modern Greece* (New York: Columbia University Press, 1940). The first concerns a major problem in Greek domestic and foreign relations; the second considers the major political changes in the century. In addition, for the development of modern Greek nationalism the issue of the relative influence of Byzantium and the Slavs is of basic significance, as is discussed in four revealing articles: Romilly Jenkins, "Byzantium and Byzantinism" in *Lectures in Memory of Louis Taft Temple*, first series, 1961–65 (Princeton: Princeton University Press for the University of Cincinnati, 1967): 137–78; Cyril Mango, "Byzantinism and Romantic Hellenism," *Journal of the Warburg and Courtauld Institutes*, 28 (1965):29–43; G. G. Arnakis, "Byzantium and Greece," *Balkan Studies*, 4 (1963)

2:379–400; and A. P. Vacalopoulos, "Byzantium and Hellenism, Remarks on the Racial Origin and Intellectual Continuity of the Greek Nation," *Balkan Studies* 9 (1968) 1:101–26.

ROMANIA

Like the literature on the South Slavs, that on the Romanians falls generally into the two categories of those who lived under Ottoman and those who experienced Habsburg rule. There is, however, an acceptable, if dated, general history covering all sections of the modern state: Robert W. Seton-Watson, *A History of the Rumanians from the Roman Times to the Completion of Unity* (Cambridge: Cambridge University Press, 1934). Professor Seton-Watson is sympathetic to the Romanian viewpoint and critical of the Hungarian, Russian, and Ottoman positions. The book is nevertheless a good introduction to modern Romanian history.

In the material in English principal emphasis has been placed on the history of Moldavia and Wallachia. For the eighteenth-century background, the cultural influences are discussed in Vlad Georgescu, *Political Ideas and the Enlightenment in the Romanian Principalities, 1750–1831* (Boulder: East European Quarterly, 1971). The decisive influence of tsarist Russia on the early political development of the Principalities is the theme of Radu R. N. Florescu, *The Struggle against Russia in the Roumanian Principalities, 1821–1854* (Munich: Societas Academia Dacoromana, 1962). An account of conditions in the country before 1848 from the viewpoint of a Russian diplomat is given in Charles and Barbara Jelavich, eds., *The Education of a Russian Statesman: The Memoirs of Nicholas Karlovich Giers* (Berkeley: University of California, 1962). The revolutions of 1848 are described in the book by the Romanian historian Cornelia Bodea, *The Romanians' Struggle for Unification, 1834–1849*, translated by Liliana Teodoreanu (Bucharest: Academy of the Socialist Republic of Romania, 1970). This work also discusses conditions in Transylvania. The European diplomatic aspects of the unification, based on extensive archival research are examined in detail in T. W. Riker, *The Making of Rumania: a Study of an International Problem, 1856–1866* (Oxford: Oxford University Press, 1931). William G. East, *The Union of Moldavia and Wallachia, 1859* (Cambridge: Cambridge University Press, 1929) concerns only the background of the double election of Cuza. The Russian attitude toward this event is given in Barbara Jelavich, *Russia and the Rumanian National Cause, 1858–1859* (1959; reprint ed., Hamden, Conn.: Archon, 1974) and in two articles, "Russia, the Great Powers and the Recognition of the Double Election of Alexander Cuza," *Rumanian Studies*, 1 (1970): 3–34, and "The Ottoman Empire, the Great Powers and the Legislative and Administrative Union of the Principalities," *Ibid.*, 2 (1973):48–83. The Romanian position in the crisis of the 1870s is presented in three articles: Richard V. Burks, "Romania and the Balkan Crisis of 1875–1878," *Journal of Central European Affairs*, 2 (July, 1942): 119–34 and *Ibid.* (October, 1942):310–20; Barbara Jelavich, "Russia and the Reacqusition of Southern Bessarabia, 1875–78," *Südost-Forschungen*, 28 (1969):199–237; and "Austria-Hungary, Rumania, and the Eastern Crisis, 1876–1878," *Ibid.*, 30 (1971):111–41. Romania's best-known historian, Nicholas Iorga, is ably presented in William O. Oldson, *The Historical and Nationalistic Thought of Nicolae Iorga* (Boulder: East European Quarterly, 1973).

The great domestic issue in the Principalities, the land question, is the subject of the classic work by David Mitrany, *The Land and the Peasant in Romania: The War and Agrarian Reform, 1917–1921.* (London: Oxford University Press, 1930). Philip Gabriel Eidelberg, *The Great Rumanian Peasant Revolt of 1907: Origins of a Modern Jacquerie* (Leiden: E. J. Brill, 1974) examines this problem further in connection with this extensive peasant rebellion.

For studies on Romanians under Habsburg rule the reader is again referred to the books previously discussed on the monarchy. In addition, conditions in Transylvania in the eighteenth century are covered in the study of Romanian historian D. Prodan, *Supplex Libellus Valachorum or The Political Struggle of the Romanians during the Eighteenth Century,* translated by Mary Lazarescu (Bucharest: Academy of the Socialist Republic of Romania, 1969). The early nineteenth century is covered in Keith Hitchins, *The Rumanian National Movement in Transylvania, 1780–1849* (Cambridge: Harvard University Press, 1969). The same author has written four outstanding articles on various aspects of the Transylvanian question and the conflicts with the Hungarian rule: "Andrei Şaguna and the Restoration of the Rumanian Orthodox Metropolis in Transylvania, 1846–1868," *Balkan Studies,* 6 (1965) 1:1–20; "The Rumanians of Transylvania and Constitutional Experiment in the Habsburg Monarchy, 1860–1865," *Ibid.,* 5 (1964) 1:89–108; "The Rumanians of Transylvania and the Congress of Nationalities," *Slavonic and East European Review,* 48 (July, 1970) 112:388–402; and "The Rumanian Question in Hungary: Auriel C. Popovici and the Replica," *Österreichische Osthefte,* 14 (1972):282–89. For a current Romanian interpretation of this period and the union of Transylvania with the Romanian kingdom, see the collection of articles in Miron Constantinescu and Ştefan Pascu, eds., *Unification of the Romanian State: The Union of Transylvania with Old Romania* (Bucharest: Academy of the Socialist Republic of Romania, 1971).

Romania's entrance into the war, including the Transylvanian question, is the subject of two fine articles by Glenn Torrey: "Irredentism and Diplomacy: The Central Powers and Rumania, August–November, 1914," *Südost-Forschungen,* 25 (1966):285–332, and "Rumania's Decision to Intervene: Brătianu and the Entente, June–July, 1916," *Rumanian Studies,* 2 (1971–72):3–29. The final year of the war is discussed in Keith Hitchins, "The Russian Revolution and the Rumanian Socialist Movement, 1917–1918," *Slavic Review,* 27 (June, 1968) 2:268–289.

BULGARIA

Although there are two general histories of Bulgaria, neither one is quite satisfactory. Mercia Macdermott, *A History of Bulgaria, 1393–1885* (London: George Allen & Unwin, 1962) is an uncritical, laudatory account. Dimitur Kosev, H. Hristov, and D. Angelov, *A Short History of Bulgaria* (Sofia: Foreign Languages Press, 1963) represents the current official view. An older history, Dimitur Mishev, *The Bulgarians in the Past, Pages from Bulgarian History* (Lausanne: Librairie Centrale des Nationalités, 1919) has a strong nationalist bent, but is useful for the period from 1800 to 1878.

For the beginning of the modern national movement, James F. Clarke has written an informative article, "Father Paisii and Bulgarian History," in H. S. Hughes, ed., *Teachers of History* (Ithaca, N.Y.: Cornell University Press, 1954), pp. 258–83. A contribution to the cultural background of the nationalist revival is Philip Shashko, "Greece and the Intellectual Bases of the Bulgarian Renaissance," *American Contributions to the Seventh International Congress of Slavicists* vol. 3 (History) (Hague: Mouton, 1973), pp. 91–121. An aspect of Bulgarian demography is discussed in Marc Pinson, "Ottoman Colonization of the Circassians in Rumili after the Crimean War," *Études balkaniques*, 3 (1972):71–85. The activities of the American missionaries in the country are the subject of two books: William W. Hall, *Puritans in the Balkans: The American Board Mission in Bulgaria, 1878–1918* (Sofia, 1938) and James F. Clarke, *Bible Societies, American Missionaries, and the National Revival of Bulgaria* (New York: Arno Press and New York Times, 1971).

As could be expected, the emphasis in historical writing on Bulgaria is on the crisis of the 1870s, the establishment of the autonomous state, and the first decade of its development. Mercia MacDermott has written a eulogistic biography of one of the principal revolutionary leaders: *The Apostle of Freedom: A Portrait of Vasil Levsky against a Background of Nineteenth Century Bulgaria* (London: George Allen and Unwin, 1967). The role of Russia in the national movement has been discussed in an article by Michael P. Petrovich, "The Russian Image in Renascence Bulgaria, 1760–1878," *East European Quarterly*, 1 (June, 1967) 2:87–105, and a book on the activities of the most controversial Russian ambassador of the time: Thomas A. Meininger, *Ignatiev and the Establishment of the Bulgarian Exarchate, 1864–1872: A Study in Personal Diplomacy* (Madison: State Historical Society of Wisconsin, 1970). The material on the events of 1875–78, so important in Bulgarian history, is given in the section below on diplomacy, but special mention should be made here of David Harris, *Britain and the Bulgarian Horrors of 1876* (Chicago: University of Chicago Press, 1939). The formation of the first modern Bulgarian government is carefully analyzed in C. E. Black, *The Establishment of Constitutional Government in Bulgaria* (Princeton: Princeton University Press, 1943). This book should be read together with the same author's article, "The Influence of Western Political Thought in Bulgaria, 1850–1885," *American Historical Review*, 48 (April, 1943) 3:507–20. The Russian role in Bulgaria during these years, together with the unification of 1885 and the rupture of Russo-Bulgarian relations is to be found in Charles Jelavich, *Tsarist Russia and Balkan Nationalism: Russian Influence in the Internal Affairs of Bulgaria and Serbia, 1876–1886* (Berkeley: University of California Press, 1958) and Barbara Jelavich, "Russia, Britain and the Bulgarian Question, 1885–1888," *Südost-Forschungen*, 32 (1973):168–91. The biographies of the first two rulers are by Egon C. Corti, *Alexander von Battenberg* (London: Cassell, 1954) and Hans Roger Madol, *Ferdinand of Bulgaria: The Dream of Byzantium* (London: Hurst & Blackett, 1933). Although perhaps overly sympathetic, A. Hulme Beaman, *M. Stambuloff* (London: Bliss, Sands and Foster, 1895) may still be read with profit. Bulgaria's entrance into the First World War is examined in two articles: Keith Robbins, "British Diplomacy and Bulgaria, 1914–1915," *Slavonic and East European Review*, 49 (October, 1971) 117:560–85 and James M. Potts, "The Loss of Bulgaria" in Alexander Dallin, et al., *Russian Diplomacy and Eastern Europe, 1914–1917* (New York: Kings Crown Press, 1963), pp. 194–234.

Economic and social issues facing Bulgaria after 1890 are discussed in Joseph Rothschild, *The Communist Party of Bulgaria: Origins and Development, 1883–1936* (New York: Columbia University Press, 1959), which centers around the career of Dimitur Blagoev, and two articles by Marin Pundeff, "Marxism in Bulgaria before 1891," *Slavic Review*, 30 (September, 1971) 3:523–50 and "Nationalism and Communism in Bulgaria," *Südost-Forschungen*, 29 (1970):128–70.

ALBANIA

The Balkan state most neglected in historical research is certainly Albania. Joseph Swire, *Albania: the Rise of a Kingdom* (London: William and Ungate, 1929) is elementary; Khristo Frasheri, *The History of Albania, A Brief Survey* (Tirana; 1964) reflects views of the present regime. Two major sources exist for factual information in the publications, Great Britain, Office of the Admiralty, Naval Intelligence Division, *A Handbook of Serbia, Montenegro, Albania and the Adjacent Parts of Greece* (1920) and *Albania: Basic Handbook*, 2 parts, (1943–1944). The one bright spot in this bleak historiographic picture is provided by the volume by Stavro Skendi, *The Albanian National Awakening, 1878–1912* (Princeton: Princeton University Press, 1967). One of the best books on a Balkan national movement, this work is a careful, detailed analysis of the national development from its inception at the time of the San Stefano treaty to the final declaration of independence in 1912. The author's article on "The History of the Albanian Alphabet: A Case of Complex Cultural and Political Development," *Südost-Forschungen*, 19 (1960):263–84 concerns an important aspect of Albanian cultural revival.

DIPLOMATIC HISTORY

Because of the importance of the area in the great power conflicts of the nineteenth century, by far the greatest number of books on the Balkans deal with international relations. Some of these, primarily covering the foreign policy of one nation, have already been cited. This section will discuss principally the works on the foreign relations of the great powers and on intra-Balkan affairs. For a general background the best study is M. A. Anderson, *The Eastern Question, 1774–1923* (New York: St. Martin's Press, 1966), which includes the events from the Treaty of Kuchuk Kainardji to the Treaty of Lausanne. Because of Russian and Austrian influence on Balkan events the two surveys by Barbara Jelavich, *St. Petersburg and Moscow: Tsarist and Soviet Foreign Policy 1814–1974* (Bloomington: Indiana University Press, 1974) and *The Habsburg Empire in European Affairs, 1814–1918* (1969: reprint ed., Hamden, Conn.: Archon, 1974) provide a background. Russian activities are further considered in Traian Stoianovich, "Russian Domination in the Balkans," in Taras Hunczak, ed., *Russian Imperialism from Ivan the Great to the Revolution* (New Brunswick, N.J.: Rutgers University Press, 1974), pp. 198–238, 352–62; in Charles and Barbara Jelavich, "The Danubian Principalities and Bulgaria under Russian Protectorship," *Jahrbücher für Geschichte Osteuropas*, 9 (October, 1961) 3:349–66; and in the relevant essays in Ivo J. Lederer, ed., *Russian Foreign Policy: Essays in Historical Perspective* (New Haven: Yale University Press, 1962). An important aspect of the relations between the Balkan states is examined in Leften S. Stavrianos, *Balkan Federation: A History of the Movement toward Balkan Unity in Modern Times* (Northhampton, Mass.: Smith College Studies in History, 1944).

On the major crises in the century Britain and her role in the Crimean War are defended in H. W. V. Temperley, *England and the Near East: The Crimea* (London: Longmans, Green & Co., 1936) and criticized in Vernon J. Puryear, *England, Russia, and the Straits Question, 1844–1856* (Berkeley: University of California Press, 1931). The Straits problem and Ottoman policy in this regard after the Crimean War are discussed in Barbara Jelavich, *The Ottoman Empire, the Great Powers, and the Straits Question, 1870–1887* (Bloomington: Indiana University Press, 1973). William L. Langer, *European Alliances and Alignments, 1871–1890* (New York: Alfred A. Knopf, 1956) provides an excellent background for these two eventful decades. The crisis of the 1870s has been studied in a number of fine books. Russian policy is emphasized in B. H. Sumner, *Russia and the Balkans, 1870–1880* (Oxford: Oxford University Press, 1937) and David MacKenzie, *The Serbs and Russian Pan-Slavism, 1875–1878* (Ithaca: Cornell University Press, 1967). These books should be read in conjunction with Michael B. Petrovich, *The Emergence of Russian Panslavism, 1856–1870* (New York: Columbia University Press, 1956). Mihailo D. Stojanović, *The Great Powers and the Balkans, 1875–1878* (Cambridge: Cambridge University Press, 1939) is a balanced, comprehensive survey. The settlement of issues at stake between the powers is covered in William N. Medlicott, *The Congress of Berlin and After: A Diplomatic History of the Near Eastern Settlement, 1878–1880* (London: Methuen, 1938).

The Macedonian question has produced an enormous number of books and articles, most of them polemical in nature. The best introduction to the complexities of the problem is through the unique book by Henry R. Wilkinson, *Maps and Politics: A Review of the Ethnographic Cartography of Macedonia* (Liverpool: University Press, 1951). The author examines about ninety maps, beginning with one of 1730, to show how the claims to the area were advanced and how individual maps reflected the interests of the various ethnic groups and the great powers regardless of the facts. Of the general studies available, H. N. Brailsford, *Macedonia: Its Races and their Future* (London: Methuen, 1906) defends the Bulgarian point of view; the Serbian side is found in Tihomir R. Georgevitch, *Macedonia* (London: G. Allen and Unwin, 1918). The Greek position is reflected in the previously mentioned book by Douglas Dakin, *The Greek Struggle in Macedonia, 1897–1913*. The role that the Macedonian issue played in the Greek national movement is analyzed by Jerry Augustinos, "The Dynamics of Modern Greek Nationalism: The 'Great Idea' and the Macedonian Problem," *East European Quarterly*, 6 (January, 1973) 4:444–53. The Internal Macedonian Revolutionary Organization, or IMRO, is the subject of Joseph Swire, *Bulgarian Conspiracy* (London: Hale, 1939).

The two major crises that preceded the outbreak of the First World War are treated in Bernadotte D. Schmitt, *The Annexation of Bosnia* (Cambridge: Cambridge University Press, 1937) and in Ernst C. Helmreich, *The Diplomacy of the Balkan Wars, 1912–1913* (Cambridge: Harvard University Press, 1938), which is the standard work on the subject. Edward C. Thaden, *Russia and the Balkan Alliance of 1912* (University Park: Pennsylvania State University Press, 1965) argues that Russia was in a stronger position after the Balkan alliances and that Austria was weakened by the success of Sazonov's diplomacy. Ivan E. Geshov, Bulgaria's prime minister during the First Balkan War, has defended his course of action in *The Balkan League*, translated by Constantin C. Nincoff (London: J. Murray, 1915).

The events leading to the outbreak of the World War are depicted in the three-volume work by Luigi Albertini, *The Origins of the War of 1914,* translated and edited by Isabella M. Massey (London: Oxford University Press, 1952–57). Joachim Remak, *Sarajevo: The Origins of a Political Murder* (New York: Criterion Press, 1959) is a well-written account in which the author contends that the assassination was planned by the Serbian chief of military intelligence, Colonel Dimitrijević. Rejecting this interpretation, Vladimir Dedijer, *The Road to Sarajevo* (New York: Simon and Schuster, 1966) argues that the plan was exclusively the work of the young students who were disaffected by the political, social, and economic conditions in Bosnia.

A good account of the war years is to be found in both Z. A. B. Zeman, *A Diplomatic History of the First World War* (London: Weidenfeld and Nicholson, 1971) and in Victor S. Mamatey, *The United States and East Central Europe, 1914–1918: A Study in Wilsonian Diplomacy and Propaganda* (Princeton: Princeton University Press, 1957). The Russian actions are examined in C. Jay Smith, *The Russian Struggle for Power, 1914–1917: A Study of Foreign Policy during the First World War* (New York: Philosophical Library, 1956). The Bulgarian, Romanian, and Serbian issues in the war as seen through Russian eyes are examined by James M. Potts, Alfred J. Rieber, and Michael B. Petrovich, respectively, in Alexander Dallin, et al., *Russian Diplomacy and Eastern Europe, 1914–1917,* previously cited.

The peace settlements in the Balkans have received considerable attention. For Yugoslavia the standard work is Ivo J. Lederer, *Yugoslavia at the Paris Conference: A Study in Frontier-Making* (New Haven: Yale University Press, 1963). The book concentrates on the disputes with Italy, but it also examines the frontier issues with Austria, Hungary, Romania, and Bulgaria. Dragan R. Zivojinović, *America, Italy, and the Birth of Yugoslavia, 1917–1919* (New York: East European Quarterly, 1972) also centers on the Italian dispute, but as seen through Yugoslav eyes. Sherman David Spector, *Rumania at the Paris Peace Conference: A Study of the Diplomacy of Ioan I. C. Brătianu* (New York: Bookman Associates, 1962) is a critical assessment. Although admiring Brătianu's successes in achieving the maximum Romanian goals, Spector is less charitable toward the man, his tactics, and his diplomacy. Georgi P. Genov, *Bulgaria and the Treaty of Neuilly* (Sofia: H. G. Danov, 1935) describes why the settlement was not the "just" peace that Wilson and the Allies had promised.

The settlement with the Ottoman Empire and the Greek-Turkish conflict has been well covered. Harry N. Howard, *The Partition of Turkey: A Diplomatic History, 1913–1923* (Norman, Okla.: Oklahoma University Press, 1931) provides a broad sweep of Ottoman affairs since the Balkan Wars. It should be supplemented by Laurence Evans, *United States Policy and the Partition of Turkey, 1914–1924* (Baltimore: Johns Hopkins Press, 1965). Both volumes examine carefully the diplomacy of the treaties of Sèvres and Lausanne. A recent book by Paul C. Helmreich, *From Paris to Sèvres: The Partition of the Ottoman Empire at the Peace Conference of 1919–1920* (Columbus: Ohio State University Press, 1974), is a detailed, thorough study of a settlement that was never implemented, but gave impetus to Kemal's eventual nationalist victory. The Greek Anatolian plans are carefully documented in Alexander A. Pallis, *Greece's Anatolian Venture and After: A Survey of the Diplomatic and Political Aspects of the Greek Expedition to Asia Minor, 1915–1922* (London: Methuen, 1937). The legacy of that disaster is described in Stephen P. Ladas, *The Exchange of Minorities: Bulgaria, Greece and Turkey* (New

York: Macmillan, 1932) and Dimitri Pentzopoulos, *The Balkan Exchange of Minorities and Its Impact on Greece* (Paris: Mouton, 1962). Greece's other defeat is recorded in Edith Pierpont Stickney, *Southern Albania or Northern Epirus in European International Affairs, 1912–1913* (Stanford: Stanford University Press, 1926).

ECONOMIC AND SOCIAL HISTORY

This field in Balkan history has been relatively neglected when compared to the material available on political and diplomatic developments. Only two books present a broad coverage. Nicolas Spulber, *The State and Economic Development in Eastern Europe* (New York: Random House, 1966) explores the role and function of the state in the economies of the Balkan nations with more attention given to the twentieth century than the nineteenth. The most recent work, by two well-known Hungarian economic historians, Ivan T. Berend and Gyorgy Ranki, *Economic Development in East Central Europe in the Nineteenth and Twentieth Centuries* (New York: Columbia University Press, 1974) is a translation of a book first published in Budapest in 1969. The authors examine demographic problems, agrarian changes, credit and transport, investments and foreign capital, manufacturing, and the emergence of capitalism. Although the emphasis is on the Habsburg lands, Romania, Yugoslavia, and Bulgaria are discussed, but not Greece or Albania.

On specific topics Traian Stoianovich, "The Conquering Balkan Orthodox Merchant," *Journal of Economic History*, 20 (June, 1960) 2:234–313 concerns chiefly commercial developments in the eighteenth century. The Bulgarian scholar Nikolai Todorov, "The Genesis of Capitalism in the Balkan Provinces of the Ottoman Empire in the Nineteenth Century," *Explorations in Economic History*, 7 (1970):313–24 argues that the growth of capitalism in the Balkans was retarded because of the nature of the Ottoman system. In another article, "The Balkan Town in the Second Half of the Nineteenth Century," *Études balkaniques*, 5 (1969) 2:31–50, the same author gives interesting statistics on urban population, ethnic composition, occupations and taxation.

On the individual states the financial plight of the Ottoman Empire and steps by which it became the economic ward of the European powers are described in two books: D. C. Blaisdell, *European Financial Control in the Ottoman Empire: A Study of the Establishment, Activities, and Significance of the Ottoman Public Debt* (New York: Columbia University Press, 1929) and Herbert Feis, *Europe the World's Banker, 1870–1914*, (New York: A. M. Kelley, 1961), pp. 258–361. The second book contains information on Bulgaria, Serbia, and Greece. Whereas these titles deal largely with the second half of the century, the first is briefly examined in E. Clark, "The Ottoman Industrial Revolution," *International Journal of Middle East Studies*, 5 (1964):65–76.

For the South Slavs the outstanding work is the previously cited Jozo Tomasevich, *Peasants, Politics, and Economic Change in Yugoslavia*. Toussaint Hočevar, *The Structure of the Slovenian Economy, 1848–1963* (New York: Studia Slovenica, 1965) is a general, informative survey. Peter F. Sugar, *Industrialization of Bosnia-Hercegovina, 1878–1918* (Seattle: University of Washington Press, 1963) provides a careful assessment of both the economic and political developments within a province whose fate helped precipitate the First World War. John R. Lampe, "Serbia, 1878–1912," in Rondo Cameron, ed., *Banking and Economic Development:*

Some Lessons of History (New York: Oxford University Press, 1972), pp. 122–67 describes how the Belgrade affiliates of the big European banks were used politically for purposes of foreign and military policy rather than to promote industrialization.

For Romania the emphasis is on the land problem. The works of David Mitrany, *The Land and the Peasant in Rumania,* and Philip Eidelberg, *The Great Rumanian Peasant Revolt of 1907,* have already been cited. There is also Ifor L. Evans, *Agrarian Revolution in Rumania* (Cambridge: University Press, 1924).

Less is available on Bulgaria. Aside from the information in Spulber and Berend and Ranki, Alexander Gerschenkron, "Some Aspects of Industrialization in Bulgaria," in his book *Economic Backwardness in Historical Perspective: A Book of Essays* (Cambridge: Belknap Press, 1962), pp. 198–234 deserves particular mention.

For Greece A. A. Pepelasis, "The Legal System and the Economic Development of Greece," *Journal of Economic History,* 19 (June, 1959) 2:173–98 concentrates on showing how the Greek legal system was a contributing factor to the nation's economic backwardness. In another article, "Greece," in a volume which the same author edited with Leon Mears and Irma Adelman, *Economic Development: Analysis and Case Studies* (New York: Harper & Bros., 1961), pp. 500–22, Pepelasis argues that it was not so much the lack of capital as its improper use that caused many of Greece's problems in the nineteenth century.

For general social conditions the most useful books available are those on village and peasant life. Although most of the works cited deal with the twentieth century, they also reflect conditions and attitudes common in the previous period. For Bulgaria Irwin T. Sanders, *Balkan Village* (Lexington: University of Kentucky Press, 1949) is recommended. Sanders is also the author of *Rainbow in the Rock: The People of Rural Greece* (Cambridge: Harvard University Press, 1961), a book that should be read with Ernestine Friedl, *Vasilika: a Village in Modern Greece* (New York: Holt, Rinehart, and Winston, 1962). John K. Campbell, *Honor, Family, and Patronage: A Study of Institutions and Moral Values in a Greek Mountain Community* (Oxford: Clarendon Press, 1964) is a sociological-anthropological study of villages in Epirus. For Serbia two basic works are Joel M. Halpern's *A Serbian Village* (New York: Columbia University Press, 1958) and, with his wife Barbara Kerewsky Halpern, his *A Serbian Village in Historical Perspective* (New York: Holt, Rinehart and Winston, 1972). They should be supplemented with Eugene A. Hammel, "The Balkan Peasant—A View from Serbia," in Philip K. Bock, ed., *Peasants in the Contemporary World* (Albuquerque: University of New Mexico Press, 1969); Hammel deals with Serbian peasant culture here and in his "Economic Change, Social Mobility, and Kinship in Serbia," *Southwestern Journal of Anthropology,* 25 (1969):188–97. For Slovenia there is Irene Winner, *A Slovenian Village: Žerovnica* (Providence: Brown University Press, 1971).

For an understanding of conditions in the Balkans in the nineteenth century, contemporary accounts and travel books can be most useful. A collection dealing with Bulgaria, Romania, the South Slav lands, and Hungary is to be found in Doreen Warriner, *Contrasts in Emerging Societies: Readings in the Social and Economic History of South-Eastern Europe in the Nineteenth Century* (Bloomington: Indiana University Press, 1965). Of the travel accounts among the best are G. Muir

Mackenzie and A. P. Irby, *Travels in the Slavonic Provinces of Turkey-in-Europe* (London: Alexander Strahan, 1866) and William M. Leake, *Travels in Northern Greece* (London: J. Rodwell, 1845), 4 vols.

LITERATURE

A brief general survey in English is available for every country: Antun Barac, *A History of Yugoslav Literature,* translated by Petar Mijušković (Ann Arbor: Michigan Slavic Publications, 1973); C. Th. Dimaras, *A History of Modern Greek Literature* translated by Mary P. Gianos (Albany: State University of New York Press, 1972); Stuart E. Mann, *Albanian Literature: An Outline of Prose, Poetry, and Drama* (London: Bernard Quaritch, 1955); Charles A. Moser, *A History of Bulgarian Literature, 865–1944* (Hague: Mouton, 1972), and Basil Munteano, *Modern Roumanian Literature* (Bucharest: Editura Cuvântul, 1943).

Index

Abdul Aziz, Sultan, 109, 112, 145
Abdul Hamid II, Sultan, 112, 147, 211, 213, 214, 215, 229
Abdul Mejid, Sultan, 104, 105
Abel, Karl von, 68-69
Abu Bekir Pasha, 31
Adalia: Italian claim to, 311
Administration: Ottoman, 3-4, 10, 36, 111; Serbian and Ottoman cooperation in, 36-37; Serbian, 37, 58-59; in Bulgaria, 160-61; in Balkans, 322. *See also* individual countries
Adrianople, Treaty of, of 1829, 55, 102, 107; terms of, 49-50, 89-90
Aegean Islands: claimed by Greece, 77
Aehrenthal, Count Alois von, 215, 257
Agrarian Union (of Bulgaria), 194, 204
Agriculture: Balkan, 7-8; Romanian, 91-92; in Greece, 172; Bulgarian, 194; in Balkan states, 201, 202. *See also* Peasantry
Akkerman, Convention of, 44, 55, 102, 324; provisions of, 89
Alba Iulia: national assembly at, 297, 306
Albania, 142, 171, 299, 316-19; Muslims in, 4; Ali Pasha of Janina in, 18; invaded by Serb forces, 219; independence of, 221, 229; national movement in, 222, 224-25; government of, 223, 318, 319; education in, 223, 226-27; and Treaty of San Stefano, 223-24; and Congress of Berlin, 224; cultural awakening in, 225-26; and Macedonia, 227-28; and Young Turks, 229; establishment of, 230-31; International Control Commission in, 232; constitution of, 232-33; during World War I, 297; and Italy, 302; Mirdite revolt in, 319
Albanian League, 224, 225, 227
Albanians, 222, 223, 227; in Macedonia, 207, 211

Albanian Writings, Society for the Printing of, 225-26
Albert, Prince of Britain, 82
Alecsandri, Vasile, 270
Aleko Pasha, 163, 164
Alexander, Prince-Regent of Serbia. *See* Karadjordjević, Alexander, Prince-Regent of Serbia
Alexander, King of Serbia. *See* Obrenović, Alexander, King of Serbia
Alexander, King of Greece, 296, 313
Alexander I, Tsar, 34, 40, 48; at Tilsit, 33, 86; and Principalities, 41-42; and Greece, 47
Alexander II, Tsar, 161, 162, 179
Alexander III, Tsar, 162, 168; and Pan-slavism, 146; and Bulgaria, 162-63, 165, 167; and Aleko Pasha, 164
Alexander of Battenberg, Prince of Bulgaria, 185, 188; and Bulgarian Liberals, 161-62; and German influence, 162; and Alexander III, 162-63, 166-67; and Rumelia, 165; defeats Serbs, 166
Alexandrescu, Gregory, 270
Algeria: France in, 23
Ali Pasha, of Janina, 39, 41, 46, 103, 108, 142, 223; activities of, 18-19; position of, 42-43; death of, 44, 109; and Mahmud II, 101; and Young Ottomans, 112
Alliance Israélite, 179
Allies, 286; and Treaty of London, 287-88; and Bulgaria, 288, 289; and Romania, 290-93; and Greece, 294-96; and Turkish revolution, 315; and Albania, 316. *See also* individual countries
Amalia of Oldenburg, Queen of Greece, 73, 81
Aman, Theodore, 280
Anatolia: division of, 313, 315